Bliss Against the World

REFLECTION AND THEORY IN THE STUDY OF RELIGION

SERIES EDITORS

Alda Balthrop-Lewis, Australian Catholic University
Jonathan Tran, Baylor University
A Publication Series of
The American Academy of Religion
and
Oxford University Press

WORKING EMPTINESS
Toward a Third Reading of Emptiness in Buddhism and Postmodern Thought
Newman Robert Glass

WITTGENSTEIN AND THE MYSTICAL
Philosophy as an Ascetic Practice
Frederick Sontag

AN ESSAY ON THEOLOGICAL METHOD
Third Edition
Gordon D. Kaufman

BETTER THAN WINE
Love, Poetry, and Prayer in the Thought of Franz Rosenzweig
Yudit Kornberg Greenberg

HEALING DECONSTRUCTION
Postmodern Thought in Buddhism and Christianity
Edited by David Loy

ROOTS OF RELATIONAL ETHICS
Responsibility in Origin and Maturity in H. Richard Niebuhr
R. Melvin Keiser

HEGEL'S SPECULATIVE GOOD FRIDAY
The Death of God in Philosophical Perspective
Deland S. Anderson

NEWMAN AND GADAMER
Toward a Hermeneutics of Religious Knowledge
Thomas K. Carr

GOD, PHILOSOPHY AND ACADEMIC CULTURE
A Discussion between Scholars in the AAR and APA
Edited by William J. Wainwright

LIVING WORDS
Studies in Dialogues about Religion
Terence J. Martin

LIKE AND UNLIKE GOD
Religious Imaginations in Modern and Contemporary Fiction
John Neary

BEYOND THE NECESSARY GOD
Trinitarian Faith and Philosophy in the Thought of Eberhard Jüngel
Paul DeHart

CONVERGING ON CULTURE
Theologians in Dialogue with Cultural Analysis and Criticism
Edited by Delwin Brown, Sheila Greeve Davaney and Kathryn Tanner

LESSING'S PHILOSOPHY OF RELIGION AND THE GERMAN ENLIGHTENMENT
Toshimasa Yasukata

AMERICAN PRAGMATISM
A Religious Genealogy
M. Gail Hamner

OPTING FOR THE MARGINS
Postmodernity and Liberation in Christian Theology
Edited by Joerg Rieger

MAKING MAGIC
Religion, Magic, and Science in the Modern World
Randall Styers

THE METAPHYSICS OF DANTE'S *COMEDY*
Christian Moevs

PILGRIMAGE OF LOVE
Moltmann on the Trinity and Christian Life
Joy Ann McDougall

MORAL CREATIVITY
Paul Ricoeur and the Poetics of Possibility
John Wall

MELANCHOLIC FREEDOM
Agency and the Spirit of Politics
David Kyuman Kim

FEMINIST THEOLOGY AND THE
CHALLENGE OF DIFFERENCE
Margaret D. Kamitsuka

PLATO'S GHOST
Spiritualism in the American Renaissance
Cathy Gutierrez

TOWARD A GENEROUS ORTHODOXY
Prospects for Hans Frei's Postliberal Theology
Jason A. Springs

CAVELL, COMPANIONSHIP, AND
CHRISTIAN THEOLOGY
Peter Dula

COMPARATIVE THEOLOGY AND THE
PROBLEM OF RELIGIOUS RIVALRY
Hugh Nicholson

SECULARISM AND RELIGION-MAKING
Markus Dressler and Arvind-Pal S. Mandair

FORTUNATE FALLIBILITY
Kierkegaard and the Power of Sin
Jason A. Mahn

METHOD AND METAPHYSICS IN
MAIMONIDES' *GUIDE FOR THE
PERPLEXED*
Daniel Davies

THE LANGUAGE OF DISENCHANTMENT
*Protestant Literalism and Colonial Discourse in
British India*
Robert A. Yelle

WRITING RELIGION
The Making of Turkish Alevi Islam
Markus Dressler

THE AESTHETICS AND ETHICS
OF FAITH
*A Dialogue Between Liberationist and Pragmatic
Thought*
Christopher D. Tirres

VISIONS OF RELIGION
Experience, Meaning, and Power
Stephen S. Bush

WRITING RELIGION
The Making of Turkish Alevi Islam
Markus Dressler

STUDYING THE QUR'AN IN THE
MUSLIM ACADEMY
Majid Daneshgar

SYNCRETISM AND CHRISTIAN
TRADITION
*Race and Revelation in the Study of Religious
Mixture*
Ross Kane

ASIAN AMERICANS AND THE SPIRIT OF
RACIAL CAPITALISM
Jonathan Tran

THE HIGHER OBJECTIVES OF ISLAMIC
THEOLOGY
Towards a Theory of Maqasid al-Aqida
Mohammed Gamal Abdelnour

CRITIQUE OF HALAKHIC REASON
Divine Commandments and Social Normativity
Yonatan Y. Brafman

ATTUNEMENT
The Art and Politics of Feminist Theology
Natalie Carnes

BLISS AGAINST THE WORLD
Schelling, Theodicy, and the Crisis of Modernity
Kirill Chepurin

BLISS AGAINST THE WORLD

Schelling, Theodicy, and the Crisis of Modernity

KIRILL CHEPURIN

OXFORD
UNIVERSITY PRESS

OXFORD
UNIVERSITY PRESS

Oxford University Press is a department of the University of Oxford.
It furthers the University's objective of excellence in research, scholarship,
and education by publishing worldwide. Oxford is a registered trade mark of
Oxford University Press in the UK and in certain other countries.

Published in the United States of America by Oxford University Press
198 Madison Avenue, New York, NY 10016, United States of America.

© Oxford University Press 2024

All rights reserved. No part of this publication may be reproduced, stored in a retrieval system, transmitted, used for text and data mining, or used for training artificial intelligence, in any form or by any means, without the prior permission in writing of Oxford University Press, or as expressly permitted by law, by license or under terms agreed with the appropriate reprographics rights organization. Inquiries concerning reproduction outside the scope of the above should be sent to the Rights Department, Oxford University Press, at the address above.

You must not circulate this work in any other form
and you must impose this same condition on any acquirer

Library of Congress Cataloging-in-Publication Data
Names: Chepurin, Kirill, author.
Title: Bliss against the world : schelling, theodicy, and the crisis
of modernity / Kirill Chepurin.
Description: New York, NY, United States of America :
Oxford University Press, [2024] |
Series: American academy of religion reflection and
theory in the study of religion | Includes bibliographical references and index.
Identifiers: LCCN 2024026076 (print) | LCCN 2024026077 (ebook) |
ISBN 9780197788899 | ISBN 9780197788912 (epub)
Subjects: LCSH: Schelling, Friedrich Wilhelm Joseph von, 1775-1854. |
God (Christianity) | Theodicy. | Alienation (Philosophy) | Civilization, Modern.
Classification: LCC B2899.G6 C43 2024 (print) | LCC B2899.G6 (ebook) |
DDC 202/.118—dc23/eng/20240905
LC record available at https://lccn.loc.gov/2024026076
LC ebook record available at https://lccn.loc.gov/2024026077

DOI: 10.1093/9780197788929.001.0001

The manufacturer's authorised representative in the EU for product safety is
Oxford University Press España S.A. of El Parque Empresarial San Fernando de Henares,
Avenida de Castilla, 2 – 28830 Madrid (www.oup.es/en or product.safety@oup.com).
OUP España S.A. also acts as importer into Spain of products made by the manufacturer.

For my mother, Irina,

with love and gratitude

Contents

Preface	xi
Acknowledgments	xiii
List of Abbreviations	xv

General Introduction: Modernity, Theodicy, Bliss ... 1
   I.1. Schelling's Plenum of Bliss ... 3
   I.2. The Genealogical Question ... 8
   I.3. A Scene of Bliss: Rousseau and Adorno ... 11
   I.4. The Fall from Bliss (into the World): Kant ... 14
   I.5. Modernity and Theodicy ... 18

PART I: *Why Must This World Be?*

1. The General Christian Contradiction ... 27
   1.1. Separation and Delegitimation ... 31
   1.2. Faith and the Not-Yet of the World ... 35
   1.3. The Epoch of Crisis: Modernity and Alienation ... 38
   1.4. With and Against the Christian-Modern ... 43
   1.5. Mysticism, Magic, and the Signs of the Times (with an Excursus on Wordsworth) ... 49

   Interlude I: Ordo quis datus? ... 58

2. The Demiurgic Subject ... 71
   2.1. To Break All Finite Spheres: In Search of Lost Bliss ... 72
   2.2. To Reproduce the World: Idealism as the Katechon ... 95

   Interlude II: "Abyss of Repose and Inactivity" ... 109

x   *Contents*

3. Evil Is but a Shadow — 118
   3.1. The One Common Being: Re-visioning the Universe as Bliss — 121
   3.2. To Dissolve as in Water, to Consume as in Fire — 139
   3.3. Everything in Its Place and Time: An Aesthetic Cosmic Theodicy — 157

PART II: *The Dark Ground*

Introduction to Part II: On Schelling's Post-1809 System Narrative — 177

4. Universal *Ekstasis*; or, Fallenness and Method — 184
   4.1. Decentering: The Fall of Adam and the Inverted World (of Modernity) — 185
   4.2. Kenosis and Construction: The Method of Philosophy — 202

5. Universal Spiral — 220
   5.1. God's Own Shelter from the World: Cosmic War and Cosmic Peace — 221
   5.2. Bliss before the Law — 241
   5.3. Recentering the Human in a Cosmic Revolution — 255
   5.4. Conclusion: Human Self-Assertion Restaged at the Meta-level — 284

   Interlude III: Clock Time as Fallen Time — 288

6. The Race to Bliss: Assembling Global Humanity — 301
   6.1. Negative and Positive Philosophy; or, Modernity and Christianity Redux — 306
   6.2. Without God, Without Possibility: Racialization and Conversion — 317

Conclusion: Bliss Against Theodicy — 340

Bibliography — 347
Index — 357

Preface

TWO AUDIENCES WERE in my mind as I was writing this book. The first is the audience of German idealism and Romanticism scholars interested in a speculative rereading of Friedrich Schelling's metaphysics of finitude, history, and the divine in relation to the question of modernity, and to the modern construction of such categories as "universal history," "humanity," "religion," and "modernity" itself (as an epoch with a specific existential program, to use Hans Blumenberg's expression). Many books have been written on G. W. F. Hegel as the paradigmatic thinker of modern negativity and alienation, of the modern striving for freedom and reconciliation, and of the so-called secularization of Christian notions of salvation and the eschaton in the wake of the Enlightenment and the advent of secularity. However, I believe that Schelling's thought also contains a distinct framework of modernity—one, moreover, that resonates strongly with the ongoing debate around the genealogy of the modern world, its modes of self-legitimation, and its constitutive exclusions and violences, a debate that can be traced from twentieth-century German thinkers such as Carl Schmitt, Blumenberg, and Jacob Taubes to Sylvia Wynter and contemporary political theology and critical theory.

Those interested in this debate, and in the entanglement between Christianity and modernity, form the second intended audience of this book. With Gil Anidjar, I am convinced that "secularized Christianity is *still* Christianity, however translated (Schmitt), metaphorized (Blumenberg) or perverted (Löwith)."[1] And although I also want to retain the basic antagonism and fundamental truth inherent in Anidjar's attendant declaration that "secularization is just Christianity by another name,"[2] I seek to explore and

---

1. Anidjar, "Interview," 229.

2. Ibid., 230. Cf. Anidjar, "Secularism."

complicate this *just* while retaining the *still*. The latter conceals a complex logic to which Schelling is singularly attuned at a key moment in its continued formation, and which I seek to interrogate by putting Schelling in dialogue, inter alia, with Blumenberg's powerful theoretical account of the modern world. Turning to Blumenberg alongside Schelling is important for me for two reasons. First, Blumenberg's tracing of the constitutive logics of modern reality and modern subjectivity arguably remains unrivaled in ambition and scope and can provide, as I hope to demonstrate, the perfect counterpoint to and a longer view of Schelling's grappling with the modern age. Second, from the political-theological perspective, Blumenberg's work can help us think the co-imbrication of Christianity and modernity while still attending to the ways in which modernity generates its own distinct logics of investment in the world, and ultimately a new world. One may regard this world, with Anidjar as with Schelling, as an overarching mutation of Christianity, but it is also recognizable as characteristically modern: it is a world of endless alienation and actualization, negativity and striving, globalization and racialization, productivity and the not-yet of progress. It is of this world, I will argue, that Schelling's metaphysics provides a unique refraction, so that what he takes to be the structure of universal reality—the "world" or "universe" (*Welt*)—is itself Christian-modern in character. To speak of the "Christian-modern" world may seem unusual to those coming from the secularist framework that programmatically separates modernity from Christianity. However, this is precisely the book's Schellingian point: one cannot understand modernity without thinking its constitutive co-imbrication with Christianity, a co-imbrication that cuts across the ostensible divide between "religious" and "secular."

Guided by that intuition, the book's chapters build toward a new picture of the development of Schelling's thought (and through it, of the Romantic impulse from the 1790s to the 1840s) as well as toward a Schellingian framework of modernity and bliss. Taken together, "theodicy" and "bliss" are my way of critiquing, through Schelling, the Christian-modern trajectory and exploring its underlying promises, ruses, and impasses. The introduction seeks to provide a panoramic overview, through Schelling but also across modernity, of the tangled problematic to be unfolded throughout the book. Following that, each chapter reconstructs a certain logic or period in Schelling's thought and draws out the various ways in which his philosophy is intertwined with—and allows us to better understand—the modern structure of reality and the formation of the Western-centric global world in whose shadow we continue to live. Along the way, the book also assembles the sites of bliss in Schelling as sites of antagonism to the Christian-modern world, and to the logics of division, not-yetness, racialization, and conversion through which this world is upheld.

Acknowledgments

AN ACADEMIC BOOK is a finite and worldly thing, even a book about bliss, and writing and publishing one requires relations of support. My gratitude thus goes to all the persons and institutions that have supported me over the years. My research has benefited from the positions I have held at the University of Hamburg, Free University of Berlin, Humboldt University of Berlin, National Research University HSE Moscow, and University of California, Berkeley. I want to thank Alexey M. Rutkevich for his generosity, and for the inspiring sobriety of his thought, to which I do my best to stay true even as I am tempted by the mystical and ecstatic. I owe an endless debt of gratitude to Rolf Schieder for the depth of his understanding and his faith in my work, to Volker Gerhardt for his encouragement and enthusiasm, and to Alex Dubilet, Anne Eusterschulte, Niklaus Largier, Dana Lloyd, Vincent Lloyd, and Giuseppe Veltri and the Maimonides Centre for Advanced Studies for their backing during a critical period, which allowed me to finish this book. To Niklaus Largier this book further owes its very beginnings: thanks to his invitation, I spent a semester at UC Berkeley, where, perhaps under the influence of the Californian sun, I started writing about bliss. Karen Feldman, James Martel, and Frank Ruda, too, have my gratitude for all their support. I am deeply thankful, finally, to Vincent Lloyd as the original series editor, to Jonathan Tran and Alda Balthrop-Lewis as the ones who saw this project through to completion, and to Steve Wiggins for guiding the editorial process from the side of Oxford University Press.

This book also would not have materialized without the colleagues and friends who have been supportive of, and provided venues for discussing and publishing, my work on bliss in Schelling and Romanticism. I would like to separately thank Charlotte Alderwick, Iain Hamilton Grant, Sean McGrath, Tilottama Rajan, and Gabriel Trop. Daniel Whistler's scholarship, combining the academic and the rigorously speculative in a singular way, has always been inspiring for me, and his comments on various drafts of my work have been invaluable. Joseph Albernaz and Alex Dubilet have likewise been the constant source of inspiration and exchange of ideas. I am generally thankful to everyone who has provided feedback on my work over the years. This includes not least the anonymous referees for Oxford University Press, whose critiques helped to improve the manuscript in numerous ways. At the same time, all errors remain my own.

This book is dedicated to my mother, Irina Trufanova, my mentor in all things intellectual, and the person whose strength of will and thought I have never ceased to admire and to whom my debt is truly infinite. I also want to thank Vladyka Nikandr, who helped to instill in me an interest in philosophical theology and philosophy of religion; this book is, inter alia, a long-term fruit of that interest. Finally, I am eternally grateful to Kyra Sutton—my constant intellectual inspiration, an incisive reader and critic of my work, and my source of bliss: with you alone, I can stand firmly both in and against the world.

Abbreviations

HKA   Schelling, F. W. J. *Historisch-kritische Ausgabe.* Reihe I: *Werke.* Reihe II: *Nachlass.* Reihe III: *Briefe.* Stuttgart: Frommann-Holzboog, 1976–present.

SW   *Sämmtliche Werke.* Edited by K. F. A. Schelling. Abteilung I (10 vols.). Abteilung II (4 vols.). Stuttgart: Cotta, 1856–61.

In this book, I mostly refer to the above two editions of Schelling's works (with preference for the historical-critical edition except where the cited text appears only in a different edition), followed by the division number and volume number (e.g., HKA I/2). Wherever available, I also provide a reference to the English translation of the respective text with page numbers. Thus, in the main body of this book, a reference to a passage from Schelling's *Philosophical Letters on Dogmatism and Criticism* may look as follows: PB 47/156, where the first page number refers to the German original and the second to the English translation. To ensure consistency, all translations from Schelling are, however, my own.

AD   "Allgemeine Deduktion des dynamischen Prozesses oder der Kategorien der Physik" / "General Deduction of the Dynamic Process, or of the Categories of Physics" (1800). HKA I/8, 295–371.

AER   "Animadversiones ad quaedam loca Epistolae ad Romanos" / "Observations on Certain Passages from the Epistle to the Romans" (1792). HKA II/4, 37–135.

ANP   *Aphorismen über die Naturphilosophie / Aphorisms on the Philosophy of Nature* (1805–7). HKA I/15, 91–143 and 213–257.

B   *Bruno oder über das göttliche und natürliche Princip der Dinge / Bruno, or, On the Natural and the Divine Principle of Things* (1802). HKA I/11, 335–451. Translated by Michael G. Vater. Albany: State University of New York Press, 1984.

BW1   *Briefwechsel* Bd. 1 / *Correspondence* vol. 1 (1786–99). HKA III/1.

C   *Clara, oder Über den Zusammenhang der Natur mit der Geisterwelt / Clara, or, On Nature's Connection to the Spirit World* (date unknown; probably ca. 1810). SW I/9, 1–110. Translated by Fiona Steinkamp. Albany: State University of New York Press, 2002.

DGD	*Denkmal der Schrift von den göttlichen Dingen / Monument to the Treatise on Divine Things* (1812). HKA I/18, 129–229.
DM	*De Marcione Paullinarum epistolarum emendatore / On Marcion, the Corrector of the Pauline Epistles* (1795). Latin text and German translation: HKA I/2, 219–295.
DMO	*De malorum origine / On the Origin of Evil* (1792). Latin text and German translation: HKA I/1, 59–147.
DMS	*Darstellung meines Systems der Philosophie / Presentation of My System of Philosophy* (1801). HKA I/10, 107–211. Translated by Michael G. Vater and David W. Wood in *The Philosophical Rupture between Fichte and Schelling (1800–1802)*. Albany: State University of New York Press, 2012, 141–205.
DNP	*Darstellung des Naturprozesses / Presentation of the Process of Nature* (1843–44). SW I/10, 301–390.
DRP	*Darstellung der reinrationalen Philosophie / Presentation of the Purely Rational Philosophy* (ca. 1846–54). SW II/1, 253–572.
EE	*Erster Entwurf eines Systems der Naturphilosophie / First Outline of a System of the Philosophy of Nature* (1799). HKA I/7, 63–357. Translated by Keith R. Peterson. Albany: State University of New York Press, 2004, 1–192.
EIP	*Einleitung in die Philosophie / Introduction to Philosophy* (1830). Edited by Walter E. Ehrhardt. Stuttgart: Frommann-Holzboog, 1989.
ESE	"Einleitung zu seinem Entwurf eines Systems der Naturphilosophie" / "Introduction to the Outline of a System of the Philosophy of Nature" (1799). HKA I/8, 27–85. Translated by Keith R. Peterson in Schelling, *First Outline of a System of the Philosophy of Nature*, 193–232.
EV	"Entwurf der Vorrede" / "Outline of a Preface [to a Planned Edition of Schelling's Historical-Critical Writings]" (1793–94). HKA II/5, 109–113.
F	"Der Frühling" / "Spring. A Fragment" (date unknown). *Die Weltalter: Fragmente*, edited by Manfred Schröter, 272–275. Munich: Biederstein Verlag-Leibniz Verlag, 1946. Translated in *Clara*, trans. Steinkamp, 79–82.
FD	*Fernere Darstellungen aus dem System der Philosophie / Further Presentations from the System of Philosophy* (1802). HKA I/12, 83–231.
FS	*Philosophische Untersuchungen über das Wesen der menschlichen Freiheit ("Freiheitsschrift") / Philosophical Investigations into the Essence of Human Freedom ("Freedom essay")* (1809). HKA I/17, 109–179. Translated by Jeff Love and Johannes Schmidt. Albany: State University of New York Press, 2006.
GG	"Geschichte des Gnosticismus" / "History of Gnosticism" (1793–94). HKA II/5, 87–99.
GPP	*Grundlegung der positiven Philosophie: Münchner Vorlesung WS 1832/33 und SS 1833 / Groundwork of Positive Philosophy: Munich Lectures in the Winter Semester 1832/33 and Summer Semester 1833*. *Grundlegung der positiven Philosophie*, edited by Horst Fuhrmans. Turin: Bottega d'Erasmo, 1972.

IN	*Ideen zu einer Philosophie der Natur / Ideas for a Philosophy of Nature* (1797). HKA I/5, 59–306.
IN2	*Ideen zu einer Philosophie der Natur*, 2. Auflage */ Ideas for a Philosophy of Nature*, 2nd ed. (1803). HKA I/13. Translated by Errol E. Harris and Peter Heath. Cambridge: Cambridge University Press, 1988.
IPU	*Initia philosophiae universae* (1821 Erlangen lectures). HKA II/10.
KF	"Kritische Fragmente" / "Critical Fragments" (1806). HKA I/15, 297–310.
KH	*Kommentar zum Buch "Hiob" / Commentary on the Book of Job* (1790/93). HKA II/1, Teilband 2.
KT	*Kommentar zum "Timaios" / Commentary on the Timaeus* (1794). HKA II/5, 149–196. Translated by Adam Arola, Jena Jolissaint, and Peter Warnek. *Epoché* 12, no. 2 (2008): 205–248.
PB	*Philosophische Briefe über Dogmatismus und Kriticismus / Philosophical Letters on Dogmatism and Criticism* (1795). HKA I/3, 47–114. Translated by Fritz Marti in *The Unconditional in Human Knowledge: Four Early Essays (1794–96)*, 156–196. Lewisburg, PA: Bucknell University Press, 1980.
PK	*Philosophie der Kunst / Philosophy of Art* (1802–3). HKA II/6, 93–405. Translated by Douglas W. Stott. Minneapolis: University of Minnesota Press, 1989.
PM	*Philosophie der Mythologie / Philosophy of Mythology* (1842, 1845/46). SW II/2.
PO1	*Philosophie der Offenbarung*, Teil 1 */ Philosophy of Revelation,* Part 1 (1841/42, 1844/45). SW II/3.
PO2	*Philosophie der Offenbarung*, Teil 2 */ Philosophy of Revelation*, Part 2 (1841/42, 1844/45). SW II/4.
POP	*Philosophie der Offenbarung 1841/42 / Philosophy of Revelation 1841/42. Philosophie der Offenbarung 1841/42 [Nachschrift Paulus]*, edited by Manfred Frank. Frankfurt am Main: Suhrkamp, 1977.
PR	*Philosophie und Religion / Philosophy and Religion* (1804). HKA I/14, 273–326. Translated by Klaus Ottmann. Putnam, CT: Spring Publications, 2010.
SA	"Fragment zur Strukturtheorie des Absoluten" / "A Fragment on the Structural Theory of the Absolute" (date unknown). In Barbara Loer, *Das Absolute und die Wirklichkeit in Schellings Philosophie*, 30–52. Berlin: de Gruyter, 1974.
SPV	*Stuttgarter Privatvorlesungen / Stuttgart Seminars* (1810). HKA II/8, 68–188. In *Idealism and the Endgame of Theory. Three Essays by F.W.J. Schelling*. Translated by Thomas Pfau, 195–243. Albany: State University of New York Press, 1994.
STI	*System des transzendentalen Idealismus / System of Transcendental Idealism* (1800). HKA I/9. Translated by Peter Heath. Charlottesville: University Press of Virginia, 1978.

UFP	*Über die Möglichkeit einer Form der Philosophie überhaupt / On the Possibility of a Form of All Philosophy* (1794). HKA I/1, 263–300. Translated in Schelling, *The Unconditional*, trans. Marti, 38–55.
UM	"Über Mythen, historische Sagen und Philosopheme der ältesten Welt" / "On Myths, Historical Legends, and Philosophemes of the Ancient World" (1793). HKA I/1, 193–246.
UPO	*Urfassung der Philosophie der Offenbarung / First Manuscript of the Philosophy of Revelation* (1831–32). *Urfassung der Philosophie der Offenbarung*, edited by Walter E. Ehrhardt. Hamburg: Meiner, 1992.
UV	"Über das Verhältnis der Naturphilosophie zur Philosophie überhaupt" / "On the Relation of the Philosophy of Nature to Philosophy in General" (1802). HKA I/12, 457–474. *Between Kant and Hegel: Texts in the Development of Post-Kantian Idealism*. Translated by George di Giovanni and H. S. Harris, 363–380. Indianapolis, IN: Hackett, 2000.
VAW	"Vorstellungsarten der alten Welt über verschiedne Gegenstände, gesammelt aus Homer, Plato u.a." / "Ways of Thought in the Ancient World Regarding Various Matters, Collated from Homer, Plato et al." (1792). HKA II/4, 15–28.
VEM	"Die vier edlen Metalle" / "Four Noble Metals" (1802). HKA I/12, 317–327.
VI	*Vom Ich als Princip der Philosophie oder über das Unbedingte im menschlichen Wissen / Of the I as Principle of Philosophy, or, On the Unconditional in Human Knowledge* (1795). HKA I/2, 67–176. Translated in Schelling, *The Unconditional*, trans. Marti, 63–128.
VJM	"Vorrede" / "Preface" [to volume 1 of *Jahrbücher der Medizin*] (1805). HKA I/15, 55–62.
VM	*Vorlesungen über die Methode des academischen Studium / Lectures on the Method of University Studies* (delivered in 1802, published 1803). HKA I/14, 51–176. *On University Studies*. Translated by E. S. Morgan. Athens: Ohio University Press, 1966.
VVC	"Vorrede zu einer philosophischen Schrift des Herrn Victor Cousin" / "Preface to a Philosophical Piece by Victor Cousin" (1834). SW I/10, 201–224.
VW	*Von der Weltseele / On the World-Soul* (1798). HKA I/6.
WA11	*Weltalter-Entwurf 1811 / The Ages of the World: The 1811 Draft*. Schelling, *Die Weltalter*, ed. Schröter, 1–107. *The Ages of the World. Book One: The Past (Original Version, 1811). Plus Supplementary Fragments*. Translated by Joseph P. Lawrence. Albany: State University of New York Press, 2019.
WA14	*Die Weltalter [Bruchstück] / The Ages of the World [A Fragment]* (1814–15). SW I/8, 195–344. *The Ages of the World (Fragment). Third Version (c. 1815)*. Translated by Jason M. Wirth. Albany: State University of New York Press, 2000.

WA27	*System der Weltalter. Vorlesung 1827/28* / *The System of the Ages of the World: 1827/28 Lectures. System der Weltalter. Münchener Vorlesung 1827/28 in einer Nachschrift von Ernst von Lasaulx*. Frankfurt am Main: Vittorio Klostermann, 1990.
WAE	*Weltalter. Entwürfe und Fragmente* (dates unknown). Schelling, *Die Weltalter. Fragmente*, ed. Schröter, 185–272. Translated in Schelling, *Ages of the World (1811)*, trans. Lawrence, 169–249.
WAF1	*Weltalter. Fragmente* Bd. 1. *Weltalter-Fragmente*, vol. 1, edited by Klaus Grotsch. Stuttgart: Frommann-Holzboog, 2002.
WAF2	*Weltalter. Fragmente* Bd. 2. *Weltalter-Fragmente*, vol. 2, edited by Klaus Grotsch. Stuttgart: Frommann-Holzboog, 2002.
WS	*System der gesammten Philosophie und der Naturphilosophie insbesondere* / *System of Philosophy in General and of the Philosophy of Nature in Particular* ("Würzburg System") (1804). HKA II/7, 99–443. Incomplete English translation in *Idealism and the Endgame of Theory*, trans. Pfau, 139–94.

General Introduction

MODERNITY, THEODICY, BLISS

The world is too much with us.
—WILLIAM WORDSWORTH

THIS BOOK TURNS to the post-Enlightenment, post-Revolutionary moment of crisis—a moment at which European modernity reflects upon itself and the global world it has created, and at which the very idea of "modernity" as a separate epoch and normative program is taking shape alongside the rapid rise of capitalism and the development of abolitionist struggle. The German idealist and Romantic philosopher Friedrich Schelling (1775–1854), I contend, is a key thinker of that moment and of the critical age and age of crisis that is modernity. Unlike his more influential rival Hegel, who comes to embrace negativity as the motor of his dialectic, for Schelling it is precisely the negativity of the modern world that, throughout his philosophical trajectory from the 1790s onward, remains the burning problem. This makes Schelling's thought deeply attuned to the aporias and impasses of modernity, and to modernity as a problem rather than the solution (as it arguably is in Hegel). After all, the modern world can be overwhelmingly negative. It demands ceaseless work and endless striving toward an endlessly deferred telos. It promises fulfillment and non-alienation in the future while using this very promise to foreclose them in the present, to reproduce the way things are, and to bind the subject to the imperatives of possession and production. Everywhere modernity can reach, it seeks to impose upon the unappropriated earth and upon alternative forms of being human the modern, dirempted structures of reality and subjectivity. Instead of overcoming alienation and negativity, modernity ends up intensifying them: the burden of the world becomes unbearable.

Over and against this negativity, Schelling insistently positions the idea of bliss (*Seligkeit*)—of a fulfilled, non-alienated existence without diremption, appropriation, or lack, a state of being that is absolutely free from the negativity of the world—as what the modern world promises yet, in the same stroke, forecloses, defers, and otherwise fails to enact. At its most radical, bliss is positioned in Schelling *against* the world and against any attempts to justify the world's negativity as somehow good or necessary (attempts that may be said to bear the collective name "theodicy"). At the same time, bliss constitutes something like the repressed underside of modernity, on which modernity feeds even while foreclosing it, and the promise of which modernity requires in order to justify the evils of the present for the sake of a supposedly better, fulfilled future. This creates what I will explore, in and through Schelling, as the antagonistic entanglement between bliss and modernity, and as the tension between bliss and theodicy at the heart of the Christian-modern world.

The same tension is located, I suggest, at the heart of Schelling's thought, providing a persistent driving force behind the (often significant) changes in his metaphysics over the decades that constitute his philosophical trajectory. As we will see, Schelling repeatedly seeks at once to affirm bliss in its anti-worldly antagonism, and to affirm theodically the modern world as ultimately necessary and good despite its negativity and violence. This contradiction, with which Schelling never ceases to grapple, is symptomatic precisely because it reflects the constitutive contradiction of modernity itself. This book thus reads bliss with and against Schelling—*with*, insofar I seek to reconstruct Schelling's concept of bliss and to draw out its conceptual implications vis-à-vis his thinking of finitude, modernity, and natural and human history; *against*, insofar as I offer a critique of the theodical tendency that permeates his thinking and stands at odds with his own imperative of bliss, and that I take to be entwined with modernity's (as well as Christianity's) constitutive foreclosure of bliss.

Over the course of this book, through a rereading of much of the Schellingian corpus, I will trace Schelling's concept of bliss in its entanglement with the modern world, and with the political-theological questions of this world's genealogy and legitimacy—questions that, for Schelling, cannot be addressed without considering modernity's emergence from and continuing co-imbrication with Christianity, and with the Christian logics of futurity and salvation. By the end of this book, a Schellingian panorama of modernity and bliss will emerge, which I take to continue to resonate today. Here, for the purposes of this introduction, I will provide a more axiomatic account of Schellingian bliss and of the relationship between modernity and theodicy. This relationship will be important both for understanding the significance of theodicy in Schelling's thought, and as that which will be confirmed and complicated by the Schellingian framework of bliss advanced in this book. I thus intend this introduction as an overview of the conceptual knot that the book's individual chapters will unravel.

I.1. *Schelling's Plenum of Bliss*

In secondary literature, Schelling's philosophical trajectory is traditionally divided into several periods.[1] Keeping in mind the imposed and imprecise character of any such periodization, one may speak of Schelling in the 1790s as a post-Kantian philosopher of human and natural subjectivity. These are the years during which he develops his transcendental philosophy and philosophy of nature (marking the broader Romantic turn to nature of which he becomes the central figure). The publication of his *Presentation of My System of Philosophy* in 1801 signals his break with J. G. Fichte and the beginning of his so-called philosophy of absolute identity or "identity philosophy." This period especially remains insufficiently understood due to the seeming strangeness of Schelling's ambition to re-vision reality not as a world of division and difference but indifferently and blissfully. Together, these two periods are often classified as "the early Schelling." His 1809 *Philosophical Inquiries into the Essence of Human Freedom*, often referred to simply as the *Freedom* essay, indexes the beginning of his so-called middle philosophy. It marks Schelling's turn from pantheism to theism and includes the monumental *Ages of the World* project, which he continues to develop well into the 1820s but never completes. What follows after that is known as "the late Schelling," a period in which he delivers his lectures on philosophy of mythology and philosophy of revelation and works out his distinction between (Christian) "positive philosophy" and (the purely rational) "negative philosophy," the latter of which he associates critically with the thought of his erstwhile friend Hegel.

As one may see, the trajectory of Schelling's thought is varied, and I do not intend to contest the fact that Schelling's metaphysics changes substantially from the 1790s to the 1840s. Over the course of this book, I will revisit the different periods of Schelling's thought and note what I consider to be some of the key shifts in his metaphysics. At the same time, I am interested not in restaging or revising existing periodizations but in offering an alternative path by tracing, across the trajectory of Schelling's thought, the antagonism between bliss and the world as well as the question of theodicy. While

---

1. For an account of this trajectory from the perspective of the history of philosophy, see Bowie, *Schelling and Modern European Philosophy*.

this alternative path is not supposed to exhaust the richness of Schelling's philosophy, I believe that it offers an important vision of a key conceptual continuity across the various changes in his thought. In its main contours, the antagonism between bliss and the world takes shape in Schelling in the early 1790s; and these contours remain strikingly consistent throughout the following decades, as though in keeping with the non-processual character of bliss itself. In Schelling scholarship, *Seligkeit* remains a neglected concept. A more traditional interpretative approach would, perhaps, focus on his concepts of "absolute freedom" or "absolute identity" instead, or even his concept of "heaven" (*Himmel*), all of which are in some way synonymous with "bliss." However, I would argue that these other concepts are ultimately more limited than "bliss," do not reflect in the same way the apocalyptic entwinement of Schelling's thought with the problem of salvation in the Christian-modern world, or are not employed by him with the same degree of consistency—whereas, as this book will show, the term "bliss" reappears at key points throughout his texts from 1795 onward. Moreover, the concept of bliss remains stable even as Schelling's concepts of freedom, identity, and the absolute undergo metaphysical shifts. Thus, the focus on bliss makes it possible at once to explore the connection between Schelling's thought and the broader Christian-modern entanglement during the late eighteenth and the first half of the nineteenth century, and to chart an alternative course through his thought from his early to his last writings.[2]

For understanding Schellingian bliss (and my choice to translate *Seligkeit* as "bliss"), it is crucial to keep in mind that, in German as in English at the time, *Seligkeit* and *bliss*, respectively, form one conceptual nexus with *beatitude*, *blessedness*, and *salvation*. There is, of course, an entire tradition behind this nexus. Importantly for us, as early as 1795 Schelling does not hesitate to use *Seligkeit* at once as "bliss," as "salvation" (the theological meaning of the German word), and as a translation of Spinoza's *beatitudo*. Earlier the same nexus can be found in Kant. Luther's Bible also renders "Blessed are. . ." (*beati*/*makarioi*) as "Selig sind . . ." In English, a similar nexus formed around *bliss* through its association with *bless*, and through what the *Oxford English*

---

2. In focusing on bliss, I also aim to complicate the common description of Schelling as a thinker of freedom (based in particular on his oft-quoted early dictum that "freedom is the alpha and omega of philosophy"; BW1 22) by insisting that finite freedom—the freedom of striving and self-assertion as well as freedom for good and evil—remains a *problem* in and for Schelling. To focus on freedom alone and not on bliss runs the risk of obfuscating both Schelling's own problematization of finite freedom through bliss and the foreclosure of bliss by the Christian and modern logics of freedom.

Dictionary calls "the gradual tendency to withdraw *bliss* from earthly 'blitheness' to the beatitude of the blessed in heaven."[3] *Bliss* and *Seligkeit* thus map onto each other rather accurately. In today's German, the word *Seligkeit* is no longer used in the sense of highest fulfillment or bliss; only its Christian sense of "salvation" remains. In Kant and the German idealists and Romantics, however—precisely due to the term's co-imbrication with the notion of salvation at a critical moment when otherworldly salvation increasingly loses its conceptual relevance—*Seligkeit* provides a decisive counterpart to the more empirical concept of "happiness" (*Glückseligkeit*).[4] Schelling's concept of bliss emerges, as it were, at the intersection of the crisis of salvation and what has been theorized as the late eighteenth-century crisis of happiness.[5] Both form a part of the broader landscape of crisis that has to do ultimately with the intensification of the constitutively alienated and divided character of the modern structure of reality.

This structure of alienation is what Schelling, starting in 1795, calls "world." One thesis this book aims to unpack is that Schelling's metaphysics of what he terms "world" or "universe" is always highly modern or, more precisely, Christian-modern in character. Since the moment of its emergence, grasped by Schelling variously as a Fall (*Abfall*) or as divine creation, the universe has for him been alienated and dirempted, and this structure of universal diremption, cutting across nature and human consciousness, *is* the structure of finite reality as such ("world"): the structure of endless negativity, productivity, and striving, in which nature and the human are equally caught. In his metaphysics, Schelling inscribes even pre-Christian forms of consciousness, such as the "pagan" mind, or pre-human natural forms into a universe that is constitutively fallen and unblissful, and whose true structure and destination are revealed to consciousness for the first time in Christianity (and then developed scientifically and philosophically in modernity). The broadly Christian-Gnostic sense of the world's fallenness, and of the subject's being bound to the world while striving to break free from it, emerges in Schelling already in the 1790s and remains integral to his metaphysics of finitude. This sense, which Schelling locates within the subject too, is what generates the subject's

---

3. "Bliss, n., Etymology," *Oxford English Dictionary*, https://doi.org/10.1093/OED/580 1613935.

4. I am interested here solely in Schelling's concept of *Seligkeit*. However, among his contemporaries, e.g., Novalis and Fichte, *Seligkeit* is also important. See further Chepurin, "Romantic Bliss." In today's German, *Glückseligkeit* is closer to "bliss."

5. Soni, *Mourning Happiness*.

longing for bliss. Bliss, in turn, may be preliminarily defined as the highest, non-empirical happiness that takes one *out* of the world, and in which all relation to the negativity of the world disappears. For Schelling, this is not merely an affective but an ontological state. Romantic love, mystical oneness with the divine, the all-consuming revolutionary fire, and the feeling of dissolution in nature provide some of the paradigmatic examples of bliss as an ecstatic state in which one is transported to the standpoint of an immediate and absolute oneness that is ontologically *prior* to the divisions and alienations of the world. This is the paradox of Schellingian bliss: although bliss is not in the world or part of the world, it is by no means illusory but, instead, what is absolutely first and absolutely real, even "divine."

As such, it is impossible to define bliss fully. Theologically put, it is the a-worldly divine fullness itself, which cannot be captured by any single definition or articulated in finite categories. Each chapter in this book, too, will orbit around and increasingly reveal the nexus of meanings inherent in Schellingian bliss without, however, exhausting it. More important than its definition is the constant function of bliss across Schelling's writings: that of antagonism toward the way the world is. In Schelling, bliss is a recurring term and recurring vision: a vision of absolute freedom as freedom from the world, and of an absolute fulfillment that is not conditioned by the world. Whereas empirical happiness is for him tied to the subject-object division and to the possession or appropriation of the desired object by the subject, bliss names a state of undivided immanence free of possession, appropriation, or striving. In bliss, all negativity and alienation, all imperatives of work and production, are dissolved into a state of absolute oneness, indifference, and non-relation. The demand of bliss is that of the abolition or, to use Schelling's own term, "annihilation" of the world qua the structure of alienation and violence. Schelling's vision of bliss is apocalyptic: bliss dissolves the world as in water, consumes it as in fire, so that nothing of the world's negativity remains. Amid the post-Revolutionary apocalyptic sentiment characteristic of early Romanticism—a sentiment that Schelling would, despite everything, always retain—he envisions this all-dissolution or all-consumption as the epoch of bliss demanded from within the present (even as the world may defer and re-mediate the immediacy of this demand). However, although bliss may appear from within the unblissful world as either a lost paradisal past or a longed-for blissful future, it is itself immanently atemporal. For Schelling, bliss simply *is*, prior to the imposition of the world; to abolish the world is but to disclose what has been violently foreclosed by it.

Especially during the early 1800s, bliss in Schelling indexes the ante-original plenitude—the infinite immanent plenum of the earth and the skies—as what is absolutely common, without particularization or appropriation, and what ontologically precedes the divisions and dominations that constitute the world.[6] (The idea of this ante-original plenitude of bliss is, I will argue, crucial for making sense of Schelling's pantheism during this period.) To intellectually intuit this bliss is to see all being as free of negativity or striving. It is to see the one life or the *it is what it is* at the heart of everything, an A = A, in which the finite being's particularity is dissolved in the pure "=": an image of absolute nonproductivity, the Sabbath of unappropriated being. The all-oneness of bliss is what is *real*, much more real than the divisions and alienations that constitute the world. In the same vein, the planetary commons of the earth possess a deeper reality preceding and exceeding the reality of the global capitalist world-order, even as the latter depends on the former for its resources and for maintaining its cycle of negativity. The modern world imposes itself upon this plenitude, this "abyss of repose" (to quote Schelling's description of the blissful essence of nature; AD 327), seeking to enclose and appropriate it. To affirm bliss as primary vis-à-vis the world, and as what the world forecloses, is to insist that this negative, alienated world is *not* all there is, and not the ultimate horizon of reality that it often declares itself to be. As "absolute," bliss ungrounds the modern world's claim to absoluteness, reminding us that there is an ontological abundance on which this world is forcefully imposed, and which this world conceals and turns into its own dark ground while continuing to exploit it. Modernity may promise abundance, non-alienation, and fulfillment in the future, but the not-yet of this promise serves only to exacerbate negativity and darkness in the present.

Bliss in Schelling thus combines a sense of the absolutely positive and absolutely negative, of radical affirmation and radical antagonism: what it unconditionally affirms is *not* the world but that which the world forecloses and excludes. This constitutive antagonism of bliss to the world persists in Schelling's thought, marking his ever-present affinity with heterodoxy and proclivity for mysticism and heresy, even following his 1809 turn to a version of Christian theism. No matter the changes in the underlying metaphysics, bliss continues to index for Schelling a state of world-dissolution in which the alienated structure of finitude is annihilated and one "cease[s] to be a finite being" (PB 79/175) in an immediate oneness with the absolutely real.

---

6. I term "ante-original" that which precedes and exceeds even the origin or beginning of the world, and which persists antagonistically against the world once the world is in place.

I.2. *The Genealogical Question*

As may be glimpsed already from the above schematic summary, Schellingian bliss is a complex concept that combines ontological, affective, ethical, mystical, and salvific dimensions, refusing to be neatly inscribed in the dichotomy of "religious" and "secular" (a dichotomy that is itself the product of modern secularism). In fact, this book argues that bliss in Schelling marks precisely the aporias of the co-imbrication of Christianity and modernity in the formation of the modern global world and its negativity. For Schelling, not only does the promise of modernity inherit and transform the Christian promise; but the modern structure of alienation, too, constitutes an intensification and mutation of the contradictions within the Christian structure of salvation. As salvation from the negativity of the world, bliss raises for Schelling the *genealogical* question: What is the relation between the modern promise of non-alienated existence and the logics of Christianity out of which European modernity emerges? It is well known that German idealism and Romanticism form an indispensable site in the rise of the modern idea of world history. In them, the question of modernity is inseparable from the question of genealogy.[7] Schelling's place in the formation of this genealogical line of inquiry (which becomes so prominent in the twentieth-century debate around secularization and political theology), however, still remains underexplored. As someone who from his early years was immersed in an intensive study of ancient philosophy and mythology as well as the Christian tradition, including heresies such as Gnosticism (see Interlude I), Schelling never ceased to reflect on the historical-genealogical trajectory of the idea of salvation—and, as we will see, his speculative constructions of "history," "mythology," and "religion" all participate crucially in the Christian-modern development of these categories in and for the post-1492 global world.

Furthermore, seeing as, for Schelling, Christianity as well as modernity end up foreclosing non-alienation and bliss, the genealogical question is constantly intertwined in his thought with the *theodical* question: How can the negativity of the (Christian-modern) world be rationally justified? What is the world-order that is given—and why must this order be, with all the suffering and violence it engenders? Most radically, we will see bliss in Schelling turn this theodical question into what may be called the *Gnostic* question: Is this world even legitimate? Or, if this world keeps foreclosing bliss, then must this world even be? These questions become the Gnostic imperative: *the world*

---

7. See also Chepurin and Dubilet, "Introduction."

must not be. The Gnostic question politically and theologically underwrites what Schelling calls "the ultimate despairing question: why does anything exist at all? why is there not nothing?" (PO1 7). The question of the meaning and purpose of the world, and of human being in the world, drives the one who raises it to despair, threatening to unground the possibility of theodical reconciliation with the world. Thereby, in an ambivalence characteristic of theodicy more broadly, the theodical question in Schelling, by highlighting the endless negativity of the world, threatens to undermine the legitimacy of the very world it seeks to justify. At the late eighteenth-century moment of crisis when, as Schelling formulates it in a 1795 letter to Hegel, "the entire previous constitution of the world" (BW1 21) appears to collapse, these questions—the genealogical, the theodical, and the Gnostic—become intensified. Schelling's thought forms a singular conceptual site in the topography of this intensification. In 1795 (not coincidentally, the year in which his concept of bliss takes shape), Schelling sees himself as living through the end of the world.

In view of the Christian-modern entanglement, to say that modernity, in Schelling as in this book, is a problem is not to imply that Christianity is the solution. Although Schelling himself turns to Christianity, rather than read this turn as anti-modern I argue that it continues to mark the problematic co-imbrication of Christianity and modernity and the foreclosure by modernity of the promise of bliss. The Schellingian framework of the negativity of modernity that I advance in this book requires a *co-critique* of Christianity and modernity in their genealogical and conceptual entanglement.[8] Understanding this entanglement is imperative for grasping and critiquing what is usually seen as an increasingly secular modernity—in its negativity, its incompleteness and not-yetness, and its foreclosure of non-alienated being. The concept of bliss is significant not least because it allows us not to lose sight of the way the promise of modernity transforms and remains co-imbricated with the

---

8. Thereby, I seek to problematize not only secularist critiques of Schelling's turn to Christianity or Christian-theological endorsements of this turn but also those readings that take Schelling to "overcome" modernity through recourse either to transcendence or to the "premodern," be it in the form of Boehmean theosophy or Christian theism. In particular, unlike Slavoj Žižek, I critique the very logic of periodization in Schelling, and of "overtaking modernity," as itself a Christian-modern logic that reproduces the hegemonic world-trajectory. Cf. Žižek, *The Indivisible Remainder*, 8. I also diverge from Saitya Brata Das, *Political Theology of Schelling*, which presents Schellingian transcendence as an alternative to the "secularized" theodicy that Das identifies with modernity and with Hegel. For me, rather, transcendence is a shared Christian-modern *problem*, and Schelling's own thought remains problematically theodical throughout—a fact that marks its co-imbrication with the aporias and violences of the Christian-modern world. Finally, unlike other political-theological readings, I take Schelling's natural philosophy to be a key site of his grappling with Christian-modern reality.

Christian idea of salvation. It also highlights the failure of this promise, with which we continue to live. In and through Schelling, we will see this promise and this failure resonate across the entire modern reality, from the strivings of the modern subject, to the enclosures of the planetary commons, to the racialized divisions and violences of the global. The modern age will emerge from this not merely as an age of linear progress but as constitutively negative and needy, as premised on the transcendent logics of actualization and striving, and as permeated at every moment with anxiety, nostalgia, hope, and longing—so that the never-ending loop of negativity characteristic of modernity constantly threatens to spiral out of control.

This book, too, is written out of a sense of crisis: a planetary crisis of the global order that modernity has produced and from which, it seems, there is no escape, not even to distant stars. The modern world remains too much with us, as its negativity continues to make life precarious and unstable, and to distribute the burden of the world in asymmetrical ways. The promise of a fulfilled, non-alienated existence, without negativity or lack, haunts the present as the longed-for future. And yet, within the cruel optimism of the late-capitalist condition,[9] this promise constitutively cannot be realized, becoming increasingly spectral and creating a renewed cycle of nostalgia, fear, and violence within a seemingly futureless horizon. At these moments, negativity intensifies apocalyptically—and it is no wonder that the figure of the end of the world, and anxiety over irreversible catastrophe, permeate the contemporary imaginary no less than contemporary critical theory. Every time this cycle becomes unbearable, every time a crisis breaks out, it is as though the atemporal idea of bliss erupts in and through the historical present, connecting it transhistorically to other moments of crisis that all resonate jointly in the now, and reminding us that history is never merely historical but constituted by its ever-present tension with what precedes and exceeds historical time. That is why pure historicism is never fully satisfactory: it cannot account for the transhistorical dimension of events such as revolution and crisis, or for the tension between the historical and the ahistorical at the heart of history. At moments of crisis, the unbearable negativity of the world generates the ultimate negation: the refusal of this world itself, demanded right now. While breaking through to the surface in specific historical contexts, the demand of bliss reveals a deeper transhistorical antagonism *to* world history in its negativity, an antagonism that exceeds any historical situatedness.

---

9. See Berlant, *Cruel Optimism*.

Thus, if this book deals with a thinker of the past, it is not simply out of an antiquarian concern. As Schelling puts it in another letter from 1795, expressing the post-Revolutionary sense of upheaval: "Who would want to bury himself in the dust of old times when the course of *one's own* time at every moment sweeps one up and carries one onward?" (BW1 16). I do not believe there to be any contradiction between the radicality of this statement and the fact that Schelling did continue to "bury himself in the dust of old times," including the deep time of planetary evolution and the oldest times of human history, and ultimately devoted decades of his life to producing a highly elaborate interpretation of ancient mythology. This was very much part of the movement of his time too, carrying him onward. The immediate post-Revolutionary moment, with its early Romantic impulse of bliss as antagonism toward the oppressions and enclosures of the world, may have been more hopeful than our seemingly futureless present, but it was destined to wane, and to be suppressed by the consolidation of capitalism in the first half of the nineteenth century—even as bliss remained excessive over its theodical foreclosure, simultaneously erupting anew, for instance, in Karl Marx's post-Romantic idea of communism in the 1840s. The dynamic of this foreclosure and renewed eruption also stands at the center of this book.

Accordingly, my argument in this book is intended to function at multiple interconnected levels: it zooms in on Schelling's philosophical trajectory so as to tell, through it, a story of the eruption and the subsequent waning of bliss during the period from the late eighteenth to the mid-nineteenth century. At the same time, this story reflects for me the broader dynamic of modernity and of the tension between bliss and theodicy inherent in the Christian-modern trajectory. This tension is precisely what I theorize in and through Schelling as the tension at the core of his own thought—so that, thereby, the meta-trajectory of the Christian-modern world loops back onto the trajectory of Schelling's philosophical development. At the center of this construction is Schelling's own diagnosis of modernity as itself a salvific epoch transforming the promise of Christianity, and his singular analytic of the modern aporias of salvation and demiurgic production.

I.3. A Scene of Bliss: Rousseau and Adorno

To understand the trajectory of Schelling's thought as traced in this book, including the centrality of natural philosophy (*Naturphilosophie*) in his concept of bliss, one context is especially important. It is the emergence of the Romantic vision of nature as the site of antagonism to the modern world, and as the a-worldly site of fulfillment. As part of the late eighteenth-century moment of crisis, Romantic *Naturphilosophie* arises over and against the alienated modern view of nature as mere object and the concomitant colonial understanding of it as the *terra nullius* meant for appropriation and resource extraction.

One version of the natural scene of bliss in particular reappears across modernity as, so to speak, a proto-scene of Romanticism. It is found in Jean-Jacques Rousseau's *Reveries of the Solitary Walker*, published in 1782. There Rousseau describes his habit of fleeing the world and of losing himself in the all-oneness of nature in which the world is dissolved:

> I would slip away and go throw myself alone into a boat that I rowed to the middle of the lake when the water was calm; and there, stretching myself out full-length in the boat, my eyes turned to heaven, I let myself slowly drift back and forth with the water.[10]

The subject becomes, in this scene, absolutely useless and idle, dissolving with the movement of the water and losing all sense of self-possession and the rigidity of a bounded self. In conjunction with Rousseau's critique of modernity and the logics of enclosure and private property in his 1755 *Discourse on Inequality*, whose affirmation of a natural state of felicity prior to the negativity of progress emerges likewise out of a resolute no to the intensification of alienation in the present, the antagonistic ease of Rousseau's scene of nature would leave a lasting impression on Rousseau's theoretical opponents and allies alike. While this scene does not exhaust the multidimensional complexity of Schellingian bliss, it may be regarded as a prefiguration of Schelling's emphasis on the one undivided natural bliss, in which the world of modern selfhood is canceled out.

In the mid-twentieth century, the same scene comes in the form of a fragment in Theodor Adorno's most Romantic text, *Minima Moralia* (1951). Entitled "Sur l'eau" ("On the Water"), this fragment sketches, against the calamitous tide of modernity, a utopia of nonproductivity. It may be, Adorno muses there, that the best way to imagine an absolutely free being is to conceive of it not as a state of endless productivity and dynamism, but as completely disinvested from the logic of production—as refusing the demand of ceaseless development and the modern pursuit of realizing possibilities to the

---

10. Rousseau, *Reveries of the Solitary Walker*, in *Collected Writings*, vol. 8, 44.

fullest. "Perhaps," Adorno speculates, "the true society will grow tired of development and, out of freedom, leave possibilities unused." "Tiredness" implies here, I would suggest, an exhaustion produced by the allure of the world's possibilities, with their constant not-yet that serves only to reproduce the world as it is. This no to the logic of productivity becomes in Adorno a vision of bliss at the end of the world, in which the world is dissolved and human and nonhuman lives are brought into a non-alienated unity, a Schellingian absolute identity without a care in or for the world: "*Rien faire comme une bête*, lying on water and looking peacefully at the sky, 'being, nothing else, without any further definition and fulfilment,' might take the place of process, act, satisfaction." At the same time, what "tiredness" also indicates here is that this bliss, while essentially one with what might be imagined as paradisal bliss, is separated from the latter by the chasm of the world. The longed-for repose—and no concept, Adorno suggests, "comes closer to fulfilled utopia than that of eternal peace"[11]—is already premised here on a process of development, an arduous path through world history, and the labor and cruelty of the negative.

In Adorno, too, bliss emerges as salvation from the negativity of the modern world—as what the concluding fragment of *Minima Moralia* calls "the standpoint of redemption [*Erlösung*]." It is in the face of the world's highest negativity that the utopia of bliss emerges in its necessity.[12] This utopia rejects the modern world's claim to absoluteness and to constituting the final horizon of reality, and persists with bliss as what is impossible yet real, as the non-place where the world's structures do not hold, and as the utopic standpoint from which the negativity of the world does not appear as omnipresent or all-powerful, or even does not appear at all. In its vast pre-human immanence that is infinitely more powerful than the world of the global, nature provides precisely such a utopic standpoint. In Schelling, whose philosophy is contemporaneous with the discovery of geological deep time, even the fire contained in the depths of the earth becomes the antagonistic site of bliss, destined to erupt against the modern world of self-assertion and enclosure (see Chapter 3). Especially in the post-Revolutionary context in which Schelling's thought emerges, the demand of bliss cannot be associated solely with repose—since, if it is to be enacted against the world, repose can come only after or in the form of (the demand for) the world's annihilation.

---

11. Adorno, *Minima Moralia*, 156–157.

12. Ibid., 247.

In this way, the metaphysical question in which everything is at stake—what is first and more essential, work or repose? scarcity or abundance? strife or peace?—plays out on the barricades of modernity. At the very least, this persistence of bliss reminds us that idleness, non-alienation, and nonproductivity are more important than negativity and work. Even modernity recognizes this, insofar as alienation and work are usually affirmed in the modern age not for their own sake, but for the sake of a better, more fulfilled future. The modern world claims for itself the promise of bliss, of endless abundance and paradise regained, inscribing this promise into its visions of progress.[13] And yet, modernity excludes the nonproductive and the idle, denigrates and racializes it, so as to legitimate this negative world as the highest. In modernity, precisely those who are declared to be by nature the most idle and immature are often made to bear the ultimate burden of the work of the world. Thereby, enlightened modernity creates and intensifies the dark ground that it exploits yet conceals, proclaiming theodically the goodness of its own creation.

I.4. *The Fall from Bliss (into the World): Kant*

It has been suggested that the German idealist thinking of subjectivity from Kant onward seeks to return Rousseau's useless (non-)subject, unburdened by care, back to the fold of the world.[14] Ironically, what Adorno imagines as a utopia of eternal peace is what Kant, the best-known proponent of eternal peace, forecloses in his anthropology and philosophy of history, as well as in his own use of the term "bliss"—so that Schelling's conception of bliss may be understood as responding to the prohibition that Kant places on bliss.

Not to let the subject escape the world of toil and strife forms a central tendency of Kant's thought, as does the forceful injunction to the subject to *care* for the world, and to bear its burden with hope. In *Critique of Practical Reason* (1788), *Seligkeit* is associated at once with atemporal divine self-sufficiency—"a complete well-being that is independent from all contingent causes in the world"—and a "blissful future" that only God can possess, a "holiness [that] is never fully attained by the creature."[15] Bliss is "attainable only in an eternity"[16]

---

13. See Merchant, *Reinventing Eden*.

14. See Sloterdijk, *Stress and Freedom*, 39: "Kant had pulled the dreamer off the boat and recruited him for the civil service."

15. Kant, *Critique of Practical Reason*, 23 and 100. Translation slightly modified.

16. Ibid., 104.

and thus, from the perspective of finite being in the world, deferred into an unreachable future. To dream of a being without striving, *right now*, of bliss as an immediate possession (*Besitz*)—by which Kant means something that one simply has or is by virtue of one's mere being, the Schellingian absolute identity—amounts to delusional "theosophical dreams." The only rational thing for us to do is to embrace this life of "ceaseless striving."[17] For Kant as for Fichte and Hegel, no activity is more in contradiction with the human as a rational being than activity without a goal. And so Kant consistently orients human being in the world toward an endlessly approximated telos.

This foreclosure of bliss becomes historical in Kant's "Conjectural Beginning of Human History" (1786), his influential reconfiguration of the biblical story of the Fall. There, in a polemic against Rousseau, Kant undertakes a dismantling of natural bliss and a justification of the expulsion from paradise. For Kant, everything—all progress of morality and freedom—hinges on the affirmation and reproduction of the world. Hegel later claims that his own philosophy of history is "a theodicy."[18] By that, he means that it justifies the negativity and suffering inherent in history as necessary for attaining what is the highest and divine—that is, the development of reason and freedom—as well as justifies the modern (Christian-European) world as the pinnacle of this development. This theodical tendency, which we will likewise witness in Schelling, already stands at the heart of Kant's essay. There is, Kant claims, no regaining of paradisal bliss from within the postlapsarian world—and, furthermore, no paradise to be regained. Paradise, he avers, cannot be anything but a brutish state of humanity's thoughtless childhood and the rule of instinct. The Fall should be understood, accordingly, as the awakening of reason. Reason drove the human out of the "secure condition of childcare, from out of a garden . . . and thrust him into the wide world, where so many worries, troubles, and unknown ills awaited him."[19] In this way the development of reason and freedom begins, always proceeding through negativity and strife. The human must now, relying on reason, assert itself vis-à-vis the alien world, across generations.

Kant's association of the world with the imperative of toil is remarkable. The work of the world is unbearable, yet reason "urges [the human] to put

---

17. Ibid., 99. Translation slightly modified.

18. Hegel, *Lectures on the Philosophy of World History*, 85.

19. Kant, *Toward Perpetual Peace*, 29. Note the opposition Kant constructs here between *bliss / the garden (of Eden)* and *the world*. "Eden" in Hebrew means precisely "bliss or joy" (Scholem, *Major Trends*, 220).

himself, despite his hating it, patiently through the toils of life." Given the world's negativity, a longing to return to an "imagined seat of bliss" is understandable.[20] However, this is but an "empty longing." The mature human being must deride the idea of "a carefree life of lazy daydreaming,"[21] with nothing to do but "rest in calm inactivity and perpetual peace and dream and fritter away his existence."[22] And while Kant may imagine a state of peace in the future, not only does he constitutively defer it ("only God knows when this would be")[23]—he also argues that this state cannot be allowed to be completely free of negativity, "so that humankind's powers do not fall into slumber."[24]

Kant prohibits the utopia of world-dissolution and doing nothing, urging the subject "to put himself . . . patiently through the toils of life,"[25] "*to be content with providence* (even though it has laid such a toilsome path for us)," and to focus on "self-improvement."[26] The negative way of the world is identified here with providence itself. Moreover, in Kant's structural displacement of guilt, deficiency and evil must be regarded as "our own" fault, not the world's, which is thereby exonerated. The call to have faith in the way of the world is repeated by Kant so incessantly, and with so many concessions to the rational observer's inevitable disillusionment with world history, that one may discern therein Kant's anxiety about how unbearable this world is. But if so, why not refuse the demands of the world? Why not call the world out for its systemic (and not "our" individual) evil? Because, Kant's theodical optimism tells us, we ought to have faith in a better future, the future that the world is supposed to provide.

This is the fundamental ruse of theodicy: to make the subject spiritually invested in the way of the world and in working endlessly on the world, through the promise of fulfillment and bliss in the future. The basic structure within which theodicy functions across the Christian-modern trajectory may be called the structure of deferral or the not-yet. In Chapter 1,

---

20. Kant, *Toward Perpetual Peace*, 29.

21. Ibid., 36.

22. Ibid., 29.

23. Ibid., 35.

24. Ibid., 12.

25. Ibid., 29.

26. Ibid., 34.

through Schelling and Blumenberg, we will see the emergence of the world in Christianity as always not-yet-fulfilled and as directed toward an endlessly postponed reconciliation in a way that is intensified in modernity. Modernity, too, promises bliss, but this promised bliss is never *now*. As in Kant's structure of endless approximation, the modern subject strives for non-alienation and fulfillment but cannot reach them, and the very promise of a future bliss binds the subject to the world. In modernity, the subject and the world are co-constituted, in a manner which the Hegelian dialectic makes explicit: the subject becomes the normative modern subject ("man") only through work on the world; and the world in turn develops through the subject's participation in what Hegel calls "the great totality, the work of the world," which provides the objective conditions for the subject's realization *as* (the "mature") subject.[27]

The co-constitution of the subject and the world has an implication that ungrounds any purely subjectivist or individualist interpretation of bliss: there can be no true, lasting bliss of the soul as long as the objective world remains unblissful—as long as the subject-world nexus, through which the subject is subjectivated, continues to persist. With the expansion of colonial and capitalist modernity, there is nowhere to escape from the world. Hence, this world itself must be annihilated or transfigured: such is the intuition underlying the Romantic obsession with the imminently demanded epoch of bliss, or with a transfigured state of all-being. In Schelling as well, bliss entails the annihilation of the subject-world conjunction in its entirety. This means, crucially, that the non-alienation and fulfillment for which I strive can never be "mine." Bliss cannot be inscribed in the modern logic of self-assertive subjectivity because, as long as one remains a bounded subject, one remains *in* the world, alienated and dirempted. In striving for bliss, the modern subject and modern world strive for their own dissolution—for the end of this unblissful structure of reality. The world and the end of the world, the world and the longed-for bliss, are co-constituted. Modernity is, beneath it all, a mystical and Gnostic epoch, striving for bliss yet never reaching it, an epoch that is full of emptiness that cannot be sated and longing that cannot be fulfilled. To immediately be in bliss, or to be immediately one with the plenum of bliss, is to lose all sense of bounded individuality, to dispossess oneself absolutely. There can be no subjective or objective bliss, since in bliss the subject-object structure cannot hold.

---

27. Hegel, *Lectures on the Philosophy of Spirit*, 99.

I.5. *Modernity and Theodicy*

One can see the centrality of the modern subject-world nexus in Kant's interpretation of the fall from bliss, which constitutes a fortunate fall in a very modern sense: as the awakening of freedom and as the self-assertion of reason and its liberation from any external dictate. Kant's subject of history is the subject of incessant work amid the alienated world, a world that the subject masters with the help of reason, thereby appropriating reality and becoming a fully developed, mature subject in this process. As such, the Kantian subject is the modern subject of self-assertion. I take the term "self-assertion" (*Selbstbehauptung*) from Blumenberg. As he defines it, modern self-assertion is an existential program according to which "man" understands his own position as historical and contingent and has to decide, rationally, "how he is going to deal with the reality surrounding him and what use he will make of the possibilities that are open to him."[28] This implies the perception of reality as reified and objective, as something other than the subject yet replete with the possibilities that can be actualized and mastered—a perception of reality as open and as producible *by* the subject. The modern world is one that is originally alien and not of the subject's own making, a hostile world into which the subject is thrown not unlike in Kant's image of expulsion from paradise, yet which is to be appropriated and remade through reason and toil. In the seventeenth century, this tendency already underlies the Cartesian and the Baconian projects of science, in which the subject seeks to become the "master and possessor of nature."[29] Such is the horizon to which modernity looks, that "of the immanent self-assertion of reason through the mastery and alteration of reality."[30] German idealism may be said to provide the normative theorization of the modern logic of self-assertion as Blumenberg understands it and thus of modernity as the normative program.

In the modern age, the totality of possibility lies no longer with God but with the world, which is freed from the voluntaristic God's transcendent meddling, and on which the subject ceaselessly works. As Francis Bacon puts it in *New Atlantis*, disclosing the end goal of the modern logic of possibility: "The End of our Foundation is the knowledge of Causes, and secret motions of things; and the enlarging of the bounds of Human Empire, to

---

28. Blumenberg, *Legitimacy*, 138. See also Albernaz and Chepurin, "Sovereignty of the World."

29. Descartes, quoted in Blumenberg, *Legitimacy*, 567.

30. Blumenberg, *Legitimacy*, 137.

the effecting of all things possible."³¹ Nothing could be further removed from Rousseau or from Adorno's call to leave possibilities unused—a call that already antagonistically responds to the project of modernity. Modernity's expansion of possibility knows no bounds, driven toward the telos of actualizing all possibility without remainder, even if this goal remains indefinitely out of reach. In Schelling as well, we will see the movement of world history coincide with the movement of actualizing the totality of what is possible, a logic whose Christian roots he discerns and affirms. This goal implies the overcoming of alienation, as it were, from within alienated reality, so that fulfillment and non-alienation continue to glimmer at the end of the subject's world-historical effort that bears the name "modernity." In the subject's spiritual investment in the world, and in the concomitant desire that this world keep going at any cost, modernity becomes "the workplace of human exertion"—the "price," as Blumenberg puts it, of modern freedom.³²

Behind this infinite exertion, however, lurks the question: *Is it all worth it?* There is an indelible uncertainty inscribed in the project of modernity and in Enlightenment thought in particular, which exhibits the combination of optimism, even hubris, with anxiety.³³ Modern self-assertion emerges in response to an all-pervasive sense of insecurity and alienation, in which the infinite openness of reality is perceived not only as possibility but also, in the absence of any pre-given transcendent guarantee, as a threat. In Kant's writings, too, one witnesses the fear that the thread of reason's development may be severed, or that its negativity may appear unbearable. Kant posits that the light of reason is finite, and that reason inhabits a world of endless suffering and darkness, so that when rational observers survey the negativity of history, they may not glimpse a rational plan or reason behind it. To this, too, Kant's response is to *theodically intensify* this negativity: to see in the dark ground of history, and in the ever-present threat to the enlightened humanity from the hostile world, the very reason for the necessity of the development of rationality and thus for the necessity of toil and strife. That this

---

31. Bacon, *Works of Francis Bacon*, vol. 3, 156.

32. Blumenberg, *Legitimacy*, 200.

33. As Jonathan Sheehan notes, the Enlightenment constituted "a moment when uncertainty embedded itself in the very bones of human experience" ("Suffering Job," 184). This uncertainty was modern, one could suggest via Blumenberg, insofar as it had to do with the rational subject's having to get by in an infinitely negative world—as Sheehan puts it, "in a ruined world of suffering, injustice, and disaster" (184): the perfect setting for engaging anew with theodical questioning.

logic only reproduces negativity and suffering is something that is obfuscated in theodicy's conciliating enclosure.

While the discourse of theodicy, as the discourse that legitimates divine creation and world-governance or providence, may be traced back at least to the book of Job, there is something specific to the modern idea of theodicy. In the modern sense, theodicy judges divine creation *rationally*, so that the world-order and God as its creator and governor appear before the tribunal of reason. Modern philosophical theodicy interrogates centrally the rational logics inherent in divine creation and providence and so in the world-process as exhibiting, to the philosopher's eye, a higher, "divine" order directed at progress or salvation. Starting at least from Leibniz, theodicy is concerned less with God as such, that is, as divorced from the world, than with justifying his function as the creator and steerer of this world—and thus with justifying this world itself, the world on which the subject works and to which the subject is bound, as a world that exhibits a rational order and is directed toward a rationally graspable telos.[34] Accordingly, theodicy in modernity belongs to the project of reason's self-assertion, and it is far from a coincidence that the term "theodicy" is coined by Leibniz in the early eighteenth century.[35] A major crisis of theodicy, added to the broader, late eighteenth-century landscape of crisis, occurs with the 1755 Lisbon earthquake, which is perceived as a major catastrophe within the Eurocentric world-order.[36] In the wake of this event, it becomes increasingly unfeasible for reason, in its judgment of divine order, to adhere to the idea of an omnipotent and benevolent transcendent God, as well as to the kind of naive optimism, ridiculed in Voltaire's *Candide* (1759), that simply discounts negativity and evil.

This does not mean, of course, that theodical optimism goes away. From Kant to Hegel to nineteenth-century capitalist visions of progress, it persists and expands, and we will witness Schelling grapple with it over and over again. But as theodicy enters the nineteenth century, it needs to engage with

---

34. This aspect is important to keep in mind since it explains the post-Leibnizian survival of theodicy in someone like Kant, who critiques the overreach of dogmatic rational theodicy while retaining the optimism of theodicy as world-justification, transforming it in an Enlightenment manner into the philosopher's faith in the providential course of world history as the progress of reason and freedom, and thus in the world as worthy of rational investment.

35. See Marquard, *Defense of the Accidental*, 8–28, and *Schwierigkeiten mit der Geschichtsphilosophie*, 52–65. In particular, Marquard emphasizes that modern theodicy is a *process*, in a sense that combines the historical and juridical—and we will see this understanding of the world-process in Schelling.

36. On the Lisbon earthquake and the crisis of theodicy, see Neiman, *Evil in Modern Thought*.

the possibility and, indeed, necessity of catastrophe and suffering more directly, tarry with them, and make them even more explicitly serve theodical goals. Revolutionary terror, the problem of land dispossession and enclosure, and the question of abolition, too, bring the dark side of the modern world to the forefront of theodical problematics. At a moment when the darkness of this world seems more than ever to foreclose the salvific horizon, Kant's, Hegel's, and (as we will see) Schelling's theodicies of history have the central function of rationally justifying the modern world itself as worthy of spiritual investment despite its negativity and violence, and as the integral part and even culmination of a universal historical process leading, despite all odds, to the promised future. The crisis of salvation and the crisis of theodicy in the late eighteenth and early nineteenth centuries go hand in hand. As part of this joint crisis, in German idealism in particular, it is reason itself, in its autonomy and history, and thus the subject-world nexus—the subject who persists in its toil and develops its reason and freedom in the face of the unbearable negativity of the world—that becomes the locus of theodicy. This tendency culminates in Hegel's description of history as a "slaughterhouse in which the happiness of peoples, the wisdom of states, and the virtues of individuals are sacrificed," even as he proclaims theodically the necessity and usefulness of this sacrifice for the progress of reason and freedom.[37] To make suffering appear *useful* is a central, and possibly most pervasive, theodical conceit.[38]

The ground of the modern world remains dark and unstable, becoming even more treacherous with the discovery of deep planetary time, and within the eighteenth-century geological catastrophism, likewise influenced by the Lisbon earthquake. Against this increased instability, theodicy has a key function. It is to *stabilize* the subject-world conjunction, so that the dark ground does not consume it and so that the subject does not become unbound from the world—and to justify rationally the subject's continuing spiritual investment in this world as (to quote Leibniz's theodical formula) "the best of all possible worlds." The ruse of theodicy arises out of the fear of instability and disorder: the disorder that would erupt from the dark ground and overwhelm the orderly process of the world. Against the hypothesis of an evil genius who would distort our perception of the world, and against any destabilization of the subject's link to the world, theodicy argues that this world is good and not

---

37. Hegel, *Lectures on the Philosophy of World History*, 90.
38. See Levinas, "Useless Suffering."

deceitful and that evil is either illusory and disappears from a point of view sub specie aeternitatis, that it is the subject's own fault (so that the subject should strive to do better and to invest in this world even more), or that evil and negativity are necessary for the higher development of what is good and divine. Already in Leibniz one finds the crucial point that, even though one could in theory imagine a world completely free of evil, one could still rationally prove that *this* world, the one in which we live and strive, would remain the best possible one. This, too, is an attempt to make the world endurable and worthy of investment, since this world is all the subject has.

Modern theodicy seeks to re-mediate rationally the negativity of reality into a coherent totality that would be good, stable, and under control. The desire for the world to cohere is theodicy's basic transhistorical desire. In modernity, to make the world rationally cohere becomes a central task in reason's self-assertion over and against the newly opened infinite expanse of reality. Blumenberg observes the historical convergence of "the opening of the world by seafaring and trade" and the emerging view of reality as boundless possibility, but also as an endless source of uncertainty unless this reality can be explored and mastered, not least following the Copernican revolution in astronomy and the growing contingency and immensity of the modern universe. This convergence marks the beginning of the modern program of expanding the "domination of nature" in all dimensions at once—across the globe, into the depths of the earth, and even into the skies.[39] As Sylvia Wynter has shown, drawing on Blumenberg, the opening of reality with the dissolution of the sacred geography (and, one might add, with the Copernican revolution) is coimbricated with the post-1492 project of colonization and enslavement, and with the emergence, as part of the modern self-assertion of reason, of a new hierarchized and racialized logic of the global. In this logic, the normative rational subject ("man") asserts itself against other forms of planetary life and of being human—and even, as we will see in Schelling too, against the entire extraterrestrial expanse of the post-Copernican universe—by reducing them to the status of mere or relative nature, of nonhuman or less than human. In this way, the appropriation, exploitation, and even extermination of those regarded as less than human or extra-human are justified as supposedly natural and as part of the modern construction of nature as resource.[40]

---

39. Blumenberg, *Legitimacy*, 388, 346.

40. See especially Wynter, "Unsettling the Coloniality."

As Chapter 6 in particular will demonstrate, the modern logics of self-assertion, possibility, and the global, as well as the world-historical path to an epoch of bliss, emerge as explicitly racialized in Schelling, too, so that Wynter's analysis makes it possible to understand the dimension of his thought—his theodical embrace of racialization and European colonialism—that has hitherto remained unexplored in scholarship. This dimension is, however, central for grasping the inseparability of modern theodicy, including German idealist theodicy of universal history, from the violence of the modern global world and from this world's constitutive production of its own dark, racialized ground. With explicit reference to the extermination of the indigenous peoples of the Americas by the Europeans and to the transportation of African slaves to North America as what is supposed to save them from world-historical abandonment and make them part of a logic of natural and historical possibility, Schelling is engaged in something similar to what Wynter calls "biodicy," or a theodicy that biologically (or, in Schelling's case, natural-philosophically) legitimates the colonial and racial logics of the global.[41] In this, even extermination and enslavement are justified and theodically made useful.

Through Schelling, this book will both confirm and develop further the diagnosis, found in Wynter and more recently in Jared Hickman's analysis of Romanticism and racialization, of the co-imbrication of modern theodicy and the global. This co-imbrication stands at the heart of the tension in Schelling between theodicy and bliss. It is as though, with the expansion of the modern world of self-assertion, its dark ground expands and deepens, too, so that the global world comes to interfere with the planetary depths themselves—intensifying at once the anxiety over the instability of reality and the theodical desire for coherence and control. The more the modern world expands, the deeper the reality it struggles to re-mediate, with devastating consequences for planetary life. Hickman has described this process as "the mediation of metaphysical totality and geocultural entirety through race," showing that this mediation of the globe underlies what he calls the new "global immanence" that emerges in and as modernity.[42]

Romanticism constitutes, as it were, a conceptual laboratory in the development of this logic of re-mediation at the post-Enlightenment moment. One could say that, during this period, the Enlightenment imposition of

---

41. See Wynter, "How We Mistook the Map," 132.

42. Hickman, *Black Prometheus*, 34.

abstract universality from above proves to be insufficiently mediational, or insufficiently attentive to the complexity of global contexts. Instead, it comes to be replaced by the Romantic interest in cultural, national, and religious particularity, serving to reassemble the global out of the particular and the local—out of local mores, deities, and cosmologies—a global synthesis that emerges seemingly from below yet continues to be underwritten by the racialized spatial and hierarchical distribution theorized by Wynter. This is a mechanism of conversion, too, in which the plenum of the earth and the skies is converted, through enclosure, appropriation, and colonial violence, into the modern Western-centric—and Christianity-centric—world of the global. Even the Romantic expansion of rationality to include the mythical and the poetic may be regarded as contributing to making the logic of such re-mediation more advanced and flexible. Through this expansion, various forms of life and thought that are grasped as pre-rational or non-rational can be co-opted into the global history of consciousness. Schelling's thought in particular forms an ambivalent part of this process, and what this book undertakes is a philosophical and political-theological critique of his metaphysics as refracting and, all too often, reproducing and universalizing the assumptions and violences of the Christian-modern world. At the same time, there always remains an antagonistic dimension to Romanticism, and to the unruliness inherent in Romantic thought, that cannot be reduced to its embeddedness in the global Christian-modern world-order. Schelling's concept of bliss contains an irreducible core of antagonism that the world cannot re-mediate: this, too, is a central thesis of this book.

PART I

Why Must This World Be?

The present world, the world without consecrated authority, seems placed between two impossibilities, the impossibility of the past and the impossibility of the future.

—FRANÇOIS-RENÉ DE CHATEAUBRIAND

*Whence and how did the discord arise?
In the common chorus of the all,
Why does our soul not sing with the sea?
Why must the thinking reed repine?*

—*Fyodor Tyutchev*

I

The General Christian Contradiction

> *That the task of Christianity lies at a great distance, and that its resolution seems to require an indefinite amount of time, inheres in the nature of this task.*
> —SCHELLING AND HEGEL (UV 470/376)

BEFORE THEY BECAME rivals—a rivalry that split the later German idealist landscape in two and has continued to define allegiances among theorists and scholars—Schelling and Hegel worked and thought closely together. "On the Relation of the Philosophy of Nature to Philosophy in General" (1802), an unsigned essay from *Kritisches Journal der Philosophie*, a journal that the two co-published, testifies to that period of collaboration and joint speculation. In this chapter, I turn to this essay alongside Schelling's 1802 lectures on theology and on the historical construction of Christianity (a part of his *Lectures on the Method of University Studies*; see VM 119–134/82–102) in order to reconstruct the Christian-modern trajectory that Schelling develops in these texts and that is crucial for understanding his thought as a whole. Although I do not thereby begin this book in a chronological manner, this chapter aims to get directly to the heart of Schelling's grappling with the modern age. I introduce here the epochal narrative and the structure of universal reality—the view of the universe or world (*Welt*) as dirempted and in need of reconciliation—that, as Interlude I and Chapter 2 will argue, Schelling starts to develop in his earliest writings. The year 1802 is when this narrative and this structure are self-reflectively grasped by Schelling as Christian-modern and as aligned with the epochal task of his own thought. Hence the importance of this chapter, and of what I will call "the general Christian contradiction," for the rest of the book.

In later, conflictual years, Schelling and Hegel would each claim authorship of "On the Relation" for himself.[1] Of the two, Schelling's claim was more

---

1. See Ziche and Müller-Lüneschloß, "Editorischer Bericht," 432–437.

direct and remains more plausible given the essay's overarching concerns with the philosophy of nature and with the idea of (the coming epoch of) absolute identity, two of Schelling's signature themes during these years. Furthermore, the essay's account of "paganism" and "Christianity" is aligned conceptually with Schelling's aforementioned lectures, delivered in Jena in 1802 and published in 1803. Still, insofar as in 1802—five years before his *Phenomenology of Spirit*—Hegel himself could be considered a Schellingian on many major issues, and insofar as "On the Relation" touches on topics that preoccupied Hegel in his own work during this period (such as the relation between faith and knowledge), the essay also indexes a conceptual and problematic convergence and, as it were, an indifference point (*Indifferenzpunkt*) between two philosophical trajectories that would soon significantly diverge. In this chapter, I will, accordingly, speak of it as a joint Schelling-Hegel piece while assuming that most of its overarching conceptual vision comes from Schelling.[2]

"On the Relation" has been neglected by scholars, and yet its significance for the history of thought is not limited to the story of the Hegel-Schelling rivalry or that of German idealism and Romanticism at large. The essay indexes, rather, the entanglement between those stories and the story of European modernity, that is, the narratives that the modern age has told about itself. Its short length and seemingly narrow title belie its world-historical ambition and the novelty of its genealogical analysis. The focus on nature—and the declaration that philosophy must begin with nature and must grasp nature as the site of non-alienation, as living and even, in its essence, divine—serves here to diagnose the denigration of nature on which modernity as the age of the self-assertion of the subject is premised. The context in which this diagnosis is placed, however, goes beyond the confines of modernity, offering a genealogy that conjoins the Christian and the modern and subverts any rigid opposition between them. Christianity, on this account, introduces an understanding of reality as a structure of alienation and contradiction, which the modern age inherits and intensifies. For Schelling, this structure is the true structure of the world and yet needs to be overcome at a higher level, leading beyond modernity as such. In this way, the 1802 essay forms a part of modernity's critical reflection upon itself—reflection of which German idealism and Romanticism form a crucial intellectual site.

---

2. Cf. Tilliette, "Hegel in Jena," 18, who emphasizes that Hegel's influence is visible in the 1802 essay. It is not hard to imagine a scenario in which this essay was written predominantly by Schelling but with Hegel's input.

Schelling and Hegel's essay takes the long view, sketching a large-scale genealogical narrative in which the premodern Christian and the modern age share an underlying logic, even as modernity transforms this logic in a specific way, exacerbating the alienation and contradiction instead of overcoming them. Schelling and Hegel's own thinking of absolute identity or absolutely non-alienated reality, and of nature as one and undivided, is positioned by them as emancipatory with regard to this genealogy of alienation, and to the forms of exploitation and domination that the Christian-modern world has produced.[3]

The genealogy offered by Schelling and Hegel proceeds from the present into the past not just to trace the conceptual origins of the modern condition but also to trouble the present and its images of itself. At the moment of the post-Enlightenment and post-Revolutionary crisis, in which the consolidating modernity looks back, not without doubt, on the world it has created, Schelling and Hegel offer an account that is importantly critical in nature—not only in the sense of a (genealogical and philosophical) critique, but also in the double sense of the Greek word *krisis* as separation and judgment, a term that would become prominent in the later Schelling. This account at once diagnoses the separation at the heart of modernity and separates *itself* from modernity while judging modernity's limits, reflecting in this "the crossroads of the modern era"[4] at which this account—and German idealism and Romanticism—are located. Schelling and Hegel's essay adopts a meta-position with regard to the modern age: it associates modernity with Christianity and partly dissociates itself from modernity in order at once to complete modernity, to overcome it, and in a way to re-commence it. This problematic nexus refracts the burning issue of the modern world's legitimacy in conjunction with the crisis of otherworldly salvation and the crisis of reconciliation due to the exacerbation of alienation and division within the expanding capitalist world-ecology. Historically and philosophically too, the 1790s, this formative Romantic decade, marks the crisis of the Kantian critical system, whose perceived inconsistencies, incompleteness, and refusal to reconcile the subject and the world prompt the post-Kantian attempts to *complete* the system, coupled with vexation at the

---

3. The 1802 essay does not use the term "bliss," speaking of "absolute identity" and "heaven" instead. However, as the following chapters will show, these terms form in Schelling part of the conceptual nexus for which "bliss" may serve as the umbrella term. Already in 1795, he speaks of "absolute bliss," "absolute freedom," and "absolute identity" interchangeably.

4. Kuiken, *Imagined Sovereignties*, 9.

impossibility of finding, in this attempt, the sense of finality and stability promised by the project of critique. The 1802 essay emerges from this complex landscape of crisis.

In what follows, I develop a reading of "On the Relation" in dialogue, most centrally, with Blumenberg's *Legitimacy of the Modern Age* and with his positioning of Gnosticism as the shared enemy of Christianity and modernity. This will be important for the overarching argument of the book, too, not least because the specter of "Gnosticism," understood broadly as the tendency of world-delegitimation and as the collapsing of the Christian-modern structure of spiritual investment in the world, haunts Schelling's thinking from the early 1790s onward. Moreover, to revisit the 1802 essay from this perspective does more than demonstrate its neglected contribution to the genealogy of modernity. If the twentieth-century political-theological debate, of which Blumenberg is a central figure, is a debate around the genealogy of modernity in its constitutive continuities and discontinuities with Christianity, then the 1802 essay provides a novel perspective on the genealogy *of* this genealogical debate itself. This essay also brings into relief Schelling and Hegel's stance toward modernity, which is more critical than Blumenberg's. For Blumenberg, modernity is the overcoming of the Christian structure of transcendence. For Schelling and Hegel, it is not. The genealogy of the modern age offered by the 1802 essay resists the typical association of modernity with immanence, or with a process of immanentization, marking a starting point for a political-theological perspective that thinks together, and affirms or critiques together, Christianity and modernity—without simply positioning one against the other, as in secularist narratives of modernity or in Christian critiques of the secular modern. The 1802 essay's proclamation of the coming epoch of absolute identity opens, furthermore, onto Schelling's broader thinking of bliss, mysticism, and magic. At the same time, in a pattern that we will see repeated throughout this book, even while, in part, co-critiquing Christianity and modernity, the essay as well as Schelling's 1802 lectures affirm ultimately the *necessity* of the Christian-modern trajectory and theodically legitimate the Christian-modern world despite this world's negativity, so that the path to the absolute future of bliss can lead, for Schelling, only *through* the modern intensification of alienation. In this manner, a tension is visible in his 1802 thought between bliss, on the one hand, and a Christian-modern theodicy of history, on the other—the tension that the rest of this book will continue to unpack.

1.1. Separation and Delegitimation

The 1802 essay's story of modernity is a story of alienation, diremption, or split (*Entzweiung*)—a diremption that begins with Christianity and persists across the presumed divide between Christianity and the modern age. In order to find "the central point of the entire modern culture," inseparable from the "fundamental error" in which modernity remains caught, one needs "to go back to a much earlier time" (UV 461/368), beyond "the narrow circle of the present" (UV 471/377). Seeing as "the whole culture of the later world" was "defined in all areas [by] the effect of Christianity" (UV 461/368), the earlier time in question is that of Christianity's emergence. Just as one cannot think modernity without going back in time, so one cannot think Christianity non-historically or without thinking its origin. The initial condition of Christianity—its nucleus or germ (*Keim*)—consists in the "feeling of a diremption of the world from God" (UV 468/374). In the paganism-Christianity-modernity trajectory that Schelling and Hegel construct, Christianity introduces a *krisis* (division) into the constitutive principle of pagan antiquity, according to which the natural world was immediately perceived as divine: an immediacy that is lost with Christianity. This *krisis* is also a trial (*Gericht*) and a judgment (*Urteil*), in which the world is judged to be ungodly, alienated from God. The Christian consciousness from the outset exists under the form of opposition and contradiction between the worldly and the divine, or between the world and salvation: an opposition with which Schelling's metaphysics, too, never ceases to grapple.

The Christian *krisis* not only separates God from the world but splits the human apart and puts it on trial, too. As a fallen being, the human is alienated from its divine essence and source—alienated, via the worldly condition, from God and salvation. The contradiction between God and the world that is revealed in Christianity amounts to a triangular structure of alienation between the self, the external (natural) world, and God. More abstractly, Schelling and Hegel express this as the contradiction between the finite and infinite. Importantly, in their analysis, this contradiction splits in two not only the self but the world (as fallen versus as one with God at the end of time). It splits, moreover, even God himself: God in relation to or mediated by the world versus God as absolutely non-worldly, who can be intuited only as an absolute identity in an immediate mystical vision. Accordingly, this split runs across each term of the entire threefold structure. Repurposing Marx, who speaks of the "general secular [*weltliche*] contradiction" inherent in modern state power, I would like to call this structure of alienation the general Christian contradiction.[5]

To reconcile this contradiction—to reconcile the world and salvation, or the worldly and the divine—emerges as Christianity's central task (UV 468/374), redoubled in Schelling and Hegel's own philosophical imperative of all-reconciliation. Implied in their account of modernity as an intensification of the Christian contradiction is the verdict that medieval Christianity fails at that all-reconciliatory task. In this claim, their genealogy resonates with Blumenberg's account of the origins of modernity as traceable back to the unresolved tension within the Christian structure of salvation. Blumenberg locates at the heart of Christianity the "ambivalence" within "the metaphysical triangle: man, God, world"—an ambivalence between (God's and the human's own) concern, on the one hand, for the world and life in the world and, on the other, for salvation and transcendence.[6] One may call this a tension between spiritual investment in the world and investment in salvation or the end of the world, or between "trust in the world" and "mistrust," "an arrangement of life with the world" versus "against it."[7] For if the world is fallen and salvation is apocalyptic, why should this world continue to exist, and what is the source of legitimacy of the world-order and of one's place in the world?

For Blumenberg, the contradictions inherent in this structure are what, as it was consolidating itself into an orthodoxy, Christianity sought to reconcile in an "attempt to hold the God of creation and the God of salvation together in *one* system."[8] Nowhere is for Blumenberg the precarious character of that attempt more evident than in the threat Christianity experienced from Gnosticism as a set of doctrines that delegitimated the world and its creator. The early second-century theologian Marcion, who posited a sharp contrast between the malevolent creator God (demiurge) and the benevolent salvific God, and thus between the world as the order of creation and a-worldly salvation, represents for Blumenberg most strongly what he regards as the Gnostic tendency. One could say that Gnosticism cuts the Gordian knot of the general Christian contradiction by refusing the "worldly" side of the binary

---

5. Marx, *Early Writings*, 226. For Marx, the general secular contradiction is that between civil society and the state.

6. Blumenberg, *Legitimacy*, 484.

7. Ibid., 131.

8. Ibid., 135.

within the entire triangular distribution of transcendence. As Blumenberg emphasizes, this radicalization emerges *from within* the Christian contradiction, exposing this contradiction as the fundamental "dilemma," "the logic that was the problem," which Christianity needed to resolve in a way that would counter the delegitimation of the world.[9]

Gnosticism is for Blumenberg a part of the apocalyptic mindset that early Christianity sought to overcome. The apocalypticist demands the immediate end of the world, stripping the world—and worldly power—of all legitimacy. But as Christianity found itself needing to explain the world's continued existence (as "the world turned out to be more persistent than expected"),[10] it was also establishing itself as just such a worldly power. As a result, it needed to justify not the end of the world, but its prolongation. Therefore, in its opposition to apocalypticism and Gnosticism, Christianity made the move of postponing the end of the world—making room for the world *in* its not-yetness. The very concept of "world" indexes, as Blumenberg points out, this structural not-yet: "What the term 'world' signifies itself originated in that process of 'reoccupying' the position of acute expectation of the end."[11] In other words, as the end grows ever more distant and the expectation of the end increasingly less acute, "the world" solidifies as the structural placeholder between the present and the postponed end—and thus as a structure of the not-yet. The place of the "acute expectation of the end," which loses its immediate relevance, is now reoccupied by the world—a world that is expected to come to an end at some point but no longer imminently. This allows for a separate age (of the world) to emerge and hold its ground, making possible, inter alia, the establishment of the church as the institution of the not-yet that is the world—the institution that "stabilizes" this not-yet.[12] Christianity produces the universal split and seeks to reconcile it via the not-yet of salvation and reunification of the world with God. Thereby, the world is produced and maintained as the structural not-yet or deferral. Just as the first effect of Christianity amounts to a destabilizing intrusion into the alleged pagan wholeness, the function of the not-yet is to stabilize the contradiction introduced by Christianity into and as the world.

---

9. Ibid., 129–135.

10. Ibid., 131.

11. Ibid., 47.

12. Ibid., 44.

As bound to the promise of its own resolution or reconciliation, the general Christian contradiction becomes a theodical structure of world-legitimation, of spiritual investment in the not-yet of the world. At the same time, the anti-theodical Gnostic tendency contained within it constantly threatens to collapse this entire (inherently precarious) structure. Peter Sloterdijk, in his theoretical exposition of Gnosticism, speaks of the "revolution in the power of negation" engendered by what he calls the Gnostic distinction between "in the world" and "of the world"—a distinction that, taken to its limit, makes it possible to think a *total* negation and refusal, even annihilation of the world.[13] That the soul or subject can be a subject who strives endlessly *in* the world but whose essence is not *of* the world, and that the soul's bliss can consist only in the annihilation of the world and not reconciliation with it—that is also, as Chapter 2 will show, the starting point from which Schelling's early metaphysics of subjectivity unfolds, standing thus under the Christian-Gnostic shadow.

The Gnostic negation does not, moreover, concern solely the world or the soul's (non-)relation to the world. It makes the God of salvation himself "unbound," a "divinized nothingness" in which the world is immediately terminated or annihilated, not reconciled.[14] This revolutionary nothingness reverberates, as a threat to the stability of the world and as the object of mystic longing, throughout the Christian-modern trajectory and never ceases to constitute an essential dimension of Schelling's account of bliss and divinity. For Schelling and Hegel as for Blumenberg, this radical negation does not threaten Christianity as something external to it. Rather, seeing as the condition of Christianity's emergence is the operation of "absolute separation" (UV 470/376), Gnosticism is from the outset, as Blumenberg puts it, an "enemy who did not come from without but was ensconced at Christianity's very roots."[15] Whereas Christianity seeks to mediate its own contradiction via the not-yet of reconciliation, the Gnostic tendency opposes and delegitimates the logic of mediation, and with it the Christian logic of futurity. The Gnostic refuses what she sees as the ruse of mediation, unbinding herself from the world immediately and totally.

---

13. Sloterdijk, *After God*, 54. Schelling and Hegel would see the distinction between "in the world" and "of the world" as Pauline-Christian rather than purely Gnostic. Gnosticism *radicalizes* this distinction.

14. Ibid.

15. Blumenberg, *Legitimacy*, 126.

1.2. Faith and the Not-Yet of the World

If, thus, the first condition of Christianity is an absolute separation, then its further direction or tendency (*Richtung*) consists in identifying the world with the not-yet of salvation and "reconciliation with God." The immediate apocalyptic demand is thereby re-mediated into an indefinite eschatological horizon. Philosophically, Schelling and Hegel conceive of this not-yet as "a becoming finite of the infinite" or "God's becoming human" (*Menschwerden*, a German word translating the Greek term for incarnation, *enanthropesis*) (UV 468/374). To read this as a secularizing finitization of the infinite would be too simplistic. God becomes human *as* God. Within finitude, the infinite or absolute must remain absolute and infinite: such is the central Christian contradiction and imperative. Even in his revelation within finitude, God must remain self-equal as the one infinite God—and that is why in Christianity there is no dispersion of the infinite into a multitude of finite natural forms as in paganism (VM 120–121/84–85).

Unlike the Gnostic Christ who brings the good news of anti-worldly salvation and refuses to negotiate with the world, Christ serves in Christianity as the figure of the universal promise of God's becoming human, or mediation between the infinite and the finite. Since becoming human is the agency of the divine or "the infinite concept" itself, the function of Christ is premised on a split within the divine. The reconciliation of the contradiction between God and the world is, at the same time, the reconciliation of God's self-contradiction. The return of the *Sohn* (son) is *Versöhnung* (reconciliation). Schelling's as well as Hegel's later philosophical elaboration of the Christian Trinitarian doctrine, including their understanding of history in Trinitarian terms, retains the idea of Christ as mediating the Christian contradiction. In 1810, Schelling explicitly identifies the final epoch of "absolute bliss" or "absolute identity" with the completion of the "becoming human of God" and the return to a oneness with God the Father (SPV 184–185/242–243). In 1802, this self-reconciliation of the divine is described by Schelling and Hegel as "the calling back [*Zurückrufung*] of the infinite concept from its infinite flight" (UV 470/376)—an image that also implies a self-splitting of the divine and that turns the Kantian motif of endless approximation into a Romantic-Gnostic image of an endless flight following the infinite call of salvation.

For Schelling and Hegel, in Christianity the world—the entire universe—emerges as fundamentally negative and dirempted, in constant need of legitimation and of reconciliation with God through salvation history. The task of Christianity consists in overcoming the constitutive negativity revealed as the universal structure of reality ("world") by Christianity itself. This creates a self-referentiality and tendency toward totality, in which the Christian consciousness is propelled by its self-produced contradiction. For Schelling and Hegel, who take up the Christian promise into their own metaphysics, this forward movement is precisely the world-movement as that of *Menschwerden* and the not-yet, to be reconciled at the end of time. In keeping with the infinity of the task of the infinite's becoming finite, the end goal of perfect oneness can arrive only in an indefinite (yet providentially destined) future (UV 470/376). As long as the promised future does not arrive, one could say that, from a Christian standpoint, the end of the world *is* the world. The world and the end of the world are co-constituted within the dual structure of the general Christian contradiction and its destined future reconciliation.

This future, which cannot be determinately known, is postulated by Christianity as the "object of faith." "Faith," as the essay defines it, "is the inner certainty that anticipates the infinite"—faith in salvation, in the world's future "unification" with God (UV 468/374). In this definition, the word "certainty" is key. By introducing an absolute diremption between God and the world—into the self too—Christianity introduces a fundamental *un*certainty into and about reality. In the formulation of Eric Voegelin (alongside Blumenberg, a key participant in the twentieth-century debate around Gnosticism and modernity), "Uncertainty is the very essence of Christianity"[16]—a point with which Blumenberg, Schelling, and Hegel would agree. This uncertainty is not just existential. It indexes an onto-epistemological condition where the divine is not immediately found in the world and where the negativity of the world is what comes to the fore, or where the world *is* the structure of negativity, at once ontological (the world as non-divine) and temporal (the world as the not-yet). With Christianity, an abyss is opened between the divine and the worldly, and so mediation—this stabilizing Christ-function—assumes the central place. The onto-epistemological condition of uncertainty and the role of mediation go hand in hand. As the pagan world is "de-divinized," Voegelin continues, "the feeling of security in a 'world full of gods' is lost with the gods themselves"—so that, "ontologically, the substance of things hoped for is nowhere to be found but in faith itself; and, epistemologically, there is no proof for things unseen but again this very faith."[17] The divide between

---

16. Voegelin, *Modernity without Restraint*, 187.

17. Ibid.

nature, the divine, and the self, a divide introduced by the general Christian contradiction, thus leads to an uncertainty that is structural, not incidental.

The hoped-for of faith is what Schelling and Hegel term "anticipation." As Schelling points out in his 1802 lectures, Christianity needs faith because the Christian processuality (of the world's reconciliation with God) is future oriented and cannot be grasped in any particular finite, stable form. In contrast to paganism, any sign or image of the divine in Christianity is "fleeting" and "transient," functioning merely as an "allegory of the infinite" that cannot be contained within the present, but manifests itself as a temporary "historical form" (VM 120/84). Faith (subjectively) and the church (objectively) correspond to, and serve to stabilize, this infinite fleetingness of Christian forms as forms of the hoped-for oneness with the infinite. The church represents as in a "living artwork" the Christian idea of history as the endless (*endlose*) revelation or appearance of God in and as the world (VM 125/90). Accordingly, the church is the objective institution of faith and objective carrier of all of the fleeting historical forms of the divine; it is precisely what I have called, via Blumenberg, the institution of the not-yet. What faith anticipates is the oneness of heaven and earth, when the church itself, as an "external" institution, will no longer be necessary: a state in which the divine substance of things hoped for is one with the substance of the world, assuming that what comes after the end of the *saeculum* can still be called a world.

Faith is itself, via the general Christian contradiction, split in two. Apocalypticism and Gnosticism are one (radical) response to the uncertainty of reality; the establishment of the church and indefinite postponement of the end is another. The two, however, are co-constituted within the general structure of alienation. In the former response, faith itself is apocalyptic, in which the only thing that is certain is the fear and trembling of the inhabitation of the end. The world is here unredeemable, without justification. In the latter response, faith becomes the guarantee of certainty about worldly reality as ultimately to be reconciled with God. The world is thereby seen as (to be) redeemed. This is the path that Christianity chooses: the path of salvation history and providence as going through the world. As Blumenberg observes, "the concept of providence" is "an essential anti-Gnostic principle,"[18] seeing as it implies what Schelling and Hegel call "the general plan of the destinies of the world" (UV 468/374)—that is, it legitimates the course of world history. Providence is a central concept of theodicy, because theodicy seeks to

---

18. Blumenberg, *Legitimacy,* 132.

legitimate the world as divinely steered, and thus as good despite whatever negativity and evil the world might contain. "The general plan of the destinies of the world" is a theodical expression. Throughout the Christian-modern trajectory, this theodical and anti-Gnostic character of providence persists, manifesting itself in Kant's injunction to be content with providence no less than in Hegel's and Schelling's own theodicies of universal history.

Christian faith is based on an ontological and theodical reversal: in it, priority is no longer granted to the apocalyptic *now* of bliss, but to the world in its unblissfulness. As Thomas Altizer has put it, Christian "orthodoxy [arises] as a reversal of an original apocalypticism."[19] Thereby, Christianity overcomes the "opposition to history and the unhistorical quality" that precludes spiritual investment in the not-yet of the world.[20] Within the structure of faith, the world is what lies between the alienated present and the reconciled future—so that the Christian germ can "have its development," via the tendency to revelation and reconciliation, only "in infinite time with the determinations of the world" (UV 468/374). Within the general Christian tension, the world oscillates between two poles: division and fallenness, on the one hand, and the destined reconciliation, on the other. Or, to employ the dynamic Schellingian language, the world-process is constituted by an interplay of two forces: the force of separation and division and the force of oneness. Faith, within this scheme, is the subjective certainty, arising out of division, in the eventual reconciliation of these forces within the world-process: the holding together in consciousness of the Christian contradiction as something that is to be eschatologically reconciled. A crisis of faith—a crisis of Christianity—is, accordingly, when this salvific construction falls apart.

1.3. *The Epoch of Crisis: Modernity and Alienation*

Modernity is the outcome of such a crisis, an age in which this crisis itself becomes universal. Importantly, modernity is for Schelling and Hegel at once a distinct epoch and a part of the world-process as determined by Christianity—an epoch whose first condition is to intensify the Christian structure of alienation. This is the key point on which Schelling and Hegel differ from Blumenberg's understanding of modernity as the age of immanence that overcomes the transcendent contradiction inherent in

---

19. Altizer, "Advent of the Nothing," 124.

20. Blumenberg, *Legitimacy*, 468.

Christianity. For them, modernity is *the* epoch of contradiction and *krisis*. The "general striving" of the modern age, as diagnosed by Schelling and Hegel in 1802—and here they have in mind the trajectory spanning from Luther and Descartes to the Enlightenment and culminating in Kantian critique and the Kantian-Fichtean philosophy of subjectivity—has been "to maintain the opposition" (UV 469/375) instead of reconciling it: to uphold the general Christian contradiction *as* contradiction.

Within the threefold divide between the subject, the world, and God, the modern tendency is for each term to become relatively autonomous or opposed to the others. This relative autonomy is visible, for instance, in Descartes's metaphysics. "Cartesian dualism," Schelling and Hegel remark, is but "a conscious and scientific articulation of the long-existing split" that emerged with Christianity—as is the trajectory of modern philosophy since Descartes. Seeing as modernity seeks to maintain contradiction qua contradiction, this split or alienation not only has not been overcome in the modern age but has been in it fundamentally "insuperable" (UV 467/373–374). Not only Cartesian rationalism but Francis Bacon's empiricism, too, one might add, contains the tendency to separate the activity of the subject from God (as creator) and from the world (as externally manipulable by the subject), with God not acting immediately in the world but leaving creation or "the universe" open for "the human race" to "extend [its] power and dominion over."[21]

The dominant tendency of modernity to maintain and intensify alienation manifests itself in several subordinate tendencies that together express "the central point of the entire modern culture" and reflect the general desire or craving (*Begehren*) for separation and division that permeates the modern age. Two of these are "the unconditional demand to have the absolute outside the self," that is, to regard God as ontologically autonomous and removed from the subject (the ontotheological or "dogmatist" tendency), and the demand "to maintain the I outside the absolute" (UV 461–462/368–369)—this crucial presupposition of the modern logics of judgment and critique. From a Blumenbergian perspective, both of these tendencies are to be regarded as co-constituted within the modern project of reason's self-assertion over and against God *and* the world. Unlike Blumenberg, however, Schelling and Hegel consider the presuppositions of modern self-assertion to be tied to a structure of transcendence and division, not immanence; and it is this

---

21. Bacon, *The New Organon* in *Works of Francis Bacon*, vol. 4, 114. On Bacon's God as leaving creation open for the human, see Matthews, *Theology and Science*.

transcendence that continues to underlie modern alienation from nature and the modern logics of domination. The trajectory of self-assertion culminates for them in the Kantian-Fichtean idealism of the I, continuing the Cartesian affirmation of the dirempted subject. As Schelling and Hegel point out, the second tendency merely inverts the first, and both remain within the structure of alienation that Christianity could not resolve. In this way, the general Christian contradiction is in modernity at once pulled apart and maintained. The modern project of self-assertion is the project of *krisis* and critique, or critique as premised on *krisis*: critique through separation and judgment.[22] In the late eighteenth century, this project leads simultaneously to the intensification of the Christian-modern structure of alienation and to an even further, revolutionary radicalization of the operation of critique as premised on separation of the new from the old, and on the judgment of the old by the new.

The separation between faith and knowledge, also intensified in modernity—as "faith that is in no way knowledge" and as knowledge that implies "unbelief"—typifies the same desire to uphold the structure of opposition (UV 469/375). Both this faith and this absence of faith separate themselves from the absolute, and critique of both remains a staple of Schelling's and Hegel's metaphysics. The same tendency thus underlies modern philosophy and modern (Christian) religiosity. Among contemporary figures, Friedrich Jacobi's emphasis on faith is singled out by Schelling and Hegel for philosophical-religious critique (UV 462/369); however, this is implicitly a critique of Protestantism, too. One may recall here, as well, Hegel's 1802 analysis of the logic of separation in Protestantism and the Enlightenment[23] and Schelling's invocation of the "solely negative" Protestant tendency toward disunity (VM 131/98)—another manifestation of the modern pulling apart of the Christian contradiction, and of the intensified negativity of modern reality.

That modernity, starting from the Reformation and the birth of modern science, seeks to inhabit a dirempted world, and that it is born of an intensification of alienation and uncertainty, may be further glimpsed in Blumenberg's account of late-medieval nominalism. In nominalism, the general Christian

---

22. *Krisis* is also judgment (*Urteil*)—and *Urteil* made autonomous is critique. In a culmination of this tendency, the modern age self-reflectively separates itself from and judges earlier centuries, too, and their conditions of possibility. As Schelling puts it in 1803, "Our epoch"— the age of critique—"not only makes discoveries, but also investigates the *possibility* of earlier discoveries" (IN2 229).

23. See Hegel, *Faith and Knowledge*, 57–61.

tension between investment in the world and investment in salvation finally implodes, paving the way at once for modern philosophy and science and for Lutheran doctrine. In this "late medieval theological absolutism," with its hypertrophy of "the theological predicates of absolute power and freedom," God is perceived as so omnipotent in his "unlimited sovereignty" as to become a veritable *deus absconditus*, completely hidden from and alien to consciousness.[24] There is here no glimpse of the unfathomable, radically transcendent will of the divine. All that remains for the human is to exist in a world that this alien God created, without the prospect, not just of changing it but of even knowing how it works, as it were, in itself. This leads to an alienation from the world, too, which "for man ... no longer possesse[s] an accessible order" and is perceived as dark, unstable, and contingent.[25] It is for Blumenberg from the attempt to inhabit this alienated world *as* alienated that the modern program of the "domination of nature" and the "self-assertion of reason through the mastery and alteration of reality" emerges.[26]

The situation of crisis out of which modernity originates is marked by a deep uncertainty about reality and an "intense consciousness of insecurity."[27] Outside the strictly nominalist context, Jean Delumeau has described this period as overtaken with a sense of anxiety, sinfulness, and fear. "Then, more than ever before," Christianity becomes a "religion of anxiety."[28] Blumenberg calls this a return of Gnosticism—again, in the sense of a tendency toward investment in salvation and disinvestment from the world. This tendency rises to the surface anew with the breakdown of medieval mechanisms of holding the general Christian contradiction together. Radical anxiety becomes the sign of an epochal threshold emerging out of the implosion of the Christian tension, a *krisis* that divides what had been, if imperfectly, held together. As an epoch that seeks to maintain the contradiction qua contradiction, modernity is the epoch of crisis par excellence—as it were, a permanent state of crisis. This *krisis* is a judgment, too, in which modernity judges the preceding epoch to have failed and seeks to assert itself as a new beginning.

---

24. Blumenberg, *Legitimacy*, 159, 171.

25. Ibid., 171.

26. Ibid., 182, 137–138.

27. Ibid., 163.

28. Delumeau, *Sin and Fear*, 1–3. We will witness Schelling's metaphysics as permeated with (Christian-modern) anxiety, too.

For Blumenberg, this new beginning marks the project of modernity as what he terms "the second overcoming of Gnosticism."[29] However, as reality in modernity continues to be contingent and unstable (and God continues to be hidden), and as the expanse of reality becomes infinitely open and cosmically alienated from the subject during the Copernican revolution in astronomy, the logic of overcoming Gnosticism and investing in the world changes. Modernity pulls apart the general Christian contradiction by radically removing God and nature from the subject: by turning God into an infinitely distant regulative idea at best, and by turning the world into a boundless empirical expanse of reality amid which the subject now finds itself. Thereby, the room that Christianity, as we saw above, originally makes for the not-yet of the world implodes into infinity, leaving the rational subject seemingly alone within infinite space, disoriented yet free to roam in any direction and to assert itself without end.

What Blumenberg understands as the modern "immanent" investment in the world should be understood as, at the same time, investment in the subject as alienated from the world and working endlessly on it, not unlike the new demiurge seeking to possess and make use of reality, and to reshape it through reason and science—thereby legitimating the subject's own project of mastery and legitimating the modern age itself. Blumenberg observes in passing this strange recapitulation by modernity of the Gnostic framework, writing of the "demiurgic activity exercised by man upon the world" and of the modern subject's "demiurgic production."[30] Complementing Blumenberg, one could say that, in spite of or, rather, *in* its very project of overcoming Gnosticism, modernity remains a Gnostic and apocalyptic epoch, an epoch of ever-intensified alienation and crisis, whose guarantee of legitimacy is forever absent and could be attained only if the demiurgic project of modernity were to succeed without remainder—if "man," this modern demiurge, could reshape the world completely, which, given the endless expanse and infinite depths of reality, remains a constitutively infinite task. How would the modern subject otherwise legitimate itself without doubt as the "good" demiurge and not as the bungling, if not malevolent, demiurge of Gnosticism? Anxiety over its own legitimacy is inscribed constitutively in the project of modernity. Hegel's philosophy of history in particular, in which human rationality ("spirit")

---

29. Blumenberg, *Legitimacy*, 126. Gnosticism thus emerges from Blumenberg as a threat that persists across the Christian-modern trajectory. Cf. Marquard, *Defense of the Accidental*, 13, on the overcoming of Gnosticism as the task of modern theodicy.

30. Blumenberg, *Legitimacy*, 205, 209.

produces at every step the conditions for its own forward movement in and as world history, may be regarded as an attempt to justify spirit as the benevolent and legitimate demiurge, and the trajectory of history culminating in modern Europe as good and even divine. Schelling's thought, too, constantly grapples with the same anxiety about the legitimacy of the modern world.

The project of self-assertion creates modernity's transformed logic of the not-yet: the not-yet of perfect mastery and possession (of reality by the subject), of the elimination of uncertainty through achieving a perfect transparency of reality to the human spirit, or through mastering fully the possibilities inherent in reality. Perhaps if reality is completely under control, then the subject will have overcome alienation, as it were, from within. In 1830, Schelling remarks that there are two ways for the subject to reach "heaven," understood not as otherworldly, but as absolute freedom from the negativity of the world: "Everyone seeks this heaven ... some through seeking to wrest everything for themselves"—that is, to appropriate or possess everything—"so as to get rid of the agony of desiring, others, by contrast, through purification from every desire" (EIP 109). The heaven of perfect possession, of becoming one with the All by claiming the All for oneself, is the image of heaven that continues to define the techno-utopian and capitalist trajectory of modernity.

1.4. *With and Against the Christian-Modern*

The 1802 essay distances itself critically from the modern logics of selfhood, possession, and use, and from the Christian-modern conjunction of interiorization, the emptying out of nature, and the removal of the divine. For Schelling and Hegel, the modern pulling apart of the general Christian contradiction entails a double process. On the one hand, the absolute is "taken up into [one's] innermost subjectivity": the self is identified as the site of absoluteness, an identification on which modern self-assertion is premised. On the other, nature thereby becomes severed from or emptied of the absolute even more radically: the above identification implies, "immediately and necessarily," "the full egress of the divine from the world, a world that is now ossified due to the withdrawal of its life-principle" (UV 461/368). This tendency was present in Christianity from the beginning. However, with the intensification of the general Christian contradiction, the function of nature as the promised site of unification collapses. Nature becomes simply what Fichte calls "the not-I," the field of mere possibility for the I's self-assertion. This operation comes to define the modern view of nature. The piety of a God transcendently removed from the world is accompanied by the world becoming a structure of instrumentalization and exploitation. Schelling and Hegel importantly write: "believing itself to have paid the highest tribute of piety to God by removing him—as an extra-worldly or above-worldly substance—from the world," the modern subject has "all the more retained free rein in this world so as to . . . make use [*gebrauchen*] of it" (UV 461/368).[31]

This kind of religiosity is essentially a cover-up operation, "the highest form of irreligiosity" (UV 461/368) that pays only lip service to piety. Francis Bacon—for whom, if God is not removed from the world, nature cannot be freely known and manipulated[32]—encapsulates perfectly this tendency diagnosed by Schelling and Hegel. The Cartesian God is likewise "the metaphysical functionary God, who has only to supply [the human as] the 'master and possessor of nature' with his license."[33] In this way, in modernity the "beauty and glory of nature" (UV 466/372) is reduced to what is useful, cognizable, and producible in a way that enhances the subject's power.

The subjugation of nature is not the only kind of domination intrinsic to Christian-modern alienation as diagnosed by Schelling and Hegel. In their account, the piety of a God removed from the world has for its flip side the imperative of blind faith and subjection, a faith in a transcendence that serves de facto to justify the subject's free rein in the world. Thereby, Schelling and Hegel target not only the modern religiosity of a faith without knowledge or any appeals to the name of God that serve to legitimate the subject's use of the world, but also post-Kantian "moral faith," a conception advocated by Fichte in which God stands in for the moral world-order, absent in nature yet present within the subject in the form of duty and command. The divine or absolute can here be given only practically (as the categorical imperative), but never theoretically (in knowledge)—an idea that forecloses, for Schelling and Hegel, any true revelation of the infinite, maintaining a transcendence from which the subject remains alienated and to which the subject remains subjected and bound. The principle of "the absolute taking-up of the categorical and the infinite into the I" is turned in this system into a bad infinity, "an

---

31. The nexus of Protestant piety and the proto-capitalist logics of use in Schelling and Hegel's diagnosis is reminiscent of Max Weber's classic account in *The Protestant Ethic and the Spirit of Capitalism* (1905).

32. Matthews, *Theology and Science*, 57.

33. Blumenberg, *Legitimacy*, 567.

endless progression" precluding any actual non-alienation and perpetuating the structure of opposition "*so that the system should remain in place*" (UV 465/371)—and so that the alienated structure of reality should remain in place, too.

Schelling and Hegel's critique of Kant and Fichte is thus inscribed in their broader critique of the modern desire to perpetuate transcendence and alienation. Moral faith exacerbates the Christian-modern tendency to indefinitely postpone unification with God. Anticipation and the conjuring up of a salvific telos are here effectively a pretense, insofar as the survival of the system, and the reproduction of the underlying structure of alienation, depend on this anticipation never being fulfilled—serving to make the subject endlessly follow the transcendent command. "The absolute has [here] no other reality except in the I's relationship of slavery and subjection to the absolute"—so that the divine can only "appear in the form of absolute command, and the I in the form of unconditional reception and acceptance of this command" (UV 464/371). Bliss is thereby foreclosed via a logic of infinite approximation that subjectivates by transcendently binding the subject to an endless striving in an alienated world.

In this way, Schelling and Hegel may be said to critique the structural continuity between Christian and modern logics of transcendence. In their political-theological and genealogical critique, the moral law indexes a false morality premised on the constitution of subjectivity through subjection, whose flip side is the enslavement of nature and the world. It is in this regard telling that Fichte cannot think nature as living or divine, and cannot think God's revelation in and as the natural world. Underlying this idealism of the I is "a self-aggrandizing enthusiasm," whose popularity (as Schelling and Hegel note) is symptomatic, seeing as this fanaticism of transcendent duty is "a deaf and hollow fruit of an age whose spirit has for a long time held high this empty form"—the form of opposition and alienation, yet another expression, among "countless" others, of "the very old split" (UV 466–7/373). Modern will to mastery and fanatical enthusiasm, instrumentalized reason and absolute devotion to the transcendent sovereign command, the subject's self-assertion and its subjection, are for Schelling and Hegel different sides of the same logic of alienation and transcendence at work in the general Christian contradiction as modernity inherits and transforms it.

Against the forms of negativity, domination, and subjection that accompany the modern intensification of Christian alienation, Schelling and Hegel position their philosophy of absolute identity as emancipatory. It is important that, in Schelling's metaphysics, the concept of absolute identity or bliss must be understood as ontologically preceding all alienation. To insist on absolutely non-alienated reality in the face of modern alienation is to insist on that which is prior to the world's structure of diremption and transcendence, yet which this structure serves to foreclose. The 1802 essay's proclamation of the arriving epoch of absolute identity, in which nature is revealed as the ante-original site of bliss or salvation that has been concealed and exploited by the logic of self-assertion, is thus (at least in part) antagonistic toward the Christian-modern structure of alienation. On the one hand, Schelling and Hegel accept the basic Christian premise that the world as such is alienated, and that universal history must be thought as leading to reconciliation and the complete revelation of the infinite in the finite. On the other, they demand, in a Romantic-apocalyptic manner, the *imminent* coming of an epoch of non-alienation and bliss: a demand that directs the original Christian promise against the Christian-modern logic of endless approximation and deferral, the logic that engenders only further transcendence, alienation, and domination.

Schelling and Hegel thus distance themselves critically from the Christian-modern and announce its approaching end. Just as Christianity constituted the first crisis and modernity the second, so Schelling and Hegel position their philosophy, in a post-Revolutionary manner, as a philosophy of crisis, in which modernity is judged to be stuck in its "fundamental error" and a new age is announced, of a new (heavenly) home in oneness with the divine and an end to the endless flight of alienation. Reconciliation alone is insufficient to overcome "the very old split." First, an all-encompassing *krisis* must take place—the *krisis* out of which Schelling and Hegel's essay is written. In this context, this *krisis* is supposed to be final, opening onto an epoch of perfect non-alienation, a world finally one with God (a kingdom of God, a *hen kai pan*). In a trajectory later continued not only by Schelling and Hegel themselves but also by Ludwig Feuerbach and Marx, this emancipation envisages freedom as non-alienation and non-domination. The general Christian contradiction must be undone if subjection and exploitation are to cease. The negativity of the world must be dissolved in a paradisal freedom without alienation or mastery, a "heaven regained" (UV 471/376). This heaven is not one attained through the self-assertion of the subject but through an insistence on the absolute oneness—the one divine, natural, and human being—that exceeds and precedes any self-assertion.

This emancipation is envisioned in the 1802 essay as an emancipation from the Christian-modern as the old age and the dawn of a new one—the age of a "new religion" (of oneness with nature and God) and the "absolute gospel [*Evangelium*]" or "true gospel" (UV 470–471/376–377). Again, this does not mean that the essay simply rejects Christianity and modernity. In a restaging of the Protestant gesture, the new religion coincides, in Schelling and Hegel's account, with the early Christian tendency of unification and revelation, abandoned by the later Christianity and modernity, "leading back to the first mystery [*Mysterium*] of Christianity and completing it"—that is, the mystery of the becoming finite of the infinite (UV 471/377). Furthermore, for Schelling and Hegel, non-alienated freedom draws on the early Christian intuition of freedom as affirmation of the infinite, distinct from the modern freedom of self-assertion and mastery (a freedom that amounts to an absolutization of finite dirempted life). In Schelling and Hegel's Romantic vision, nature must be recognized as the "ground and source" (UV 471/376) of the infinite, foreclosed by the alienated world. Undivided nature is to be affirmed *against* the world, so that the human and the divine can be immediately one within it. "To call back into nature the life that flew away from it" with the emergence of the Christian contradiction is an "instinct" that Christianity already possessed in its idea of the revelation of the divine within finitude, but that was later obscured (UV 472/377). In this, Schelling and Hegel's philosophy of absolute identity seeks not only to overcome but to complete the Christian-modern trajectory. To do so, as we will repeatedly see in Schelling, is to complete modern science, too. The Copernican revolution in astronomy and the rational standpoint of universality developed by modern philosophy and science disclose a truth about the universe, yet this truth remains one-sided as long as alienation and self-assertion persist. To overcome alienation, human reason needs to grasp itself as immanently grounded in nature and in God, and this is the world-epochal mission that Schelling's own philosophy of absolute identity serves. Only in this way can the original Christian promise be fulfilled.

The return to early Christianity indexes a "rebirth of nature" (UV 471/377) that not only has undertones of a Christian logic of conversion or turning but also maps the entire tripartite movement of history (paganism, the Christian-modern age, the epoch of bliss) onto the Christological scheme of life, death, and resurrection. The philosophy of absolute identity becomes thereby a philosophy of immanent resurrection opposed to the transcendence or beyondness of God and nature alike. However, that means that, in its overcoming, the Christian-modern world joins back with paganism, so that the opposition between the two is canceled out as well, and the truth of the Greek mysteries is revealed to coincide with that of "the first mystery of Christianity." The new absolute identity indexes a higher "restoration of the lost identity" and "re-sublation of the split" (UV 471–472/378). In the resulting wholeness, even the negative one-sidedness of modernity has its place as part of the dialectical movement *toward* this wholeness—so that Schelling and Hegel justify the entire Christian-modern trajectory, despite its negativity, as the dialectical "path to completion" (UV 470/376). They thereby embrace the Christian-modern providential vision of history as one progressively unfolding whole, a vision that is central to the process of the ongoing self-reflection of the Eurocentric global world out of which the 1802 essay is written. In this way, they end up falling into a theodical justification of the trajectory of history that they construct retroactively out of the crisis of the present. And although they proclaim a return to a quasi-pagan oneness, one should not take this to be a straightforward elevation of the Greeks above the Christian moderns. There is, Schelling and Hegel insist, "no prospect of returning" to paganism. Nor would a mere going back to what they position as the lower historical level or "potency," already transcended (*überschritten*) by the movement of history, be desirable. Instead, the point is to press forward: to overcome the split "at a higher potency" (UV 472/378).

The "return" thus goes necessarily *through* the Christian-modern trajectory and occurs at a higher level already premised on the truth of the general Christian contradiction and on the achievements of modern rationality. The new immediacy to be reached—the absolute future of bliss—can be mediated or attained only through the negativity of the Christian-modern world, a negativity that makes it possible for reason to develop before it can reconcile itself with nature and with God in a conscious manner. What makes the 1802 essay a theodicy of world history is that it ends up legitimating the Christian-modern trajectory as the path to the absolute future instead of simply refusing or abolishing the structure of alienation and the not-yet—the structure that, with Christianity, emerges as "the world." For Schelling and Hegel, while pagan oneness may complement the one-sidedness of modernity, it is itself one-sided and incapable of attaining the true historical standpoint that emerges in Christianity and remains Christian in character (to "intuit [cosmos] as *history*" is, for them, the central Christian achievement, on which modern philosophies of history build; VM 120/83). Nor does paganism attain the idea of the one infinite God, which is likewise fundamental for Schelling and Hegel's metaphysics. The "return" to paganism announced by the 1802 essay is therefore not to be understood as a regression to the lost origin. It has, rather, the structure of an ascending spiral that incorporates paganism, Christianity, and modernity as the levels of ascent of consciousness toward the epoch of bliss.

Moreover, insofar as the essay announces the task of the new philosophy and new religion to consist in a return to the early Christian contradiction so as to overcome it once and for all, and insofar as it proclaims the failure of modernity to resolve that contradiction, the essay's gesture of a new beginning restages what Blumenberg sees as the founding move of modernity itself—namely, the overcoming of the Christian structure of transcendence as a way to liberate the human and the world. Schelling and Hegel would, however, disagree with Blumenberg that the modern logic of self-assertion constitutes such a liberation. At the post-Revolutionary crisis-point, Schelling and Hegel seek in an important way to re-commence modernity in opposition to the failed modernity that inherited the general Christian contradiction and turned it into an "empty form" of alienation, exploitation, and subjection. Such a re-commencement, insofar as it picks up the original Christian task, re-commences Christianity, too, fulfilling in this the anticipation inherent in the early Christian faith—a fulfillment that Christianity itself failed to accomplish. In this fulfillment, Christianity is destined to disappear as a religion of the not-yet, dissolving together with paganism in a divine all-oneness.

1.5. Mysticism, Magic, and the Signs of the Times (with an Excursus on Wordsworth)

The ambivalence toward what the 1802 essay, together with Schelling's lectures from the same year, calls "mysticism"—an ambivalence in which Schelling at once identifies medieval and early-modern mysticism with the essence behind Christianity and justifies the Christian church in its historical opposition to the mystical impulse—marks most clearly the conjunction in Schelling of the antagonistic or anti-worldly tendency and the theodical one. The reasons for his ambivalent position vis-à-vis mysticism are instructive and worth examining at some length.[34]

The reassessment of Christian mysticism over and against dirempted modern reason constitutes an important antagonistic motif of early Romanticism. Thus, Friedrich Schlegel in 1798 speaks against the association of mysticism with the kind of piety without knowledge that we have seen the 1802 essay criticize. Instead, Schlegel connects mysticism to the essence of "absolute philosophy, at the standpoint of which spirit regards as mystery

---

34. In this section, I speak of Schelling alone, even with regard to the 1802 essay, since this essay's conception of mysticism is clearly Schellingian and recapitulated in his 1802 lectures.

and as miracle everything that it otherwise, from other perspectives, theoretically and practically takes to be naturally self-evident."[35] For Schelling too, unlike the modern religiosity that de facto legitimates alienation from nature, mysticism indexes "the highest kind of religiosity for which the mystery of nature and the mystery of the becoming human of God are one and the same" (VM 122/86). This mystery of absolute identity or oneness, which constitutes the true core of Christianity, is what the mystic seeks *immediately* to inhabit. Mysticism expresses the "esoteric" "innermost spirit" of Christianity: the mystic immediately intuits the infinite in the finite (VM 125/90; UV 469/375), thereby undoing the general Christian contradiction. In the mystical vision of bliss, the world is annihilated in the atemporal *now*. This vision, moreover, remains essentially the same throughout the Christian trajectory, persisting across the schism between Catholicism and Protestantism (UV 469/375). If "miracle," as Schelling configures it, points to an immediate being of the infinite within the finite that bypasses all relation to time and all not-yet ("miracle . . . emerges in time yet without relation to time"; VM 124/89), then mysticism in Schelling may be defined as the immanent inhabitation of the miraculous.

At work in Schelling's description of mysticism is the apocalyptic identification of what is essential, and of the blissful core behind Christianity, with what is immediate and a-worldly, and with what cancels out the logic of mediation through which salvation history unfolds. Thereby, although it expresses the inner essence of the Christian promise as the promise of all-oneness, mysticism disrupts the providential apparatus of the not-yet that holds the general Christian contradiction together—the apparatus upheld subjectively by faith and objectively by the church. One could say that, despite Schelling's characterization of mysticism as expressing the transhistorical core of Christianity, mystical bliss immediately and apocalyptically closes the split that Christianity seeks to mediate. Thereby, mysticism ungrounds that which makes Christianity distinct from apocalypticism and Gnosticism: namely, the Christian contradiction and the not-yet of its universal reconciliation. Christianity requires the promise of bliss in order to maintain its not-yet, re-mediating the immediacy of bliss into a promised salvific future. Hence, in insisting on bliss *in the now*, mystical vision cannot be properly equated with Christianity. What makes absolute identity or bliss as accessed by the mystic essential is also what makes it excessive over and even antagonistic to

---

35. Schlegel, *Kritische Friedrich-Schlegel-Ausgabe*, vol. 2, 184.

Christianity. Or, put differently: what in Christianity exceeds and refuses the theodical apparatus of the not-yet is not Christianity as such but bliss as what persists transhistorically both with and against it. In its persistent re-emergence across history, mysticism erupts against the foreclosure of bliss by the Christian not-yet. In this manner, Christianity and mysticism are antagonistically entangled.

Perhaps that is why, in his own Christian-modern view of history, Schelling seeks to counterbalance his affirmation of mysticism with a justification of the church in its antagonism to mysticism. It is unsurprising, he emphasizes, that the church opposed the mystical impulse as too subjectivist and at odds with the orderly process of salvation history, and that "the church almost at all times contradicted and in part even persecuted" the mystics who proclaimed the immediacy of divine vision—since the mystics "sought to make the esoteric [dimension] of Christianity exoteric" without regard for the not-yet of the world as the gradual, and not immediate, revelation of the infinite in the finite (VM 125/90), and without regard for the church as the institution of the not-yet. The enactment of the Christian promise is supposed to be premised on faith (in the future), and on the objectively unfolding task of God's becoming one with the world, not on the immediate intuition of divine oneness that has no need of justification or reconciliation. The church could not but oppose the mystics "because they turned faith into a vision [*Schauen*], and wanted to pluck too soon the fruit of time that was not yet ripe" (UV 469/375).

In other words, the mystic seeks to enact bliss right now, whereas (as Schelling insists with the Christian church) everything has its place and time. This implies a theodical logic that is characteristic of Schelling's thought and that we will witness throughout this book. Already here one may note, however, that this logic is different from the modern theodical logic of the self-assertion of the subject. What Schelling advocates for here is a kind of theodical waiting, rather than striving, and a patient witnessing of history as standing in constant tension with, and being gradually overtaken by, eternity. This kind of witnessing of the Christian-modern not-yet from the standpoint of eternity reveals something important about this not-yet: namely, the not-yet of the world cannot be reduced to an empty forward movement but remains full of anticipation and longing, and of a fundamentally mystical sense of unfulfillment, even if Christianity and modernity seek to sate this longing and reach fulfillment in different ways. This, too, is why bliss remains the underside and telos of the Christian-modern world even as, considered immanently, bliss has no relation to the world's not-yet—and why mysticism keeps erupting, out of the not-yet of history, against history, which never seems ready for bliss. Still, his 1802 proclamation of the epoch of non-alienation and bliss means that Schelling is convinced: if one reads the signs of the times correctly, one can see that the time is objectively ripe for a *krisis* ushering in a "heaven regained."

Schelling's theodical legitimation of the church, and of the not-yet in which everything has its time, has, however, an antagonistic dimension too. The church's criticism of mysticism as too subjectivist, while ideologically motivated, harbors a fundamental truth about absolute identity or bliss. As I emphasized in the introduction, there can be, strictly speaking, no subjective bliss or "my" bliss, since bliss cannot be appropriated and the subject-object divide cannot hold in it. Similarly, what the mystic experiences in her vision is never just her "own" oneness with God, but all-oneness itself, without distinction between subjective and objective, a oneness in which all the divisions and not-yets of the world are annihilated. That is why Schelling insists that, in mystical vision, nature is not denigrated but intuited immediately in its oneness with the infinite (VM 122/86). Thus, what he seems to imply (in his announcement of an entire epoch of absolute bliss, too) is that, while the mystical impulse is essential and true, historically mysticism was never quite sufficient, since *reality itself* must be transfigured if bliss is to be really enacted—and all division, enclosure, and egoism must be cleansed as in a divine fire.[36] It is for this universal task that "subjective" mysticism comes too early.

Hence, it was important that the church uphold, objectively and exoterically, the Christian world in its negativity and not-yetness over and against the mystical desire for immediacy. It seems that, for the final *krisis* to arrive, this negativity must for Schelling be maximally intensified, and universal reality itself must first be alienated to its limit, so that absolute bliss, as a total negation of the alienated world, might erupt out of this alienation. It is in this manner, too, that time must be ripe. This brings to mind Adorno's reflection in *Minima Moralia*, cited in the introduction, that it is only out of the highest negativity of the world that the thought of redemption or salvation emerges in its necessity. Adorno, however, refuses to justify theodically the negativity over and against which redemption appears, whereas the 1802 essay does exactly that, demonstrating the way in which bliss and theodicy form the two opposed poles within Schelling's thinking.

---

36. On this vision see further Chapter 3.

To see in mysticism transhistorically the affirmation of nature as the divine site of bliss, over and against the Christian-modern structure of diremption, is a highly Romantic motif that resonates, out of Schelling's *Naturphilosophie*, across European Romanticism. It is often analyzed under the rubric of Romantic "pantheism"; however, this term by itself serves more to conceal than to highlight the *antagonistic* character of the Romantic idea of the all-oneness of bliss. Via the 1802 essay, we have also traced the way that, for Schelling, this idea, and thus his own pantheism during this period, are coiled already at the apocalyptic roots of early Christianity. The Romantic scene of nature, such as the Rousseauian scene of lying on water and looking at the sky in which the world and the self are dissolved (see introduction), may be said to express, from what Schelling would call the "real" side of nature, the same vision of all-oneness that the mystics intuited "ideally" or intellectually.

Poetically, the same vision of oneness with the real manifests itself, during the late 1790s and early 1800s, in William Wordsworth's vision of what he calls the "one life" or the one "unappropriated bliss" of unenclosed and undivided nature, the "blended holiness of earth and sky."[37] In a perfectly Schellingian manner, in Wordsworth's "Lines Written a Few Miles above Tintern Abbey," the bliss that suspends the world indexes simultaneously the soul's solitude, completeness, and oneness with the All. The "wild secluded scene" merges here with the "more deep seclusion" arising as the mind "behold[s] these steep and lofty cliffs," which, in turn, serve to merge together the earth and the sky.[38] The resulting identity is a "serene and blessed mood" in which

> *we are laid asleep*
> *In body, and become a living soul,*
> *While with an eye made quiet by the power*
> *Of harmony, and the deep power of joy,*
> *We see into the life of things.*[39]

This seeing sees not the world of objects, but the one absolute being (the "one life" or "the life of things"). This plenitude of non-separation reveals an

---

37. Wordsworth, *The Prelude*, Book II, in *Major Works*, 403 (line 430), and "Home at Grasmere," in *Major Works*, 176 (line 85), 178 (line 163). In my reading of Wordsworth here I draw on Chepurin, "Romantic Bliss."

38. Wordsworth, "Lines Written a Few Miles above Tintern Abbey," in *Major Works*, 131 (lines 4–6).

39. Ibid., 132–133 (lines 46–50).

absolute identity in "the light of setting suns, / And the round ocean, and the living air, / And the blue sky, and in the mind of man"—the absolute cosmic power that "rolls through all things," preceding them and abolishing any rigid division between them.[40] Or, as Wordsworth writes in *The Prelude*, looking back at his experience of bliss:

> *with bliss ineffable*
> *I felt the sentiment of Being spread*
> *O'er all that moves, and all that seemeth still.*[41]

For this enacted oneness with the real, or with the vast, more-than-human being of nature, Schelling has a further name: magic (*Magie*).[42] Starting from the 1800s and at least until the 1820s, Schelling thinks of the epoch of absolute bliss as the epoch of magic. "Magic" expresses for him the absolute power of nature itself, with which the speculative philosopher of nature becomes one, not unlike the mystic's becoming one with the divine in her vision. It is the fundamental premise of Schelling's natural philosophy that the philosopher does not approach nature in an alienated or reflective way from the outside, but dispossesses herself toward a oneness with nature's power and movement, which she speculatively traces. The concept of magic names what is excluded by the modern structure of rationality yet what continues to underlie, as the absolutely real of nature, the modern imposition of alienation and exploitation that turns nature into mere resource for self-assertion and forecloses its divine essence.

Thus, in his 1821 lectures, Schelling identifies "eternal magic" with the "eternal power [*Macht*]" at work in or underneath all reality (IPU 189)—the same power of which Wordsworth speaks as "the power / Of harmony, and the deep power of joy," where the self grows quiet, entrusting itself to the one infinite life. It is, so to speak, the power of the absolutely real itself, embodied by the cosmic or natural reality, so that all reality rests upon this power and

---

40. Ibid., 134 (lines 98–103).

41. Wordsworth, *The Prelude*, Book II, in *Major Works*, 402 (lines 419–421).

42. "Magic" is a shared Romantic preoccupation (cf. Novalis's "magical idealism") because the Romantics perceive the moment of crisis they inhabit as a crisis of modern alienated cognition, to which "magic" serves as a counter-term within their vision of a "higher," non-alienated science. One may further note that Schelling's use of "magic" is close to Boehme's "divine *Magia*" as the power of "the wisdom of God," "whence the *eternal nature* doth always arise from eternity" and wherein nature is "known from eternity" (*Epistles of Jacob Behmen*, 84). Schelling likewise associates "eternal magic" and divine wisdom (IPU 262).

knows itself to be absolutely one: a pre-human kind of absolute knowledge that nature possesses and enacts. Magic, Schelling writes, is "the pure, resting knowledge, infinite in itself," which is inherent in all finite forms (IPU 189). Similarly, in 1806 he asserts: "Nature knows not through science but through its own essence—in other words, magically" (KF 298). Just like the Romantic poet, the philosopher of nature, her "mortal eye" (KF 300) made quiet by the power of being, becomes immediately one with the sky and the earth, from the movement of planets to the growth of plants—disclosing Romantic natural philosophy as an all-encompassing mysticism of the real:

> In its quietest existence and without reflection, the plant reveals eternal beauty. And thus it would be best for you to know God in silence and, as it were, unknowingly [*nichtwissend*]. . . . Only in the highest science does the mortal eye close, where not the human sees, but the eternal seeing [*Sehen*] itself becomes that which sees within the human. (KF 299–300)

This vision, in which the magical realism of *Naturphilosophie* turns the "subjective" mystical intuition "objective" and real, is what is enacted by the arriving epoch of absolute identity. "The time will come," Schelling proclaims, when "immediate cognition" without mediation will take the place of the individual sciences (KF 298).[43] The separation of the sciences emerged in the first place only "due to the lack" of such immediate knowledge. To illustrate this, and as though to complement the example of the plant as what is below, Schelling turns to astronomy as a science of what is above. "For instance," he declares, "the whole edifice of astronomical calculations" was erected "because it was not given to the human to immediately see the necessity inherent in heavenly movement, or to co-live [*mitleben*] spiritually the real life of the All" (KF 298). The role of modernity is in this regard ambivalent for Schelling: starting from Bacon and Descartes, modern science wants to develop a universal cognition that would make possible the kind of perfect knowledge and mastery of reality that would turn alienation and mediation into immediacy, and the world into a paradisal garden under the control of "man."[44] Yet this goal is constitutively unreachable if modernity does not give up the very logic of

---

43. Cf. WA11 9/63: "At that point there will no longer be any difference between the world of thought and the world of actuality. It will be One World, and the peace of the golden age will first announce itself in the harmonious unity of all the sciences." Benz, *Schellings theologische Geistesahnen*, 65–69, takes this vision to be influenced by F. C. Oetinger's eschatological proclamation of the "light-science of the end times."

44. Cf. Merchant, *Reinventing Eden*, 65.

self-assertion—and this is why a *new* epoch, a re-commencement of modernity in a true reconciliatory way, is necessary (without, however, losing what is true about modern science, including the standpoint of universality itself). This entails for Schelling recognizing bliss and magic as the underside of modernity that modernity forecloses yet longs for. Only on the basis of true philosophy as reconciling the modern sciences—a philosophy that Schelling equates with his identity philosophy—can Christianity, mysticism, poetry, and science finally flow into one.

Schelling's insistence that a time will come in which calculation and science will turn into magic may sound similar to the oft-repeated adage of science fiction writer Arthur C. Clarke, the third of his "three laws," which argues that "any sufficiently advanced technology is indistinguishable from magic." Another of Clarke's laws states, relatedly, that whenever someone claims that something is scientifically impossible, "he is very probably wrong." Science ventures beyond "the limits of the possible . . . into the impossible":[45] this, too, is the salvific telos of modern science. Still, a confusion is to be avoided here. Like Bacon's, Clarke's vision of the unity of technology and magic continues the modern project of mastery over reality. Schelling's vision at its most radical is, instead, *antagonistic* to this project, and antagonistic to the mainstream trajectory of modernity, even as it emerges out of modernity's own crisis. For Clarke, "technology" and "magic" jointly mark the culmination of the self-assertion of reason, including the logic of realizing possibilities to the fullest that, as I observed via Blumenberg in the introduction, the project of self-assertion involves. In its endless doing and striving, the modern rational subject never leaves possibilities unused, instead braving ever-new frontiers and bending reality to the subject's will. This, too, shows that modernity longs for immediacy and non-alienation, and implies a utopian vision of magic and bliss at the end of the modern world. However, this bliss is supposed to be reached through perfect possession and control, and through mastering the totality of possibility inherent in reality understood as something opposed to the subject, the not-I to the demiurgic modern I. This logic, through which alienation is in fact reproduced and upscaled rather than overcome (a fact to which the trajectory of capitalist modernity attests), is ultimately individualist and appropriative, a kind of modern wish-fulfillment through science and technology. Here the subject wants the world to conform entirely and immediately to modern dirempted reason.

---

45. Clarke, *Profiles of the Future*, 14, 21.

Schellingian magic, by contrast, abandons the logic of self-assertion and dispossesses the self, refusing to control or manipulate reality but rather becoming immanently one with the real—with the stillness of natural beauty and the power of planetary depths, the one life of things, the growth of the plant, the infinite void of the sky. Magic for Schelling is not a dream of reality-manipulation or an engineering of manifestation. Nor is it the use of signs or calculations to produce changes in objective reality. Free from the fantasy of calculated order and the colonial image of the frontier, Schellingian magic follows the absolute and makes its practitioner—the speculative philosopher of nature or the Romantic poet—one with the divine or inhuman power that fundamentally cannot be controlled by the subject. The utopia of magic is immanently unlimited, preceding and exceeding the world of self-assertion, and dissolving the general Christian contradiction—just as, in Schelling's vision from his 1800 *System of Transcendental Idealism*, the world that philosophy cognizes is destined to be dissolved in "the ocean of poetry" (STI 328/ 232). Perhaps one could say that Schellingian magic is poetry enacted, the poetry of the real. In Schelling's thinking of mysticism and magic, an antagonism erupts from within the negative and dirempted trajectory of world history and from within the modern subject's striving in an alienated world. That this unblissful striving inevitably casts doubt on the world's entire structure of legitimacy is a problem that looms behind Schelling's concepts of mysticism and magic in the 1800s and that already haunts his earliest thought in the 1790s.

Interlude I

ORDO QUIS DATUS?

QUID SUMUS ET quidnam victuri gignimur, ordo / quis datus? What are we, and for what life are we born? What is the order, or the distribution of place and rank, that is given? These lines from the first-century poet Persius (*Satires* III.67–68) are quoted by the seventeen-year-old Schelling as the epigraph to his 1792 thesis *On the Origin of Evil*, devoted, significantly, to a central problem of theodicy. In this interlude, I want to suggest that the question of (world-)order—of its structure, genesis, and legitimacy, and of the modern subject's demiurgic striving within this order—forms a crucial point around which the wide-ranging nexus of the young Schelling's theoretical concerns may be seen to crystallize by 1795, the year in which he declares "the existence of the world" to be the main problem of all philosophy (PB 82/177) just after observing, in a letter to Hegel cited earlier, that "the entire previous constitution of the world" at present stands in question (BW1 21).

Schelling was famously a philosophical prodigy. During the early 1790s, he was still a student at the Tübingen Seminary, to which he had been admitted at the precocious age of fifteen, and where Hegel and Hölderlin were his roommates: a powerful trio that would be to a large degree responsible for shaping the course of German idealism and Romanticism. The scope of Schelling's preoccupations during these years is impressive. In addition to commenting on the book of Job, the Psalms, the prophetic books, the Gospel of John, and the Pauline Epistles, he studies heresy, including different varieties of Gnosticism, and the early Christian world and the figure of Jesus. He also writes on Plato's *Timaeus*, the spirit of Platonism, ancient myth and poetry, and the origin of evil. All of this leads up to his 1795 dissertation, *On Marcion, the Corrector of the Pauline Epistles*, and to his first significant philosophical works, *On the Possibility of a Form of All Philosophy* (1794) and *Of the I as Principle of Philosophy* (1795). To separate the more standardly philosophical among these preoccupations (such as his interest in Plato or Kant) from the rest is to run the risk of neglecting the sheer ambition underlying this range of concerns; and there is, of course, always the temptation to dismiss this formative period as too youthful and eclectic. It does not help that Schelling himself proclaims in 1795 to have left his historical-theological studies behind (BW1 16), climbing instead onto the barricades of post-Kantian philosophy.

However, it is precisely the scope of Schelling's interests during these years that I seek to highlight and rethink here. What in 1795 Schelling could only suspect, yet what is clear if one surveys retrospectively his range of preoccupations in the early 1790s, is that his entire early thought is intertwined with the movement of his time and with the self-reflection of the modern age at the critical late eighteenth-century moment.

I1.1. *The World-Historical Constellation*

From a Blumenbergian perspective, the young Schelling's constellation of concerns is striking, and indeed appears world-historical, insofar as it reflects the foundational logics of modernity in its overcoming of Gnosticism through the self-assertion of the rational subject. Schematically, I will arrange this nexus around five interconnected lines of inquiry: (1) the modern epoch and its task; (2) ancient world and thought, or the beginning of human history; (3) Christianity and Gnosticism or heresy; (4) theodicy; and (5) modern philosophy of subjectivity (via Schelling's rereading of Plato in a Kantian vein), a line of inquiry leading up to the next chapter.

I1.1.1. The Modern Age: Revolution and Completion

One of Schelling's overarching early interests is the essence and task of the modern age and modern thought—a burning issue for the young Schelling and Hegel at a time when all eyes, including those of students at Tübingen, were set on Revolutionary France as heralding a truly universal future. Schelling and Hegel are, during these years, on the lookout for the signs of the times; and in one of his letters, Schelling raises the key concern with "our age [*Zeitalter*]": What is its essence? What has it produced (*hervorgebracht*) and what can it yet produce? Where does its greatness lie? Seeing as the old constitution of the world is crumbling and an eschatological battle "until victory or demise" is taking place, what is it that separates this age from "the preceding times" (BW1 20–21)? The same concern breaks through in Schelling's allusion to the French Revolution at the end of his 1792 dissertation on evil, and in his proclamation, in the 1795 *Philosophical Letters,* of a revolutionary "covenant [*Bund*] of those whose spirit is free" (PB 112/196).

At this stage, Schelling's interest in the contemporary epoch has not yet developed into what we have seen as his later exploration of the genealogy of modernity or modern alienation. It is still centered mostly around the Revolution in the political realm and Kantian philosophy in the realm of thought. It is, nonetheless, significant that the same revolutionary impulse is for Schelling at work in both; and in both, it is an impulse of oneness—perceived even more acutely from within German political backwardness and disunity at the time. The essential oneness of global humanity (in reason and freedom) and the expected oneness of philosophy mutually imply each other. The completion of the post-Kantian system coincides, world-historically, with the completion of the task of the age. This raises, however, the question of what it is exactly that is being completed, and what it is about "the preceding times" that is being overcome. The movement of the age itself engenders the political-theological question of periodization.[1] "Each time," Schelling writes around 1793/4, "has its own forms under which its concepts appear" (EV 113). This periodization is assumed to culminate universally in and through the modern European logics of self-assertion of reason, and is co-imbricated with the European colonial domination within the global order. The world-historical master narrative is already encoded in Schelling's thinking during the 1790s.

I1.1.2. The Ancient World: Re-mediation and Immediacy

Making sense of the above narrative in its re-mediation of the richness of the global is impossible without grappling with the ancient world as what Schelling would traditionally construe as the first epoch of history. With regard to this epoch, the young Schelling is interested not only in Greek mythology and philosophy but also the world of the Hebrew Bible and early Christianity in the empirical multitude of this world's languages and geographies. This forms the second sub-nexus of Schelling's earliest concerns. His more metaphysical 1794 commentary on Plato's *Timaeus* notwithstanding (see below),

---

1. On the logic of periodization as entwined with the self-legitimation of Western modernity, see Davis, *Periodization and Sovereignty*.

these concerns appear largely philological and historical-critical in character. If one surveys Schelling's fragmentary pre-1795 commentaries on the Hebrew prophets, the Psalms, or the book of Job, one can see the linguistically gifted Schelling taking notes on and offering his interpretation of various obscure expressions, exegetical issues, and even astronomical events (such as the darkness covering the moon and the stars in Job; see KH 154).

However, not only does Schelling not limit himself to interest merely in textual, mythological, or linguistic detail, often venturing into the conceptual. This interest itself, as I have previously emphasized, is part of the formation of new knowledge and new ways of thinking required to grasp the endless historical complexity and particularity of the global world, and to re-mediate particular cosmologies into the Christian-modern universal-historical image of the globe. Philology too, with its interest in etymology and the origin of language, is part of the modern grappling with the idea of the oneness of humanity and its complex global distribution. Schelling's later philosophy of mythology would also develop out of this kind of attention to the particular (albeit grown more speculative).[2] Even the fascination with astronomy and celestial bodies, visible in Schelling's commentary on Job, would speculatively unfold into his natural-philosophical interest in the deep time of the solar system and the earth's planetary history. The "system of the world" equals for Schelling the heliocentric cosmic *Weltsystem* in which the earth is one of the heavenly bodies. As this book will show, the modern age of global human history is for him an age of planetary and cosmic history, too (see Chapter 3). The transcendental order of thought, the world-historical order of the global, and the cosmic order are conjoined in Schelling's thought in a singular way.

Alongside what would become the logic of world-historical (re-)mediation, another logic takes shape in the young Schelling as part of this sub-nexus: the logic of immediacy.[3] Of this logic, myth and poetry constitute two important sites.

---

2. As Johannes Zachhuber emphasizes with regard to Schelling's later thought, "There is little doubt that the power of Schelling's message resulted from his affirmation of the need and the justification of critical, empirical, historical work while fully upholding the speculative dignity of history as a mirror of the world-spirit" (Zachhuber, "Schelling and the Rise," 28). This combination emerges, in a more rudimentary form, already in Schelling's studies from the early 1790s.

3. See also Matthews, *Schelling's Organic Form*, 39–68, who foregrounds the influence of "the unmediated experience of the divine" (42) in the Pietist tradition on the young Schelling, and highlights the latter's goal of "overcom[ing] the alienation of human existence" by integrating "religion" and "logos" (67–68).

Thus, Schelling's 1793 essay "On Myths" not only contains a treatment of pre-lapsarian paradisal felicity as something to be found, in a Platonic-Augustinian manner, within the soul (UM 229–230), prefiguring his 1795 concept of bliss. It also shows speculative interest in the mind of the ancient mythmaker and the transcendental history of consciousness, and in what would continue to underlie Schelling's understanding of paganism: namely, the idea of an immediate natural oneness preceding the diremption introduced by Christianity. In ancient myths as Schelling interprets them in 1793, consciousness stands in thrall to the natural in a way that is still "childish," not least because this consciousness cannot yet form the idea of the one infinite essence of nature, but only perceives immediate oneness polytheistically within particular sensible phenomena. What the phenomenon signifies and what it is are one and the same; there is no separation of "the phenomena" from "the thing in itself" (UM 238), no structure of separation or reflection.[4] Recapitulating in a Kantian manner the logic of self-assertion, Schelling speaks of the awakening of reason from the "deep simplicity" of historical childhood (UM 205). "Previously, the human was the friend or son of nature; now he is its law-giver"—the demiurgic subject who finds, transcendentally, "the archetype [*Urbild*] of nature in *his own* understanding" (UM 233). Within the narrative of history, sensible immediacy comes first and is the lowest. As such, this immediacy itself becomes part of re-mediating the "pre-rational" elements of the global into one continuous history of rationality.

Aside from this lowest kind of immediacy, there is another, absolute or divine logic of immediate oneness in which the young Schelling shows interest, and which comes closer to his later association of bliss with the immediate operativity of what precedes or cancels out the mechanism of mediation. In his 1792 notes on Plato's *Ion*, this kind of divine immediacy is what is at work in poetry, in a way that resembles proleptically Schelling's later conception of poetry, magic, and miracle. Through poets, "divine force" spreads magnetically, overflowing the listener—so that "the listeners (to build on [Plato's] metaphor) constitute, as it were, the last ring in the magnetic chain, onto which the poet's divine force pours out" (VAW 17). Schelling excerpts passages from *Ion* that speak of the Corybantes and Bacchants as possessed, lost in a trance in which their minds are not in them: a self-dispossession toward a non-mediated oneness with the same divine power that acts in poetry. However, unlike ritualized dancing, which Schelling would never place

---

4. Later, Schelling develops this into a theory of mythology as "tautegorical" and not "allegorical." See Whistler, *Schelling's Theory*.

quite at the same level as poetry,[5] a poetic product is an enacted "miracle for which natural causes cannot be found," and which emerges in a way that is *urplötzlich*, "primordially sudden" or "pre-sudden," revealing what precedes the logic of mediation (VAW 18). Although Schelling would constantly attempt to inscribe these logics of immediacy, too, into the not-yet of history, they enact immediately that which abolishes the not-yet as such.

I1.1.3. Early Christianity and Gnosticism: Between Orthodoxy and Heresy

The young Schelling's engagement with what, in a letter to Hegel, he calls "the spirit of the first Christian centuries" (BW1 16) continues his concern with the historical and mythological contexts of the ancient world, and with the break that Christianity enacts. The figure of Paul especially fascinates Schelling. Through Paul, he seeks to theorize the world-historical turning point that "the pure doctrine of Christ" announced (AER 80)—yet that could not *immediately* become universal due to the opposition to it from the power of the old world, embodied by the Roman Empire: an idea that must have been additionally important to Schelling because of what he saw as the comparable contemporary event, the French Revolution, and the resistance to it in Germany in particular. "Paul," Schelling notes, "saw that humanity was ripe for a great transformation," but also that it was held back in its progress by the external "iron force [*Gewalt*]" of the empire (AER 80). The first Christian centuries were thus, for Schelling, crucial to the formation of the Christian-modern dialectic between the immediacy of truth, on the one hand, and its world-historical deferral and re-mediation, on the other.

In 1793–94, Schelling wanted to write a volume of historical-critical essays that would presumably include his commentaries on Paul's Epistles to the Romans and the Galatians and on the early life of Jesus according to Luke and Matthew, providing an intervention in the contemporary debate over biblical hermeneutics.[6] At the same time, Schelling's sensibilities during these years appear remarkably Gnostic, especially in light of the fact that in 1795 he wrote his theological dissertation on Marcion and Paul—and importantly,

---

5. In his later thought, Schelling historicizes and racializes this kind of trance-like ecstatic dancing as too wild, opposing to it the deep peace revealed in the Greek mysteries. See, e.g., UPO 389. For a more "transgressive" speculative reading of collective bodily rhythm in Schelling, see Trop, "Politics of Speculative Collectivities."

6. See Danz, *Schelling und die Hermeneutik der Aufklärung*.

the above Pauline epistles were among those included, together with a version of the Gospel of Luke, in Marcion's New Testament canon. Moreover, Schelling planned to compose a whole treatise under the title *History of Gnosticism*. His intended structure for that work (GG 81–83) reveals an impressive panorama of heresy—not only of Gnosticism narrowly defined in its Marcionite, Valentinian, and other varieties but also all sorts of sources and offshoots of Jewish, pagan, and early Christian thought, among them "oriental religions" (including Hinduism and Manichaeanism), apocalyptic and magical thinking, Pythagorean and Platonic systems, the Kabbalah, and heresies such as Docetism and Montanism. As such, this was to be a history of the Gnostic tendency as a tendency toward heretical *gnosis* and heretical salvation.

The above has led Christian Danz to characterize this as Schelling's heretical counter-program.[7] For Schelling, this counter-program is aligned with the Kantian spirit of critique in its opposition to any dogmatism (cf. BW1 21), and with the Revolutionary age—thus connecting with the issue of the essence and task of the contemporary epoch (but also with the question of the entwinement of heresy and orthodoxy in the formation of the Christian-modern trajectory, not unlike the antagonistic interplay of mysticism and the church familiar to us from Chapter 1). As we will see, even Schelling's 1795 writings in post-Kantian philosophy are replete with elements that can be grasped as Gnostic or that can be traced back to Paul and the separation enacted by Christianity. This includes the distinction between *in the world*

---

7. See Danz, "Die Philosophie der Offenbarung," 170. Danz emphasizes the persistence of the spirit of this counter-program into Schelling's later philosophy. Cf. the recollection of one of Schelling's classmates that, "during his years at the seminary . . . Schelling predominantly studied the Gnostics, especially the Ophite and the Valentinian systems" (cited in HKA I/2: 203). Ophite teachings in particular valorized the Serpent's injunction to eat of the Tree of Knowledge, and Schelling's interest in them converges with his legitimation of the Fall. The point is not, however, to reductively call Schelling a Gnostic but to highlight the persistent antagonistic dimension of his thought. What he studied as "Gnosticism" was derived from Christian heresiologists, for whom "Gnosticism" stood in for the dangerously heterodox *tout court*, "mark[ing] the erroneous, the heretical, the schismatic, as well as all things threatening, anomalous, esoteric, and arcane" (King, *What Is Gnosticism?*, 18). Schelling's counter-program may be called "Gnostic" in this broad sense, too. Cf. his striking notes for a conclusion to *History of Gnosticism*: following "the downfall of Gnosticism," one sees "an almost complete disappearance of heretics from history—[with the exception of] here and there the Monophysites [and] the Nestorians—also the Tritheists in the third century—the Monothelites in the sixth—afterward only few names—lights in the night" (GG 100). At the same time, whatever one understands by "Gnosticism" (a term I employ as a Blumenbergian shorthand for the tendency of world-delegitimation), in Schelling the Gnostic tendency always stands in tension with the theodical tendency of *legitimating* the world and the demiurgic (divine or human) agent.

and *of the world*, and the possibility of a total negation of the world toward a salvation understood as a-worldly and even annihilative of the world. It also includes the conception of the infinite's revelation in and as the finite, as well as the Pauline structure of already/not-yet and the Pauline-Gnostic opposition between salvation and the externally coercive law.

We will see Schelling's philosophical writings from 1795 reveal this counter-program to be co-imbricated with the modern logics of alienation, futurity, and demiurgic subjectivity, and with modernity itself as a demiurgic, heretical, and critical epoch (no matter whether one might want to call this modernity's "Gnosticism" or by any other name). At stake here, as in Schelling's planned *History of Gnosticism*, is less the historical name "Gnosticism" than a heretical speculative tendency out of which his concept of bliss qua salvation develops—a tendency that we will see culminate in the question: If bliss is something a-cosmic or a-worldly, and an absolute freedom from the negativity of the world conjoined ethically with absolute virtue, then why must this world even be there? This is a question of world-justification or theodicy, too.

I1.1.4. Theodicy and the Role of Evil

Theodicy remains an essential concern for Schelling throughout the 1790s and beyond—so that, for instance, when considering his explicit discussions of Leibnizian theodicy in the subsequent decades, it should be kept in mind that he already plans to write a treatise on Leibniz and theodicy in the 1790s (see BW1 171). Schelling's first philosophical work, his 1792 master's thesis, *On the Origin of Evil*, is a work of theodicy; and his extensive notes on the book of Job—which he calls "a theodicy" concerned with God's "governance of the world" (DMO 105, KH 239)—likewise stem from these earliest years.

The epigraph from Persius at the beginning of this chapter marks Schelling's 1792 thesis—an analysis of the "myth" of the Fall from the book of Genesis—as concerned with the question of order and, through the concept of evil, with the legitimacy of the world-order. In theodicy generally, inquiry into the origin and role of evil points to the deep concern with legitimacy. Evil is what most radically threatens the legitimacy of established ("divine" or "worldly") order; that is why the question of evil is located at the forefront of theodical questioning, as well as at the forefront of heresy.[8] Besides seeing

---

8. As Tertullian characteristically points out, "morbidly brooding over the question of the origin of evil" is precisely what led Marcion, like many others with "a heretical proclivity," to stray

it as a threat, theodicy seeks to consider evil in its *usefulness* to the good. Thereby the threat of evil can be converted into what confirms and upholds the order's legitimacy. In this regard, it is important to observe the further theodical spin that Schelling puts on the Kantian framework that he follows in the 1792 work.[9]

This framework, as we remember, conceptualizes the Fall as the original act of reason's self-assertion and liberation. Starting from the refusal of the pre-given distribution of rank and place in paradise—a disobedience Schelling captures via the concept of spontaneity—reason's "ever-urgent striving" (DMO 105) produces the endless negativity of the world that the subject, now counting only on itself, creates and inhabits. However, this negativity is ultimately justified and reconciled by the destined fulfillment (*Vollendung*) of freedom at the end of reason's toilsome world-historical path. The book of Job, says Schelling, this "oldest and truly divine poetic work," sought to justify the goodness of divine order. Yet—and this is the aforementioned spin—a theodicy that merely emphasizes goodness is insufficient. The book of Job "contented itself with the same proposition at which the philosophy of Leibniz stopped, too: 'All things have been created by God; ergo, he created them as good'" (DMO 106). From Job to Leibniz, Schelling suggests, theodicy tends to conceal the principle of evil.

However, at the post-Lisbon moment of theodicy's crisis coupled with the crisis of otherworldly salvation, reason in its self-assertion can no longer simply refer to transcendent divine goodness as a way to justify the infinite negativity of the world whose dark ground threatens to engulf the light of reason. Enlightened reason sees the negativity of the world it has created and fears its dark ground more than it fears God. What theodicy must now do is confront this darkness head-on, investigate its origin and character, and assert reason's world-historical goal *over and against* this darkness—making negativity and evil themselves useful for the development of reason and freedom, or making the principle of evil serve theodically what is divine, absolute, and good. That is what, in the introduction, I have called reason's theodical intensification of the dark ground; and that is why Schelling asserts symptomatically, in the first sentence of his work, that "reason itself has the highest interest" in

---

from the vision of the one true God and to "vilify" the divine world-order, or "the world itself [as] inscribed *with the goodness of its Maker*." Tertullian, *Five Books against Marcion*, 272 (I.2), 281 (I.14), 310 (II.17).

9. On the Kantian-Enlightenment dimension of Schelling's thesis, see Jacobs, *Gottesbegriff*, 173–210.

tracing the origin of evil (DMO 105). Theodicy must tarry with negativity and evil, and this becomes the project of Schelling's theodicy for the rest of his life.

Of course, this intensification of darkness for the purpose of its theodical enclosure runs the risk of turning order itself dark. It reveals the abyss of darkness that is *prior* to divine order. Throughout his life, Schelling seems to subscribe to the theory of the book of Job as "extremely ancient and pre-Mosaic."[10] This makes the problem of theodicy older than the account of creation and the Fall in Genesis, so that creation conceals the darkness that theodicy first reveals. Satan as the principle of temptation and evil, too, must for Schelling be regarded as subordinate to the providential goodness of the created order if this goodness is to be upheld. Schelling's abiding interest in the figure of Satan—who appears already in Schelling's first footnote to the 1792 work—should be understood in light of the above. In his later philosophy of revelation, Schelling develops this interest into a full-fledged theodicy, speaking of Satan in Genesis and in Job as the divine "instrument" whose role it is to bring evil to the surface as in a divine "trial" (UPO 621–623, 636). Satan is the principle that "brings [one] into suspicion" from the point of view of what is divine, or that "pulls out" evil from underneath divine order (UPO 623).

At the same time, in this theodical construction, the fault for the entire trial narrative of history falls not on God but on the will that fails the divine trial, thus *confirming* the trial's necessity. (Divine world-order, after all, wants the will to conform to it voluntarily, not just externally, since only that secures its upholding.) This original failure, however, is already in Schelling's 1792 text revealed retroactively as good from the standpoint of the fulfillment that is promised at the end of history—a fulfillment that must be deserved by reason and won through freedom (DMO 146). "It is," Schelling emphasizes in a way that connects the beginning and the end of history into a narrative of redemption, and that later becomes central for his positioning of the existence of the world as a key philosophical problem, "a rightful question to ask why we had at all to fall from the condition of original happiness and what ultimately the future goal of all human things is supposed to be" (DMO 142–143). Only from this standpoint does the first trial of the human will reveal its theodical significance. "And now," Schelling proclaims, "the entire history of humanity ought to explain for us this ancient story" (DMO 140), that is, the story of the Fall, whose significance is revealed in and as human history qua the development of reason toward freedom and autonomy and toward

---

10. As he puts it in an 1820 letter; quoted in HKA II/1, 2: 21. Cf. DMO 106, KH 239.

the oneness of humanity in reason "on the entire globe" (DMO 144). This goal of the formation of the rational unity of the global compensates for the negativity and evil it generates along the way, and this negativity itself proves useful, within the "most wise plan" of history, for the attainment of the end goal (DMO 145).[11] Hence—goes Schelling's Kantian injunction—one must have faith in this goal and not despair. Just as his text begins with an epigraph on order, so it ends with a justification of the "order of the whole," to which all parts of humankind are subordinated. Schelling does not foreclose fulfillment via infinite approximation the way Kant does, instead proclaiming "the new golden age" (of reason) as reachable—with allusion, significantly, to the language of the French Revolution (DMO 146–147). The theodical arch in Schelling's earliest thought is co-imbricated with the essence of modernity as the age of self-assertion, and with the modern vision of the demiurgic rational subject who asserts itself in the Fall.

I1.1.5. The Demiurgic Subject: Plato with Kant

From the question of the contemporary epoch, to his interest in myth, heresy, and disobedience, to his theodical narrative of global history, the young Schelling grapples with the issue of the world-order as generated in its negativity by the demiurgic activity of reason. That this logic is explicitly grasped by Schelling as demiurgic is clear from his unfinished 1794 commentary on Plato's *Timaeus*, where he interprets the Platonic demiurge—this "world architect" (KT 159/232) central to Gnosticism too—through the lens of the modern subject-world conjunction.

Of pivotal importance to Schelling's interpretation is the fact that the demiurge in Plato fashions preexisting material, disorderly and formless, into an orderly cosmos with the help of ideal forms. For Schelling, this prefigures the activity of the Kantian transcendental subject, who arranges the disorderly material of sensation into the phenomenal world through the imposition of categories or forms. Material reality, Schelling asserts in his reading of the *Timaeus*, does not originally possess form; the world is given shape by the demiurgic subject, who contains forms in its mind. The world is thus a subject-object structure in which orderly reality arises through the subject's

---

11. The allusion to the rational oneness of humanity "under a single law and single goal" proclaimed by the French Revolution makes it clear that for Schelling the beginning of this new coming epoch is *now*. Cf. BW1 21 on the present as "the dawn" before "the sun" or "the full day."

imposition of form. As we have seen, starting from ancient mythology, this demiurgic logic has for Schelling been true world-historically, too: every epoch is marked by the specific way consciousness shapes the world (e.g., the mind of the ancient mythmaker is more sensual than rational, and so are the forms with which it arranges the world). In modernity, this becomes *explicit* or self-reflective; demiurgic subjectivity becomes autonomous and grasps itself as such.

The parallel with the modern subject of self-assertion in Blumenberg—as finding itself amid an alien and contingent reality out of which the subject must produce a world that would be rational, orderly, and under control—could not be more evident. Schelling underscores that the original principle of the material reality that the demiurge faces before proceeding to reshape it is pure contingency and unlawfulness (KT 154/210). These are also the characteristics of the reality in which, in Blumenberg's account, the subject finds itself at the outset of modernity, and to which the subject must impart order and rationality. Through the forms imposed by the subject, contingency and disorder can be tamed, brought within the regulated limits set by the subject.

In Plato, this logic is not yet grasped as subjective ("Plato everywhere carries the subjective over to the objective"; KT 156/212). Nonetheless, Schelling maintains, we moderns can see that "the philosophical ground" for the order and intelligibility of the world must be "in us." We do not merely "empirically receive" the world; we shape it (KT 157/212). Plato's "ideas," too, are the ideas of reason. In thinking of these ideas as non-subjective, Plato belongs to the epoch of paganism, since nature for him precedes and binds rational subjectivity. In the same vein, Schelling ties the Platonic dialectic of oneness and multiplicity to the modern synthetic activity of cognition, in which the subject synthesizes what is manifold into conceptual unity (KT 161/215). In this way, the subject masters through self-assertion the reality that is originally alien. While it is easy to read this as Schelling's unwarranted Kantianization of Plato, the point is not only that this approach is programmatic on Schelling's part in light of his view of the continuous history of reason from antiquity to the modern age.[12] "Kantianism" and "Platonism" remain meaningless terms unless one grasps the significance of Schelling's turn to Plato and Kant at a key moment of modernity's self-reflection, a moment to which Schelling is attuned. This turn indexes the self-reflection, in Schelling and in German idealism generally, of the modern subject upon

---

12. See Gloyna, *Kosmos und System*.

itself *as* demiurgic and upon the legitimacy of this world that the subject has demiurgically produced. Schelling's reading of the *Timaeus* is also a thinking through of the demiurgic logics of modern subjectivity in its construction of reality as mere material for self-assertion and synthesis. In the figure of the demiurge as Schelling reconfigures it, the transcendental question of genesis (of the world-order) is inseparable from the world-historical genesis and from the problem of this order's legitimacy.

For Plato, the demiurge is good; thanks to the demiurge, a beautiful cosmic order arises out of disorder (KT 150/208). However, is the modern subject a good demiurge? Is the modern world beautiful and good? The modern subject's demiurgic striving seems rather to exacerbate alienation (as Schelling admits in his comment on the modern age as the world-historical peak of negativity; DMO 145). The unblissful character of this striving stands at the center of Schelling's 1795 thinking of the world and bliss—to which we now turn.

2
The Demiurgic Subject

IN HIS PHILOSOPHICAL works from 1795, *Of the I as Principle of Philosophy* and *Philosophical Letters on Dogmatism and Criticism*, Schelling offers a singular analytic of the modern demiurgic subject, and of the unblissful world that this subject produces in its very striving for fulfillment and bliss. These works as I understand them continue his earlier engagement with the nexus of Christianity, modernity, and Gnosticism, rethinking the fundamental Gnostic and Christian-modern themes in a strictly philosophical manner. It is in these works, too, that Schelling first develops his concept of bliss, identified with the "absolute" or "unconditioned" being that is foreclosed by the dirempted structure of the world. The modern world especially, in which the divine guarantee holding the general Christian contradiction together collapses, is structurally negative and cannot provide itself with reality. Schelling's 1795 metaphysics is highly abstract, and terms such as "the unconditioned" or "the absolute" may sound cryptic. What they express, however, is Schelling's search for a freedom and fulfillment, and for the absolutely first ontological principle, that would not be conditioned by this alienated world or reducible to the subject's unblissful striving in it.

In modernity, only the world that the subject produces can be called the subject's own; however, the subject also senses the endless negativity of this world. The intuition that this world is *not* the absolute horizon of reality intensifies in the 1795 Schelling, and it is out of this intensification that the concept of bliss emerges in his texts as what is Romantically antagonistic to the logics of self-assertion, productivity, and striving, and what is absolutely first vis-à-vis the world. In 1795, Schelling does not yet identify bliss or the absolutely real with the one undivided being of the earth and the skies. His 1795 philosophy remains too Kantian-Fichtean, still moving largely within the confines of philosophy of subjectivity, even as the antagonism of bliss *to* modern dirempted subjectivity marks his thought as excessive over this confinement. This chapter traces this antagonism together with the constitutive aporias of modern subjectivity that result in the subject's being bound to the (reproduction of the) world even as the subject seeks to break free from it. Ultimately, by way of his spiritual investment in the revolutionary task of modernity as the time of a decisive battle between the true and the false, Schelling's 1795 thought ends up embracing the modern program of self-assertion and the theodical foreclosure of bliss that is characteristic of modernity and of the broader Christian-modern trajectory. The endless deferral or non-arrival of bliss, into which Schelling falls, is something that he then seeks to overcome in his philosophy of absolute identity, which he develops in the early 1800s and which will be examined in Chapter 3.

2.1. *To Break All Finite Spheres: In Search of Lost Bliss*

The ultimate end goal of the finite I and the not-I, i.e., the end goal of the world, is its annihilation [Zernichtung] as a world, i.e., as the exemplification of finitude.

—SCHELLING (VI 128/99)

In Schelling's 1795 metaphysics, the world seems more of a prison than a beautiful and orderly cosmos. "The world," as he defines it in the above-quoted passage, identifies the structure of finitude as such with a world that we may recognize as quintessentially modern. It is a world of diremption between the subject and object, or the I and not-I, a structure of conflict (*Widerstreit*), striving (*Streben*), and "original opposition [*Gegensatz*]" (VI 93/90). This world must, in the end, be abolished or annihilated. This annihilation is what we will see Schelling call "absolute bliss."

In this alienated world, the I is faced with the not-I as external reality, something other, yet to be known and appropriated—something over and against which the subject asserts itself. However, Schelling complicates this (characteristically modern) logic of self-assertion in a Platonic and Gnostic manner. The reason that, discovering itself in the world, the I strives to find a way *out* of it—a striving that defines for Schelling all of the I's activity—is that the I somehow intuits its own essence (*Wesen*) to *not* be of the world. As a result, the modern subject's entire existence in the world that it demiurgically creates is reconfigured by Schelling as an endless flight from the world. Three lines of questioning arise here. First, what is this essence of the I that makes it strive to assert or, as Schelling puts it, "save" itself as it finds itself caught in the nets of the world? Second, why is the I, its essence not of the world, caught up in the world in the first place? More speculatively: Why the world at all, this world of opposition and self-assertion? And finally: What happens to the I *in* the world? What is the dynamic of their encounter? As we will see, Schelling's 1795 metaphysics conceals an overarching story: of how the subject finds itself in the world, strives to break free from it toward absolute identity or bliss—but ultimately ends up reproducing the world, paradoxically, *through* this very striving to break free.

2.1.1. Ungrounding the Subject, Annihilating the World

The modern subjectivity that stands at the center of Schelling's analysis is the Kantian subjectivity that we have already encountered in his reading of the *Timaeus*. In this transcendental framework, all reality is "for the I": the empirical manifold (the not-I) is "posited" in the I, or endowed with conceptual form by the subject. The subject faces a materiality that is empirically contingent and disorderly, yet that the subject arranges or structures in an orderly fashion with the help of the Kantian forms of intuition and categories of the understanding, which circumscribe the entire "sphere of our knowledge" (VI 88/73) and "all that there is" (VI 85/71), the phenomenal world in which the subject exists. Crucially, the subject is always subject *in* the world: subject and object, Schelling says, are reciprocally "determined" or "conditioned" (VI 88/73).

Yet the subject is not entirely of the world. Within itself, the subject intuits a being that is not finite but absolute, or the absolutely real itself: the divine essence of the human soul. In this intellectual intuition (as Schelling calls it), the subject-object opposition disappears (*verschwindet*). Since this essence is absolute, it is neither a finite thing nor a finite self. Within the depths of one's soul, the subject-object structure that is the world ("objects in general and the unity of synthesis") is canceled out (VI 105/85). In the disappearance of the world, an absolute being is revealed that is foreclosed by the world yet must be thought of as *preceding* it: "the unconditioned" or "the absolute" itself. The term "unconditioned" is antagonistic for Schelling to the conditioned character of existence in the dirempted world, expressing that within us that is not of the world. Everyone, according to Schelling, can intuit an absolute being within oneself that makes one dissatisfied with mere being-in-the-world: an essence that we share yet none of us can appropriate.

One may approach this by way of a Platonic-Gnostic idea: the soul carries within itself a memory of its ante-worldly provenance, a longing that marks this dirempted world as not our true home. This idea, however, is not just a theological curiosity, but speaks to the condition of the modern subject, who senses that this dirempted world of endless things, which the subject produces and consumes, cannot bring fulfillment and is, in truth, *not* all there is.[1] Only if we refuse to regard this world as the absolute horizon of reality—the refusal that each of us can enact precisely because we cannot be reduced or bound without remainder to the way the world is—can we discover what is truly absolute and fulfilling: and this is a constitutive Romantic idea, as well. The sense that true freedom and fulfillment cannot be conditioned by this world of things (*Dinge*) is likewise implied by the term "unconditioned" (*das Unbedingte*). Only by inhabiting immanently or dwelling with this sense or this intellectual intuition—only at the standpoint of our non-worldly essence—can we decouple ourselves from the constant striving and irreconcilable alienation that define our existence in the world, and that threaten to make us forget that the world cannot fully claim us.

Since the absolute fulfillment that we intuit and long for within ourselves is antagonistic to the dirempted subject-object structure of reality, Schelling calls it "absolute identity": the one undivided being that must be thought of as preceding our thrownness into the world. This absolute identity cannot be inscribed in the world's logics of mediation, reification, and division. Only what, as Schelling puts it, "*can never become object at all*" may be called (the) unconditioned (VI 90/75). In other words, what is absolute is absolutely non-objectifiable, and without transition to the logic of thinghood. In *Of the I*, Schelling calls the essence of one's soul "the absolute I." In *Philosophical Letters*, written later in the same year, Schelling abandons the term "absolute I" as too subjectivist, speaking instead simply of "absolute identity" and "absolute freedom."

For Schelling, "the absolute I"—or, more precisely, absolute identity as revealed within the I in intellectual intuition—thus discloses a standpoint that is *not* subjective, but free from the subject-object division. It is only within the I–not-I opposition that the distinction between subjective and objective appears, an opposition absent at the absolute standpoint that reveals what simply *is* (absolute being) without any diremption (absolute oneness), or what is solely "through itself" (absolute identity). Within my soul, I *simply*

---

1. In his *Naturphilosophie*, Schelling speaks in the same vein of the ante-original condition of non-alienation: "The Platonic idea that all philosophy is recollection [*Erinnerung*] is, in this regard, true: all philosophizing consists in recollecting the state in which we were one with nature" (AD 365).

am, without any further qualification. Importantly, one's essence is for Schelling not some pre-given substance; nor does the term "absolute identity" imply that we are all the same. It marks rather the absolute freedom of *simply being what one is*, without any external demand, reason, telos, or any expectations placed on one by the world or by other finite subjects. These freedom and immediacy are what the world forecloses. And although in 1795 Schelling identifies this freedom only with the essence of the human soul, and not the essence of all nature as he starts doing by 1800 (see Interlude II), in *Of the I*'s utopian vision of *sheer being and letting-be* one may likewise glimpse the Rousseauian freedom of lying on water and looking at the sky, a nonproductive freedom from the world in which the world is dissolved.

Schelling likes to speak, in a Platonic manner, of the standpoint of the essence as "the highest [standpoint]," since it is absolute, and since compared to this standpoint the world emerges as secondary and negative. At the same time, in this absolute identity, there is no distinction between lower and higher, primary and secondary. It is free from hierarchy and division, disclosing "immediately all truth and all reality" (VI 119/93), a being immanent only to itself. I may glimpse this being within my I, but it is nothing proper, nothing to call my own. As indexing what is in itself, without relation or transition to any outside, this being cannot contain any otherness. In the dirempted world, this identity is divided into subject and object, and the one absolute being (*Sein*) is separated, appropriated, and enclosed into a being-there (*Dasein*). The absolute standpoint itself is, however, a zero point that precedes and immanently refuses this division. Below we will see Schelling explicitly call this the state of salvation and bliss.

Schelling's ungrounding of the finite subject of self-assertion is arguably the most radically heterodox operation that emerges in his 1795 texts and continues to permeate his later thought. Having introduced the intellectual intuition of an absolute being that exceeds and overwhelms the bounds of the subject, Schelling proceeds, furthermore, to unground the entire categorial grammar of the world via an immediate philosophical and mystical oneness with the absolute. His language of "identity," "oneness," and "being" transforms these standard ontological terms—by applying them to the unconditioned itself—into a metaphysics of divine attributes or names that contravenes the finite usage of these categories. If the modern world is a world of original division and synthetic unity, of the particular that is to be remediated into a universality, of enclosed identities that negate what is other to them, and of endless possibilities that the subject must strive to actualize—then it is this finite world that is here completely ungrounded.

Thus, the absolute is an identity (it "simply is what it is"; VI 101/82), but in this abyssal identity all finite identity, as premised on relational division and otherness, disappears. Not inscribed in the logic of the world, absolute identity is "without condition or limitation" (VI 130/100); it is non-relational and radically *without*. The absolute is one, but not in the sense of a synthetic unity of what is conceived as originally divided. It is, rather, an ante-original and immediate oneness, so that not even the possibility of division or twoness is here thinkable or needed. Its *"utter oneness"* is, as Schelling puts it, "indeterminable through number." This oneness is non-conceptual, too, since concept is "what gathers multiplicity into unity," but the absolutely one must be thought of as preceding multiplicity and synthesis. It cannot be a universal either, "For the universal is *conditioned* through the particular" (VI 107–109/86–87). Nor can it be grasped in terms of the relation between part and whole (VI 117–118/93)—unlike the world, which functions through particularization and enclosure. Finally, absolute being is atemporal and a-modal. It is "in *no* time" and "without any duration" (VI 130/100). There is, at the standpoint of absolute identity, no before or after. Accordingly, no process of actualization can take place in it, and the distinction between modal categories makes no sense with regard to it. "For the absolute I, there is no possibility, actuality, or necessity" (VI 163/120). Another fundamental characteristic of the world is thereby refused, just like all others.

This absolute refusal of and freedom from the categories through which the world operates is precisely what Schelling defines as "absolute freedom" (VI 106/84–85). This freedom is at once absolutely negative (as non-relation and withoutness) and absolutely positive—as the purely affirmative being that simply is what it is, and that "unconditionally posits all reality in itself" through the unmediated power (*Macht*) of the absolutely real.[2] In its absolute positivity itself, it functions as without any outside or otherness. Absolute freedom is infinite, and has no place and no need for the world. Indeed, it is "completely incompatible" with the world and cannot bear it (VI 104/84), just as this world is completely incompatible with the fulfillment of *simply being*. Absolute freedom is free from even the temptation of succumbing to the world. Instead, it immediately and absolutely "precludes" the possibility

---

2. "Defined *negatively*," absolute freedom functions "as complete independence from, indeed, even complete incompatibility with all not-I." Absolute negation is to be distinguished from what is "negative" in the finite sense, i.e., as related to antithesis and comparison, and to the reciprocal being-conditioned of the finite I and not-I. Similarly, absolute freedom is absolutely "positive" *qua* "unconditioned" (VI 104/84).

of the world or any transition to it.³ The absolute is absolutely nonproductive of the world.

As such—Schelling escalates—absolute freedom is *annihilative* of the world. A unique metaphysics of nothingness emerges at this point, which continues to mark Schelling's thinking of bliss during later years. The power of the absolute is that of the absolute *nihil*, which "completely annihilates" the logic of opposition and striving. "This idea" (of absolute freedom), says Schelling, "is so far removed from anything empirical that it not only stands far above it but even *annihilates* it" (VI 122/95). There are two aspects to this affirmative reduction to nothing. First, from the point of view of the world, the absolute "can be neither object nor not-object, i.e., cannot be anything at all [*gar nichts*]"—it can be only a zero or nothingness, "nothing at all (= 0)" (VI 101/82, 119/93). The world cannot mediate the absolute through finite categories, and thus declares it to be a nothing. The absolutely real is foreclosed by the world, from within which it appears as a utopian no-thing and no-where. Conversely, since absolute being has no place or need for diremption or otherness, it is the world that is *nothing at all*, annihilated by the power of the absolute as the absolutely nothing. The absolute functions, in effect, as the full absence of a world. Not that it would *care* for any world, either. Absolute freedom does not lack, desire, or will. It possesses "no will" and "is never [the] will" to anything (VI 122–123/95–96). It is, one might say, the power not to dialecticize itself, not to fall prey to the world or be caught in the circle of negativity and otherness. The world is a world of mediation and striving but, Schelling proclaims, "The absolute can never be mediated," and there is "no striving" in absolute freedom (VI 109/87, 104/85).

To summarize, not only the modern world as the subject-object structure of negativity and lack but the modern I, too, whose finite freedom of ceaseless striving and willing serves to uphold this world, is dispossessed and emptied out—declared to be nothing essential—in absolute freedom. If the absolute is, as Schelling calls it, the "primordial ground" (VI 85/71) or "unconditioned condition" (VI 100/81), this ground and this condition are of a very strange, nonproductive kind. Considered immanently, this absolute zero point does not condition the world. Instead, the entire categorial grammar of the world is, in this absolute ground, absolutely ungrounded.

---

3. Schelling uses here the term *Ausschließung*, best translated in this context not as "exclusion" but as "preclusion." The absolute "precludes all object," refusing to be inscribed in the subject-object structure. *Ausschließung* signals the absolute as *preceding* and *precluding*, ruling out the world: it is "prior to any not-I, and precluding all not-I" (VI 93–94/76–77).

2.1.2. This Negative World—or, A Paradise Lost

"Absolute freedom" is the absolutely first that is "utterly immanent" and "has no need to go outside itself" (VI 167/122). It is annihilative of any "outside" and is without any need or care, any striving or "ought" (*Sollen*; VI 164/121). This leads to a crucial issue. If the absolutely first is without world—and nonproductive of a world—then why must the world be there? And how is its being-there thinkable? There is metaphysically *no transition* from absolute being to the world. To intellectually intuit the absolute is to remain within absolute identity and freedom, without the possibility or necessity to proceed to anything else.

In order to think this finite world, however, we need to think otherness. The world is, after all, identity *and* difference. This implies the structure or, as Schelling calls it, "form" of opposition and otherness. The world as a subject-object structure is thinkable only if we think the not-I; and to think the not-I is to negate absolute identity. Resulting from this is a twoness that cannot be derived from oneness: from absolute identity itself, "No not-I can originate [*hervorgehen*]" (VI 113/90). The subject can only find itself thrown into a world whose origin it cannot grasp, facing a not-I that appears as completely alien and other. All that the subject can see is that the not-I is contingent and endless: an empirical chaos that the subject strives to synthesize into conceptual unity. It is through this synthesis that a reified world of finite things (products of synthesis), of limitation and condition, of particular and universal, of division and relation, appears before the subject's eyes. This world, as a result, never expresses identity or oneness except in a synthetic, originally alienated way.

Schelling calls the empirical chaos that the subject faces the "absolute not-I" or "original not-I." This chaos is not yet an object or a thing. It is but material for the I's self-assertion and synthesis, an "absolute nonbeing," pure multiplicity (VI 114/91). The "absolute not-I" occupies in Schelling's 1795 metaphysics the (non-)place of pure matter from Plato's *Timaeus*, whose origin the I—not unlike the modern subject in the wake of nominalism—cannot fathom. This non-place coincides with what I have theorized in the introduction (and will trace in detail in Part II) as the dark ground of the modern world of self-assertion. In modernity, all that is declared to be "nature" in the sense of pure extension and otherness, or the not-I, is co-constituted within this dark ground. Nature *as such* (prior to the imposition of the alienated world), the multiplicity of nonhuman or less-than-human forms of life declared to be merely natural, remains invisible to the subject except as mere matter or resource for production and synthesis. This adds a further dimension to Schelling's early metaphysics of nothingness. Absolute being is a nothing from the perspective of the world since it cannot be inscribed in the world's structure of diremption; but this diremption or negativity is itself a nothing since it is merely a "not-I" that has not been arranged into a world. It is important to add here what in 1795 Schelling himself does not yet seem to realize: these two nothings are, in truth, one and the same. It is the one absolute being, the infinite plenum of the earth and the skies, which is converted by the modern subject into the empirical not-I, a denigrated and alienated nature against which the subject asserts itself. In the next chapter, we will see this insight underlie Schelling's later identity philosophy and its vision of the blissful plenitude of the undivided All.

The alienated structure of finite subjectivity is ambiguous for Schelling. On the one hand, as the I becomes conscious of its limitation through the not-I, the I becomes aware of itself—a reflective doubling at the origin of self-consciousness, which is central for the development of reason and science, and for Schelling's construction of the world-process as the process of such development. On the other hand, the subject continues to sense that this reality was imposed upon it, that it is thrust into a world in which it must now struggle and strive, and from which it cannot seem to liberate itself. The freedom of the modern subject of self-assertion, as always subject *in* the world, is at the same time deeply unfree. "Self-consciousness," as arising from within the I's self-assertion against the not-I, "harbors the danger of losing the I"—of losing it *to* the chaotic not-I. Self-consciousness, Schelling emphasizes, "is not a *free* act of the immutable [essence] but an imposed striving of the mutable I that, conditioned through the not-I, strives to save [*retten*] its identity and to grab hold of itself again in the sweeping stream of change." (Observe the language of salvation here.) However, Schelling adds, the "*empirical* I would never strive to save its identity" if it were not for absolute identity as the I's ante-original absolute essence (VI 104–105/84–85).

In other words, what the subject strives to save is precisely its *simply being what it is* in the face of the world. In the depths of its essence, the subject intuits the absolute reality of non-alienation and oneness. This essence precedes the world as the structure of alienation yet is foreclosed by the world, and so appears to the subject from within the world as something that the subject is in the danger of losing, or something that has already been lost and needs to be saved ("grab hold of itself *again*" suggests that it has indeed been lost). The subject senses itself to have fallen from bliss, so that the subject's self-assertion amid the alien world into which it has been cast is prompted by a recollection of the absolute identity that was lost with the imposition of the world, and by the desire not to be consumed by the not-I perceived as dark, chaotic, and threatening. The structure of opposition in which the subject finds itself is a "conflict between the I and the not-I" (VI 115/91), where to assert one is to cancel out the other.

This creates, on the part of the I, a striving that is simultaneously nostalgic and future-oriented: a longing for the lost essence and for a future salvation from the world. From within the world, the atemporal essence—absolute being and absolute freedom—appears to the I at once as the idealized past and the wished-for future. Out of multiplicity and dispersal, the subject seeks to regain the absolute identity and non-alienation it feels itself to have lost.

And yet, again, why must this world even be there, if all the subject wants is to be free from it? "The main business of all philosophy consists," writes Schelling in *Philosophical Letters*, "in resolving the problem of the being-there of the world" (PB 82/177). "The absolute in us" is something the subject immediately intuits. "It is, however, incomprehensible how we exit the absolute so as to oppose something"—that is, how the structure of the original opposition arises, or why the subject finds itself in this alienated world in the first place. To the subject, this is "the most mysterious" (PB 79/174–175).

The world is a riddle or mystery (*Rätsel*), an enigma whose origin, to the subject, is veiled in darkness. One cannot think otherness from within the state of absolute identity; to think otherness is to already find oneself *at* the standpoint of otherness or the subject-object divide. If, says Schelling, we were to intuit only the one absolute reality, we would all be united (*einig*) within the one common being, without any divisive particularity. Therefore, "the problem ... of all philosophy" is the question, "How does it even happen that I go out of the absolute and toward an opposition?"—in other words, the question of "the stepping-out from the absolute" ("Heraustreten aus dem Absoluten"; PB 60/163–164). If we were all intuiting absolute oneness, this question would not arise. However, we are already in the world, and therein lies the problem:

> If man could succeed at some point in leaving this realm [of the finite world] in which he found himself through the stepping-out from the absolute, that would spell the end of all philosophy, and even of this realm itself. For it arises only through the conflict [between subject and object] and has reality only as long as the conflict continues. (PB 59/163)

The possibility of the world as the "realm of experience"—as the subject-object structure—can be thought only under the assumption of the world:

> I ask anew: Why is there even a realm of experience at all? Any answer that I provide to this question already assumes the being-there of a world of experience. To be able to answer this question, then, we need to have already left the realm of experience; if we were at some point to leave this realm, however, then the question itself would cease to apply. (PB 79/175)

There is thus no answer to the question *Why must the world be?* To think the possibility of the world, we need to think the original opposition—and yet there is no reason for this opposition that the subject can discern, and as soon as one thinks this opposition, one is already caught within it.[4] In the absence of the world's guarantee of origin, the world appears to hover in an endless empirical void (of the not-I) that makes the subject fear losing its sense of self and leads the subject to assert itself demiurgically over and against this void. Just as absolute identity is itself groundless (*grundlos*; PB 76/173), so too is the world. Within it, the subject is simultaneously separated from the not-I and from the absolute, which the subject intuits mystically inside itself but cannot discover in the world. This corresponds, again, to the constitutive condition of the modern subject as alienated, with the falling apart of the general Christian contradiction, at once from nature and from God.

To find oneself outside the absolute, one's essence lost, is to fall away from the absolute. Thus, the subject's condition is grasped by Schelling as the Fall:

> A French philosopher[5] says: since the Fall [*Sündenfall*], we have ceased to intuit *things in themselves*. . . . We suppose this philosopher to have been thinking of the Fall in the Platonic sense, [i.e.,] as the stepping-out from the absolute state. But in this case, he should have said, conversely, that it is since we stopped intuiting things in themselves that we have been fallen beings. For if the word *thing in itself* is to have any meaning, it can mean . . . only something that is for us no longer an

---

4. In *Of the I*, too, Schelling insists that the mystery of the origin of the world—the mystery of the original opposition—cannot be solved: "For *the fact that* [*Daß*] the I opposes to itself a not-I, one cannot provide any further reason" (VI 113/90). One may read this as pointing to the fundamentally *contingent* character of this dirempted world.

5. Schelling here refers to Condillac.

object, or no longer offers any resistance to our activity. It is, after all, precisely our intuiting of the objective world that tears us out of intellectual self-intuition—out of the state of bliss. (PB 95/185)

The I is fallen, and so it strives to save its essence. The term *Sündenfall* returns us to the theodical dimension of this narrative. As fallen, the subject strives to break free from this world of negativity and suffering toward an absolute freedom from any negativity or need. This absolute freedom coincides with what the subject sees as its essential and ante-original state, "the state of bliss."

The world is determined as the negation of bliss; as long as there is bliss, there is no world, and vice versa. We may observe the ambivalent temporality of bliss in this passage—mapping onto the temporality of salvation in the I's striving to save its identity. Bliss indexes, on the one hand, the absolute past preceding the Fall; on the other, Schelling speaks of the state of bliss accessed in intellectual intuition as what is consequent upon the world—a future state in which we intuit something that is "*no longer* an object for us," "*no longer* poses any resistance." Bliss designates the absolute oneness from which the I is torn away and toward which it strives; and the world appears as the tearing apart of the one atemporal bliss that remains accessible solely in intellectual intuition. If so, however—if the structure of finitude is constitutively negative and unblissful—then really, must this world even be? The question is intensified. Schelling's Platonic and Gnostic refraction, via Kant, of the modern logic of self-assertion is imbued with a deep sense of crisis—as *krisis* too, a separation and a judgment (of the world). This sense of crisis transforms significantly the Kantian paradigm of prelapsarian felicity as a brutish state of instinct and external dictate. Instead, paradisal bliss emerges from this as the same absolute identity and absolute freedom that the subject, within itself, intuits as that which is the highest and in which the world is annihilated.

2.1.3. To Gather the Dispersed or to Annihilate It: Synthesis and Morality

So far we have established the following. The subject finds itself in an alienated world yet intuits that the absolutely real is not the world, but absolute identity and absolute freedom. Therefore, from within the world, the subject seeks to regain the absolute identity that it can access only, mystically and briefly, in intellectual intuition. Two logics arise for Schelling from this: synthesis (the "theoretical" logic) and morality (the "practical"). As late as in 1830, as we may recall, Schelling would conceptualize them as two ways of seeking heaven or bliss: through absolute possession, the subject's seeking to claim everything for itself, and through self-purification toward a freedom from all desire. In his 1795 metaphysics, synthesis and morality provide precisely such alternative "worldly" paths to the same salvific goal—two sides, as it were, of the modern logic of self-assertion.

Synthesis is the subject's demiurgic activity that begins as soon as the subject discovers itself amid the empirical multiplicity of the not-I. Synthesis arises for Schelling from a contradiction or conflict between the I and the not-I. On the one hand, it is the I itself that "posits" the not-I by converting what is other than the subject—the plenum of nature—into mere empirical material for the subject's self-assertion. On the other, the not-I appears to the I as something that is originally alien and *not* of the subject's own making: something that resists and delimits the subject. To think the not-I is therefore to "cancel out" the I (VI 114–115/91), and this cannot but appear to the I as a threat to its identity.

This threat is what generates the subject's activity of synthesis: namely, one way for the I to "save" its identity is to gather this chaotic manifold into an orderly conceptual unity. The logic of modern self-assertion is a logic of mastery: through synthesis, the I imposes its form of identity upon the not-I, reshaping what is disorderly into a rationally cognizable reality ("the world") that is no longer chaotic but under control. As part of this, the not-I is perceived by the subject as the endless expanse of space and time, the conquest of which becomes the subject's telos.[6] Space and time are synthetic forms, the I's way of coping with multiplicity without losing its identity. Synthesis is the process of unifying the endless empirical manifold into a world by producing endless things in order to fill the unfillable void of what is perceived by the subject as the empty expanse of space and time, as mere material for appropriation and object-production. As such, modern synthetic reality is a world that has been produced or "created" by the subject, and that is structured by a logic of productivity. Characteristically, "creation" is defined by Schelling as the exhibition (*Darstellung*) of absolute identity—the infinite essence of the I—"within the limits of the finite," which takes place in synthesis (VI 145/109). Thus defined, creation begins as soon as the I finds itself facing the not-I. In this way, the Fall and the beginning of creation coincide: a highly Gnostic conjunction that, from a Blumenbergian perspective, indexes precisely the position of the subject at the outset of modernity. The I, this modern demiurge, is constantly

---

6. On the generation of space and time (the Kantian forms of intuition), see VI 120/94.

"creating" the world; at every moment, the world is re-produced. This brings us back to what we may remember from Chapter 1, via Blumenberg's remarks on the modern subject's "demiurgic production" and the "demiurgic activity exercised by man upon the world," as modernity's unwilling recapitulation of the Gnostic framework.

Since to produce this synthetic world of things is to exhibit the infinite within finitude, this process seems, however, constitutively without end. The empirical not-I is endless and cannot be mastered unless the subject can produce all possible objects out of it—a truly infinite task. Such is the logic of modern temporality as arising from Schelling's analysis: it is the not-yet of gathering empirical multiplicity into an all-encompassing rational oneness. As Schelling puts it, it is the "identification of the not-I with the I" as the "ultimate end goal" (VI 124/96). As long as the not-yet of synthesis persists, the world endures, too.[7] The logic of possibility and actualization, absent at the standpoint of the absolute, also arises from within the process of synthesis (VI 158/117). This corresponds to the fact that, as was observed in the introduction, to enact all things possible, or to turn all possibility into reality, is the end goal of modern self-assertion. The world as produced demiurgically by the modern subject is a synthetic world of endless actualization and the not-yet directed toward a dream of absolute possession—a dream that arises out of the I's original conversion of the plenitude of the real into an alienated not-I, and out of the I's fear of the not-I and anxiety about being consumed by it.

All synthesis is, in the end, nothing but the operativity *of* identity in or upon multiplicity in the givenness of multiplicity. The I is capable of gathering the not-I into oneness only because the I essentially *is* identity and oneness or possesses the form of oneness that it can impose on the empirical manifold. As *Philosophical Letters* reiterates, "*Synthesis* in general . . . arises only through the conflict of multiplicity with the original oneness" (PB 60/164). Oneness and twoness are both necessary for synthesis as the operativity of oneness upon twoness in which oneness becomes telos. "First," Schelling writes, "synthesis [must] be *preceded* by an absolute oneness . . . Second, no synthesis is thinkable except under the assumption that it itself [must] *end* in an absolute *thesis*" (PB 63/165). Synthesis "ultimately aims for absolute

---

7. The temporality of finitude is the temporality of synthesis, and of the continuous self-assertion to which the presence of the not-I forces the I. The world is always in time. "*Time* is the condition of all synthesis," which is at the same time "produced by the imagination in and through synthesis" (VI 158/117). The absolute simply *is*, whereas the finite I and the world last or endure (*dauern*; VI 130–131/101).

oneness" (PB 63/166), because this oneness is where it proceeds from. To think the possibility of the world vis-à-vis the absolutely first, we need to think at once oneness and twoness, where oneness *suspends* twoness (there is no twoness at the standpoint of absolute oneness) and is operative *in* it (as bringing it into unity). Considered immanently, absolute identity does not ground—but completely "precludes"—the world; it becomes the transcendental ground only within the structure of opposition or twoness. Note also how what is, considered immanently, absolutely first, without transition to otherness, becomes second or telos from the perspective of finitude. This reversal or inversion of priority is how teleology emerges; the world is the structure of this inversion. As soon as multiplicity is given, oneness starts to function as empirical synthesis whose goal is its own self-termination in and as absolute identity.

In this way, the status of the world is complicated. Synthesis is what produces the world. And yet synthesis becomes, in Schelling's account, the operativity of absolute identity upon multiplicity, whose goal is not the synthetic product (the world) itself, but the dissolution of multiplicity in identity and of all synthesis in absolute thesis. *The world's own goal is the end of the world.* Faced with the not-I, the I proceeds to posit it under the form of identity, whereby the world gets produced. The I could not, however, care less about the process of synthesis—and it cares about the synthetic *product* (the world) only to the extent that this product represents identity. The I has essentially no interest in the finite *as* finite. All it does is reassert identity in the striving to save itself—simply because identity is what it is, and so it must remain what it is amid multiplicity. In Schelling's analysis of modern reality, this alienated world is produced, and keeps getting reproduced, only through the subject's salvific striving for absolute identity. Absolute identity remains, as such, without relation to the world—however, from within the world (in the givenness of multiplicity), it is re-mediated through a process in which identity becomes the goal. The modern subject longs for bliss. Yet, through this very longing as converted into the activity of synthesis, possession, and production of endless things, the subject keeps re-producing the world as alienated and unblissful: such is the aporia of salvation inscribed in modernity, an aporia that is at once tragic and Sisyphean or absurd.

Synthesis is thus a secondary or imposed way in which the absolute manifests or "reveals" itself: all activity of the I "reveals an original freedom of the absolute I" (VI 133/102). Let us observe the double-sided character of synthesis, corresponding to the I–not-I structure of the empirical. On the one hand, synthesis brings the not-I to the form of identity, "assimilating" it to the I: the objective side. On the other, the I insists therein on its own essence of identity. Considered from either side, the goal of this insistence is the same: absolute identity. And yet the logic is different, corresponding to the Kantian division between the theoretical and the practical. As Schelling says, "Reason aims in its theoretical as well as in its practical use at nothing other than . . . the statement $I = I$" (VI 160/118). To reach this telos of identity would be to abolish the world as the structure of opposition. The theoretical and the practical constitute the I's two paths toward this goal.

The theoretical logic is synthesis considered from the point of view of multiplicity. The more the original multiplicity is gathered into unity, the closer the end goal of "absolute thesis." Theoretical philosophy seeks to unite all "finite spheres" into "one infinite sphere," coinciding with all reality as fully "encompassed" or seized (*befaßt*) by the I (VI 145/109). At the conclusion of this process stands "the highest synthesis." In this way, the I seeks to "resolve the conflict between the I and the not-I" by uniting them into "one ultimate exemplification of all reality" (VI 115–116/91). Reason "strives to elevate the not-I to the highest unity" (VI 160/118). Yet—a Kantian motif—in doing so, it falls into contradiction with itself as the I.[8] Paradoxically, the more the subject possesses, the less of a free subject it becomes. To produce or synthesize the one all-encompassing objective sphere (of possession and mastery) is to let the not-I swallow the I—which is what the I fears the most. At the end of the logic of reified possession become absolute, once the subject has appropriated all possibility and all things for itself, the subject itself becomes reified: the I turns into an absolute object. *Total reification*, of nature and the human alike, is the outcome of modernity's striving for the bliss of perfect possession.

The practical logic is different: it is the insistence of the I on its essence. It emerges out of the contradiction, not directly between the I and the not-I, but *within* the finite I—between its conditioned nature and its essential (absolute) freedom from the world. As we recall, within the structure of the general Christian contradiction, the human is also dirempted; this diremption, too, is intensified in modernity and leads the subject to sense itself to be irreconcilably split. It is within this split that Schelling locates morality. The subject's

---

8. As Schelling puts it, in the statement $I = I$, the I is "posited [simply] *because* it is posited." In the highest or total synthesis, the I strives to posit all not-I under the same form: "to posit the not-I [simply] because it is posited, that is, elevate it to unconditionedness" (VI 160/118). The not-I itself, the object, thereby becomes total. "The ultimate exemplification of all reality" becomes "the I = *not-I*," "canceling out the absolute I" (VI 116/91).

essence of absolute identity "*demands* utterly that the finite I should become equal to *the absolute*, i.e., that it should utterly annihilate within itself all multiplicity and all change." While absolute being simply is what it is, the finite subject is self-alienated: I am, so to speak, my own not-I, never fully identical with myself. For the subject, the demand of becoming one with its essence becomes "the moral law." "The highest law for the finite being is: *be absolutely identical with yourself*" (VI 125–126/97–98). The moral law appears from this perspective as the law of constancy, and the categorical imperative coincides with the imperative of absolute identity. Here the subject seeks to annihilate all not-I within itself, instead of gathering it into an all-encompassing objectivity. "The practical I," writes Schelling, "strives toward pure oneness, to the *exclusion* of all not-I" (VI 101/82).

Modern (Kantian) morality is for Schelling tied to finitude, emerging because the I, *within* the confines of finitude, insists on its absoluteness. "The moral law," Schelling observes, "holds only in relation to finitude" (VI 126/97). Only a finite being can be, or is called upon by its essence to be, moral. Absolute freedom is neither moral nor amoral—it is the sheer power of the absolutely real. No imperative could even arise within it (VI 165/121). The absolute "knows no moral law whatsoever, determined as it is in its causality only as absolute *power*, equal to itself." It follows solely the "law of identity" or "law of being," not the moral law (VI 126–127/97–98). In other words, the modern logic of moral purity, too, is premised on the structure of alienation and division, from which the subject strives to break free.

The moral law's character as a demand ("Be absolutely identical with yourself!") already betrays its finite, synthetic character: the absolute simply *is* absolutely identical. From the perspective of the finite subject, however, identity is represented "as demanded." Here normativity appears, absent in absolute being. The moral law is merely "a schema" of the law of identity, or its representation from within finitude (VI 126/98). As finite, the subject cannot immediately *be* absolutely identical; it can only strive to *become* so. In this way, the immediate demand of identity is re-mediated into a telos that can be progressively approximated or "produced in time" (VI 126/98). Everything that is finite about the I is now imagined as gradually stripped away, with moral purity or absolute freedom as the end goal. In this way, the I may be imagined to *expand* toward $I = I$. Expansion (*Erweiterung*) is what Schelling calls the moral demand as mediated by the world—an image expressing the shrinking of the not-I, and of its power over the I (VI 128/99).

The annihilation of finitude that, at the standpoint of the absolute, is what the absolute *immediately* does—prior to the very possibility of finitude—becomes now, from within finitude, the end goal. "In order to resolve the conflict between I and not-I," which theoretical reason or the process of synthesis cannot do, "nothing else remains except complete *destruction* [*Zerstörung*] of the finite sphere"—"(practical reason)," adds Schelling in parentheses (VI 118/92). What the subject futilely tries to synthesize by combining all finite spheres—by "forming" (*bilden*) finite spheres in the hope that they may contain the infinite empirical manifold, or putting infinity together piece by piece until nothing remains except the total synthetic product (whereby, however, the I is lost)—must be achieved by way of the practical *breaking* of the spheres, an all-out destruction of the alienated structure of finitude. It is only if "we pierce through [*durchbrechen*] these spheres," Schelling asserts, "that we find ourselves in the sphere of absolute being" (VI 145/109). Practically, philosophy must equal the annihilation of the world.

Thus, to envision the resolution of the question *Why is there even a world at all?* is not to conceive a theoretical answer. It is to *resolve* the question practically by *dissolving* it (the two senses of the verb *auflösen*)—to dissolve the very logic of finitude indexed by the question:

> As a result, this question cannot be resolved except the way Alexander the Great resolved the Gordian knot, i.e., through the canceling out of the question itself.... Such a resolution of this question, however, can no longer be theoretical, but necessarily *practical*. For, in order to be able to resolve it, I must myself leave the realm of experience, i.e., suspend for myself the limits of the world of experience, or cease to be a finite being. (PB 79/175)

There can be no justification of the world except by tracing the way it undoes itself. If "the main business of all philosophy consists in resolving the problem of the being-there of the world," then this resolution can consist only in the complete dissolution of the world. It is in the breaking of all finite spheres—the tearing down of all idols, all representations, all finite vessels, so as to break through to the unveiled absolute oneness—that the only solution to the mystery of the world consists, and the only way to "restore" absolute identity and freedom (VI 130/100), to regain paradise or heaven. "Practical reason enters, not in order to untie the knot, but to cut it into pieces by means of absolute demands" (VI 100/82). To the question *Why must the world be?*, the answer is *The world must not be*. Since Schelling configures the world as constituted by the operativity of absolute identity and freedom *within* the structure of opposition, the world is thinkable only as demanding its own dissolution.

Precisely because, as such, the absolute functions in and as the absence of the world, its operativity *in* the world becomes that of collapsing or annihilating the world. In this manner, a Gnostic apocalyptic vision of counter-worldly salvation persists at the core of Schelling's 1795 metaphysics.

2.1.4. The Bliss of World-Annihilation

The world must not be is the imperative of all striving. To reach this goal—to annihilate the world, to be free from striving and one with the absolute—would be, for the I, pure bliss. The term "bliss" first appears in *Philosophical Letters*, but "pure happiness" is what Schelling calls it already in *Of the I*. Here we encounter the crucial distinction between happiness and bliss. Happiness (*Glückseligkeit*) is for Schelling the "agreement of objects with our I," of "the not-I with the I." I am happy when objects please me, or there is no conflict between them and myself. This happiness is "empirical," since I continue to depend on the not-I for my happiness. There is a strong element of chance to it, of dependence on external circumstances; that is why Schelling calls it "contingent" (*zufällig*). Happiness presupposes the gap between I and not-I.

As empirical, happiness cannot belong "to the (ultimate) end goal." It does, however, asymptotically imply an idea aligned with the end goal: the idea of the full absence of any gap between the not-I and the I, and in that sense their perfect oneness. This idea arises from theoretical philosophy, and yet, if the practical demand were to be realized—amounting to the "complete annihilation of the not-I"—this would lead to a state in which there is necessarily no gap between the not-I and the I, but now in such a way that the element of externality and chance is precluded. Morality, therefore, leads to *pure* happiness as the oneness with the absolute that the moral law demands. Such is the only "practical significance" of happiness, in which "it is also fully *identical* with the ultimate end goal" (VI 124/97).

Seeing as pure happiness indexes absolute oneness, at the standpoint of pure happiness the distinction between theoretical and practical disappears. After all, neither synthesis nor morality is itself the end goal; absolute identity is. "Pure happiness" is a name we can give to this identity, to the extent that all resistance on the part of the not-I is here absent. In this, the term "happiness"—as grounded in the empirical—becomes, with the addition of "pure," ungrounded or self-subverting. "Pure happiness consists," says Schelling, "precisely in elevation above empirical happiness; the pure necessarily precludes the empirical" (VI 124–125/97). Thereby, however, the very need to be happy vanishes:

The ultimate aim of all striving is not empirical happiness, but complete elevation above its sphere, so that we must strive toward the infinite, not in order to *become* happy, but in order to never have need of happiness, indeed, to become completely *incapable* of it. (VI 124–125/ 96–97)

The point of pure happiness is not to be happy (or, for that matter, unhappy), but to occupy the standpoint at which this binary itself does not apply. The separation between nature and freedom, "natural causality" and "the causality through freedom"—another modern divide—disappears at this standpoint, too, together with the divisions between theoretical and practical, mechanism and teleology, or possibility and actuality (VI 172–175/125–127). Pure happiness collapses all binaries and relations that define the world, spelling a "complete canceling out" of finitude (VI 173/126). It is on this note—the end of the world in pure happiness—that *Of the I* itself ends.

It is, perhaps, due to the self-undoing inherent in "pure happiness" that, in *Philosophical Letters*, Schelling adopts the term "bliss" instead. Bliss (*Seligkeit*) and happiness (*Glückseligkeit*) relate here the same way that pure and empirical happiness did in *Of the I*—with the added conceptual benefit provided by the words themselves. *Glückseligkeit*, observes Schelling, contains the component of *Glück*, "luck," as that which happens *to* us or comes from the outside, and which is thus tied to the contingent character of the not-I. "We owe our happiness... not to ourselves, but to *lucky chance*." Happiness is tied to the subject-object structure and gives us over to the circumstances of the world. Happiness is empirical and finite—and the "purer" we imagine it to be, "the closer it comes to morality and the more it ceases to be *happiness*" (PB 92/183). Hence the need for a different concept. *Seligkeit*, as delinked from chance—and as connected to the soul (*Seele*)[9] and (in its meaning as "salvation") to the end goal of striving—answers this need perfectly.

Having considered the unity of pure happiness with the end goal of all striving—the end of the world—in *Of the I*, we find the logic of bliss in *Philosophical Letters* to be familiar. "Morality," reiterates Schelling there,

---

9. *Seligkeit* ("bliss") is not etymologically connected to *Seele* ("soul"), but Schelling connects them conceptually, not only speaking of the soul's bliss, but also spelling *Seligkeit* as *Seeligkeit*. In fact, *seelig* had been a common alternative spelling of *selig* at least since the seventeenth century, facilitated precisely by the perceived affinity with *Seele*. See "SELIG, adj.," *Deutsches Wörterbuch von Jacob Grimm und Wilhelm Grimm*, digital edition, Version 01/23, https://www.woerterbuchnetz.de/DWB?lemid = S26373, accessed December 11, 2023.

"cannot itself be what is the highest," consisting only in the "striving toward absolute freedom," which itself "does not know any [external] law anymore, only the unchangeable eternal law of its essence" (PB 91–92/183). This goal of all striving, that is, absolute identity and freedom, is precisely absolute bliss. "Where *there is absolute freedom, there is absolute bliss*, and vice versa" (PB 94/184). Bliss is oneness with the absolute—a state of pure identity, absolute non-relation and intransitivity, to which we are transported in intellectual intuition. In this way, we have direct access—via the essence of our soul—to the end (goal) of the world; or, rather, immediately are at this standpoint. In intellectual intuition bliss does not, in other words, appear *as* goal. It is where the soul simply *is* in its essence—"our self [as] stripped [*entkleidetes Selbst*] of everything that came from the outside" (PB 87/180).

Thereby, bliss is identified by Schelling not only with the prelapsarian past or the longed-for non-alienated future, but explicitly with absolute being itself in its atemporality or eternity, and with the entire metaphysics of absolute identity in which the world is immediately ungrounded and annihilated. Bliss appears vis-à-vis the world as an absolute past, an absolute future, and an absolute *now* in which the world is abolished and its very possibility is precluded. This tripartite antagonistic entanglement of bliss with the world (as the ante-worldly past, post-worldly future, and anti-worldly impulse or demand) would always remain at the core of Schelling's thought.

Within bliss itself, there is no such tripartite division. It simply *is*, in no time, without telos and without relation to the world. It contains no demand and demands no justification. It is only *out of* the space-time of the world that the subject longs for bliss, and bliss appears as re-mediated into past and future bliss. In bliss itself, we are taken utopically out of time and space and are the one immanence, without temporal succession or otherness. From the perspective of the world, we can be transported *to* or *out of* this state, so that there is a before and after, past and future, inside-the-world and outside-the-world. In bliss, however, the world is completely dissolved—the knot of finitude is immediately resolved—for, as we recall, in order to resolve it, "I must . . . cease to be a finite being." One could envision here the bliss of the mystic who might appear, from the point of view of an external observer, to enter and exit a state of oneness with the divine—but whose mystical state, considered immanently, transports her immediately to the atemporal *now* in which all time and externality, and all sense of finite selfhood, are consumed as in a divine fire. In fact, as a-worldly and without relation to time, the bliss of intellectual intuition corresponds directly to what in Chapter 1 we saw as the standpoint of the mystical and miraculous.

Schelling connects this cessation of the world in bliss to Spinoza's *beatitudo*, quoting "the statement with which [Spinoza] concluded the whole of his *Ethics*, '*Bliss is not the reward of virtue, it is virtue itself!*'" (PB 91/183). Bliss cannot be a reward, since the logic of reward is external and transcendent, premised on the gap between what I am or do and what I receive. With "reward," we are thinking of something that pleases us. As such, it is tied to happiness, not bliss (PB 93/184). "Insofar as we still believe in a happiness that rewards us, we are assuming happiness and morality ... as conflicting principles." "This conflict," however, "ought to utterly cease." The closer we are to virtue, the less value (*Wert*) rewards have for us (PB 92/183). One simply *is* virtuous and thus immediately one with the absolute. Bliss consists precisely in this immediate oneness and not in any kind of reward or possession:

> Should we, asks an ancient writer,[10] deem the immortal gods unhappy because they possess no capitals, no gardens, no estates, no slaves? Should we not rather praise them as the only blissful ones precisely because they alone, thanks to the sublimity of their nature, are already deprived [*beraubt*] of all those goods [*Güter*]? (PB 93/184)

The logic of reward entails the conceptual nexus of possession, value (capital), domination (even slavery), and justification. What the image of the Stoic-Epicurean gods signals is bliss's refusal of this nexus and of the world as a whole. Note also the immanent inhabitation of nothingness by the gods, "deprived" of everything—just as, in the earlier description of intellectual intuition, the self was *entkleidet*, bare. Bliss indexes an immanent dispossession, an absolute, divine poverty.

The sudden turn to pagan antiquity in the above passage in conjunction with the reference to Spinoza marks this passage as antagonistic to the Christian-modern structure of alienation or diremption. It is on this structure, as intensified in modernity, that the empirical logic of happiness as Schelling presents it is premised—that is, happiness as contingent dependence on the not-I, as alienated desire for reified possession, perpetuating the I–not-I division and the subject's unfulfilled striving. This kind of reduction of happiness to the modern logic of the empirical, which Schelling at once critiques and relays, is characteristic of what Vivasvan Soni has described as

---

10. The writer in question is Seneca.

the late eighteenth-century crisis of happiness.[11] Two important symptoms of this crisis emerge from Soni's analysis. The first is the mutation of happiness, around this time, into a "hopelessly privatized, sentimentalized, and trivialized" empirical concept, appropriated into the rising bourgeois sensibility, and into the logics of possession and reward.[12] The second, conjoined with the first, is the endless postponement of fulfillment in modernity, through which the subject is bound to an endless pursuit of empirical satisfaction that, however, constitutively cannot lead to non-alienation but serves only to reproduce the subject's alienated striving. This postponement, too, becomes inseparable from the idea of happiness by the end of the eighteenth century. It is out of this crisis of happiness that Schelling's concept of bliss may be said to erupt.

Again, one might suggest with Schelling—to complement Soni's analysis—that at stake in the late eighteenth-century landscape of crisis (of happiness, salvation, legitimacy, theodicy, and so forth) is a deeper underlying issue. This issue is the modern alienated structure of finitude, and the binding of the modern subject of self-assertion to this structure, from which the subject strives to yet cannot break free. For Schelling too, the problem is the structure of finitude itself, which, in a Christian-modern vein, he understands as constitutively alienated. His turn to bliss in lieu of happiness is significant, since it restages antagonistically the question of freedom *from* and not just *in* the world and implies a bliss to be found in the annihilation of the very need for happiness—because happiness in modernity is a logic through which the subject is bound to this unblissful world. In empirical happiness, we may momentarily feel ourselves to be free of the negativity of the world. Yet this freedom conceals the persistence of alienation on which the logic of possession is based, and accordingly it only upholds and justifies the world's negativity. Schelling's thinking of bliss is generated from this aporia, while carrying within itself a transhistorical utopian and Gnostic demand of the kind that happiness cannot bear. Mysticism, Gnosticism, bliss: all of them break through to the surface through the crisis of the world, yet in specific, historically situated ways—in this case, as antagonistic to the simultaneous "trivialization" and foreclosure of fulfillment and to the logic of subjectivity underlying this foreclosure.

---

11. Soni, *Mourning Happiness*, 3.

12. Ibid., 430.

In collapsing *all* binaries at once, absolute bliss is apocalyptic. Bliss is an "infinite activity" and, as absolutely non-empirical, "the cessation of *all* passivity"—yet it is also a radical passivity, since it does not strive toward anything and possesses no will (PB 101/189), "no consciousness" (PB 94/184), and "no arguments of reason." "Here, at the moment of absolute being," Schelling asserts, "highest passivity is one with the most unlimited activity. Unlimited activity is absolute repose [*Ruhe*], perfect Epicureanism." Bliss spells the end of the world—and of the I in the world. "The highest moment of being is for us transition to nonbeing, the moment of *annihilation*" (PB 93–94/184–185). The "for us" is important here. It marks the finite subjective perspective, as does "transition," which implies succession. "For us" in our finitude, entering bliss can appear only as a "transition to nonbeing" or a (transitive) "moment of annihilation." From the standpoint of the absolute, however, there is no transition, and no world, but only pure nonbeing and bliss, where the soul simply *is*. At this absolute standpoint, it is the world that is *not*—exposed as a secondary, negatively imposed reality. As absolute freedom from the world, bliss equals the joy of world-annihilation.

From the point of view of this life in the world, bliss, as the annihilation of striving, is comparable only to death. "We awaken," says Schelling, "from intellectual intuition as from the state of death. We awaken through *reflection*, i.e., through a forced return to ourselves" (PB 94/185). In the Kantian-Fichtean framework especially, life is identified with teleology and ceaseless striving, and death with the absence of will and striving; hence the comparison of bliss with death. Bliss, however, is not physical death, which is itself part of the finite life cycle and the life/death binary. It is a mystical death to the world and antinomian death to the law.[13] It is an absolute death, but also absolute life: a state in which all distinction between life and death disappears and "unlimited activity" coincides with "absolute repose," absolute being with absolute nonbeing.

Still, since our I is finite, we are "forced" to exit this state: forced to go back to the (imposed) existence of opposition and striving. We are, as it were, forced to live (in the world). "Were I to maintain intellectual intuition [indefinitely], I would cease to live" (PB 95/185)—and yet I have to return into

---

13. In his 1792 notes on the Epistle to the Romans, Schelling excerpts passages on death, e.g., 7:4 ("Wherefore, my brethren, ye also are become dead to the law by the body of Christ") and 6:3 ("Know ye not, that so many of us as were baptized into Jesus Christ were baptized into his death?"), adding that Paul speaks of "the dying away of sin" (AER 62). In 1795, Schelling draws on this image of a "higher" death in a more metaphysical manner: the world is the structure of fallenness, abolished in the absolute death of bliss.

the world. This forcedness to live corresponds metaphysically to the fact of "the stepping-out from the absolute." *The world must not be*, but it is there. The joy of the world's annihilation, the bliss of nonbeing is, for the subject, the highest moral demand. And yet the subject can experience the state of absolute oneness only briefly in intellectual intuition, since the world is not only alienated and unblissful, but prevents the soul's bliss. Unlike Spinoza, for Schelling bliss is world-annihilative and can be achieved or glimpsed from within the world solely for a moment ("the moment of absolute being"). Only apocalyptically, at the end of the world, would one be able to attain permanent bliss without being forced to return to the world. Bliss appears, from within the world, at once as the ante-original past, the desired future, and the subject's striving for bliss—which, however, cannot be reached without undoing the world itself.

2.2. *To Reproduce the World: Idealism as the Katechon*

2.2.1. Moral Progress and Faith (in the Not-Yet)

The radical self-dispossession in bliss is not to be confused with the subject's striving, amid the empirical world, to purify itself from the not-I or to become moral—which is part, in Schelling's analytic, of the logic of self-assertion. The intellectual intuition of bliss is, from the point of view of the subject's being in the world, only momentary, and one is forced to return from it to the life of striving, and to the opposition between the I and not-I. Moral purification, too, is directed at the striven-for state of absolute identity or bliss, but it takes a different path that can be only *gradual*: the subject must learn, as it were, to discipline itself and to cleanse itself of its dependence on the not-I. As such, this may be perceived as an ascetic practice of purification but also very much a part of the modern subject's existence in a scattered and distracting objective world, with regard to which the subject must become independent *so as* to be able to withstand the world without giving in to it, or to empirical circumstances and impulses. In this way, morality and possession or synthesis as the two sides of the logic of self-assertion emerge as fundamentally co-constituted.

As we have seen, the moral demand leads to the necessity of moral becoming. The schema of becoming not only makes the moral law applicable to the finite subject, but also leads to the temporality of "moral *progress*" as Kantian infinite approximation, or "progress into infinity." The absolute, says Schelling, is one and eternal—"which means that the finite I, in its striving to become identical with the absolute, must also strive for pure eternity." To that end, the I must "posit within itself eternity as *becoming*, i.e., as empirical, or as *infinite duration*" (VI 128/99). In other words, the subject strives for eternity, but eternity can be imagined, from within finitude, only as infinite duration—so that moral becoming itself becomes infinite. This re-mediation of morality by the temporality of finitude is the "moral" or "practical synthesis" (VI 164/121), and thus part of the synthetic logic of the world. From the pure *is*, we thereby get to *Sollen*, the "ought." The finite subject cannot strive for anything without representing it as the determination of its will, so that synthesis is required in order for that which cannot be represented in finitude (i.e., atemporal absolute identity) to become representable—to become *possible* as goal.

The demand of absolute identity becomes the law of possibility inscribed in the world's logic of actualization and striving; and morality really becomes practical (and not impractical). Through moral synthesis, "practical possibility, actuality and necessity" arise. In its absolute purity, the moral law appears to the subject as the demand for an immediate moral revolution: *be* identical with the absolute! Caught in the world, the subject, however, perceives it as an impossible demand. Within the structure of diremption, the finite I cannot even represent this demand other than as a demand for (possible) gradual change or becoming. In order to determine the will, the moral law must be re-mediated into an ought. "Only for the finite being," underscores Schelling, "is there an ought, i.e., practical possibility" (VI 163/120)—whereas in bliss one ceases to be a finite being, and the entire form of diremption is annihilated. Not unlike in Kant himself, morality in Schelling re-mediates the bliss of world-annihilation through the logic of possibility and infinite approximation. This leads to the structure of a not-yet in which morality appears as an "incremental *approximation* to the end goal." Through the logic of possibility, bliss can be represented only as "an infinite task for the I ... realizable only through infinite progress" (VI 124/97). To configure bliss as the telos of possibility—instead of antagonistically leaving possibilities unused and demanding the abolition of the structure of alienation in the now—is to defer bliss to an indefinite future via the process of endless striving. In morality as in synthesis, the absolute "only ought to be *produced*"; however, "to *produce* an *absolute* reality is an empirically infinite task" (VI 166–167/122). Through the logic of production, which is entangled with synthesis, possibility, and the not-yet, the world is reproduced—even if all that the subject of self-assertion really seeks is to become absolutely free.

Paradoxically, we must think the end of the world in order to think identity and freedom *in* the world; but insofar as we think them in the world, we can never get *out* of the world. As finite, the subject can imagine the end of the world only from within the world. The paradox is that the demand of annihilation must be applicable to that which it wants to fully annihilate, i.e., the empirical. To be applicable to the empirical, however, it must be represented in terms of the empirical. "The finite being can ... progressively expand the limits of its finitude"—a progress into infinity "because, if this expansion were ever to cease at some point, this would amount to the infinite itself having limits" (VI 174/126). That which is supposed to annihilate the world becomes a position in the world, a telos toward which the world is directed. The absolute demand of immediate annihilation is impossible, and so gets postponed to a possible future that is, constitutively, *never now* as long as the world remains. The world is supposed to be, in the end, annihilated, but this annihilation is always not-yet. Thereby, the world re-mediates bliss as telos, splitting it into a past bliss and an unreachable future bliss. Via possibility and the not-yet, the world endlessly postpones its own annihilation: the Christian-modern structure of deferral familiar to us from Chapter 1, yet here emerging from Schelling's analytic of the demiurgic subject.

Knowledge and morality signal the finite I's inability to get out of the world, even as the I's absolute essence demands it—so that, re-mediated by the world, this demand becomes the infinite not-yet through which the I is tied to this world (of striving) even further. At this point, in Schelling's 1795 metaphysics, the concept of faith emerges in its entanglement with the not-yet. As a finite being in the world, I can only *believe* in the end goal, without expecting to reach it. "Since you are tied to objects," says Schelling, "your intellectual intuition destroyed," even your immanent essence "becomes for you at the *end* of your knowledge only an object of *faith*: as it were, something that is different from yourself, and something that you infinitely strive to exhibit in yourself, and yet never find as actual inside you" (VI 146/110). Where knowledge ends, morality *as* faith begins, in which the end goal is represented as "different from" one's essence, and thus as transcendent and unreachable. In faith, the divine essence is re-mediated by the world and alienated from the I. Moral faith becomes here, in effect, faith *in* the end goal *as* unreachable. It is because one cannot reach the goal that one is called upon to have faith. This move is Christian-theodical, too: by having faith, by not despairing and infinitely striving forward, one accepts the world's not-yet. Your faith in the telos of the world justifies the striving to reach it—the striving that *is* the world itself, in its infinite not-yet. The world destroys our (immanent) bliss, and all that is left for us is (transcendent) faith.

2.2.2. The Heroism of Striving and the Foreclosure of Bliss

In *Philosophical Letters*, Schelling goes further. Here he affirms idealist philosophy itself as upholding and legitimating the not-yet of the world, revealing idealism's theodical character. As we may recall, Schelling says that, if we were simply to intuit absolute identity, there would be no conflict or disagreement. The idea is that thereby would cease not only the conflictual character of the world—but also the conflict between different philosophical systems. If everyone were to remain one with the absolute, without stepping out of it, "There could never be any quarrel [*Streit*] between different systems" (PB 59–60/163), and more specifically between (post-Kantian) idealism or criticism and (Spinozan) dogmatism as, for Schelling, the two main opposed systems of thought. Idealism asserts the absolute self (the Fichtean I), and dogmatism the absolute object (the Spinozan substance) as the first principle, but in both cases this principle, considered immanently, is but an absolute affirmation or absolute identity: the first unconditioned principle can be only "an absolute *asserting*," without negation or otherness (PB 80/176). This holds for idealism and dogmatism alike.

It is over the world that the battle rages. One could say that the world *is* the battle. It is only in the realm of finitude that it can even begin (seeing as "No quarrel is possible over the absolute itself"; PB 76/173). That is why Schelling can claim that the "existence of the world" is the main problem of *all* philosophy. Dogmatism and idealism can be distinguished only within finitude, in terms of the world's relation to the absolute (since the absolute itself is the pure oneness at the standpoint of which there is no world). Since finitude has the structure of the I–not-I opposition, we can either take the side of the subject (idealism) or the side of the object (dogmatism), making one or the other into the first. But when it comes to the problem of how this opposition originates, seeing as absolute identity is absolutely intransitive, the finite world remains a mystery for both systems: "*No* system can *accomplish* the transition from the infinite to the finite. . . . No system can *fill* the gap that is entrenched between the two" (PB 83/177).

Both systems want to mediate between the world and the absolute, "so as to bring about the unity of cognition," and both find this impossible. Yet they continue to strive for that unity, and absolute identity remains for them the end goal: "the endless striving" on the part of the finite "to lose itself in the infinite" (PB 83/178). We recognize in this the general logic of striving, now applied to philosophy itself. Finitude re-mediates the demand *Be identical with the infinite!* into an endless striving toward completion. Since this demand is, as we know, ultimately practical and not theoretical, that leads Schelling to focus on the difference between criticist and dogmatist *morality* as the opposed paths that these two systems take toward the shared goal of absolute identity or oneness. It is "not through the *goal*," but "in the way they *approach* it," that the two systems diverge (PB 103/190). Seeing as one prioritizes the subject and the other the object, they proceed, as it were, in opposite directions. For the dogmatist, to lose oneself in the absolute is to let the self be consumed in a Spinozan infinite substance, the absolutized not-I. For the idealist philosopher, it is to become one with the absolute essence she intellectually intuits within herself. Nevertheless, both dogmatist morality and idealist or criticist morality arise out of the dirempted, modern structure of finitude as divided into subject and object, the I and the not-I. Just as the modern world is the structure of opposition between the I and not-I, so modern thought, too, remains caught within the same structure.

The dogmatist moral agency is submission, the dissolution of the I in the absolute object: a morality of purification through passivity and receptivity, not through expanding the power of the I. This passivity, however, is distinguished by Schelling from the radical passivity of bliss as coinciding with unlimited activity. The way Schelling construes it, dogmatist passivity, like the more active Kantian morality, is a gradual process of *becoming* that is directed, from within the divided world, toward absolute oneness and approximates it, albeit in a different way. One could summarize this schematically as follows: idealism is the self-assertion of the subject; in idealist synthesis, the subject seeks to gather the not-I into a unity over which the subject would have perfect mastery, and in idealist morality, the subject seeks to purify itself from any influence of the objective. The dogmatist, however, seeks simply to give herself over *to* the object, to enhance the power of the not-I over the I. This dogmatist processuality remains bound to the same I–not-I split; the idealist and the dogmatist simply affirm the opposite sides of this split.

Thus, Schelling maintains, the demand that "the finite become identical with the infinite" equaled for Spinoza, this supreme dogmatist, the demand that the finite "perish in the infinity of the absolute object." The subject was for Spinoza secondary to the absolute object and so "belonged to," and had to return to, the latter. The absolute demand "had, accordingly, to be fulfilled not through the subject's own causality, but through an alien causality within it." This demand of passivity and, as it were, absolute self-alienation may be expressed in the maxim "Behave *utterly* passively vis-à-vis the absolute causality!" (PB 85/179).

At this point, Schelling's ambivalence toward mystical oneness with God breaks through to the surface too, as he proclaims: "'Return to divinity, the primal source of all existence, unification with the absolute, annihilation of the self'—is this not the principle of all fanatical philosophy?" (PB 85–86/179). It is highly important to note the direction of the movement here: the self as giving itself up to the objective, not as expanding so as to preclude it (as in Kantian moral progress). To increase the reader's revulsion at dogmatism, "this scary thought" of self-annihilation (PB 85/179) is positioned by Schelling in terms of existential dread. Thereby, "Philosophy is abandoned to all the horrors [*Schrecken*] of enthusiasm" (PB 102/189). "Where am I supposed to flee from the power [of the absolute object]?" asks Schelling rhetorically, as there is nowhere to flee. The self is "deprived" of power (PB 104/191), abandoned to the alien and external world. Importantly, the Spinozist logic of absolute self-alienation, too, is positioned in Schelling's analysis as a counter-logic *within* the modern structure of finitude, constituting the flip side of the logic of self-assertion. Moreover, as we remember, the fear of being overtaken by the external world, or the perception of the not-I as infinitely dark and hostile and as threatening to consume the I unless the I can withstand the alien power of reality and shine the light of reason into this dark ground, is the foundational fear of the subject in Blumenberg's account of modern self-assertion. Dogmatism emerges from Schelling's text as the evil power at the roots of modern reality and thus as co-constituted with the "good" demiurgic logic of self-assertion.

Idealism or criticism, by contrast, takes up the banner of self-assertion and striving. Already in *Of the I* Schelling speaks of "the bold deed of reason": "to rid humanity of the fear of the objective world" (VI 77/67). In *Philosophical Letters*, he takes the side of the finite freedom of striving even more emphatically, to the point that it becomes heroic. Whereas dogmatism "progressively constricts the boundaries of my freedom so as to expand those of the objective world," idealism reverses the direction: "By expanding the boundaries of *my* world, I constrict those of the objective world" (PB 104–105/192). In this, idealism combats the constitutive modern fear of objectivity—by combating dogmatism, too.

In the final, tenth letter, the battle against dogmatism becomes a battle over the world and the human soul, of highest eschatological intensity, the decisive battle of the modern age. Dogmatism as the principle of the not-I's infinite dark power occupies here the place that would be occupied in Schelling's later philosophy of revelation by Satan as the principle of evil and deception that is supposed to be defeated by God in the final battle (UPO 623). The narrative setup of the tenth letter is interesting in this regard. It begins with the image of heroically fighting an overwhelming external power—and perishing in this fight:

> One more thing remains: to *know* that there is an objective power that threatens our freedom with annihilation, and, with this firm and certain conviction in our hearts, to fight *against* it, to mobilize our entire freedom, and *thus* to perish.... This possibility, even after having vanished before the light of reason, must still be preserved for art—for the highest of art [i.e., tragedy]. (PB 106/192)

A discussion of ancient tragedy follows, in which the tragic heroine, fighting against the external *fatum*, asserts her freedom in her fight against this power, in being punished for the crime she was doomed to commit (this punishment indexing the recognition of the freedom inherent in the fight), and in her very demise. "It was," Schelling proclaims, "a *great* thought, to suffer punishment willingly even for an *unavoidable* crime, and so, through the loss of one's freedom, to prove this very freedom, and to perish with a declaration of free will" (PB 107).

It is arguably the part where the heroine perishes—where the alien power is presented as unconquerable—that makes Schelling declare that this heroism belongs in the past from the standpoint of rationality (it has "vanished before the light of reason"). This kind of doomed heroism belongs to paganism as the epoch in which the human mind stands in thrall to externality. At the same time, the parallel between the idealist and the hero is obvious, and the entire conclusion of *Philosophical Letters* becomes, from here onward, coded through heroism. Schelling's *modern* point, in other words, is not to present the power of objectivity as undefeatable, but to combat it. Heroism does have a place in the contemporary world—the letter ends on a heroic-revolutionary note with the proclamation of a "covenant of those whose spirit is free" (PB 112/196)—but the thought of an overwhelming external power must be opposed. To save humanity from corruption by exposing the lie of dogmatism and revealing the truth of freedom is the task of the contemporary epoch. "It is [our] duty," says Schelling, "to uncover the whole [dogmatist] deception" (note again the identification of dogmatism with the Satanic principle of deception) and to fight for the principle of freedom. "In this alone, the last hope for the salvation [*Rettung*] of humanity lies": in insisting on and fighting for "the freedom of the will" (PB 109–110/194–195). The I's striving to "save" itself from the not-I, running throughout Schelling's 1795 metaphysics, is ultimately identified by him, in keeping with the modern logic of self-assertion, not with the a-worldly repose of bliss, but with opposition and conflict. Thereby, the world as the structure of opposition is forcefully affirmed, not annihilated. The theodical tendency of world-justification overtakes the demand of bliss.

The freedom of the will is, decisively, *not* absolute freedom or bliss. It is the freedom of striving. Salvation consists here not in the state of bliss, but in the very striving to reach it—a striving that must, as such, *never* reach its goal. The ninth letter makes this clear. Just after discussing bliss as the end goal, Schelling turns to criticize it precisely for its apocalyptic, world-destroying character. Modern freedom is the assertion of the power of the I, the expansion of the self toward absoluteness. However, in bliss, the self *and* the world are equally annihilated. Bliss is the immanent inhabitation of nonbeing and not the finite life of striving. It annihilates all binaries, including those between subject and object, freedom and necessity—or, indeed, idealism and dogmatism (PB 98–99/187–188). Both systems, Schelling reminds us, strive toward absolute identity. Dogmatism may strive toward it by submitting the I to the not-I, and idealism by affirming subjectivity over and against objectivity—but this opposition itself holds only within the world as the structure of finitude. If idealism were to reach the goal of absolute bliss, this would spell its self-annihilation:

> Where an activity, no longer limited by objects and wholly absolute, is no longer accompanied by any consciousness; where unlimited activity is identical with absolute repose; where the highest moment of being begins to border on nonbeing: there criticism is bound for self-annihilation just as much as dogmatism is. (PB 96–97/186)

At this point, all knowledge and morality cease. There is here nothing to know, nothing to strive for, no doubling and no reflection. The world goes down, and the opposition of dogmatism and idealism goes down with it. Schelling does not, however, want to allow this. Idealism is too important, too co-imbricated with the essence and task of modernity, to let it blissfully perish. The principle of idealism, the I, must be preserved. *The world*, as the realm in which the opposition and the apocalyptic battle take place, must be preserved and legitimated, too. With this opposition eradicated, how would the moderns be able to strive so heroically? Dispossessed, blissful, how would they be able to save humanity from fanaticism and deceit? Schelling views philosophy and the modern world itself as a never-ending theodical trial, in which the subject must ceaselessly prove itself to be on the right side of salvation history, on the side of the good in its battle against evil, and in which any other sense of fulfillment and freedom is prohibited and bliss foreclosed.

Idealism must be preserved, and it can be preserved only by insisting on the unreachability of bliss. Oneness with the absolute must remain the universal vocation (*Bestimmung*) of the human being, but, in a typically modern aporia, it must not be understood as actually reachable or even desirable. Bliss must not be allowed to annihilate the (value of the) world. "In criticism, my *vocation* is the *striving for* unchangeable selfhood, unconditioned freedom, unlimited activity" (PB 106/192)—a renewed binding of the I to the world of self-assertion and striving. At the standpoint of bliss, unlimited activity would coincide with unlimited passivity and all selfhood would dissolve, something that idealism cannot allow: *strive*, but do not *reach*. In *Philosophical Letters*, Schelling introduces bliss yet ends up foreclosing it, turning it into an unreachable regulative ideal. The unification of all philosophy is theorized only to be denied, since it would spell the annihilation of philosophy as such, and critical-idealist philosophy in particular.

It is, ultimately, only the existence of the world that provides the possibility that idealism will avert the horrors of dogmatism. And it is only by acting as the bulwark against the end of the world that idealism can stave off humanity's corruption. In this, idealism acts as what Carl Schmitt has called the *katechon*, that which withholds or restrains. Taken originally from Paul, this term indexes for Schmitt "the power to restrain the appearance of the Antichrist and the end of the present eon."[14] Accordingly, the katechon has an ambivalent function: it is the defense against chaos, but also the indefinite deferral of salvation (as spelling the end of the world). Idealism has this double function, too. "For the sake of everything in the world I would rather not be blessed [*selig*]!" repeats Schelling after Lessing, adding: "For someone who does not feel *just this way*, I cannot see philosophy as of any help" (PB 96/186; note the philosophy-world conjunction here). Idealism opposes dogmatism, and so it must justify the world and oppose bliss. As Schmitt asserts, "One must be able to name the katechon for every epoch.... The place has

---

14. Schmitt, *Nomos of the Earth*, 60.

never been unoccupied, or else we would no longer exist."[15] Idealism occupies for Schelling this world-upholding place in the modern epoch—the age of self-assertion, and of the battle against dogmatism.

Bliss is absolutely uncaring, a zero point at which no world is possible or needed. Idealist philosophy, however, ultimately cares too much about the world as the structure within which it functions, seeking to uphold and justify this structure as required for idealism's survival. Therefore, idealism *encloses* bliss, divides the absolute in two—the I and not-I—and champions the former. This division in place, idealism *expands*, assimilating the not-I to the I: idealism's own colonial logic. To maintain that logic, it needs the division to remain. It is on this division alone that it lives and feeds; and so it affirms freedom as the life of self-assertion and struggle, over and against what it perceives to be nonbeing, dispossession, death. Meanwhile, it is this nonbeing that, denied by the world and converted by the subject into the not-I, remains the absolutely real on which the modern world is imposed—and where the soul simply is in its essence, prior to the imposition of the world.

Not that, however, idealism really cares about the world. What it cares about is its own striving—the expansion of the I over the not-I—and it needs the world (the structure of opposition) solely for this striving to be possible. Striving remains the operativity of absolute freedom, as non-relation and preclusion, within the confines of finitude. And yet, not unlike in the case of moral progress, it is this (finite) freedom that serves, in practice, to foreclose absolute freedom—and to reproduce the world *as* the infinite not-yet. By means of morality and freedom, the immediacy of the apocalyptic demand is mediated into an indefinite eschatological horizon. Thereby, we return to what in the introduction I called Schelling's living, in 1795, through the end of the world: at this decisive moment of modernity, bliss erupts apocalyptically against the world yet must be katechontically postponed so that the eschatological struggle can continue.

In 1795, Schelling programmatically defers the power of bliss, refusing to insist on world-annihilation and investing instead in the world's not-yet. It is as though, in *Of the I*, Schelling conceives of absolute identity as the unificatory principle of philosophy but then sees that, in its radicality, this principle might abolish the very structure of opposition on which modern philosophy is premised—only, in his idealist commitments, to turn in

---

15. Schmitt, *Glossarium*, 47.

horror from the consequences of such an abolition. No wonder that the language of existential dread, and the motif of the alien, inhuman power of absolute identity or bliss, become so prominent in *Philosophical Letters*. Beneath the heroic rhetoric lies a fear of nonbeing, of the more-than-human nature that is turned by modern self-assertion into its dark ground, yet that exceeds, in its vastness, the world of self-assertion. The fear of dogmatism reflects the modern anxiety about the fact that the world against which human reason asserts itself could swallow it whole, and that the subject's existence amid this infinitely contingent post-Copernican abyss of reality is ultimately groundless. Instead of embracing the absolute groundlessness of bliss and abolishing the world—an operation that would reveal the plenum on which this world is imposed—the modern subject seeks to ground itself and its negative world through the restless demiurgic activity of self-assertion and production. The eschatological battle against dogmatism *must* be won for this world, in its infinite violence and hubris conjoined with infinite fragility and contingency, to remain in place, and not to plunge into the universal abyss.

The phantom bliss of absolute mastery and possession, including self-possession, is generated by the modern world precisely due to modernity's ungrounded character and its anxiety about this groundlessness. That is why the subject is doomed to demiurgically toil even if it would prefer not to, even if what it intuits within itself is nonproductivity and repose. And that is why the subject, as longing for bliss yet facing the negativity of the world that it creates, looks to justify itself as the *good* demiurge, generating the very idea of the modern epoch and its supposedly universal task so as to legitimate the subject's own compulsive demiurgic productivity. Like no other epoch, modernity is endlessly anxious about its legitimacy. In truth, of course, there is no heaven *of* possession and mastery. There is but one bliss, refusing all opposition and justification, all selfhood and all reward—a bliss that can erupt only from the world's underside that is one with the depths of the soul, consuming the split between the I and not-I. This bliss, however, remains foreclosed as long as the modern world persists and expands. Modernity emerges from the Schellingian analytic as an epoch that is as violent as it is unblissful and tragic. Its own subject feels the deep illegitimacy of this world and yet is bound to maintain and legitimate it. Its essence not of this world, the modern subject is condemned to a melancholic and Gnostic condition in which demiurgic production is, for the subject, a curse, not a blessing. By construing this condition as revolutionary and heroic, Schelling ends up justifying the unblissful order of the world.

2.2.3. Between World-Justification and World-Refusal

The world must be, concludes *Philosophical Letters*. Just as it begins with the imperative of world-annihilation, Schelling's 1795 metaphysics ends with a justification of the world. The strategy of this justification is twofold. First, synthesis and morality are justified as the demand of the absolute—as the actualization of the absolute in the world, the exhibition of the infinite in the finite. Schelling declares: "Finite beings must exist in order for the infinite to exhibit its reality within *actuality*," that is, in the process of actualization. "All finite activity"—and therefore the world as constantly recreated in synthesis—"aims at this exhibition" (VI 172/125). However, this exhibition demands the dissolution of the world in bliss and is thus insufficient to justify this dirempted world. And so, in *Philosophical Letters*, this world is additionally justified *over and against* absolute identity and bliss. Here Schelling asserts that the value of the world consists precisely in its finitude as what makes the freedom of self-assertion possible and prevents bliss from spelling the world's termination. Modern freedom commands its subjects—"those whose spirit is free"—to set aside their bliss, to strive and struggle. At the same time, in the cunning of idealist reason, modern freedom continues to justify itself through reference to bliss, even though bliss as such refuses all striving. The struggle serves as the proof of goodness and freedom, and yet, as if to conceal the fact that "freedom" here *is* the unblissful struggle, freedom refers to bliss as its telos. Modern demiurgic freedom is parasitic on the absolute power of bliss that it at once feeds upon and endlessly defers. In this way, modern freedom and bliss remain antagonistically entangled. The world is haunted by bliss as the necessity of its abolition; however, in place of that necessity, theodicy substitutes the false necessity of maintaining the striving through which the world is justified and reproduced.

Importantly, while Schelling's 1795 metaphysics reflects the modern subject-object structure, this metaphysics holds true for Schelling throughout the history of consciousness. For him, consciousness has always been demiurgic, starting from the mind of the ancient mythmaker—the subject itself simply did not know it yet. Not unlike the tendency of the self-assertion of reason in Blumenberg, the logic of the transcendental is in Schelling transhistorical, yet becomes self-consciously affirmed only in modernity with the falling apart of the general Christian contradiction and the concomitant autonomization of alienated finite reason. As such, bliss too, while emerging in Schelling's 1795 writings as antagonistic to the modern dirempted world of synthesis and the not-yet, marks what is transhistorical: a transhistorical antagonism to the theodical logic of history itself. This cosmic antagonism between bliss and the world, at work ever since the Fall, is what the transcendental perspective on history reveals, even as this perspective arises out of the constitutively modern understanding of freedom.

The Schellingian logic of modern freedom as an endless actualization of what is essentially absolute is marked by many of the traits of freedom in modernity that make it so violent. It is, in effect, a colonial logic of expansion, universalization, and the increasing of the power of the I over what is relegated to the status of the not-I. Since actualization is a process, this inevitably leads to some people getting ahead in the progress of freedom compared to others—not to mention those who refuse to participate in it or work actively against it, or those who in modernity do not count as fully human or as rational subjects at all. This leads in turn to a division between lower and higher as based on the advancement toward freedom. *Philosophical Letters* explicitly speaks, in this regard, of "the better humankind" to which freedom is revealed (PB 58/163) and claims that the conflict between idealism and dogmatism will persist "as long as not all finite beings are standing on the same level [*Stufe*] of freedom" (PB 75/173). No such hierarchized succession of levels or stages is possible within the absolute freedom of bliss considered immanently, only within the modern freedom of actualization, striving, and progress. The idea of the oneness of humanity, postulated by Schelling as the end goal of history (VI 79/68), is also premised on the progressive actualization and universalization of freedom, the logic that underlies all German Idealist philosophy of history.[16] The racial logic of modernity is premised on this, too—and indeed, as has been mentioned, in the later Schelling we will see how the narrative of actualization leads to a vision of the ascending ladder (*Stufenfolge*) of world history as explicitly racialized in character, in which the higher levels (*Stufen*) are metaphysically justified in using the lower as mere material. The seeds and presuppositions of that are already contained in the early Schelling's doctrine of finite freedom.

At the same time, Schelling theorizes bliss as an absolute refusal of the world—including the refusal of justification, since bliss simply *is* and does not seek to justify itself. Even Schelling's tracing of the constitutive logics of the world may be seen as pointing to the fact that, as long as this world persists, it remains constitutively impossible to *be* in bliss—to *simply be*,

---

16. That human reason around the globe develops level by level (*stufenweise*), forming a *Stufenfolge* in which parts of the one humanity are arranged, is postulated already in Schelling's 1792 thesis (DMO 111, 147).

without any justification, any investment in the world, or any striving (to get ahead in the freedom race). Within itself, in the absence of the world, bliss is non-domination and nonviolence—and so, in the presence of the world, it turns into an immediate apocalyptic demand: the demand that this world, as a world of domination and violence, *must not be*. Since bliss appears from within the world as "death" and "nonbeing," it is no wonder that the world has to re-mediate bliss in order to survive.

Yet, at the heart of this re-mediation, there remains for Schelling the core of absolute identity, non-relation, non-mediation, and indifference or non-will. Both demands, *The world must not be* and *The world must be*, are premised on the fact of the world—so that, in order to think its possibility, one needs to think opposition, negativity, and striving. However, the core of one's soul, the absolutely real that one accesses in intellectual intuition and in which the world is annihilated, remains absolute identity and freedom. Even though it appears from within the world as the goal of all striving, this absolutely real remains without relation to or care for the world. In neither of its modes of operativity (synthesis or morality) does the I truly care about the world it creates through synthesis. The world may be a mystery, but this mystery is, in effect, nothing but a hindrance, an inescapable nuisance—the I's constitutive unblissfulness—the annihilation of the world amounting, for the I, to pure joy and bliss. The goal of the I's striving in the world is to break the vessels of finitude; to finally be at rest; to cut the Gordian knot of mystery and be absolutely free from the world. And yet the world is there, and the subject continues to struggle in its nets of mediation and the not-yet—doomed to infinitely long for bliss from within the world. This is Schelling's own philosophical struggle, too: Why the world at all? Why must it be? And so, in his thought, he continues to seek ways to justify the world, even as bliss remains for him pure non-relation, refusing all justification and refusing the world.

Interlude II

"ABYSS OF REPOSE AND INACTIVITY"

IT HAS BECOME common knowledge, almost cliché, that Romantic nature is a dynamic nature, a nature in a state of constant striving and transformation. Arguably, although he had many predecessors such as Kant, Herder, or Goethe, no one contributed more than Schelling to the formation of the Romantic view of nature as a lawful and purposive dynamic whole. When one thinks of Romantic natural philosophy or philosophy of nature (*Naturphilosophie*) as a systematic enterprise and a school, it is Schelling's name that first comes to mind. While his 1795 metaphysics was that of the demiurgic human I, and nature remained therein a mere not-I, in his 1797 *Ideas for a Philosophy of Nature* Schelling proclaims a "system of nature" to enhance that of the human mind (IN 93). With the publication in 1798 of *On the World-Soul* and in 1799 of the *First Outline of a System of the Philosophy of Nature*, Schelling strengthens his reputation as the leading natural philosopher of his time. By 1799, moreover, he overcomes the (broadly Fichtean) view of nature as secondary to the I, coming instead to regard the natural world as an independent realm of productive forces that precedes and genetically grounds human consciousness.[1] From this point on, Schelling holds that the genesis of consciousness is to be sought in nature as ascending, through inorganic and organic life, to the I. In human consciousness, nature itself comes to self-awareness.[2]

---

1. See Nassar, *Romantic Absolute*, 187–202.

2. On Schelling's "transcendental naturalism," see Beiser, *German Idealism*, 483–524.

In this interlude, which leads up to the next chapter's analysis of Schelling's identity philosophy—or the philosophy of absolute identity, which he starts to develop in 1801, and of which natural philosophy is the foundation—I briefly introduce Schelling's view of nature as it develops by 1800. Like his construction of the I, his construction of nature is a construction *with a view to bliss*: a bliss for which all nature strives. And just as the world of human spirit in Schelling's 1800 *System of Transcendental Idealism* is supposed, in the end, to dissolve blissfully in the ocean of poetry, so, too, does he posit that the natural world seeks a similar dissolution. Although it is customary in scholarship to extol the infinite productivity of Schellingian nature, what has remained generally unobserved is that, by 1800 at the latest, nature's productivity and striving are configured by Schelling as a *problem*—as a circular unblissfulness from which nature cannot break free. What I will sketch here is *the curse of production*, in which the natural subject, too, appears as highly modern, one that is caught in the same aporia of endless striving as the demiurgic human subject. More broadly, at stake in what follows is the question: Can bliss be produced from within the structure of finitude?

Schematically, one may outline the basic conceptual logic of Schelling's *Naturphilosophie* by returning to the original opposition between the absolute I and the absolute not-I in *Of the I*. As we may recall, there the I, or the principle of identity, posits the not-I as what is opposed to the I, or as the principle of sheer multiplicity and scatteredness. Within this original opposition, the world then unfolds via the synthetic activity of the I as it attempts to re-collect multiplicity into oneness. *To think immanently the I in its opposition to the not-I* is to find oneself transported to the standpoint of a contradiction that can be resolved only through the I's synthetic activity as the operativity of absolute identity within multiplicity. There is, however, a paradox, a kind of absolute abstraction involved in thinking the original opposition as posited by the I: to think the positing of what is absolutely opposed to the I is, as Schelling puts it, to cancel out the I, to fully abstract from it.[3] Accordingly, *to think immanently the not-I in its opposition to the I* is to find oneself transported to the standpoint of the same contradiction, except from the perspective of the not-I: to glimpse within the absolute not-I the

---

3. I owe this observation to Daniel Whistler, on whose work on abstraction in Schelling I also partly draw here. See Whistler, "Abstraction and Utopia," and Berger and Whistler, *Schelling-Eschenmayer Controversy*, 170–175. See also Grant, *Philosophies of Nature*, 158, on Schelling's project of providing "a physical grounding [to] the powers of abstraction"—which are nature's own powers at a higher level.

contradiction between its being-posited by absolute oneness and its character as pure scatteredness.

The origin of Schelling's natural philosophy as what he configures, in the years leading up to 1801, as the "parallel" science to transcendental philosophy lies then in the following insight: the contradiction must be resolved from the side of the not-I, too. Because the absolute not-I was posited by absolute identity, it remains (in its "essence") absolute oneness, which, however, exists under the form of scatteredness. The absolute not-I may be envisioned as *the original scattering of oneness, of what remains essentially one*. This contradiction within it generates the inner striving inherent in the not-I to restore itself to oneness, or to level out its inadequacy to its own essence by ascending from scatteredness back to self-conscious identity, that is, to the I. This is the manner in which nature genetically grounds consciousness, and it is this genesis that the natural philosopher constructs. The not-I is not merely not-I: it is a nature that strives toward consciousness. Once nature has generated consciousness, the same striving for the re-collection of oneness continues *within* consciousness as the activity of the I, now traced by transcendental philosophy.

To put this differently, the natural philosopher must abstract from her own I so as to "*participate* in the work of nature,"[4] to retrace nature's immanent unfolding as *natura naturans*, the nature-subject of constant metamorphosis and ceaseless productivity. The philosophical construction of nature is one with nature's self-construction. The natural philosopher, in Schellingian parlance, "de-potentiates" herself. Just as the activity of nature is the gradual ascent or potentiation (*Steigerung, Potenzierung*) toward the I, so the philosopher of nature begins by placing herself at the lowest level or stage (*Stufe*) from which this entire ladder (*Stufenfolge*) of nature begins. This lowest level is that of the construction of matter. In Schelling's dynamic conception of nature, matter is not a preexisting substance, but is constituted in the interplay of the dual original forces, the expansive and the contractive, which together fill the three-dimensional space.

In this original duality, one may recognize again the absolute not-I and the absolute I, reconfigured as the forces of nature. One is the force of scattering or expansion, and the other is the force of limitation, retardation, or contraction, *counteracting* the expansive force. This counteraction prevents

---

4. Nassar, *Romantic Absolute*, 211. Wirth, *Schelling's Practice*, 17, calls this "doing philosophy in accordance with nature."

the dissipation of the expansive force into infinity and makes possible the shaping of material being. The contractive or limiting force is designated by Schelling as "A," and the expansive or scattering force as "B." In the shaping of material being, B comes first: all actual materiality emerges from a delimitation of the expansive force. If, however, the expansive force comes first, why does Schelling designate it as B and not as A? This has to do with the fact that A maps onto identity and B onto non-identity, or multiplicity as what is *not* A. This nomenclature is important because it implies that, although B comes first within the structure of opposition that defines finitude, in truth *A is the first* from the standpoint of absolute identity. A, or the contractive force, is the operativity of absolute identity that prevents scattering by re-collecting it into a finite oneness or material being. Each finite natural being captures a local balance or indifference between these two forces. Hence, Schelling's formula for material being is A = B, where the copula marks a relative unity between the two forces. Each product (*Produkt*) thereby expresses, without exhausting, the productivity (*Produktivität*) of nature as an ascending interplay of the two forces, which continue to act throughout inorganic and organic nature. The exact way in which these forces act at the level of the stone compared to the "higher" level of the plant, or the even "higher" level of animal life, is precisely what the natural philosopher must construct. Thereby the philosopher grasps all forms of natural being as the hierarchized expressions of the productivity of nature within the confines of the original duality, that is, within the structure of finitude.

How can one picture more concretely the beginning of this interplay of forces that fills the entire material space? Here we may observe that Schelling's natural philosophy is also a heliocentric post-Copernican cosmology, drawing at once on the early-modern cosmologies of Giordano Bruno and Johannes Kepler and on the astronomical and cosmological advances of the time, made by figures ranging from Kant, J. H. Lambert, and Buffon to William Herschel. Although philosophically it is our solar system and our earth that interest Schelling the most, "nature" refers in his writings to the universe (*Universum, Welt, Weltall*) or the All (*das All*), this vast immensity of space composed of a multitude of star systems or even, as Kant and Lambert speculated, galaxies beyond the Milky Way.[5] Cosmologically, *to speak of the beginning of the*

---

5. As mentioned previously, the term *Welt* in Schelling, in keeping with the usage of the time, refers variously to "world" or "universe" (as in the expressions *world-system / système du monde / System der Welt / Weltsystem*, used to designate the post-Copernican system). Accordingly, I will speak of either "world," "universe," or "the All" in Schelling depending on the context.

interplay of forces is to speak of the beginning of the universe. For Schelling, the universe originates in a kind of big bang: the first cosmic explosion that still continues, so that what we usually call the expansion of the universe is grasped by him as a "continuing explosion" (EE 154/89; cf. EE 318/90). To conceive of what is prior to this ur-event is to think something that precedes space and time: an absolute utopic center point (*Mittelpunkt*; EE 318/89; cf. EE 158/93), a point of "absolute involution" (EE 265/187) or absolute contraction, containing within its infinite intensity what will evolve or unfold as the All. It is to this ante-original point that the two forces must be applied so that the material expanse of the universe can be constructed, starting with the primordial sun (*Ursonne*) as the proto-material mass that then divides, producing stars and planets (EE 318/89).

To think the application of B and A to the absolute point is to think its explosive scattering: the ur-cosmic contingency, which must be assumed in order to explain the fact that the world is there (since if one thinks *only* the absolute point, one cannot deduce the universe from this pure oneness). As usual in Schelling, one needs to think the original opposition or duality in order to think the (possibility of the) world. Once B starts its expansive movement, A emerges as the centripetal force that counteracts the dissipation. One can see here the same dynamic as in the emergence of the finite I in 1795. As soon as absolute oneness finds itself amid multiplicity or scatteredness, it cannot but start to re-collect this multiplicity *into* oneness, emerging as the synthetic or synthesizing activity (*synthetische Tätigkeit*; AD 300): the third as the relative unity of the two. In his 1800 essay "General Deduction of the Dynamic Process," Schelling attempts, through the triad of A, B, and their relative synthesis, to construct the three dimensions of the material All.

It is already at this lowest stage that Schelling observes the unblissfulness of natural productivity. Synthetic activity, he notes, is thinkable only under the assumption of nature's self-alienation or split (*absolute Entzweiung*), the same term that, in 1802, he uses to describe the alienated Christian-modern universe. Natural productivity as arising from the original opposition indexes the fact that nature has been estranged from itself, and its essence of absolute identity has been left behind (AD 327; cf. ESE 63/219–220). As "absorbed within itself," or in its absolute nonproductivity, "Absolute identity cannot be forced to exit or reveal itself": a description in which we recognize the fact that, considered immanently, the bliss of absolute identity has no transition to otherness. The revelation of absolute identity can happen "only once absolute identity has been canceled out *as* absolute identity." Schelling continues:

> From this it self-evidently follows that absolute identity *as such* cannot at all, under any circumstances, reveal itself, for *as such* it is an abyss of repose and inactivity [*Abgrund von Ruhe und Untätigkeit*]—and within activity it is no longer *absolute* identity. Nonetheless, under the condition of diremption [*Entzweiung*], it becomes operative as the force that reveals absolute identity. This [synthetic or constructing] force is therefore not foreign to nature; its ground is the original [essence] within nature, or *nature itself*: the ground that becomes operative [*wirksam*], or reveals itself as a force, under the condition of absolute opposition. (AD 327)

In absolute identity as the essence of nature ("nature itself"), we see the same ungrounding ground that we encountered in Schelling's 1795 metaphysics. Considered immanently, this ground grounds only its own bliss, ungrounding any transition to the world. As such, it cannot be mediated or revealed. In the givenness of the structure of opposition, however, or in view of the fact of the world, this ground becomes operative as the activity that "reveals" identity out of scatteredness by re-gathering it into a oneness. From the outset, the movement of nature is thus a search for rest. In its present forced state, nature is severed "against its will" from its essence of absolute identity and "split from itself" (AD 300). Nature's striving is therefore deeper, or more abyssal, than a striving toward the I: it is the striving for bliss as salvation *from* striving itself. What Schelling also confirms in the above passage is that, although he calls it a third synthetic force, it is in fact the activity or self-revelation of absolute identity itself, torn out of its blissful repose and seeking to return to it, "reveal[ing] itself as a force."

If *all* scatteredness could be gathered into oneness, or if an absolute identity—an absolute product or sphere (*Sphäre*)—could be produced, nature would attain "absolute repose" again, and its productivity would cease (ESE 34/197, 45/206). All that nature strives for is to fully reveal, and thereby restore, itself as the "abyss of repose and inactivity." Yet, in this very striving, nature is doomed to reproduce and uphold the original opposition. Nature's striving is self-alienated and circular, and even what seems at rest in nature (e.g., a resting stone) is but a seeming, transitory relief. Every relative balance is in fact a nonstop reproduction of balance, constantly under the threat of being lost. A product, once produced, immediately gets consumed by the abyssal forces (*Abgrund von Kräften*; ESE 73/230), that is, the forces that emerge from the abyss of absolute identity after its oneness has been split; and once consumed, the product must be momentarily reproduced again only to be again consumed, and so on ad infinitum. While one may celebrate this "constantly renewed creation" (AD 330) as a phoenix-like image of endless rejuvenation, this is decidedly not an image of bliss. Every seeming stability is a vortex (*Wirbel*), a strife of forces: "something that vanishes at every moment, and every moment emerges anew" (ESE 46/206). With the product's (re-)emergence, "The opposition that underlies it re-emerges," too, "in perpetuity" (AD 327).

Thus, nature seeks to produce absolute identity but can only (re)produce finite, particular identities. We may see these identities as an overabundance of natural forms, but behind it lies a constitutive unblissfulness, an endless craving that cannot be sated. In this, one sees the origin of Schelling's later (even more pronounced) emphasis on the unblissful circularity and melancholy of nature, which we will witness in Chapters 4 and 5. Even in its relative repose, nature is toiling without rest (cf. ESE 43/204), producing ever-new products and forms whose destiny is to be immediately consumed, yet without diminishing or fulfilling the natural subject's abyssal desire that is likewise reproduced without end. Unceasing productivity, premised on the structure of alienation, seeks a future fulfillment that, however, constitutively cannot arrive, since no matter how many products are produced and consumed, the alienation and unfulfillment are only reproduced. The tragic irony of all finite productivity—a highly modern motif—is that it is driven by the desire to be free of productivity, to achieve the non-alienation that is, however, foreclosed by the alienated constitution of productivity itself. The Schellingian natural subject, too, is a modern demiurgic subject who is forced, out of a dirempted reality, to endlessly (re)create the natural world through its (i.e., the natural subject's) striving to produce an immediate fulfillment or bliss that *cannot* be produced, instead only reproducing the world as the structure of diremption. In this manner, Schelling inscribes a salvation history into nature (in its striving for salvation or bliss), which, however, cannot attain its goal—at least not within pre-human nature itself.

That his view of nature-as-subject is highly modern is, further, something that Schelling himself recognizes when, in his 1802 lectures, he places modern natural philosophy within the trajectory of the general Christian contradiction. Phenomena such as electricity and chemical reactions, he notes, could not be properly theorized until recently (VM 122/86). That is because, to be able to grasp them, one needs to have a sense of the duality or polarity at the heart of nature (or what in the expanded 1803 edition of his *Ideas* Schelling calls "the general law of diremption"; IN2 287/203), conjoined with a sense of the fleetingness of natural appearances as they strive to exhibit the infinite out of alienation—a view of nature that, as we remember from Chapter 1, emerges with Christianity. "The highest problem of all the sciences," which his natural philosophy aims to resolve, is formulated by Schelling in 1799 in the same terms that we have seen him apply to the central problem of the Christian view of reality: "the possibility of the exhibition of the infinite in the finite" (EE 79/15). Modern natural philosophy and science thus scientifically disclose and confirm the condition of nature's alienation that Christianity reveals to be the true condition of the universe, alienation that Schelling's *Naturphilosophie* seeks to overcome *on the basis* of modern philosophy and science.

Schelling wants to overcome this alienation and mobilize the perpetual circularity of nature through a logic of universal ascent, or by directing nature's restlessness *upward*: a move that likewise remains fundamental for his later metaphysics. Although the Schellingian universe is a modern, post-Copernican universe, one peculiar (and highly Romantic) thing about it is that, throughout his thinking, it is envisioned by Schelling not as de-hierarchized (the way, for instance, the Newtonian universe is) but in terms of an ascending ladder (*Stufenfolge*) of being.[6] This hierarchy is not imposed on nature by God, but immanently produced by nature in its repeated attempts at self-transcending, or at transcending its own unblissfulness. Its absence of repose is what drives nature to produce increasingly "higher" products, or more complex forms of natural being, which the natural philosopher classifies, tracing their directedness toward the highest form to which nature attains: the human. Here, nature reaches its peak (*Höhe*), and the human can *cognize* nature only because, in the human, nature itself breaks through to "ideality" or reason (AD 364–365), or because human (self-)consciousness is the highest organization of the powers at work throughout nature. The human I, however, is just as restless as nature, and exists within the same opposition: the contradiction that drives the world of spirit onward, too, until it reaches the ocean of poetry in which, as the highest revelation of absolute identity, it will finally be able to rest.

From the above, three insights follow that pave the way for Schelling's turn in 1801 to the identity philosophy. First, since absolute identity is the essence of both nature and the I, and since there cannot be two different absolute identities, it is one and the same absolute identity that, out of the same structure of original opposition, re-collects itself throughout the natural

---

6. On this tradition and Schelling's place therein, see Lovejoy, *Great Chain of Being*.

world and the world of human spirit. Since it is nature that thinks itself through the human, or since self-consciousness is "nothing but nature in the highest potency" (STI 46/17), this is but *one* subject that undergoes an all-encompassing process of organization: "What cognizes and what is cognized are one and the same," as Schelling later summarizes it (EIP 57; cf. WS 105/141 [§1]). If so, however, if this is but one overarching story of a heaven or bliss to be regained, then there is no need for any transcendental philosophy outside of natural philosophy: the latter suffices to ground the one philosophy of absolute identity. Second, if the bliss of absolute identity cannot be synthetically produced yet is attained if universal reality is re-visioned from the standpoint of poetry, perhaps it is the very logic of synthetic productivity and striving that needs to be rejected. How, though, is reality to be viewed if not through the lens of productivity and synthesis? Given that synthesis arises as soon as the original opposition is given, one would—Schelling's third insight goes—need first of all to stop viewing reality on the basis of this opposition, or, more precisely, on the basis of the primacy of this opposition vis-à-vis "synthetic" oneness. The entire metaphysics of reality needs to be transformed.

The first step toward this transformation is to admit that there is, in truth, no such thing as a third synthetic force. Schelling himself notes, in a passage quoted above, that what appears as the third (i.e., synthetic unity) is but the revelation of the absolutely first (i.e., absolute identity). The second step is then to emphasize not the structure of opposition but the common essence at the heart of nature and spirit. Within nature as within spirit, within the real as within the ideal, everything exhibits or reveals in its own way the one essence of absolute identity. This essence precedes the binary of the I and not-I, or spirit and nature, even as it is revealed by both. To view the planet, the stone, the plant, and the human mind as revealing equally, if in different ways, the one blissful essence is to affirm the ontological primacy of identity over and against division, and to *re-vision universal reality as a plenum of bliss-in-common*. The All is the one undivided being, and bliss is its one non-appropriable essence. This metaphysical vision, directed at the overcoming of the modern alienated condition, underlies Schelling's 1801 turn to a philosophy of pantheistic immanence that is supposed to cut the Gordian knot of the aporias of endless productivity and striving.

3
Evil Is but a Shadow

THIS CHAPTER IS devoted to Schelling's philosophy of absolute identity, or identity philosophy—a remarkably radical period of his thought that begins in 1801 with the publication of the *Presentation of My System of Philosophy*, in which he defiantly proclaims his break with Fichte and allegiance to Spinoza. Indeed, the identity-philosophical system may be understood as a version of Spinozistic pantheism wherein every form of being and thinking expresses the divine bliss of the All. However, as the possessive "my" in the title indicates, Schelling is offering here not a restating of Spinoza, but something new and singular—something that is, moreover, aligned with the world-historical task of the post-Enlightenment, post-Revolutionary moment within the movement of the modern age as Schelling sees it. While many readings of the identity philosophy have focused on its more abstract metaphysical dimensions,[1] in this chapter I want to embed Schelling's metaphysics of identity in the context of his vision of universal (cosmic and human) history and his ambivalent relation to the Christian-modern world. Despite often being presented *more geometrico*, or as though it were ahistorical, identity philosophy is a philosophical theodicy of history that contains a tension of truly apocalyptic proportions. On the one hand, Schelling seeks here to construct universal history as guided by a necessary logic through which the course and telos of history are philosophically legitimated. On the other, he insists on the (immediate and absolute) primacy of bliss as what annihilates the mediation of history, dissolving the not-yet of the world as in

---

[1]. On Schelling's identity metaphysics, see in particular Whistler, *Schelling's Theory*; Nassar, *Romantic Absolute*, 225–256; and Berger and Whistler, *Schelling-Eschenmayer Controversy*.

water or consuming it as in fire, and revealing the one blissful being on which the world is imposed.

What Schelling regards as the task of modernity is familiar to us from Chapter 1 on the basis of his 1802 lectures and "On the Relation": texts that, not coincidentally, appear during the identity-philosophical period. For Schelling, the condition of modernity is that of the intensification of the general Christian contradiction, or the threefold structure of alienation between God, nature, and the human. Within this structure, mind and nature, mind and God, and nature and God all appear divided. Unlike in 1795, when he associates Spinoza with the threat of dogmatism, starting from 1801 Schelling finds in Spinoza a thinker who is rational and scientific, employing a strict deductive method, and who is, at the same time, antagonistic to the dualities of modern thought: a thinker of beatitude or bliss, and of the *one undivided and unenclosed cosmos* that is immediately divine. It is for similar reasons that Schelling draws, during this period, on Bruno, Kepler, and Leibniz, who all offer a (scientific-cosmological and cosmo-theological) vision of the universe as a divine plenum. It is not the influence of Spinoza and Bruno that leads to Schelling's identity philosophy. On the contrary, what he sees as the universal task of the present, a vision that arises from the immanent development of his own thought as responding to the post-Revolutionary and post-Enlightenment moment, necessitates for him a turn to the standpoint of identity and an accompanying revisiting of modern philosophical archives.

The fact that Schelling's identity philosophy builds on the above thinkers marks not an eclecticism, but a vision of a philosophical trajectory that is distinct from the trajectory of modern dirempted thought, and that Schelling makes programmatically his own, pitting it against the alienated kind of knowledge whose representative he finds in Fichte. Unlike Spinoza or the early-modern Platonic cosmologists, however (and this is where his Romantic-Christian allegiances come into play), Schelling views the modern world through the lens of the intensified general Christian contradiction: modern cognition and the self-assertion of the modern subject *are* fallen and unblissful. The task of the present moment, as he proclaims in 1802, consists not simply in rejecting, but in redeeming and reconciling fallenness—in ushering in an age of heaven regained. The task of the identity philosophy is aligned with this revolutionary epochal task as well as the original task of Christianity. Throughout the changes in his metaphysics, true philosophy always has for Schelling a revolutionary-prophetic function, and the identity philosophy is no exception.

In keeping with this task, there are two steps that the identity philosophy must take to further things along toward the promised epochal turn, which will have fulfilled the original Christian promise of universal reconciliation. First, it must present an alternative to the modern standpoint of alienated thought, religion, and science, and to the modern primacy of dirempted subjectivity. It must pursue nothing less than a *metaphysical-phenomenological revolution*, a revolution in consciousness and perception: a total, systematic re-visioning of reality with a view to non-alienation and bliss—and this is precisely the role that the turn to pantheism plays. However, while antagonistic to modern alienation, this philosophical revolution is not simplistically antimodern. The identity philosophy is not just a pantheistic cosmo-theology; it is a scientific-philosophical system of the post-Copernican universe, premised on the modern assumption of the regularity and formalizability of the law of universal genesis. Its meta-standpoint of universality, too, from which the one universal system, one universal history, and one universal humanity are to be constructed, would have been impossible prior to the Romantic moment at which it emerges—and Schelling himself asserts, starting from "On the Relation," that what the identity philosophy offers arises out of the present moment of crisis.

From this, the second step becomes clear. The identity philosophy must point a way beyond the structure of alienation, a way that would not simply reject but reconcile the modern world, incorporating into the standpoint of true philosophical science the central results of modern philosophy and individual sciences.[2] The modern intensification of alienation is for Schelling necessary insofar as it makes possible the achievements of universality and abstraction that are required for the development of modern science—even as, in its current turn to organicism and a dynamic view of nature, science itself starts, the way Schelling sees it, to move beyond its earlier alienated viewpoint. That the identity philosophy, as grounded in *Naturphilosophie*, takes up the epochal task is evident in Schelling's ambitious call in 1805 to do what, as he asserts, has presently become possible for the first time in "many centuries": to engage in the "joint labor" among "philosophers and natural scientists of all kinds," reconciling the disparate sciences via "the one divine

---

2. Without grasping the proclaimed epochal task of the identity philosophy, it is hard to understand the rationale behind the conjunction between Spinoza and the Christian-modern not-yet that Schelling advances during this period. From a purely Spinozistic perspective, Schelling's 1802 proclamation of a Christian view of history would appear as incomprehensible or jarring.

vision . . . of the universe" that philosophy puts forward and that unites human spirit by the same "holy bond" that binds the All (VJM 55–57). In new natural-philosophical and scientific developments, Schelling sees a key sign of the times, pointing to the eschatological horizon of all-reconciliation. As paving the way to this reconciliation, Schellingian philosophical revolution re-mediates modern unblissfulness into a vision of bliss that is essentially already there, but that is empirically yet to come in a joint labor of nature and spirit. An antagonistic vision of immediate bliss in which the world is dissolved becomes a mediated historical movement toward an epoch of bliss, a movement within which modernity forms a necessary stage. *Antagonism* and *reconciliation*, mapping onto the tension between bliss and the not-yet of world history, and between bliss and theodicy, form the two poles or foci, themselves antagonistically entangled, around which the identity philosophy orbits.

3.1. The One Common Being: Re-visioning the Universe as Bliss

Through birth, temporal life, and death each being is divested, in accordance with divine order, of what it owes to its mere finitude, its mere embeddedness in God. Each being exists in time by virtue solely of that part of itself which is relational, and this relationality [Relation], which is eternally annihilated in God, is the only part that is likewise annihilated in each being as it goes through time.

—SCHELLING (ANP 116–117 [§125])

Schelling's identity system is a cosmo-theological or theo-cosmic system: a system of pantheism, in which "absolute identity" equals the essence of God, and "God" is synonymous with the universe or the All. Schelling is occupied during this period with the broadly Spinozan *deus sive natura* or the *hen kai pan*, which he proclaims to be the essence of the coming epoch of immediacy: of magic, heaven, or bliss. To understand the identity philosophy, it is crucial to keep in mind that, as Schelling emphasizes, bliss is *essentially already there* from the viewpoint of God or the All, or the standpoint of "divine order" proclaimed in his 1805 *Aphorisms on the Philosophy of Nature*. In this order, finitude as a structure of diremption and the temporal not-yet is immediately "annihilated in God," and all forms of being express the All and shine with divine light.

Crucially, Schelling does not conceive his identity philosophy as constructing a system, so to speak, ex nihilo. For him, the All itself is the one true system, the *Weltsystem* or system of the universe. Human thought and true philosophy are themselves part of this system as its highest point, at which human reason coincides with what the 1801 *Presentation* terms "absolute reason," or, one might say, the mind of God. To speak of the divine "mind" here is not to speak of a transcendent intelligence beyond the universe, but of the All as a cohesive real-ideal whole, or a natural whole that conceptually coheres and cognizes itself through human reason, and whose structure can, accordingly, be grasped by the philosopher's mind. The All unfolds itself, articulates the one divine essence, expresses or reveals itself through natural forms and forms of human thought. The insight that the universe may be regarded as auto-poietic, an auto-organization and auto-revelation, is inherited by the identity philosophy from Schelling's earlier philosophy of nature.[3] Each being, accordingly, reveals itself, in its essence, as one with God, and in its finitude as conceptually embedded (*begriffen* or *eingebildet*) in the All, or as part of the relational network of finite forms through which the phenomenal universe articulates itself and evolves.

God in his pure essence of identity is, however, absolutely indifferent to this articulation, which appears as such only from within the fallenness of reality in its having fallen away (*Abfall*) from absolute identity. All of us, and everything that is, are but fragments immersed in the one common being of the All, which is perfectly equal to itself (the "common substance," or the "substance, root, and identity of all things"; WS 261 [§167], 364 [§243]). These fragments reflect the bliss of the All with various intensity and, as it were, from different sides—and the task of philosophy is to reassemble this seeming scatteredness into the oneness that it essentially *is*. Through intellectual intuition, an operation that remains central for the identity philosophy, the philosopher attains to the divine standpoint while tracing the relational structure of God's revelation in finitude, and the system as she articulates it in writing seeks to mirror, in a transparent formal manner, the auto-articulation of the All. Hence Schelling's repeated attempts at a geometric or deductive mode of presentation found in the *Presentation*, the so-called *Würzburg System*

---

3. See Grant, *Philosophies of Nature*.

from 1804, and the *Aphorisms* as his three most systematic works during this period.[4]

3.1.1. To See Bliss but Not the World: The A = A

In the identity philosophy, the All is immediately one with itself and absolutely blissful, even though what we perceive as finite things are not. Such is the central meta-opposition or meta-antagonism inscribed in the beginning and methodology of the identity philosophy: the antagonism between the true philosophical standpoint of absolute identity or bliss and the standpoint of false cognition, associated by Schelling with Fichte and with modern alienated cognition more broadly. This false standpoint is that of the self-assertion of the subject as premised on the division between subject and object. In natural philosophy, it is likewise the standpoint that identifies nature with an irreconcilable duality or opposition of forces. From this standpoint of what Schelling calls "reflection" or "purely finite cognition" (WS 402 [§291]), both nature and the I appear as dirempted and as striving ceaselessly for a fulfillment and bliss that constitutively cannot be attained.

Such is, Schelling announces, the "fundamental error" of all thinking: to begin with the "distinction between subject and object" (WS 105/141 [§1]). We are used to perceiving the universe as a world of separation and division, in which things are originally disconnected and can only be synthesized *into* a unity that is secondary and not primary. The All appears, from this perspective, as an endless collection of things that fundamentally cannot be recollected into oneness. As such, both nature and mind exist here, as Schelling puts it, "outside" the All, or in separation from the one all-encompassing being. This is the standpoint of sheer fallenness, of *Abfall* considered "for itself," that is, as though diremption were the absolute structure of reality—as though things truly were "alien and without community [*Gemeinschaft*]" (ANP 243 [§CXLIX]).

What is needed is to *refuse* to see this alienated world as the ultimate reality: to refuse to "take the particular to be the real" (WS 139/171 [§31]). The false standpoint must be abandoned if true knowledge is to be achieved: this is the antagonistic condition of the identity philosophy. The identity philosophy,

---

4. I should note that the existing translation of WS into English is incomplete. Hence I provide references to the page numbers of the English-language edition only where it includes the respective passage.

Schelling writes, "removes itself completely from the standpoint of reflection," that is, the subject-object division, overturning the principle on which this standpoint rests: namely, the principle that opposition is primary vis-à-vis identity (DMS 115/145). In the *Würzburg System*, Schelling likewise reiterates: intellectual intuition "abandons forever the sphere of reflection," of negativity and diremption, transporting us to the viewpoint of absolute identity where "our subjectivity and our finitude ... fully disappear" (WS 107/143 [§1]). "In [absolute] reason, all finitude perishes" (WS 111/146 [§4]).

What becomes visible with the disappearance of the structure of finitude is the Wordsworthian "one life" and "unappropriated bliss" that we encountered in Chapter 1. In this blissful *now*, the particular coincides with the universal immediately, without the negativity of synthesis but also without foreclosing the being of the particular. Immediate dissolution of the particular in the universal is precisely how Schelling characterizes bliss (FD 133). To intuit this bliss is to see the *it is what it is* at the heart of everything, an A = A, in which each finite being's particularity is dissolved in absolute identity or what one might call the pure "=." The first thing we intuit in any A = A, Schelling claims, is not the "A" (the *what*) but the "=," "identity itself" or the pure "is" (DMS 119/147 [§6])—a bliss that cannot be captured by the dialectic of mediation and otherness. The pure "=" is neither the leftmost nor the rightmost A in A = A, nor the form of their unity, but the absolute copula that binds prior to any doubling or reduplication.

"Identity itself" is the essence (*Wesen*) of all things, or the way they are in their idea (*Idee*) and not in their particularity. A = A is the form (*Form*) in which the essence of identity exists: the archetypal form of blissful being. Form is for Schelling what, in all beings including God or the All, expresses or articulates the one essence of absolute identity. Each being, insofar as *it is what it is* or simply *is*, exists under the form of self-identity (of being identical with itself), or as an A = A that thereby expresses absolute identity. For Schelling, there is no gap between the essence, or "identity itself," and the form of A = A. *To simply be what one is* is to immediately express, and be dissolved in, the essence. All forms of being, insofar as they simply are what they are, or insofar they immediately affirm themselves, express the same essence of absolute identity. That is to say, *the animal is the animal, the plant is the plant*—any A = A—expresses, from the standpoint of absolute reason, "identity itself" immediately, equally, and fully. Paradoxically, to see, for instance, the flower as *simply being what it is* is to cease to regard it as a particular "what" (a flower) and to view it as a sheer identity that dissolves it *as* flower. In this way, A = A and B = B dissolve equally into the pure "=," so that A's and B's particularity vanishes.[5] Absolute identity is absolutely indifferent, and absolutely without relation to any difference or specificity, to any specific position of identity. It is the whatever identity, or whatever manifestation or revelation of absolute identity. Finite things may come into being and perish, but the "=" persists, eternally or atemporally, in each and every one of them. In Schelling, *the copula is the common*: "the copula, or absolute identity" is the one substance (ANP 220 [§§XXIX–XXXI]), the "community of all that exists" (ANP 216 [§IV]), expressed by A = A as the form(ula) of the All.

From this a highly Romantic vision emerges: one can glimpse bliss, equally and materially, in the ocean or the burning fire, in each stone, each flower, each animal or human form of life, and every common thing, *if only one ceases to view them through the lens of particularity, objectivity, telos, and use*. It is in this manner that the one undivided and non-appropriable bliss is revealed. The absolute being of the All, as expressing the one divine essence or the pure "=," cuts through the divisions of the world, collapsing the borders between particular and universal, lower and higher, human and nonhuman into a radical immanence common to all things. To intuit this being-in-common is to see each finite being non-relationally, without comparing it to other beings, without viewing it as lacking or superior, or even as (relationally or comparatively) different or other. To intuit the one being-in-common is to let everything simply be what it is: an absolute letting-be.

This absolute freedom could not be more antagonistic to the modern freedom of self-assertion, possession, and mastery, which serves only to bind the subject to the imperatives of the world. To intuit a thing in its idea is to see it flare up as if struck by a divine lightning (*Blitz*; ANP 115 [§116]) that immediately burns down its particularity, so that only the non-relational "=" remains. "In truth, or in their essence, [all things] are mere radiations or flashes of the infinite affirmation" (ANP 113 [§101]) that coincides, in the same stroke, with infinite annihilation (*Vernichtung*). "Considered in itself, nothing is finite" (DMS 121/149 [§14]), and so, from the standpoint of absolute identity or the *An-sich*, there is no finite relational world. What is revealed in this world-annihilation is but "eternal equalness" (*Gleichheit*; WS 108–111/143–146 [§§3–4]), the pure "=" whose being is "all-blissful" because it "contains no opposition" (B 354/132).

---

5. Cf. FD 132: "The whole universe, be it plant, animal, or the human, is in the absolute—but since in each [of them] is the whole, each is therefore in the absolute not *as* plant, *as* animal, *as* human, or as any particular oneness, but as absolute oneness."

Theologically, during this period Schelling is equal parts a Spinozist and a mystic, especially in his continued emphasis on the annihilation of the world in bliss. Absolute identity as "the absolute at-once" "annihilates" the phenomenal world of division and duration (DMS 173/180 [§95]). "God," Schelling writes, "is equally the eternal night and eternal day of things" (ANP 113 [§102]): the absolute light of bliss, in which the world's distinctions are undistinguished. As "all-blissful," God is absolutely nonproductive: he "effects nothing" and "cares for nothing" (ANP 93 [§4], 108 [§77], 115 [§118]). God is immanently dispossessed in that he does not possess anything—not even himself in a way that a self-conscious subject would. There is no self-relation in the pure "=." As absolutely non-relational (*Beziehungslose*; ANP 101 [§50]), God is incapable of relating. He may manifest himself in all identity in the world—in whatever identity—but he manifests himself in it only *as* absolute indifference. In his bliss, God is unconcerned with the conflicts (*Widerstreit*) that constitute finitude (ANP 115 [§118]) and is "utterly without determination" (ANP 134 [§215]). This nonproductive *nihil*, an absolute being that is at the same time an absolute nonbeing, a reason that is so absolute as to cancel out all thinking *of* anything or thinking that could belong to a subject: this is what the name "God" indexes in Schelling's identity philosophy. The most radical thing about this God is that, even as he is absolutely annihilative, he is absolutely affirmative and by no means otherworldly. He is intuited directly in each and every form of being to the extent that this being simply *is*, without any determination. As such, "God" names the one immanence that the structure of fallenness shatters or fragments.

Translating this into cosmological terms, to say that all being is essentially God is to say that, in its essence, everything is the universe or the All: not just something that is *in* the All, but the All itself. This, too, is a Romantic way of looking at things: everything that is part of the universe essentially *is* the universe. This universe may appear infinitely fragmented, and full of endless eccentric trajectories and deviations that seem to serve no purpose. Yet the Romantic glimpses that each fragment is not something other than the whole, but the whole itself, expressing the one absolute identity of the All.[6] Similarly, each seeming deviation, in its very absence of telos, immediately expresses the one absolute truth: the pure "=," the divine essence. From this

---

6. In this way, the identity philosophy may be regarded as a singular variation on the Romantic theme of the coincidence of whole and fragment as analyzed in Lacoue-Labarthe and Nancy, *The Literary Absolute*.

cosmic perspective, nothing is outside absolute identity, and there is nothing other than absolute identity.

As Schelling's recourse to the images of "center," "radius," and "periphery" across his writings shows, he pictures absolute identity as the primordial divine point that coincides with the absolute circle or sphere: an immediate all-oneness in which the all and the one are undistinguished. And although the post-Copernican universe is dirempted and decentered, the identity philosophy programmatically adopts from early-modern Platonic cosmology a theo-cosmic vision in which the center of the All is everywhere and its periphery nowhere. As Schelling summarizes it in a letter from 1801, the standpoint of absolute identity is one at which *all is central*, in contrast to the "peripheral" view of the universe.[7] If Schelling continues at the same time to subscribe to the cosmological idea of the original cosmic contingency as a falling away of finitude from the primordial point, leading to the phenomenal unfolding of the post-Copernican universe in space and time, then this is not a contradiction but part of the program: to discern an absolute oneness within the decentered and seemingly disharmonious universe, to re-vision the post-Copernican universe as the blissful All, and to impose the form of absolute reason (A = A) upon it.

However, if absolute identity is the standpoint at which this fallen world is annihilated as such, how can philosophy even think finitude? The universe is a system that philosophy needs to be able to think in its variety and differentiation too, and not only in its absolute oneness. The fact that, at the standpoint of bliss, *there is no finite world* remains the pressing issue that the identity philosophy needs to resolve. To make it slightly less abstract (if no less speculative), one may illustrate this problem cosmologically with the example of the opposition between the earth and the sun, as Schelling does in his 1802 *Further Presentations from the System of Philosophy*. In the post-Copernican view of the universe, which Schelling considers to be scientifically true, the earth is decentered vis-à-vis the sun, and there is a conflict (*Streit*) between our planet's "own indifference (the particular) and the sun's (the universal)," manifested in the earth's elliptical orbit around the sun (FD 150). It is as though the earth asserted its particularity over and against the sun while also being attracted to it as the universal light (cf. already VW 91). There is thus a *distance* between the particular (the earth) and the universal (the sun), originating in what Schelling pictures as the breaking up of the primordial

---

7. Letter to C. J. Windischmann, May 8, 1801, quoted in the editor's introduction to DMS in HKA I/10, 43. It is, Schelling writes, "the only *central* standpoint," a view "from the center."

proto-sun, from which individual celestial bodies fall away (this is the cosmological model of the cosmic Fall or *Abfall*).

Yet, Schelling continues, from the standpoint of "the absolute or in-itself," one cannot think the decenteredness of the earth or its trajectory. In absolute identity, there is no decenteredness, only the absolute center-point, so that "one cannot even differentiate between a point and a different point." As a result, in intellectual intuition the earth and the sun simply coincide within the "One Point" (FD 150). The absolute is "the eternally equal, eternally resting center" (WS 122/156 [§15]). The earth and the sun exist in a state of reciprocal relative indifference, but not *absolute* indifference, in which they would be immediately undifferentiated. "To consider a celestial body from the standpoint of absolute indifference" would mean that "the point that represents the earth and the one that represents the sun immediately collapse into one" (FD 174). To re-vision the All as bliss is to re-vision it as the pure "=," in which one can glimpse the earth and the sun as equally all-blissful yet cannot see or think any difference or relation between them. To be in bliss, for the human as for the planet, is *to be as the absolute center-point unto oneself*, without relation, differentiation, or otherness. There can thus be no science at the standpoint of bliss, and science is what Schelling wants to have.

All of the above is to underscore that, at the standpoint of absolute identity, there is no phenomenal world with its divisions, only the bliss of the pure "="—and yet the world *is* there, and philosophy needs to think its divisions and distances, too. We have again the meta-antagonism between the standpoint of fallenness and that of the absolute: from the former, one can see finitude but cannot see oneness and bliss; from the latter, one can see bliss but not finitude. *How to think the differences of finitude as themselves expressing the identity of the All?* Such is the problem that the identity philosophy needs to resolve. For that, it needs an additional standpoint that would mediate between fallenness and absolute identity in order "to bring appearance back to identity" (FD 174).

3.1.2. Re-collecting the All: The Standpoint of Potency (A = B)

The mediating standpoint is that of the potency (*Potenz*) of being as the *relative power, or degree* (*Grad*) *of intensity*, with which every finite being expresses the absolute identity of the All. To understand this standpoint, we may recall that, for the identity philosophy, the All itself is a system: the primordial point unfolds, articulating or revealing itself through all the particular forms of being in the universe. The identity philosopher knows that there is nothing outside absolute identity and that separation or division is secondary with regard to the All. Unlike those who remain at the standpoint of reflection, she can see that what appears as a separate individual thing—say, a stone—is but a *localization or particularization* of the All: a particular form of being in which the All is revealed in a particular way, a fragment that is conceptually embedded in the All.

The identity philosopher can, accordingly, recognize the conceptual embeddedness (and, so to speak, the cosmic place) of every particular being in the All, re-collecting this being into an overarching oneness, as though assembling the puzzle (*Rätsel*) of the universe so as to reveal its mystery. The mystery is that of the revelation of the absolute in finitude.[8] The identity philosopher says: true, the phenomenal universe originates in a Fall from oneness and its fragmentation, but it also *remains* essentially one. Each particular thing is an identity fragment, a relative identity. And in each and every such fragment, the power of absolute identity—the power of the absolutely real—continues to reside. While the All as a whole possesses the fullness of this power, finite forms of being, qua particularizations of the All, cannot fully expresses the power of the All, but only partially, or to a certain degree. Yet all finite being seeks precisely to express this power with as much intensity as it can. This is true of the darkest and most inert matter no less than of the plant, the sun, or human reason, even if these are located at different levels (*Stufen*) with regard to how visible the power of the All is in them. From the standpoint of absolute identity, these levels are immediately and equally dissolved in absolute bliss. From the standpoint of relative power or potency, they become visible—and thus the world becomes visible, too, not as a world of things, but as what expresses the one underlying power of the All.

This means, Schelling insists, that finitude *as* finite does not exist for itself, and does not have any being or power of its own. This dirempted world cannot ground itself; it is needy, and dependent on the bliss that it forecloses and pulls apart. This structure of diremption must not be viewed as an independent reality: the finite world as finite, or the universe considered through the lens of particularity and thinghood, is a nothing, illusion (*Schein*), mere relationality, *ens imaginarium* (ANP 114 [§111], 121 [§152]). To occupy the standpoint of potency is to view finitude as existing by virtue of borrowed being and shining (another meaning of *Schein*) with borrowed light, or merely

---

8. Which is, not coincidentally, for Schelling the mystery of Christianity (see Chapter 1).

reflecting (in a *Reflex* or *Widerschein*) the true light of the All.[9] Only the All has being; the particular qua particular does not. Yet—and this constitutes the identity-philosophical double vision—the speculative philosopher can discern in the very nonbeing of the particular an expression or revelation of the absolute being of the All, shining through this nonbeing as the power that sustains the world of appearance. As Schelling asserts, "Since the particular is posited as mere nonbeing only through the All itself, this nonbeing as such, through the fact *that* it is mere nonbeing, is the *expression* of the All." In finite being, this expression is "not immediate but mediated." Thus, the standpoint of the potency of finite being, that is, its relative power as expressing the power of the All and its relative light as reflecting the light of the All, is the standpoint of mediation between finitude and absolute identity. In what fallen cognition regards as independently existing particular beings, true cognition sees that which reflects, with various potency or intensity, the one divine light. Thereby, fallenness is re-mediated into what reveals the one common being and power of the All. "With this," Schelling continues, "the whole meaning of [the world of] appearance is articulated for the first time" (WS 150–151/182 [§41]).

At stake in this conceptual switch from *Schein* as illusion to what *shines* with divine light, and from *Reflex* as the false standpoint of reflective cognition to what *reflects* the light of absolute truth, is more than Schelling's penchant for wordplay. The phenomenological revolution that the identity philosophy undertakes must rethink the logic and terminology of our perception. In her double vision, the identity philosopher can see that a particular being has no light of its own, but just as the earth's light is that of the sun, so the very darkness into which the particular is submerged if stripped of the universal reveals that there is only *one* universal source of light. "Dissolving the particular," Schelling writes, "the infinite affirmation leaves behind, like lightning, only the empty shell, the shadow, the pure nothingness of the particular—yet it is precisely through this nothingness of the particular that the All expresses itself *to the utmost* as the all-powerful, innate, eternal substance" (WS 151/182 [§41]). In its fallenness, finitude has no power. Its potency is, in truth, the expression of its inherent *powerlessness*, so that all finite identity is but the operativity of absolute identity within fallenness. The world of modern dirempted cognition is the shadow world: modernity is Plato's cave,

---

9. Cf. FD 128: to grasp something as a "*reflex* of absolute oneness" is to grasp its "organic" and "necessary" subordination to "the absolutely whole," i.e., the fact that the life of any particular being is *not its own* but that of the All—just as its light is borrowed from that of the All.

inhabited by alienated modern subjects and the Kantian-Fichtean philosopher of subjectivity ("Kant was, more or less, together with them in the cave"; WS 402–403 [§291]). The identity philosophy alone can lead one out into the absolute sunlight that, for the first time, allows one to recognize shadows *as* mere shadows and to re-vision finite forms as the reflection of the absolute light.

To summarize, potency is for Schelling the degree of intensity with which a form of being expresses the absolute being and power of the All.[10] As such, potency is the power of re-collection within all things: out of fragmentation, everything seeks to restore itself to oneness, even if, as finite, being can attain only a relative indifference or oneness, not absolute indifference. Only the All itself and human reason as coinciding with absolute reason in intellectual intuition exist under the form of A = A. Finite being, by contrast, even as it *is* (relative) identity, always expresses in its finitude a tension between the particular and the universal. This tension is captured by the form A = B, which Schelling calls the formula of potency (*Ausdruck der Potenz*) or finitude (*Ausdruck der Endlichkeit*; DMS 137/158 [§44]). A = B, in other words, is at once the form of identity (since all being is relative identity) and the form of deviation or imbalance: the deviation of this particular form of being, or this particular kind of finite identity, from the All. It is thus form, and not essence, that mediates between fallenness and the absolute—and this is why Schelling needs the form-essence distinction.

Schelling believes that, with the help of A = B as the formalized relation of relative indifference between the universal (A) and the particular (B), the identity system can capture *all* the gradations with which finite being

---

10. Schelling also calls it "quantitative difference," i.e., difference in the degree of intensity, and not "qualitative difference," i.e., difference in substance, since there is only one substance. Quantitative difference, or potency, is non-substantial and nonessential. It "cannot be posited with regard to *the absolute itself*, [only] with regard to what is separated [*abgesondert*] from the absolute, and only insofar as it is separated from it. . . . Quantitative difference is in general posited only through the *act of separation* [*Absonderung*], and it holds with respect to this act" (DMS 128–129/251–252 [§30]). This separation transports the philosopher to the standpoint of *Absonderung* or *Abfall*, from which, in her double vision, she can re-mediate or re-collect fallenness. Cf. WS 424 (§307): "The ground of finitude [i.e., A = B as the formula of potency] consists, according to our view, solely in the not-being-in-God of things qua particular, which . . . can be expressed as a falling away [*Abfall*], *defectio*, from God or the All." While the term *Abfall* in the theo-cosmic sense emerges in the 1804 Schelling, I see the structure of separation from absolute identity already in the invocation of *Absonderung* in the 1801 *Presentation*, and in the Christian contradiction as the structure of the universe in 1802. Cf. VM 122/86, where *Abfall* designates the falling away from pagan oneness, and thus the transition to the general Christian contradiction, and VM 125/91, where redemption is configured as "the reconciliation of the finite that has fallen away [*abgefallen*] from God."

expresses the All, throughout the universe, on the earth, and even within the human mind: our thoughts, too, are finite identities in the realm of "the ideal," whose intensity reflects the light of truth to a certain degree. The standpoint of potency is a relational standpoint: the distinction between various degrees of intensity "*can be made only within the relation* of one thing to another particular thing or to the entirety of things," or by way of relative negation (particularization) and comparison (ANP 128 [§196]). What potency expresses is the relative "manner in which [a part of the All] reproduces the fullness of the whole within itself," a manner that is formal and nonessential, merely "comparative" (ANP 129 [§197]). To put this differently, the extent to which the power of a being's identity approximates or deviates from the power of the All defines the relative (nonessential) difference between it and the All, and between it and any other being—such as the relative distance and conflict between the earth and the sun. Thereby the identity system, in its classification or articulation of all possible forms of finite being, is envisioned by Schelling as coinciding with the system of the All's auto-articulation as the unfolding of the absolute point across the phenomenal multiplicity of the real as well as the ideal.[11] This is not an absolutely indifferent re-visioning of the All, since at that standpoint everything collapses into bliss. It is, rather, a relatively indifferent re-visioning: a philosophical construction of finitude *with a view to the bliss of the All* as what finite beings express to the best of their ability. The All is envisioned here as a nested network of intensities, or particular nodes within the All that shine more or less brightly, and not as a world of things. *Thinghood* is re-mediated into *potency*.

The potency of a finite being is not the absolute power of bliss itself, but an approximation of or deviation from bliss: the relative (un)blissfulness of this being. Only the All in its bliss remains "without potency" or "potenceless" (*potenzlos*; ANP 131 [§208], ANP 133 [§215]). Other beings are confined to potency to the extent that they are not perfectly blissful. The higher the being's degree of intensity, or "the higher the degree of reality or perfection of a thing, the more it approaches the divine and the more it participates in the bliss of the divine" (WS 420 [§305]). In fact, for its seemingly static character, A = B

---

11. Sometimes Schelling uses in this respect the image of ideas in the divine mind, actualized in the All's phenomenal unfolding. Cosmologically, this means that, within A = A as the primordial point, what will become the articulated All is virtually contained. Logically, it means that *to think identity (A = A) is also to think the possibility of difference, and thus the possibility of A = B*. In the absence of the actual universe, however, A = A remains a point, and the possibility of difference remains virtual. To think the actuality of difference, one must occupy the standpoint of *Abfall*, or of being "outside" absolute identity.

captures for Schelling a *tension* within all being, and the identity system offers a dynamic and historical view of the All, if indifferently expressed. Since the world is the fragmentation of what remains essentially one, the power of identity inheres in each fragment, striving to re-collect itself into oneness. From the standpoint of potency, the All's differentiation and its re-collection or reassembling coincide. Finitude is a falling away from oneness that strives to return to a higher, more differentiated oneness, driving cosmic history across the space-time of the phenomenal universe: such is the Schellingian schema of cosmic history, including human history. What is peculiar about the identity philosophy's reframing of the world as the universe of potency is how, in its concern with the pure form of finitude, it wants to preserve the character of finitude as processual and as driven by contradiction, striving, and conflict or battle (*Kampf*; DMS 150–151/167–168 [§§58–60]). This conflict marks the persistent unblissfulness and striving for bliss within all being—the unblissfulness and striving that remain at the heart of the identity philosophy. "All phenomenal things," Schelling writes, "are reproductions [*Abbildungen*] of the whole, even if highly imperfect reproductions, which strive in their particular form, as particular, nonetheless to express the universe." Their particular form of being, in its imbalance with the universal, "does not attain the perfect bliss that may truly be enjoyed only by the ideas"—that is, "to be the law unto itself, to encompass in its particularity the universal and in its universality the particular." "In this double drive [*Trieb*]," Schelling concludes, "everything lives and moves" (FD 133).

This dynamic reflects the All's fragmentation, which scatters and dims the one bliss. Even as the identity philosophy re-visions the All as bliss, it seeks not to lose sight of the world's unblissfulness. Finite being is a being of contradiction (*Widerspruch*) that, while merely formal, captures the conflict that defines this being's particularity—but also determines the telos that drives it: to approach "perfect bliss." What defines the dynamic evolution of the phenomenal universe is that all being strives *to actually become the center unto itself*: "to be the law unto itself," to imitate the bliss of $A = A$ as the absolute center-point. In this manner, the law of absolute being ($A = A$) becomes the law of phenomenal becoming: of $A = B$ striving to become $A = A$. This law defines the gradual unfolding of the All. To be blissful is to be as an $A = A$ unto itself, and as such to be free from imperfection, conflict, or striving—and in this, to copy or reproduce (*abbilden*) out of finitude the bliss of the All.

This explains the conflictual dynamic between the earth and the sun, too: the earth used, for Schelling, to be one with the sun, but now it has fallen away from it and asserts itself against it precisely to become the center unto itself. What appears as the centrifugal force of the earth is its self-assertion or self-insistence: the insistence on being, in its particularity, no less of a center-point than the sun. This rivalry between the earth and the sun is what appears phenomenally as the former's orbiting around the latter. At various levels of intensity, a similar rivalry—a universal structure of self-assertion—defines all finitude. Each finite being has a particular selfhood (*Selbstheit*) out of which it seeks to attain a centrality vis-à-vis other beings, thereby imitating the All. Each of us in our mental life, too, wants nothing but to assert oneself as central and others as peripheral. All finite being wants to become a relative All unto itself and, in this, manifests relationally the one power of the All. For a being to actually reach bliss—to become one with its non-relational idea—would amount to the annihilation of its particularity and to its transparent oneness with divine being: to salvation from the conflictual and negative character of finitude. The *hen kai pan* as the promised telos would be the utopian state in which everything actually is the center unto itself, or in which the standpoint of the idea or essence coincides with that of potency. In this state, there would be no conflict or striving, and all relationality would dissolve: to be a monad-like $A = A$ is to immediately dissolve in the one bliss of the pure "=," so that, as Schelling provocatively suggests, the Leibnizian and the Spinozan universe are, in essence, one and the same (ANP 143).

3.1.3. Classifying the Phenomena: The Three Potencies ($A = B$, A^2, A^3)

So far, I have spoken of "potency" in the singular as the intensity of a being's relative identity or relative indifference. For Schelling, potency can be further structurally divided into three aspects or dimensions, so that, even as he calls $A = B$ the general formula of potency, he also speaks of "three potencies," each of which is *a specific dimension of how finite appearances reflect the structure of the All*. Namely, taken as a whole, the phenomenal universe has three logical-metaphysical aspects or dimensions:

- *Allness.* First, the universe encompasses all particular being (or, which is for Schelling the same, all particular being is a particularization of the All).
- *Oneness.* Second, the universe is immediately and essentially one.
- *Wholeness.* Third, the universe is *at once* infinitely particular and infinitely one: it is a whole as oneness-in-differentiation, or the unity of particular and universal.

All finite being in the All reflects these three dimensions, so that, with their help, Schelling seeks to deduce space and time and to classify all physical phenomena in the world of appearance. These three dimensions are precisely the three potencies, or the three structural dimensions of potency, which characterize not only the structure of the All, but also of each and every being within it insofar as it expresses the All.[12] Let us consider these potencies in more detail.

The first potency: gravity (A^1, or $A = B$). The first structural dimension of all finite being is that it occupies a certain place or position (*Position*) within the All. To say this is to focus on the way in which all particular being exists in tension with the All: it is particular to the extent that it is a particularization of the All. Through $A = B$ as expressing a relative indifference between universal (A) and particular (B), Schelling believes that he can deduce physical phenomena such as cohesion and rigidity (*Starrheit*). Cohesion is, so to speak, the holding together of A and B within a material position, which prevents it from simply dissolving in the All, and therefore grounds its particular "rigid" existence. From this perspective, $A = B$ is the formula of the material filling of space, and of the rigidity of a being's particular cosmic position, insofar as, in its particularity, it "tears itself away from" the one identity and gains its own (relatively independent) place (WS 220 [§124])—as if it were saying: *I have my own place in the All*. Each being gravitates to and around its place, a fact that at the most basic level defines its "selfhood," the "I-ness [*Ichheit*] of things" (WS 220 [§124]). A stone or a planet, from this perspective, possesses a particular selfhood just like an animal or a human. Particular selfhood forms the basic level through which the universe differentiates and unfolds itself, and based on which higher universal life (including the life of the mind) can develop.

Since the three potencies also constitute Schelling's way of classifying natural being, there is for him a class of being in which gravity dominates: these are metals, minerals, and physical things such as stones. In his identity-philosophical works, Schelling goes to great lengths to deduce not only different types of minerals and metals, including platina, diamond, and gold, but also the relative positions of the planets in the solar system solely from $A = B$ as the formula of cohesion. The first potency is the lowest level of potency or intensity: the darkest, the most obscure and inert. Gravity, or rigid selfhood,

---

12. One may see that these dimensions correspond to the three aspects of the identity form (A = A or A = B), where one can distinguish the subject or universal, the predicate or particular, and their unity or balance.

is what in each being, including the human, resists the light of the universal and dims it. Yet this resistance is necessary, and gravity forms universally the dark "ground of reality" (WS 204 [§105]), for without it no particular would be discernible, and no world of appearance could exist or be thought. (The ontological structure of the world and the structure of its thinkability or articulability coincide in the identity philosophy.)

The second potency: light (A^2, or $A = (A = B)$). The second dimension of all finite being is that it is processual and so exists in time. This is true of the stone too; it is just that the processuality of the stone is weak and obscured by its rigidity. In all dynamic process, Schelling maintains, the All affirms itself as one *across* its particular positions, as though negating the fixedness of particular place or overcoming the rigidity of particularity. Yet this rigid selfhood at the same time resists the All's attempt to immediately cancel it out; and this resistance is what engenders processuality and change. In gravity, the All affirms every particularity as essentially belonging to it (the dimension of allness). In light, the All may be said to (relatively) negate any particularity insofar as particularity does not have a being that would be independent from the All (the dimension of oneness). Schelling's formula for the second potency is $A = (A = B)$, where the parenthetical $A = B$ expresses material particularization, and the leftmost A its relative overcoming. At the level of the second potency he places the three kinds of the dynamic process: magnetism, electricity, and the chemical process, hierarchically arranged according to the degree to which they overcome rigid corporeality. In magnetism as the universal process of repulsion and attraction between bodies, cohesion and particularity (and thus the relative fixedness of the particular place) still dominate; in electricity, light appears to move through materiality and negate its relative independence; while the chemical process involves equally corporeality and light, undifferentiating them into a higher whole. On this example, we can see how, within a particular potency (in this case A^2), the principle of tripartite division is recapitulated: a nested structure that is typical of Schelling's thought.

All nature is but "a series of oppositions between gravity and light" (WS 203 [§104]): a series that appears only from the standpoint of potency, and not absolute identity ("considered absolutely, light and gravity are one"; WS 203 [§105]). This (highly Romantic) battle between gravity and light as two relational cosmic principles manifests itself visibly, too. The stronger the force of cohesion, the more light is obstructed by it, and so the more intense light (or lightning, fire, etc.) has to be in order to penetrate it. Light is, again, but the operativity of absolute identity ("in light is absolute identity itself"; DMS 162/174 [§93]) as "shining through" relational particularization (ANP 124 [§170]) and seeking to reaffirm oneness: a process which particular selfhood at once grounds and inhibits or opposes. The relative opposition of gravity and light turns thereby into the relative balance between darkness and light within all being.

The third potency: organism (A^3, or $A = (A = (A = B))$). The first two potencies exist, however, only within and for the sake of the third: the auto-sustaining oneness-in-differentiation, or organism, incorporating into itself the strife of gravity and light. This potency dominates in organic life in the broadest sense. The universe itself is an organism, equal to itself throughout its evolution and differentiation. But Schelling likewise declares each planet—picking up on a motif from Bruno—to be an auto-evolving, internally balanced organism, encompassing other organisms that inhabit it (such as animals and plants). A plant is an organism of a lower kind, whose freedom of movement is more limited, but which unfolds or auto-articulates itself from the seed, and which is rooted in its place in the earth yet strives toward the sun as the universal. In Schelling's formula of the third potency, $A = (A = (A = B))$, the leftmost A expresses a higher potentiation of light as its gathering into an independent, lawfully self-unfolding being that persists across its differentiations and transformations, manifesting a "perfect balance" between gravity and light (ANP 127 [§188]). The organism is therefore the highest reproduction of the All out of finitude.

Together, A^1, A^2, and A^3 form the ascending ladder (*Stufenfolge*) of nature brought "to completion, or to the exhibition of a true likeness of the All" (ANP 128 [§195]). The potencies are the generic structure through which the All is reassembled as an auto-articulating whole. Since these potencies are the necessary dimensions of phenomenal reality, all three are there from the beginning of the universe, even if they only gradually unfold into their present state. In this way, as a contemporary reviewer put it, although Schelling's "primordial oneness . . . is a mathematical point, it becomes everything by the hand of the speculator; from it, the universe is born in an evolution that knows no limit."[13] The standpoint of potency may be that of nonessential relationality and of illusion, since essentially there is only one all-blissful being. However, potency is a *necessary* illusion: it is illusory insofar as it is relational and emerges from the *Abfall*, yet it is necessary in order to think the auto-generativity of the phenomenal universe without viewing it as irredeemably divided and unblissful. The formulas of potency express absolute identity as the underlying power of the universe even within conflict and

---

13. Schweighäuser, "L'état actuel de la philosophie," 200.

division. They disclose that a "concrete thing... in its very nonbeing is a necessary reflection of the All" (WS 150/182 [§41]). Only in this manner can the Gnostic vision of universal unblissfulness be mediated and reconciled, and Gnosticism overcome. Although from the standpoint of absolute identity the potencies "do not ground any difference either within God, or between things, or within the thing itself," they *are* the structure of phenomenal nature in its unfolding qua the re-collection of bliss (they are, Schelling emphasizes, "actually expressed in nature"; ANP 127–128 [§189, §193]). Through the potencies, Schelling seeks to formalize with a view to the bliss of the All what he regards as the achievement of modern science: the insight that, as Iain Hamilton Grant summarizes it, "the laws of the whole are also the laws of the subordinate systems, so that the whole recapitulates itself in particulars."[14] This universal nested logic makes possible, in Schelling's utopian imperative, the collaboration between philosophy and science that is necessary for the age of reconciliation to come.

Even in this brief outline of the identity philosophy, one sees the complex interplay of standpoints that Schelling mediates into the system of the All in its phenomenal unfolding. There is, first, the standpoint of absolute identity or bliss; second, the standpoint of potency, or of the approximation of absolute identity out of particularization; and third, the standpoint of dirempted and synthetic knowledge for which separation is primary vis-à-vis identity, or the standpoint of fallenness "for itself." One can observe here a cleft not only between the standpoint of synthetic cognition and that of bliss—but also between the standpoint of bliss and that of potency as indexing the particularization of the All and finitude's mere reflection of, and striving for, bliss. One should not downplay this latter cleft, or turn the identity system into a "smooth" Spinozism that would postulate an uninterrupted continuity between the immediately blissful being of $A = A$ and $A = B$ as the formula of the actual world. $A = A$ and $A = B$ may both be forms of identity, but since the latter is a formula of particularization and relational division, there is a "holy abyss" (B 380) separating the two.[15]

---

14. Grant, *Philosophies of Nature*, 163.

15. To underscore: one can *think* $A = B$ virtually (as merely possible differentiation) on the basis of $A = A$, but only the catastrophic event of the *Abfall*—the fact of the finite world—makes $A = B$ into the actual formula through which to grasp the phenomenal world in its particularization of the one all-blissful being. Absent this unblissful world, $A = B$ would be no more than an empty form that would dissolve back into $A = A$.

As always in Schelling, there is *no transition* between bliss and the phenomenal world except through a positing of what is *not* absolute oneness, a positing that the identity philosophy grasps as the *Absonderung* or *Abfall*, which is underivable from absolute identity and re-mediated by the philosopher via the form A = B. The identity philosophy is a catastrophic Romantic Spinozism. Behind its formalism, the identity-philosophical universe is that of a cosmic shattering of identity: A = B is the formula of universal conflict and contradiction, even as these remain within the one substance. Without grasping the chasm separating absolute identity from potency, it is impossible to understand Schelling's speculative vision of the pure "=" in which there is no earth *as* earth, and no sun *as* this sun that is not the earth. At the standpoint of potency, by contrast, the divisions and particularizations of the world remain in place, even as they are re-visioned into an evolving network of intensities that jointly re-collect bliss-in-common. Re-mediation is an alternative logic or view of the phenomenal world, in which the world itself remains intact. Not so in bliss, where the world is annihilated, and what is revealed is the one undivided being foreclosed by the world. It is in this world-annihilation that the antagonistic core of the identity philosophy consists.

3.2. *To Dissolve as in Water, to Consume as in Fire*

> *The Earth, you see, is already kindled; blow but the Coal, and propagate the Fire, and the Work will go on.*
> —THOMAS BURNET, *The Sacred Theory of the Earth*

In what follows, I want to dwell on the antagonistic core of the identity philosophy as a kind of solar thought, which places Schelling in the tradition exemplified in the twentieth century by thinkers such as Georges Bataille and Alexander Chizhevsky. If one persists with this antagonistic core, coinciding with the standpoint of bliss-in-common, the revolutionary character of the identity philosophy becomes visible—even if Schelling himself ends up downplaying this dimension of his system. Hans Urs von Balthasar has observed that, "whereas for John, Plotinus, and Fichte the highest appears in the image of *light*, for Schelling *fire* is what is ultimate."[16] This absolute

---

16. Balthasar, *Der deutsche Idealismus*, 250.

fire—the fire of bliss—is, I argue, apocalyptic: it is the fire of the sun burning down the divisions of the world.

3.2.1. Natural Bliss and Divine Agency: Indifferentiating the World

To dwell at the standpoint of solarity is to enter Schelling's thought at its most speculative and esoteric, in its Romantic conjunction of the scientific and the apocalyptic. As we remember, at the standpoint of absolute identity the earth, the sun, and all the divisions of the world dissolve in the bliss of the pure "=." This absolute point is itself imagined by Schelling to be solar: the absolute ur-sun, as it were, orbiting around itself. "In the true universe," he writes, "there are no suns or planets, but only One infinite and omnipresent sun, the light itself, and only One infinite planet, that is, gravity" (WS 276 [§179]). This "true universe" is the being of absolute identity: within A = A, the left A (universality or subjectivity) stands for light, and the right A (particularity or being) for gravity, yet they immediately coincide within the pure "=." The true sun's planetary being (gravity) is the immediate carrier of its fiery subjectivity (light). In geometric terms, within absolute identity there is no difference between center (light) and periphery (gravity). The two constitute one absolute point coinciding with absolute totality, and come apart only within the finite solar system, where the (relatively peripheral) planet orbits the sun as the center and "ur-source of light" (WS 204 [§106]). Our "empirical sun" is but the image and operativity of the true sun breaking through the relationality of finitude (WS 277 [§179]).

To intellectually intuit the one common being is to glimpse this divine solarity, in which absolute day and absolute night are undifferentiated. The sun is sheer light, but it is absolutely blinding, indifferent to and consuming the differences and divisions that uphold the phenomenal world. At the standpoint of absolute identity, blindness and revelation coincide: one must become blind to the world to be able to see the one blissful being. This being is neither immaterial nor otherworldly. It is immediately visible, and immediately operative, in the two principles that Schelling declares to be the highest within gravity and light, respectively. These principles are *water* and *fire*, the two manifestations of nature's bliss as what actively *indifferentiates* the world.[17] Within absolute identity, water and fire, too, are completely undistinguished;

---

17. Somewhat ungrammatically, I speak of "indifferentiating" to preserve the concept of "indifference" therein.

in finitude, at a distance from the sun, they come apart.[18] And yet both water and fire, breaking out of their respective potency, directly enact the power of the absolutely real, exceeding their phenomenal confinement to the structure of potency and revealing that which *precedes* this structure: that is, the one bliss. Water and fire constitute the "last principles of all things in nature" (WS 285 [§181]), where "last" should be understood in the apocalyptic sense, too, as when one speaks of "last things."

Phenomenally, what appears as water reflects the All at the level of the first potency (A^1), or that of the material filling of space. The bliss of water is that of *pure passivity and dissolution*. Driven by the power of absolute identity within it, each body "strives for totality" or strives to undo its separation from the All (DMS 157/171 [§80]). The more the body is immediately one with the All, the more blissful it is. Hence "the constant striving of things for dissolution [*Auflösung*]," and the "general tendency" of matter to be reduced to water in chemical indifferentiation (ANP 120 [§144], WS 267 [§175]). *To be the mere filling of space*—and in this, the utter passivity of decomposition, a mere permeability (the capacity to simply *let pass, Durchdringlichkeit*): this is a state of the absolute calm of the substance, the "abyss of eternal repose and hiddenness" (WS 203 [§105]). The bliss of passive materiality is a watery bliss: not even a lying *on* water as in Rousseau and Adorno, but a becoming water as that which, considered immanently, dissolves, dissipates, indolently rolls, or flows without telos. The liquid flux indifferently fills all particular positions, indifferentiating them. If one could imagine existing in this state, it would amount to letting the world dissipate and to letting oneself dissipate with the dissolution of the world, without any otherness, will, or care. Liquidity (*Flüssigkeit*) is the material logic of decomposition without a "higher" subjectivity—a decreation and dispossession, "the absolute privation of difference," "a fully indifferent substance" that swallows all particularity (WS 226 [§129], DMS 170/179 [§95]). The logic of potency is here dissolved into a "difference-less state of matter": into "the potenceless water, which, as Pindar says, is the greatest of all things" (WS 274 [§179], DMS 181/185 [§111], WS 238 [§141]). Thereby, water overflows the confines of A^1, becoming as potenceless as absolute identity itself, and transfiguring cohesion ($A = B$) into $A = A$. Water is one with God in his passive or indolent aspect: the bliss of all-dissolution.

---

18. Water only appears *as* water, Schelling points out, because the earth exists at a certain distance from the sun (DMS 171 [§95]).

Schelling identifies the principle of water with the dimension of depth (*Tiefe*) into which "length and width disappear" (WS 223 [§129])—and one may think here of the abyssal oceanic depths that precede and dissolve all worldly cares. Into these primordial depths, natural and human selfhood longs to dissolve in the kind of oceanic feeling against which Herman Melville's Ishmael famously warns: an ecstatic, dreamlike all-oneness that might make the sailor, "lost in the infinite series of the sea," also "lose his identity." Becoming "diffused through time and space," the sailor might then forget, in this "enchanted mood," to hold on to the mast, falling into the deep.[19] It is the same feeling, too, that Sigmund Freud decries as the "primitive" opening of the ego, this basic reality principle, onto what is inhumanly "outside."[20] To call this only a feeling, though, fails to do justice to the *ontological* unconditioned state of bliss as all-dissolution, for which all material being really strives, and which exposes individuality and selfhood as secondary impositions, revealing the one non-appropriable being that no particular self can claim as its own. If A = B is the formula of the particularization and enclosure of the one common being, then, through the lens of fluidity thus understood, the enclosures of being themselves emerge as fluid, as de-absolutized and dissolved.

If the watery bliss is the highest being of the pure "=" to which passive materiality attains, then the dynamic process (A^2) is the *active* annihilation of the particular. To envision the bliss of the dynamic process is to focus on the other aspect of bliss: not its absolute passivity but absolute activity. "[All] dynamic movement is the return from difference to identity, the striving to go back from duplicity to oneness" (WS 261 [§167]). This is true of magnetism, electricity, and especially the chemical process as the actual transformation (*Verwandlung*) of materiality. The chemical process embodies "the totality of the dynamic process, in which all forms of the latter come together and equal each other out": an indifferentiation of form grasped as the active self-affirmation of the All, generating "the potenceless from potency" (IN2 123/65, WS 261 [§167]).

This actively impotentiating principle, the highest manifestation of the dynamic process, is *fire* (*Feuer*) as the all-consumption of form, or "what dissolves all forms of dynamic life" (WS 282 [§181]). "Fire," Schelling writes, "is nothing other than the pure substance breaking through in corporeality" (IN2 123/65). Just like in the case of water, in fire the confines of potency are

---

19. Melville, *Moby-Dick*, 126–129. "Heed it well, ye Pantheists!" mocks Ishmael (129).

20. Freud, *Civilization and Its Discontents*, 66–68.

consumed, and the very logic of potency is annihilated: "The annihilation of all potency, the highest goal of all dynamic activity, is reached with the outbreak of fire, or in the process of combustion." All fire is the fire of divine self-affirmation, and the bliss of fire is that of nature's self-annihilation as essentially one with absolute identity. Fire exceeds and *precedes* the three levels of the dynamic process (magnetism, electricity, and chemical processuality), just as "the absolute identity of the divine" exceeds and precedes "the three potencies of nature" (WS 268–269 [§176]). What is seen phenomenally as an outbreak of fire is but a relational appearance. Considered immanently, "Fire does not emerge; it is the clear primordial substance itself, co-eternal with matter, but here it consumes—seeks to dissolve—the holy Vesta," the goddess of fertility and natural (re)production (WS 282 [§181]). In its fiery bliss, nature insists on the one common being that is absolute and not produced, and in relation to which all productivity emerges as secondary and inessential. Fire, one could say, reveals nonproductivity and world-annihilation as the essence of nature.

Water and fire, Schelling notes, are equally consuming (*verzehrende*) principles, "hostile to selfhood" (WS 238 [§141]).[21] Divine being is absolutely one; therefore, the bliss of gravity (watery bliss) and the bliss of light (fiery bliss) constitute a mere relative distinction, which disappears in God, whose absolute agency *is* absolute indolence. In his unfinished novella, *Clara*, whose titular character's name may be taken to refer to the "clear [*klare*] primordial substance" mentioned above, Schelling speaks of the soul's bliss as a state where one "disappears in God like a drop in the ocean, a ray of light in the sun … [or] a single tiny spark in a fire" (C 72/52).

In speaking of the bliss of the soul, we are transported to the level of human, not just natural bliss. For Schelling, however, "the ideal" (spirit) has the same structure of potency as "the real" (nature). Accordingly, watery and fiery bliss have their counterparts in the realm of human spirit. To the watery bliss of all-dissolution, there corresponds "absolute cognition," or the essential cognition of the All, in which relationality and opposition disappear, and the philosopher's selfhood, too, is cast off (*abgelegt*; WS 408 [§292], PR 302/33). Absolute cognition, as Schelling defines it, is "the dissolution of spirit back into the allness of things" (WS 408 [§292]): a dispossession of the I and a

---

21. Chemically, too, fire and water go together: water serves as the "basis" (WS 262 [§168]) of the combustion process, and it is the same "consuming principle"—oxygen (WS 241 [§142])—that, in combination with hydrogen (the principle of the negation of cohesion), is operative in both water and fire.

decreation of the dirempted structure of knowledge. In the intellectual intuition of absolute identity, "what is divine within the soul" alone remains (WS 412 [§300]). This standpoint discloses precisely the pure "=" that constitutes the non-relational core of the phenomenological revolution proclaimed by the identity philosophy.

Just as the bliss of fire is the bliss of all-dissolution considered from the side of activity—or as an active all-consumption of the world—so, too, absolute cognition (water) grounds absolute agency (fire). To the phenomenological revolution, there corresponds a revolutionary agency as *the bliss of the immediate enactment of what is divine*. Generally, agency (*Handeln*) is for Schelling an acting out of one's concept: every being *does* or *enacts* what it *is*. In absolute cognition, however, the soul is not a finite self, but one with the divine—and so, at the level of agency, the soul enacts the one divine being without any care for the divisions of the world, for its own selfhood, or for what is sensible or even possible. An agency that is absolutely free or blissful springs (*quillt*) immanently from the divine, without any "alien mediation" (WS 415–416 [§304], UV 472/378). Such is for Schelling virtue (*Tugend*) or holiness, which he distinguishes from a commandment (*Gebot*) or ought (*Sollen*) as what externally dictates, and from any intention (*Absicht*), telos, or choice (*Wahl*). For this blissful agency, there is no external moral law, only the divine "love, passion, and beauty" (WS 434 [§314]). At the standpoint of bliss, absolute knowledge and absolute virtue immediately coincide. This is the true ethical principle: to intellectually intuit and enact what is unconditioned or what cannot be conditioned by the world.

In 1804, Schelling calls virtue "the highest resoluteness for what is right, without any choice" (WS 429 [§310])—a formulation repeated in the 1809 *Freedom* essay (FS 159/57). This immanent refusal of choice signals a divine indifference, in which one does not act *as* human, but lets the All act in and through oneself. To enact this indifference, as Schelling further explains in 1810, is to let the impersonally divine "act in you" or to "act as a holy man" (SPV 166/235). In this state, the soul is a totality, blissfully complete in itself, so that virtue, as the immediate expression of that totality, operates here without any deliberation or any regard for the world. This state is atemporal in the sense of being without relation to the world's temporality or regime of reproduction, simply enacting what is divine.

Consumed as in fire or dissolved as in water, the soul in bliss does not negotiate or construe dialectical relationships with the world; it intervenes in it. The agency of the virtuous person, whose soul is in bliss, is indifferent to the world while being operative *in* it. It is an absolute inoperativity that becomes operative *as such*, while remaining immanently non-relational and nonproductive. Such an agency may appear impossible from the point of view of our worldly relations and entanglements, yet this is exactly the point: to cut through the world's logic of possibility, and to enact bliss as what is impossible yet real, much more real than the world itself. The "holy man" is akin to a fire that, as the power of the absolutely real, burns down the enclosures of the world and reveals forcefully the one common being that the world forecloses. In both nature and spirit, fire is a magical agency in the Schellingian sense of "magic" as decoupled from voluntarism or subjectivism: it is the enacted power of bliss breaking through the chains of alienation, and indifferentiating the divisions that the world imposes on bliss. Only in one's dissolution— in the dissolution of one's selfhood—can one shine like divine lightning, illumining the one blissful being. To be holy is to be the immediate carrier of divine agency, of the cleansing fire of God that no diremption can withstand. Like all fire, this divine fire can spread from soul to soul, engendering a blissful agency in common, on which one could base a Schellingian conception of revolutionary collectivity as a covenant of those whose spirit is holy— of those who have no relation to the world or even to each other as particular individuals, but only faithfulness to the divine idea, a faithfulness in which they act as one. Considered in its impossible purity, the revolutionary cause demands precisely a combination of the highest indifference and non-relation with the a-worldly fire of "love, passion, and beauty," with which the revolutionary collective burns.

Grasped as water and fire, Schellingian bliss reveals itself to be not an expression of order or harmony (concepts that are theodical in character), even if Schelling often wants to associate order and harmony with bliss. The enactment of bliss is, rather, a total indifferentiation, a divinely indifferent storm of water and fire.[22] In this divine storm, all hierarchy and not-yet are dissolved and the order of the world is disclosed as a secondary, illusory structure that has no power of its own, but whose potency comes solely from partitioning and appropriating the underlying power of bliss. Only in this absolute indifferentiation, as responding to the call of bliss as a call of revolt against the world of particularity and enclosure, a call breaking through the prison walls of the world, does the soul become one with the common chorus of the All, singing Romantically with the ocean and the fire, and inhabiting the one bliss-in-common against the alien mediation of the world. What is disclosed

---

22. The apocalyptic conjunction of water and fire in Schelling thus combines the biblical imagery of the deluge and the fire of the Last Judgment, purging the world's wickedness.

in the bliss of an absolute letting-be without domination or possession is the all-oneness of being, the one immanence prior to the world. This bliss is not transcendent, it is what underlies the world ("according to the viewpoint of true philosophy," writes Schelling in a rejection of hierarchy within bliss, "God is not the highest," but simply absolute oneness; WS 116/150 [§8]). Bliss persists *below* the imposition of the world and erupts materially *against* it; and to persist in and with bliss is to dwell at the standpoint of antagonism that precedes the world and refuses to reconcile itself with it.

Such is Schelling's way of thinking bliss apocalyptically in the now, against what Balthasar has aptly termed "the curse of infinite approximation,"[23] or what Schelling critiques as "merely an endless approximation of the absolute" (ANP 134 [§215]). If I emphasize so strongly this dimension of the identity philosophy, it is because it offers a singular post-Revolutionary Romantic vision of a revolution in perception and agency that is unbound to the world and antagonistic to the logics of modernity, while emerging out of the late eighteenth-century moment of modernity's crisis. Although one should not read this as a conscious critique (especially given his justification of modern colonialism to be considered below), Schelling's opposition during the early 1800s to *the enclosure of being* can be read as a powerful critique of the partitioning of the earth by the modern subject and the intensified capitalist enclosure during this period—enclosure that is premised on the modern logics of self-assertion, objectification, and possession qua appropriation, all of which are annihilated in bliss. The standpoint of bliss insists that the earth and the All must not be enclosed, since thereby the plenum of the All is obscured. This abundant plenum is not something transposed into an indefinite future. It is already there, and needs to be uncovered and inhabited as such, without being subjected to the imperatives of futurity and production through which the alienated structure of reality is reproduced. Intellectual intuition does not transport one to a Platonic realm beyond. It re-visions *this* reality as an immediate plenitude that the world converts into division and scarcity. In this, a Schellingian critique of political economy may be said to consist: in refusing to view reality in terms of the primacy of scarcity over abundance and the individual over the common.

The radicality of this vision is such that its spirit may be taken to reappear in such thinkers as Pierre-Joseph Proudhon or the early ("Romantic") Marx. In his 1844 manuscripts in particular, Marx understands communism

---

23. Balthasar, *Der deutsche Idealismus*, 232.

not least as a phenomenological revolution. Under the regime of private property, he maintains, human feelings and perceptions—from sight and touch to love—are filtered through the lens of self-assertion, appropriation, and objectification. Our perception is inverted and alienated under capitalism: we view the world of objects (to be produced, appropriated, consumed) as the true horizon of reality, calling only that *ours* which we possess as object. Communism, by contrast, entails a "complete emancipation" of perception and an undoing of self-assertive selfhood. It is for Marx a total re-visioning of reality: the very senses of the one who *lives in common* become transformed, as do the notions of wealth and plenty. From the socialist standpoint, the being of humanity and of nature is revealed to be the one plenum, and "the eye," that is, our sight, becomes *essential*, so that in each object, too, we see what is one with our common essence and not what is possessively "mine." This is also a vision of what Schelling calls absolute identity, dissolving the egoism of the self and freeing nature from the imperative of "mere utility."[24] Although in Marx this vision carries a more humanist and less natural-philosophical tone, it is imbued with the same antagonistic impulse that one finds in the identity philosophy: the impulse that, by 1844, becomes much less discernible in Schelling himself. In this manner, the antagonism inherent in the ideas of bliss and the one common being survives, transformed, into the time of the consolidated capitalist modernity that is the mid-nineteenth century.

3.2.2. The Earth against the Sun: Cosmos and History

The identity philosophy ultimately defers bliss to a distant future, inscribing it in a cosmic-historical not-yet. This deferral occurs through Schelling's conception of temporality as that through which the immediate world-annihilation in bliss is mediated into a gradual becoming-more-blissful of the world. History arises for Schelling from the standpoint of potency as that of the fragmentation of the phenomenal All. If A^1 (gravity) is the potency of space, A^2 (light) is that of processuality, and therefore of time. A^3 (organism) expresses the fact that everything in the All exists within the one "organic" space-time of the All's overarching differentiation and re-collection. Generally, temporality for Schelling is the material processuality of a form of being—its going through the process of change, or "its own life" (WS 206 [§§110–111]). Since the structure of potency is nested and recapitulative, the

---

24. Marx and Engels, *Collected Works*, vol. 3, 299–306.

temporality of a part of a larger relational whole is subordinated to the temporality of this whole. Accordingly, the one universal temporality is the temporality of the universe, the processual life of the All that is distributed among all particular beings—and this is precisely cosmic history.

What Schelling configures as the earth's self-assertion against the sun is also a historical process that exceeds the present state of the solar system, and that includes the history of humanity on the earth. In giving rise to the human, the All generates the "potenceless image of potenceless identity," the highest indifference point between the real and the ideal: the human is the only being capable of developing philosophy and science and grasping the totality of the All (WS 375 [§259]). As the cosmic indifference point, the human is not bound to the earth. In the 1804 *Philosophy and Religion*, Schelling envisions humanity's future existence "on higher stars," a being "less subordinate to matter": a cosmic "palingenesis" of the human soul (PR 319/49).[25] Even in its present dirempted state, the human is at once "the organ of the earth" and "the organ of the sun," the highest "connecting" being (WS 376 [§259])—a being whose current dirempted condition reflects that of the solar system, and which constitutes the real-ideal organ through which the All cognizes itself. As the organ of the earth, the human is part of the earth's own life: "Like every planet, the earth is the identity not only of everything that is on it [presently], but also of everything that was and that will be" (WS 365 [§244]), including humanity in its past, present, and (terrestrial) future. The earth strives to be an All unto itself, and humanity falls into the orbit of this (relative) All, encircling the globe in a circumnavigational movement.

However, humanity is *also* the organ of the sun, with which the earth exists in conflict. In keeping with his cosmological theory of the ur-sun, Schelling postulates the original oneness of the earth and the sun, followed by their separation and the rigidification (*Erstarrung*) of the earth (PR 315/46). Thereby, the earth proceeds to claim a selfhood for itself—a selfhood that is in all beings connected to rigidity (*Starrheit*). Torn away from the ur-sun, the earth strives to claim the divine solar fire for itself, concealing this fire under its rigid planetary shell so as to make its own separate life possible. In its Promethean self-assertion, the earth turns solar power into its own dark ground so that terrestrial being can develop. This "eternal fire" remains sealed (*verschlossen*) in the earth's core (FD 230), manifesting itself in the

---

25. This idea was widespread in eighteenth-century thought, and Schelling may have been influenced here by, among others, François Hemsterhuis and J. G. Herder. On Hemsterhuis's cosmic vision of humanity, see Chepurin, "Theodicy across Scales."

earthquakes and volcanic eruptions that disturb the planet's rigidity. It is, as it were, the fiery remnant of a geo-cosmic past when the earth was one with the sun. In a typical Schellingian logic of inversion, planetary selfhood begins with a negation or particularization of the solar essence in order to subordinate this essence to itself—so that what was primary in the sun (i.e., fire) becomes secondary and concealed in the earth. Thereby, however, the power of solar bliss continues to operate not only from without, but *from within* the earth as that upon which the earth's planetary selfhood lives and feeds.

The human condition and the terrestrial history of humanity reflect this cosmic conflict, so that global humanity is itself split, as it were, between the dominion of the sun and that of the earth. The Christian-moderns are, as Schelling calls them, the "children of the earth" (VEM 327). Modern consciousness, or the self-assertive I, presupposes the structure of the general Christian contradiction, and thus alienation or *Abfall* from the divine, just as, cosmically, the earth is fallen away from the sun and strives to assert itself. In the fabled past, after the earth was separated from the sun, a "higher species"—Schelling speculates—lived on this earlier, "milder" (i.e., less rigid) earth. Originally, these "primordial beings" had been one with God, perhaps inhabiting the sun. This angelic or spiritual species (*Geistergeschlecht*) possessed "in an unconscious glory" the true cognition of the All (PR 315/46). Theirs was, in other words, an immediate magical cognition, which human reason now strives to *consciously* reach.

At some point following the Fall, these spiritual beings found themselves on the earth, from which they later "disappeared." It was these "higher natures"—arguably, Schelling's take on the fallen angels or the biblical giants—who were the "spiritual educators" of the nascent humankind.[26] This is, Schelling maintains, the only hypothesis that can explain how "the human as it now appears" could first have its reason "awakened," as well as the "common origin of all arts, sciences, religions, and legal institutions." It is from the shattering of this originally unified angelic wisdom that pagan polytheism, the epoch of the scattering of the human mind, originated. The humans at the present stage of their evolution continue to be a residue (*Residuum*) of these spiritual beings and a "lower potency" in comparison to them: the heavier, more rigid kind of being, the lower remnant of a higher chemical process that formed the primordial beings' materiality, which must have been closer to fire

---

26. Schelling thus may be read as taking up the old idea of the angelic origin of human culture; cf. Pseudo-Dionysius, "Celestial Hierarchy," 157.

than our present body.[27] The development of humanity marked, simultaneously, "the gradual deterioration of the earth"—that is, its rigidification and growing selfhood, marking the planet's descent into external materiality and corresponding to humankind's increasing independence from, and oblivion of, its solar origin (PR 314–316/45–46).

For all of its fantastic character, we would do well to tarry with this theocosmic vision of human past because it tells us something crucial regarding the way Schelling envisions humanity's present and future. Global humanity is for him still in development, and this development cannot be disentangled from the history of the earth. It is as though Schelling ascended here to a higher cosmic scale from which to consider the trajectory of human history, identical for him with the evolution of humanity as a species and with the development of human consciousness. Looking at history from the cosmic vantage, the identity philosopher can see that the present state of humanity and the earth is defined predominantly by their fallenness, so that, while there is in humanity the possibility for the perfect universal reason that would transcend this terrestrial condition, this reason is not yet actualized. However, the philosopher also sees that this joint fallen condition of humanity and the earth is *necessary*: it is a necessary stage in the evolution of the solar system, which, like everything in the All, develops through self-assertion and differentiation and must go through particularization and division to attain a higher oneness-in-differentiation. "The I" or "I-ness" is both "the universal principle of finitude," or "principle of fallenness," and the necessary basis of universal reconciliation (*Versöhnung*), reunification, and return (*Rückkehr*) at a higher level (PR 300–301/30–31). When Schelling speaks of human history as manifesting a higher necessity with regard to which empirical history is a mere "instrument" (*Werkzeug*; VM 123/88), this necessity is for him cosmic, too: it is dictated by the one law of (the unfolding of) universal nature that "works in nature and in history, determining the life of the whole and the destiny of each part" (WS 360 [§238]).

This cosmic viewpoint engenders Schelling's *planetary and cosmic legitimation of the modern age*, including the colonial violence that is constitutive of global Western-centric modernity: specifically, the European conquest and extermination of the indigenous South American peoples who still worshiped the sun and were thus a scattered remnant of humanity's solar past

---

27. The image of "residue" may allude to an intermixture between this "higher species" and humans, and thus to the story of giants, "the sons of God," impregnating "the daughters of men" from Genesis 6:4.

(with South America coinciding for Schelling with the geographical point of the highest influence of the sun over the earth). The respective passages that Schelling writes in 1802 constitute, significantly, his first explicit justification of European colonialism and thus his first theodical legitimation of the post-1492 world of the global:

> There [i.e., in South America], an immediate instinct taught the natives, for the first time, to worship the sun, just as the earth, subjected from within to fiercest convulsions, was proving its independence. The eruptions of primordial fire, too, mark this spot as a hearth of life.... The subjugation and destruction, through European violence [*Gewalt*], of those peoples that were formed under the influences of the sun has a similar necessity as the first directedness of the earth's individuality against the sun: it was a victory of the children of the earth over the children of the sun. (FD 230, VEM 327)

For Schelling, the modern age is the peak of the earth's self-assertion against the sun, and so, from this perspective, the victory of "the children of the earth" over "the children of the sun" (the self-designation of the Incas, to which Schelling here alludes) is a necessary reflection, in the realm of the history of spirit, of the formation of the earth's independent planetary individuality. Human, planetary, and cosmic history are for Schelling *one* in the strongest sense. Strikingly, he takes the modern European subject, which asserts itself by striving to become the master of reality, and which develops the principle of I-ness to the highest degree, to carry the earth's own struggle and striving.

For Schelling, even in its violent expansion, modernity is driven, consciously or not, by a higher mission: to unify humanity. It is something of an idealist axiom for him (reiterated in his later philosophy of mythology) that the scattering of humanity into different cultures and religions is also a scattering of consciousness, and the universalizing promise of Christianity, merging with the post-Revolutionary promise of modernity, consists in the re-collection of consciousness into a higher oneness. Already in 1794, Schelling speaks of the awakening demand in humanity (by which he means European humanity as the vanguard of history) "to finally reach a oneness of knowledge, faith, and will," claiming thereby its "allotted" destiny so as to "heal the evils of humanity" (UFP 299–300/55). This (Christian-modern) universalizing and theodical ideal of reconciliation qua salvation ("to heal," *heilen*, also invokes "salvation," *Heil*) stays with him throughout his life. As striving to become a unified All unto itself, the earth itself demands the unity of humanity as its organ of self-consciousness, and this demand can be realized only under the aegis of the Christian-modern world. Unlike "pagan" sun worship, Christianity is for Schelling the true religion of light and universality, which, in its proclamation of "the cross [as] the sign of world-conquest" (PK 160/58), is also the enemy of all false solar cults such as that of the Incas. Humanity may be fragmented, yet these fragments must be reassembled into a oneness of consciousness and oneness of knowledge, and this is the Christian-modern mission.

The fact that the reassembling or "reconciliation" of humanity is so violent does not disturb Schelling: from the standpoint of potency, reality *is* conflict and battle, and this natural-philosophical vision applies equally to human history. From the scientific perspective, too, the unification of humanity can be premised solely on the universalization of (Christian-)modern consciousness: of modern science and philosophy, whose task it has been precisely to develop the true universal standpoint, the task that Schelling's identity system is meant to complete. Just as Novalis proclaims in his 1799 essay "Christianity, or Europe" that it is "one part of the [human] species," the European, that has awakened for universal spiritual life and sets the course toward "a new history [and] new humanity,"[28] so for Schelling too, the Christian-modern subject is the carrier of the planetary future. Although Schelling often critiques the deficiencies of modern alienated subjectivity and knowledge, it is still for him *through* this subjectivity and knowledge that the path to the promised future leads. This, too, is an operation of theodicy: a legitimation of the negativity and disunity of the present as that through which the salvific future of oneness is to be attained.

In the Christian-modern world, the history of consciousness thus reaches for Schelling its present apex, and it is, paradoxically, through the Christian-modern subject's very enclosure and appropriation of the globe that the subject re-collects the global into a "higher" oneness. The victory over the children of the sun is the victory of the present and future over the past and of true philosophy, religion, and science over error. That the modern subject's *theoretical* claim to universal reality, and to the standpoint of universality, doubles as the *practical* claim of modernity's expansion illustrates well Blumenberg's observation that modern self-assertion is a practical, not just theoretical, program of mastering the world.[29] For Schelling during his

---

28. Novalis, *Philosophical Writings*, 147.

29. Blumenberg, *Legitimacy*, 208–209.

identity-philosophical period, the earth itself is the driving geo-cosmic force behind this program, mobilizing humanity as its own organ and instrument in the battle against the sun. This cosmological vision is important for grasping the stakes of Schelling's identity philosophy, and its neglect in scholarship can be explained, I believe, not only by its unabashedly speculative character but also by the prevailing modern tendency to separate human from natural history—the tendency that Schelling radically opposes.

3.2.3. The Sun against the Earth: The Solar Future and Divine Violence

The future, however, does not belong to the earth as such, and even as children of the earth, humans remain collectively, at the same time, the organ of the sun. Ultimately, for Schelling, there can be no victory over the sun: the sun-king cannot but prevail over the rebellious earth, which encloses and suppresses the one solar power of bliss. In the Schellingian schema of history, the opposition between the earth and the sun serves, in the end, their higher reconciliation. The modern age may at present be the highest stage in the evolution of humanity and the earth, yet this stage, too, must be overcome when humanity and the earth return to their solar essence.

At this point, Schelling's vision again becomes apocalyptic. The human remains presently bound to the earth; the essence of the human, however—just like that of the earth—remains one with the divine and with the fire concealed within the planet and breaking through in volcanic eruptions. So far, planetary history has stood under the dominance of rigid selfhood. The next epoch, then, must be one at whose peak fire and light will consume this "external" materiality, purifying it, through a chemical process of combustion, toward a higher, less rigid state. The re-collection of the earth and humanity into oneness serves ultimately the purpose of their transfiguration, through which the human will return, at a conscious level, to the higher angelic being of which it is presently a residue.[30]

---

30. Grant takes the passing reference, in a transcript of Schelling's 1830 *Introduction to Philosophy* lectures, to "a new race [*Geschlecht*] equipped with new organs of thought" (EIP 57) to imply that nature for Schelling does not culminate in the human (*Philosophies of Nature*, 13, 55). I find Grant's reference to the indicated passage to be too quick; it would seem that Schelling there retrospectively characterizes the broader spirit of the time ("es lag in der Zeit," he says) of which his identity philosophy was a part, and which called for overcoming human alienation from nature by way of developing a true philosophy of nature. The "new race" in question is for Schelling arguably *still humanity*, if in a higher potency (not unlike in Novalis's invocation of "a new humanity"): a humanity that has regained, at a higher level, its lost

"The final resolution of the conflict between the earth and the sun," Schelling prophesies, will consist "in an eruption of the eternal fire of the sun concealed within the earth." This combustion event will "not require any external condition." It will originate from within, "develop[ing] immediately out of the absolutely innermost"—that is, the earth's core—"toward a corporeality that is pure." Schelling's apocalyptic vision remains materialist-chemical: the eternal fire will impotentiate and essentialize terrestrial corporeality. This will signal nothing less than "a liberation of life from death," a liberation "of which the vulcanism of the earth, in which the central fire struggles for freedom without being able to gain it, is but a remote intimation" (FD 230). Not just volcanoes, these "preludes to the general fire" (as Thomas Burnet had called them),[31] but "every process of combustion" presents for Schelling an image of "a victory of the sun over the earth, which the former celebrates with the eruption of fire" (WS 270 [§176]). This victory will be final in the general eruption to come, leading to the (external) death of the earth through which our planet is meant to gain a purer materiality: a solar explosion out of the planetary depths, annihilating the *nomos* of the earth as based on rigidity and egoism.

In this prophecy, one may discern the modern cosmic anxiety about the perishability of the earth and its possible consumption by the sun, an anxiety that is, however, resolved by Schelling in a vision of a more blissful being that is "less subordinate to matter." That this being arrives from within the earth is significant: it as though the earth, in a kind of kenosis, voluntarily gave up its self-assertion and submitted to the sun. "Every combustion process," Schelling writes, "is a sacrifice of individuality," and the same is true of the earth's future transfiguration qua conflagration (WS 270 [§176]). Given the weight of the world that will have accumulated by then, is it any wonder that bliss will arrive as the all-annihilative fire, tearing all of this down—this earth grown old, this rigid terrestrial body?

In Schelling's so-called "Spring Fragment," which was presumably intended to be a part of *Clara*, the transfiguration of the world in divine fire is proclaimed in similar terms—and as involving not only the earth, but the entire cosmos (*Weltbau*):

---

immediate cognition. One may indeed say with Grant that, for Schelling, "man is necessarily transitional," yet this "progressivity" (55) does not imply an abandonment of the vision of humanity, in its entire historical metamorphosis, as the privileged site of the All's self-cognition.

31. Burnet, *Sacred Theory*, vol. 2, 78.

Indeed, not only ourselves, the whole of nature craves God, from whom it was originally taken. And even though it may be currently subjected to the law of externality, . . . this solid structure of the universe will too dissolve into the spiritual. However, it is only this external form that will disintegrate. The inner force and essentiality will persist, so as to be revealed in [this] new transfiguration [*Verklärung*]. The divine fire, which rests sealed within [nature], will one day gain the upper hand, consuming everything that was introduced into the truly inner solely through the violence of external suppression. Then, returning to its initial state, [nature] will no longer be the self-assertive agency holding the divine forces, as it were, captive within itself—and, in this purified being, the spiritual and the divine will freely reunite. (F 274–275/80–81)

What is concealed (*verschlossen*) will be revealed (*offenbart*), this revelation cutting through the world and consuming it as in divine fire. The universe originates from divine light, and into divine light it must return. This is a familiar utopian loop: primordial bliss, the falling away from it, and the (longed-for) universal return. This loop defines the temporality of the phenomenal All. World-annihilation is thus re-mediated into a cosmic historical not-yet. This eschatological cosmic tale is a tale of the deferral of bliss, but also of its ultimate arrival: a positive Romantic-apocalyptic expectation that characterizes Schelling's thinking of bliss starting from around 1800, and that is distinct from what we saw as the infinite postponement of bliss in his 1795 metaphysics.

This entire cosmic narrative may also be read as an account of the condition of modern reason. That the human is at once "the organ of the earth" and "the organ of the sun" marks a conflict within reason between itself as particular and as universal. The earth is the cradle of humanity, yet modern reason wants to assert itself as truly universal and not merely terrestrial—as a central organ of the universe's self-cognition, or as capable of cognizing the entire expanse and evolution of the All. One may recognize in this the central ambition of modern philosophy and science, an ambition that continues to drive current proponents of space colonization and active evolution. Reason needs to master or subjugate the earth, so that, having become the one who has actually mastered the globe and in whom planetary history thus culminates, reason can affirm itself as something higher than a contingent and transient terrestrial product. Reason wants to prove itself to be the *necessary* and *highest* planetary being; yet even that is not enough. As universal, reason cannot limit itself to being bound to the earth but seeks to transcend the terrestrial condition. In the very meta-standpoint of universality inherent in modern reason, there is inscribed a conflict between the terrestrial and the universal. This conflict is what Schelling speculatively narrativizes, legitimating it from a cosmic vantage as the conflict that defines planetary and human history, and in which the universal, as reason's true essence, must in the end prevail. If this necessary conflict manifests itself, inter alia, by way of colonial genocide, then this is, for Schelling, merely an inevitable shadow-side of the development of reason as truly universal: after all, it is not coincidental that the so-called age of discovery—of European exploration and colonial conquest—is also the foundational age of discovery in modern science. To generate $A = A$ out of $A = B$, the universal needs to make the particular one with itself, be it dialectically or, if necessary, by force. From the vantage of the absolute future, the result is the same. In this way, at the standpoint of potency, the violence of history is theodically justified.

Of course, bliss also carries with it a violence of its own. The violence of the divine is absolute: it is an all-dissolution and all-consumption, the bliss of the world's annihilation. Schelling seeks to downplay this violence by configuring it as liberation, transfiguration, or a return to God for which the world longs. Still, the violence is unmistakable, and Schelling knows this, speaking of "the violence of fire" or "the violence of the consuming principle" (WS 269–270 [§176]). One can discern in the identity philosophy a meta-opposition between two kinds of violence: *external* (or worldly) and *divine*. The world is a structure of violent conflict. Its violence is that of enclosure, suppression, and self-assertion—exemplified by European colonialism and the entrapment of divine light by the earth. "Rigid selfhood" seeks to "suppress" the one common being (WS 298 [§196]). To this, another agency is opposed: the striving of finitude for bliss. This striving is the operativity of absolute identity itself, caught in the nets of finitude and seeking to break free. The divine essence seeks to counteract the violence of selfhood, to dissolve or indifferentiate all conflict. This cannot, however, be done without *breaking through* the enclosure of finitude, an activity that itself inevitably appears violent—as the violence of universal emancipation, the freeing of the solar essence from captivity, the consumption of the divisions that make up the world, the tearing down of all walls, all property, all subjugation. As the operativity of absolute identity, this violence is, in truth, absolute indifference: it annihilates finitude not because it regards itself as opposed to it—but because all particularity is *nichtig*, a mere nothingness, before its power. The deferral of bliss in Schelling serves not least the goal of attenuating this divine violence, so it can be re-mediated into the not-yet of terrestrial and cosmic history. By combining the standpoints of absolute identity and potency, the identity system thus plays the two kinds of violence against each other, turning them into the two poles through which the phenomenal All differentiates and unfurls itself. Thereby Schelling universalizes the constitutive tension between bliss (as world-annihilation) and theodicy (as world-justification), inscribing this tension into the heart not just of the Christian-modern trajectory, but of cosmic history as a whole.

3.3. Everything in Its Place and Time: An Aesthetic Cosmic Theodicy

Content to come, content to go,
  Content to wrestle or to race,
Content to know or not to know,
  Each in his place;

Lord, grant us grace to love Thee so
  That glad of heart and glad of face
At last we may sit, high or low,
  Each in his place;

Where pleasures flow as rivers flow,
  And loss has left no barren trace,
And all that are, are perfect so,
  Each in his place.
    —CHRISTINA ROSSETTI

3.3.1. Theodical Indifference and the Beauty of It All

One may ask the obvious question: Does Schelling consider the European act of colonial genocide against the South Americans, which we saw him justify as part of terrestrial history, to be an act of evil? Within the framework of the identity philosophy, the answer to this question is a resounding no. In theory, Schelling could have admitted the evil of colonial conquest and extermination even while justifying it as necessary, or as a necessary evil inevitable at this stage of planetary history. This, too, would have been a theodical argument. However, the identity philosophy goes further. As part of its complete re-visioning of reality, the identity system wants to *see no evil*.

Here too, the interplay between the various standpoints we have traced is crucial. At the immanent standpoint of absolute identity, there is no evil, but also no world-justification, because all the divisions and conflicts of the world are here immediately annihilated. From this standpoint, one cannot proclaim European colonial violence to be necessary; on the contrary, it is de-absolutized and shown to be but an imposition on the one common being. At the standpoint of potency, things are more complex. This standpoint re-mediates the universe's apparent unblissfulness into a vision of reconciliation, and of the omnipotence of God or the All. From the standpoint of potency, it is not unblissfulness that is primary, but the light-trace of (the absolute light and power of) bliss within all being. Thus, although there is an original transgression (the *Abfall*) inscribed in the universe, there is no evil or sin since the agency of all that is consists in reflecting and approximating bliss. To *act* for a finite being is to enact one's concept (*Begriff*) or one's relational *what*, which defines the conceptual position or place through which this being is embedded (*begriffen*) in the All. From this perspective, all conceptual positions are necessary, and none are evil, since all serve equally the purpose of the All's unfolding. It is only the false philosophical standpoint of finite fallen cognition—the standpoint of fallenness "for itself," redoubling in consciousness the original transgression—that takes the universe to be evil.

For the identity philosophy, one could say, all evil is *the evil of false cognition*.[32] There is no sin or evil except through human reason, or through reason's adoption of the standpoint of fallen knowledge, from which things appear to be essentially separated and not essentially one. The sin (*Sünde*) of modern philosophy is to think of this finite "world of nothingness" as the true reality (WS 424 [§307]). Modern dirempted cognition adopts the standpoint of rigid selfhood (the I) as primary, and it is this standpoint that constitutes the fallenness of modernity. "Finitude," as the subordination of the universal to the particularity of selfhood, and thus as transgression and fallenness, "is the punishment unto itself" (PR 309/40, 318/48). This punishment consists precisely in the rigidity of selfhood (including the philosopher's selfhood), which

---

32. The evil of, and evil emerging from the standpoint of, erroneous cognition includes moral evil, suffering, and imperfection. These appear only from the point of view of reflection, or I-ness taken for itself, and disappear at the true "divine" standpoint. One might argue that, thereby, Schelling preserves the idea of moral evil at the meta-level, since the standpoint of reflection is apparently sinful. However, this standpoint is itself necessary from the divine point of view, and thus immediately redeemed or reconciled by true philosophy. This is in line both with Schelling's theodical justification of the Fall, and with his simultaneous criticism and legitimation of modernity as the age whose task it is to develop the fallen standpoint of the self-assertive I—the task that is providentially necessary.

dims the absolute light of bliss. Thus, all finite beings and finite dirempted cognition, to the extent that they persist in their finitude, find themselves removed from the bliss of the All. The identity philosopher, however, sees that although the light may be dimmed and fragmented, it is still the light of the one bliss—and the universe, this all-organism, already *is* blissful. This is a Romantic axiom, too: there is nothing evil in nature, and it is only insofar as the human tears itself away from all-oneness that evil appears.

In speaking of good and evil, we seem to have transitioned from the realm of nature into the ideal or moral realm. For Schelling, however, there is no division between the two, or between natural and moral evil. What we call "evil" is simply what appears lower or relatively more imperfect, in nature and in spirit alike. In truth, nothing is evil, since all finite beings are one with God. Just as "finitude is nothing positive" (PR 319/49), so evil, too, is but a shadow, and the world of evil is that of Plato's cave, out of which true philosophy leads. To see something as imperfect or deficient, Schelling reasons, is to compare (*vergleichen*) it with other things and to judge it to "lack something that should belong to its nature." Thus, in Schelling's example (for which he credits Spinoza), a blind person is compared to the general concept of the human and deemed to be lacking. To judge a form of being in this manner is to focus on imperfection (*Unvollkommenheit*): on either physical or moral imperfection, or "vice." This, however, is the wrong approach, for thereby the *necessary*, and even divine, character of blindness is obscured. Blindness, too, has its necessary place within what Schelling calls "divine order" or "the order of nature." If there were no blindness, the world would not be what it is. "Just as it necessarily belongs to the essence of a square that it is not round," Schelling insists (by "essence," he means here the relational essence or concept), "so, in the case of the blind man, it necessarily belongs to his essence that he does not see." "For," Schelling continues, "if it were compatible with the order of nature that he could see, then he *would* actually see." Evil or imperfection no longer even appears to the identity philosopher as privation (*Privation*), but as a necessary position within the All or an affirmative part of divine order, a part expressing the all-affirmative power of the universe (WS 417–419 [§305]). Thereby, through a kind of philosophical naturalization, everything is justified as in its proper place and as enacting its relative *what*, or concept, within the relational network of the cosmic whole.

The standpoint of potency is a relatively indifferent standpoint—and the (cognitive and ethical) attitude that recognizes the necessity of the whole is likewise associated by Schelling with indifference. With regard to what appears as imperfection, he argues that the appropriate term to use is not "privation" but "negation," understood as an indifferent statement of fact: to say that blindness is the negation of sight is not to judge blindness as lacking but to claim that sight does not belong to the concept of the "blind man." If someone is blind, sight is simply not part of what the person is, and that is all (WS 418 [§305]). Given that all apparent evil is grasped by Schelling as relative imperfection, this example can be expanded to include colonial extermination: if the South Americans are slaughtered by the Europeans, this, too, belongs to the order of nature and should be contemplated with indifference. For Schelling, the American indigenous peoples had their place within the world-order and continue to have their place *as* this order's exterminated or conquered and as belonging to the relatively darker historical past of humanity. The *deus sive natura* is indifferent to what humans may perceive as evil or suffering, and indifference is thus the highest attitude the philosopher can adopt, too. One may see in this a Stoic move, beneath which, however, lurks the indifference of the modern post-Copernican universe—over and against which Schelling seeks a justification of this universe in its apparent non-relation to our categories of good and evil. In this register, the cruelty of indifference and its absence of care are very different from the indifferent divine violence that dissolves the world as in water or consumes it as in fire. Schellingian indifference is an ambivalent attitude, which can be directed against the world or used to justify it.

This ambivalence of indifference, I would suggest, is an ambivalence inscribed in the modern universe itself as it simultaneously fascinates and troubles the Romantic imagination.[33] On the one hand, the contingency of the universe means that any particular cosmic world or form of life can be annihilated seemingly without reason, or for any contingent reason, and is ultimately groundless and without any "higher" justification. Not even the human as rational creature is from this standpoint a necessary kind of being: just as humanity appeared, so it might disappear, and the universe would not care. The universe de-absolutizes any world and any form of life. On the other hand, every star system, planet, or form of life in the universe *is* the universe itself, and expresses the power of the universe as the source of all being, and of all relational configurations of various kinds of beings, across the universal expanse. From this perspective, since every form of being has been produced by the universe as *this* kind of being in *this* particular place, this form of being is relationally necessary precisely where it is, and nothing

---

33. See further Gode-von Aesch, *Natural Science*, and Chepurin, "Reading Novalis and the Schlegels."

can really be out of place. If a form of life becomes extinct, this, too, is relationally necessary, and may be seen as conditioned by the universe as a whole. From this point of view, every conflict and every war—colonial war, too—is a cosmic war, since it is through the relative conflict between various forces, material forms, and forms of life that the universe dynamically evolves. The tension between these two perspectives within the one universe, mapping onto the tension between bliss and theodicy, is what the identity system seeks to hold together.

At the standpoint of potency, what appears evil is thus revealed to be, in truth, necessary and good from the perspective of the All. The identity philosopher theodically relates the *what* of every being, including the kind of being that one might judge to be deficient or evil, to its necessary place in the universal whole. This operation is redemptive: the transgression of the Fall (*Abfall*) is thereby itself redeemed or pardoned, freed from guilt (*entschuldet*). In his finitude, "a man who acts wrongly" is relegated to "the lower degree of reality" or intensity: the wrongdoer is, as it were, darker or less luminous than the one who does good. However, this does *not* mean that the wrongdoer is evil. "Considered absolutely," Schelling proclaims, "this man too, as a member of the universe [*Glied der Welt*], is necessary, and from this point of view he is not punishable but even excusable [*entschuldbar*]." The analogy that Schelling employs here is typical of his naturalistic theodicy: "The stone," he writes, "can also be excused for not being human, and nonetheless it is condemned to be a stone and to suffer what the stone suffers." Similarly, the "weakness [of] whoever cannot tame his desires and passions" is "necessary if it is *considered in its place* [*Stelle*]." It is cosmically necessary, because "all degrees of perfection from the lowest to the highest must have their place in the universe" (WS 420–421 [§305]). The ambivalence of this vision runs deeper than this example suggests. What if we consider not someone who inflicts but one who suffers wrong? According to this logic, this person, too, must suffer as the stone suffers—just as the South American peoples are cosmically condemned to suffer at the hands of the Europeans.

Positionality itself is a theodical logic, engendering a theodical *indifference of world-acceptance*, which regards everything as necessary from the perspective of divine order. "The doctrine according to which everything in the universe is what it is through God, and that, therefore, nothing is in truth imperfect before God," Schelling says, "contributes to a serene and calm life." The wrongdoer, too, while relegated to a lower level of perfection, is acquitted from a God's-eye view, since "at the same time in this very level [of perfection] the wrongdoer belongs to the totality of the world-phenomenon, which we must honor in him" (WS 421 [§305]). The simultaneous naturalization and divinization of evil, undoing it *as* evil, is "the fruit of a universal philosophy that leads the human back to nature," and to a "serene contemplation of the human and the universe" (WS 418 [§305]). Indifference becomes here a *Duldsamkeit*, "tolerance" or "forbearance," and even an honoring and acceptance of the world: "true forbearance" consists in "conceiving of all things as contained within the totality [of the All], and respecting them as being in their place" (WS 421 [§305]). This includes their being in their time, too, since the time of a particular being is its processuality as part of the processuality of the whole. Thus, a human being's *time* is this being's relative *place* within the space-time of humanity, and this applies to both an individual and a people. Following their conquest by the Europeans, the Incas no longer have a time of their own within the terrestrial process of humanity. This, too, is what Schelling means when he says that relationality is what is "annihilated in each being as it goes through time" (ANP 116–117 [§125]). The Incas may have disappeared, and the modern subject will as well, but the idea of humanity—its non-relational A = A—persists, and will persist even after humanity's possible evolution into a species inhabiting "higher stars."

We should take note of the theodical ruse in the above, whereby the annihilation of finitude, and of the very logic of place, within the pure "=" is turned by Schelling into a justification of the negativity of finitude through the logic of place or position. The blissful *simply being what it is* of every being becomes, in this theodical double vision, the (relative) *what* that determines the necessary *place* of this being in relation to the whole. In bliss as such, hierarchy and division are annihilated; in the identity philosopher's double vision, however, they are justified. All punishment is, in this way, turned into pardon—a pardon coinciding with the theodical acquittal of God from responsibility for imperfection or evil. "Serenity and calm" must take the place of the empty desire to change the world, Schelling maintains, denouncing "those who imagine themselves to be world-educators and world-improvers," and who "end up accusing the creator whose infinite fullness reveals itself in all degrees of perfection" (WS 421 [§305]).[34] Thereby the negativity of finitude is justified by Schelling as part of divine creation qua revelation, or the exhibition of the infinite in and as the totality of phenomenal being. Every agency, even what appears to be self-assertion or wrongdoing, is the agency of

---

34. "Creation" in not to be understood here in the voluntaristic sense that we will see in the later Schelling, but as the unfolding of the divine essence as what continues to underlie and power the phenomenal All.

the one substance, which acts out of each cosmic position, testifying to "the harmony of the universe." To the identity philosopher, everything, including seeming evil, reveals "the good" and follows with necessity "the order of the whole," even if only as this order's unconscious "instrument" (WS 423 [§306]; cf. WS 286 [§182]).

For the identity philosopher, all is good with the world. Finitude may be "a falling away from God," yet "it immediately turns into reconciliation," and God thereby "posits the world as a world that is perfect" (or "complete," *vollendet*; WS 435 [§315]). Outdoing Leibniz, Schelling bets on this world as not just the best possible, but the immediately perfect one. He tames the catastrophic vision of the *Abfall*, together with the conflictual and fragmented vision of the universe captured by the formula A = B, by re-mediating this vision into a cosmos of immediate harmony. In this cosmos, there is in truth no discord, decenteredness, or darkness, and even conflict is not dissonance but part of the perfect, consonant, and orderly unfolding of the absolute divine point. In its own way, this theodical outcome is radical, too. The contingency of the modern universe and the theo-cosmic shattering of bliss are transformed by Schelling into *an orderly distribution of universal place*, a formal synoptic table of the universe and divine revelation, a table in which the relative place of each form of being is quantified as the degree of its relative imbalance vis-à-vis the overarching A = A. Schelling's all-reconciliatory ambition is one with the original ambition of modern science: to resolve analytically the system of the universe. His theodical vision is one with his vision of the longed-for unity of philosophy, theology, and science. The re-commencement of modernity at a higher level implies for him a doubling-down on spiritual investment in this world as the one and only perfect universe.

The question of fallenness, however, continues to haunt this vision as what the postulation of an immediately perfect divine order of all-identity constitutively excludes or explains away. It may be formulated as the question that we will also encounter in Schelling's later thought (cf. FS 168/66): Why does the revelation of the divine essence consist in a gradual unfolding and not an *immediate* overflowing of divine bliss? Schelling's answer to this question is circular, looping through the fact of the world: because this is the way it must be for this world to exist—or because one needs to think the separation (*Absonderung, Trennung*) or falling away (*Abfall*) from absolute identity in order to think the fact of this dirempted phenomenal world. Because of fallenness, there is the rigidity of selfhood that arises out of the particularization of oneness and that *resists* or dims the immediate overflowing of universal light. This resistance, while relatively unblissful, is necessary for the world to be thinkable, since the world is thinkable only as a structure of actual twoness, not oneness. Within an immediate all-expansion of the divine essence, as Schelling points out as early as 1800, nothing would be discernible (AD 299). In a way, an immediate overflowing would be too disorderly and could not give rise to a world; nor could one here speak of a world-*order* or an orderly distribution of place. Hence, Schelling needs the fallenness of selfhood as a kind of inhibiting force so that the unfolding of the All can be gradual and orderly. This further explains why the re-collection of oneness goes for him hand in hand with its differentiation and why the development of self-assertive selfhood (including planetary and human selfhood) has, despite its negativity, a positive role in the plan of the whole.

In the *Aphorisms*, Schelling borrows in this regard a physical example from Leibnizian theodicy: what appears evil is but the inertia (*Trägheit*) of rigidity or rigid selfhood. However, this inertia, which slows down and mediates the immediacy of revelation, is nothing independent: it is a "nothingness or mere relationality" (ANP 142–143). Since relationality is what is annihilated in time, inertia is destined to be overcome, and the world is bound to reach its blissful destination—as the identity philosopher knows, therefore contemplating the not-yet of the world with indifference. This not-yet is the "successive development" of the already-perfect, already-completed creation, and the "[successively] appearing annihilation of . . . everything that does *not* belong to the idea of God" (WS 435 [§315]). Thus, the earth's relational self-assertion against the sun indexes the phenomenal not-yet, in which the earth simply has not yet transfigured its relative darkness through solar fire, or has not phenomenally caught up with itself as essentially no less divine or central than the sun.[35]

In Schelling's claim that all agency constitutes the instrument of the absolutely good, the rhetoric of instrumentality should not be overlooked. The lower may reveal the divine, but despite Schelling's insistence that the lower is valuable in itself despite its lower degree of perfection, it remains auxiliary to the higher. The lower is useful "only as an instrument in the hand of

---

35. Similarly, in *Philosophy and Religion*, the rigidification of the earth in its falling away from the sun exhibits the growing "power of the evil principle" (PR 315/46), likewise to be understood as the rigid selfhood that subordinates the universal to the particular—an inversion of true judgment (as what subordinates the particular to the universal), manifested materially in the suppression of the solar fire underneath the earth's crust. This relative or relational evil is, however, also the relational instrument of the All's self-exhibition: the All must unfold *through all possible positions*, including those we take to be evil or deficient. To recognize this is to restore true cognition and true judgment—to philosophically re-subordinate all particular self-assertive positions to the universal—and thus to reveal that there is, in truth, no evil.

the artist, which serves without knowing it, and in this service becomes worn out [*abgenutzt*] and used up [*verbraucht*]." The relatively higher, too, in turn serves the highest—God or the All—and "becomes more perfect through service" (WS 420 [§305]). This logic of instrumentality and devotion (or instrumentality *as* devotion) also flows into the stance of theodical indifference. True piety (*Frömmigkeit*), Schelling maintains, consists in a serene acceptance of the ways of the world as divine ways, in knowing one's place and calmly following (the unfolding of) the All (WS 437 [§316]).

This piety is, at the same time, an aesthetic piety, as Schelling's recourse to the figure of the artist shows: an awe at the beauty of the universe, and a poetic and prophetic contemplation that discerns the necessary unfolding of the absolute future out of the present. In his lectures on the philosophy of art from the early 1800s, the true aesthetic viewpoint coincides with that of the All as a harmonious whole. "In God," Schelling says, "the universe is formed [*gebildet*] as an absolute work of art in its eternal beauty," a beauty manifesting the "infinite intention" of God as the creator-artist and the "infinite necessity" of this intention's perfect realization (PK 128–129/31). The universe is an artwork wherein every detail, however small, is perfectly balanced and assigned its proper place in relation to the whole. *Everything has its place* is also an aesthetic principle. The apparent negativity of phenomenal reality discloses a higher, divine beauty. Every individual thing or agency, no matter its seeming imperfection or ugliness, is beautiful from the standpoint of the All: a position that divorces art from judging things to be good or bad or beautiful or ugly and connects it to divine indifference.[36] The standpoint of aesthetic-theodical indifference merges here with a Platonic-Christian aesthetic theodicy such as the one found in Augustine, who likewise claims that God is the greatest artist and that those who speak of what appears evil in nature "do not notice how splendid such things are in their own places and natures, and with what beautiful order they are disposed, and how much they contribute, in proportion to their own share of beauty, to the universe as a

---

36. Gabriel Trop suggests that this Spinozistic position is highly modern precisely because it divorces aesthetics from the binaries of "good/bad" and "beautiful/ugly," engendering "a dramatic defamiliarisation and delegitimisation of . . . normative distinctions," and opening the possibility of a "radical aestheticism . . . in which *all things* can become a source of intellectual joy." See Trop, "Spinoza," 185–189. The same may be argued with regard to Schelling—but, at least within the Schellingian framework, this position entails the claim that wrongdoing, oppression, and colonial genocide are beautiful, too. As a result, the theo-cosmic viewpoint of the beauty of *whatever thing* runs the risk of legitimating, and not delegitimating, the order of the world.

whole."[37] For Schelling as for Augustine, to deny that everything is beautiful from the viewpoint of the whole is to raise an accusation against God and against the orderly distribution of place that is the world as governed by divine providence.

The bliss of dispossession shows here its theodical flip side, too. To be according to reason is "to forgo freedom as selfhood" (WS 424 [§307]) in order to recognize the necessity inherent in the world. It is to let go of one's self and to simply let the universe be, or to let the world have its way without resistance. Self-dispossession runs the risk of being possessed by the world. In this way, paradoxically, the logic of position or place survives and is justified precisely through the philosopher's voiding of her particular place and becoming immanently one with the All. Through this operation, even more paradoxically, the philosopher *gains* her place as the part of the All that cognizes and acknowledges the necessity of the whole, becoming one not just with absolute identity in intellectual intuition, but with the not-yet of history. The philosopher asserts, with Leibniz, that the universe *is* the Garden (ANP 129 [§198])—it is just still in the process of growing, still branching out, producing life until it (ful)fills the All and rests in unity with God.

3.3.2. The Faith That Stands Still and the Christian View of the Universe

The philosopher turns thereby into a fatalist (*Fatalist*) who cognizes everything in its necessity. The philosopher, Schelling proclaims, should not press forward but *stand still*, because eternal bliss is not an object of striving or feverish progress but something that precedes all striving and must be insisted on as such, not in the sense of a return to an idealized past, but as the recognition of the divine nature of the Garden that is the All. To stand still (*zum Stehen zu kommen*) is to attain "a divine temperance through which one takes up the infinite into oneself and grounds one's life eternally" (WS 425 [§308]). It is in this standing still that heaven (*Himmel*) consists, as well as "our rebirth into the All" (WS 424 [§307]). The philosopher achieves consolation, reconciliation, and fulfillment through acknowledging the necessity of the

---

37. Augustine, *City of God*, 477 (XI.22). Augustine also likes to emphasize that, from the divine point of view, everything is set in its proper place and "activated" at its proper time, and nothing is in truth bad or deficient; see Augustine, *Confessions*, 369–371, and *City of God*, 708 (XVI.8). A key pre-Christian source for this theodicy of the All is Book X of Plato's *Laws*, where God is compared to the ideal craftsman or demiurge (902e) responsible for the perfect providential distribution of proper place within the world-whole.

course of the world, and through becoming one with the eternal calmness that counteracts the fever of the world:

> In one who has reached such a point [of standing still], true calmness is attained. Heaven arches itself over him as the transfigured image of totality, and just as the polestar shines for the mariner through the groundless depths, so the eternal identity of this point shines [for the philosopher] through all the storms and inconstancies of life. This is what calms us and elevates us forever above all the empty longing, fear, and hope: to know that it is not *we* who act, but that a divine necessity acts in us, by which we are carried to the goal, and with which nothing that proceeds from absolute freedom can conflict, since it is itself this absolute freedom. (WS 425 [§308])

This calmness is an active embrace of passivity in the broadly Stoic sense: a heroic endurance and free acceptance of cosmic necessity. This attitude equals "unconditional faith" (WS 426 [§308]) in the goal of the world. The co-imbrication of faith and the not-yet thus reappears here. Schelling distinguishes faith (*Glaube*) from hope (*Hoffnung*) because hope is not dispassionate or indifferent enough—in a way, not accepting or tolerant enough of the present state of the world.

The philosopher, in this manner, inhabits immanently the here and now: a blissful, eternal *now* that is, however, not world-annihilating but world-affirming. The end goal of the world is already reached in God, and the world has been the Garden since (before) its beginning: such is the world's an-originary origin that *persists*, coinciding with the philosopher's persistence. Through this persistence in God, "what is holy" is disclosed—through "the firm confidence [*Zutrauen*] in absolute necessity, which acts in *all*." "Only therein," Schelling continues, does "the holiness that man requires" consist (WS 426 [§308]). The figure of the "holy man," as one who acts immediately out of the divine, is thereby turned theodical. The holy person's faith becomes a "trust [*Zuversicht*] in the divine, which cancels out all choice" not by intervening in the world but by accepting the way things are (WS 429 [§310]).

In a speculative Lutheran gesture, Schelling enlists Christ (or rather, Christ as filtered through Paul) in support of this understanding of faith: "We have on our side the creator of Christianity himself, who says: not *good works* but faith brings salvation" (WS 430 [§310]; cf. Romans 3:27–28). In the context of trusting the world to bring us to our destination, the contrast between "works" and "faith" transforms faith into a doing nothing, a passivity whose character as *Zutrauen* and *Zuversicht* consists in its theodical indifference, a free giving oneself over to divine order so as to let oneself be carried by it. It is a radical passivity of world-acceptance (of accepting and legitimating the course of the world as divine), and a doing nothing that leaves the world be, *thereby* upholding it. Not only self-dispossession, but also passivity and doing nothing reveal here their theodical flip side.

Traditionally, in accounts of German idealism and Romanticism, this kind of divinization of the objective and insistence that the movement of world history reveals the divine is associated with Hegel rather than Schelling. However, over the course of this book, we have witnessed a similar theodical tendency in Schelling starting from the 1790s. This tendency finds its culmination in the identity philosophy—and, as we will see, continues into Schelling's later thought. The identity philosopher subscribes, in her own way, to the Hegelian dictum that the philosophy of history is a theodicy that discloses history to be the process of divine revelation and reconciliation. As Schelling puts it, "History itself is nothing other than the development of the reconciliation of the finite" with God, a reconciliation that "in God himself is eternal or atemporal" (WS 435 [§315]), and that coincides phenomenally with the exhibition of the divine within finitude.

This view of history returns us to what in Chapter 1 we saw as the specifically *Christian* view according to "On the Relation" and Schelling's 1802 lectures. From the broader cosmic vantage of the identity system, we can now discern the theo-cosmic role of Christianity as a view of the All in which, as we remember, cosmos is for the first time "intuited as *history*" (VM 120/83). The general Christian contradiction is not something that Christianity simply invents. It is for Schelling the true structure of the world, and the light of Christianity is what discloses the universe as the historical universe that, in truth, it had been since the beginning—it is just that the pre-Christian mind could not yet grasp it *as* historical. Modernity, too, develops this originally Christian historical standpoint, as does Schelling's own exposition of cosmic and human history. Schelling's construction of "the world" and "world history" is thus programmatically Christian-modern in character. He speaks in this regard of "the great historical orientation of Christianity" and "the higher Christian view of history" (VM 122–123/87)—"higher" compared to the ahistorical pagan view of the cosmos. Paganism and Christianity are thereby hierarchized in Schelling: paganism is inscribed as an epoch in a view of history that, as such, emerges only with Christianity. In this manner, paganism is subordinated to the Christian standpoint. Due to the Christian emphasis on the one infinite God in conjunction with the fallenness of the world, the universe is revealed in Christianity to be charged with contradiction, which drives the universe forward and endows universal history with a higher meaning qua salvation history, or the history of the finite's reconciliation with the infinite. This promise is that in which the philosopher must have faith.

For Schelling, no tension between the finite and the infinite, which would necessitate a Christocentric mediation and historical reconciliation, is present in paganism. The periodization of human history (as the history of the human consciousness of the divine) into paganism, the Christian-modern age, and the coming, more blissful epoch is itself grasped by Schelling through the doctrine of the three potencies. Paganism stands under the dominance of gravity (A^1) as the potency of the particularization of oneness, as well as the potency of material space. This explains the polytheism of pagan mythology and the proliferation of particular corporeal deities that fragments (the human consciousness of) the one divine essence and "subordinates [the divine] to finitude" (VM 120/84). With Christianity (A^2), the light of the essence breaks through material particularity and gets announced to consciousness. This is the good news that Christianity brings: the revelation of the general Christian contradiction as the true structure of universal reality to consciousness, emphasizing the opposition between the worldly and the divine. As standing under the dominance of the second potency, Christianity introduces processuality and time, and therefore history, into the human consciousness of God and the universe. Modernity, as the continuation of Christianity by the combined means of modern philosophy, religion, and science, intensifies the structure of opposition so that selfhood, abstraction, and universality can develop before their higher unification within A^3 as the "organic" epoch of reconciliation to come. In this future epoch, philosophy, religion, and science are to flow into a new immediate oneness.

It is not entirely clear whether for Schelling this epoch will be an epoch of the material transfiguration of the earth, too, or whether that event will be the beginning of an even higher cosmic history yet to follow. Either way, on the example of this tripartite division of terrestrial human history, we can see how the structure of potency engenders a logic of periodization. For Schelling, this periodizing logic—first made possible by Christianity—is truly universal because it applies to any organism, including the All. Thus, the human individual, too, develops from an immersion in particularity (childhood) via an age of opposition (adolescence) toward a higher wholeness (maturity), in which one's particularity is supposed to be subordinated to the universal such as the state, the church, or artistic, scientific, or philosophical activity. Thereby, maturity is associated in Schelling with having a socially recognized vocation, an association that is itself cosmically legitimated. In the same stroke, he associates paganism with the epoch of childlike immediacy, of consciousness's immersion in the particular: a darker, more naive, and more immediate epoch than the light of reflection that Christianity brings.

Since in paganism the infinite divine essence is concealed from consciousness under the "external," corporeal existence of the particular gods, there is here no distance and *no relation* between the finite and the infinite properly conceived. That is why pagan gods can exist so unproblematically alongside humans in mythological consciousness. In paganism, the finite and the infinite are immediately one, and there is no true divine infinity to which finitude could be related as something other or non-divine. By contrast, Christ, this figure of mediation as God's becoming human (*Menschwerden*), is what makes the finite and the infinite *relatable* from within their separation. This means, however, that the key part of Schelling's identity-philosophical double vision—namely, the relationality of the potencies as expressing the relation of finite forms of being to God and the striving of finitude to express the divine, which as such is without relation to the finite—is premised on the Christian logic of historical mediation. The pantheistic standpoint of the identity philosophy is decidedly distinct from pagan pantheism, in which there can be no such relationality, premised as this relationality is on the assumption of the fallenness of the world, or on the general Christian contradiction.

Based on his opposition between paganism and Christianity, Schelling declares that the principle of paganism (gravity) and the principle of Christianity (light) represent the only possible kinds of "religion" in general. "This opposition," he avers, "is the only possible one when it comes to religion, and that is why there are only paganism and Christianity, and outside these there is nothing except absoluteness [i.e., absolute identity], which is common to both" (UV 470/376). It would, however, be wrong to claim that Schelling thereby relativizes Christianity, turning it into but a particular and limited kind of religion.[38] To make that claim is to obscure the fact that the very standpoint from which Schelling advances the distinction between "paganism" and "Christianity" is Christian in character. Paganism is constructed retroactively as the other to Christianity, only to be

---

38. Sandkühler seems to suggest as much in "Philosophie der Geschichte."

incorporated into the Christian structure of the salvific not-yet, absolutized by Schelling as the structure of the universe itself. The constructed pagan oneness (under the dominance of A^1) becomes a part of the return to oneness at a higher level (under the dominance of A^3) as the fulfillment of the Christian promise. In Schelling, Christianity is the retroactive condition for the consideration of history as totality, as well as for the division into epochs. Christianity first makes possible the idea of the continuous development of something called "religion," from its first transmission from the higher angelic species at the dawn of history to the variety of pagan religions to Christianity. The universal-historical viewpoint that true philosophy must adopt is itself Christian.

This is generally a crucial point to keep in mind when speaking of "the Greeks" in German idealism and Romanticism. As one can see on Schelling's example, the construction of "pagan religion" is a Christian-modern construction that theorizes "paganism" retroactively as the other to Christianity and as an ostensibly naive pre-Christian unity (hence Schelling's configuration of the pagan mind as tautegorical, or immediately one with its deities). This unity is ambivalent. On the one hand, it marks a non-alienated oneness that Christianity lost, and thus a Christian-modern construction of Christianity's own origin that is posited as *the past* with the emergence of Christianity. In this regard, paganism carries an impulse that remains, in an important sense, antagonistic to the negativity and alienation inscribed in the Christian-modern world. On the other hand, as identified with the pre-Christian past, paganism is positioned as lower than Christianity because it fails to reach the standpoint of historical reflection. This standpoint becomes possible only with the revelation of the general Christian contradiction to consciousness as the true condition of the *Weltall*, a condition that Schelling applies, in a supersessionist manner, to the pre-Christian past, revealing this past as fallen and lower. Any return to oneness can happen only as the reconciliation of paganism and Christianity at a "higher" level, a reconciliation that goes necessarily through Christianity and fulfills the Christian promise, at once overcoming and *completing* Christianity. As a result, instead of being relativized, Christianity becomes the meta-standpoint from which the entirety of history is arranged and justified through the (Christian-modern) logic of proper historical place. The Incan solar religion in particular, as a "pagan" religion that exists as late as the sixteenth century of the Christian era, constitutes from this viewpoint something that cannot but disappear under the onslaught of Christianity. The universal category of "religion," of which Christianity is ostensibly only a part, is constructed by Schelling through Christianity—confirming the scholarly diagnosis that the concept of religion is a Christian-modern construction that has been extended in a colonial manner, at once diachronically and synchronically, across the entire globe.[39]

Only by persisting at the standpoint of the pure "="—of the "absoluteness that is common" and that refuses the logic of periodization—could one escape the assimilation of reality to Christianity's universalizing ambition. That is, however, not Schelling's intention. Instead, he programmatically forecloses the antagonistic dimension of his philosophy by inscribing bliss into a theodical vision in which the course of the (Christian-modern) world becomes cosmically legitimated. Even as he announces a phenomenological revolution, he identifies it not with annihilating the world in the now, but with transforming our manner of looking at the world into a theodical indifference that binds everything to its place, binding the philosopher, too, to the position of world-acceptance. The non-relational *idea* is turned into a relational *concept*, the *what* that marks all being's particular place as embedded in the relationality of the All. "The copula, or absolute identity" is turned into that which binds, instead of a radical *unbinding* that would inhabit immanently the contingency of the universe as a way of delegitimating the Christian-modern world and its pretensions at necessity and universality. The binding through the copula to the logic of place is a theodical sleight of hand. The copula does not have to bind; it can express simply *one's being whatever one is*: simply being, without being tied to a place. One can see the whole in every fragment without justifying either the fragment or the whole, and so without falling into theodicy as the justification of the world or God the creator: this, too, is what the standpoint of bliss discloses.

In a letter from 1844, transforming the Archimedean "Give me somewhere to stand and I will move the earth," Elizabeth Barrett Browning writes: poetry "is my *pou sto* ['place to stand']—not to move the world, but to live on in."[40] Poetry allows one to stand still *despite* the world. There is a sense of antagonism in Browning's words, insofar as, without a place to stand that poetry provides, the world would be unfit to live in. The "place to stand" is opposed to "move" and to "world," thereby grouping world and movement

---

39. See Masuzawa, *Invention of World Religions*; Nongbri, *Before Religion*; Barton and Boyarin, *Imagine No Religion*.

40. Browning, *Letters*, 178.

together, and rejecting them both so as to be able to live, to survive. Poetry thus provides refuge from and refuses the movement of the world.

Can Schelling's identity-philosophical ethics of bliss qua standing still be configured in a similar vein? To a certain extent, it can. In standing still, the philosopher intuits the absolute identity foreclosed by the dichotomies and enclosures of the world. This standing still refuses to long or strive, finding a divine refuge in this refusal. However, for Schelling, in standing still the philosopher is supposed to have trust in the way of the world. The refuge is found in the fact that the philosopher contemplates that everything is right with the world, despite any appearance to the contrary. "Peace with God" (WS 432 [§313]) entails peace with the world, and with one's own place therein. The Schellingian standing still functions not against but *with* the world, as a serene certainty that the space-time of the world reveals the divine.

By 1809, Schelling abandons the identity system. His later thought relinquishes the desire to see no evil, tarrying instead with the real darkness and decenteredness of the universe, and with the fundamental reality of evil and suffering. Starting in 1809, the All for Schelling can no longer be immediately reconciled. Whatever the exact reasons for his 1809 turn, one thing is clear: his identity philosophy is haunted by a tension between bliss and theodicy qua world-justification. Throughout his identity-philosophical writings, Schelling combines the postulation of the nothingness of the world with a justification of the necessity of its structure and the divine character of its temporal unfolding. This tension leads to a double vision that, instead of leading to a serene life, essentially tears the identity philosopher's consciousness apart, calling on her not to see evil and suffering, to see nothing but goodness and beauty. In a way, Schelling falls here into the same tautological theodicy that, in Interlude I, we saw him criticize in his dissertation on evil: the theodicy that claims that all things are good simply because they are divine. Given the increasing negativity of the post-Copernican universe and of modern reality at the onset of the nineteenth century, this kind of immediate world-acceptance could hardly be sustainable. Two possible ways out of this position seem to present themselves. One would involve embracing the antagonism to the world of self-assertion and enclosure, resulting in either an apocalyptic-revolutionary path or a trajectory of fugitivity, a flight from the imposition of the world. The other would entail no longer discounting negativity and evil as illusory but acknowledging evil *as* evil and facing it, even while attempting to justify the course of history *despite* all of its negativity. This second path is the one Hegel takes when he admits that, indeed, history is a "slaughterhouse," yet it is inevitable that a road to higher freedom should lead through sin and suffering: the destination makes it all worth it.[41] What I want to suggest is that, after 1809, Schelling follows a similar path within a different metaphysical account of reality, an account that retains bliss and the world as the two meta-poles. It is thus the above tension, which the identity system refuses to resolve and which comes back to haunt it and tears it apart, that may in part explain Schelling's move away from the system of identity and his renewed attempt at a *Weltsystem*, to be considered in Part II. The immanent logic of bliss is so at odds with the logic of the world that the conflict between bliss and the world shatters the identity-philosophical equilibristic from within. This shattering reveals the post-Copernican universal darkness that must be confronted as such.

---

41. Hegel, *Lectures on the Philosophy of World History*, 90.

PART II

The Dark Ground

Most people turn away from the things hidden within themselves, just as they turn away from the depths of all life, and are afraid to gaze into the abyss of the past that is still all-too present within them.

—SCHELLING (WA14 207–208/3-4)

*Who set into motion the great strife,
which will not be resolved for an eternity?
Who caused the breach on high,
which will not be mended for an eternity?
Who will be the guardian of the house,
as far as the enclosure of the worlds?*

—The Mandaean Book of John

Introduction to Part II

ON SCHELLING'S POST-1809 SYSTEM NARRATIVE

SCHELLING'S IDENTITY PHILOSOPHY was torn apart by the irreconcilability of bliss and the world. Through this tear in the one common bliss, it is as though the abyss of negativity and darkness became visible that could not be reduced to illusion or quantitative imbalance. In the geo-cosmic depths of gravity, and in the violence of history, this darkness was what the system of identity sought to contain. Yet, in view of the ongoing discovery of deep time and countless other galaxies and cosmic worlds, which served to radically decenter the human and the earth, Schelling's identity philosophy seemed doomed in advanced. Universal harmony could not be given in intellectual intuition, and it is as though the modern universe itself resisted Schelling's desire to re-vision it as a cosmos in which all is divine, the center is everywhere, and periphery nowhere.

In the collapse of the identity philosophy, universal darkness is let loose, permeating Schelling's further attempts at a system. In Schelling scholarship, it is customary to speak of a break in his thought signaled by the publication of the *Freedom* essay (1809), a dense sketch of a new system that Schelling keeps iterating in the subsequent decades. One way to describe this break is to say that, starting from 1809, Schelling's metaphysics grows darker, and universal decenteredness and contingency become the foci around which his thought orbits. Reality turns for him irreducibly scattered and explosive—and the cosmic abyss treacherous and full of horror. "God" ceases to be the synonym of the blissful All, the way he still was in the *Aphorisms*, becoming split into the divine essence and the darker abyssal forces concealed within divine selfhood.

Schelling's post-1809 metaphysics is a metaphysics of the fallen divine will (*Wille*). In an intradivine strife, the divine will breaks God's oneness, falling into the darkness of scattering, out of which universal history must ascend, step by step, to bliss reconfigured as transcendent light. This ascent to bliss constitutes the history of the universe and the human, a history that is marked by the ever-present, highly modern threat of losing its providential course and succumbing to the forces of contingency and decentering. This path is also that of creation (*Schöpfung*), grasped by Schelling as continuous and ongoing, and as coinciding with the process of universal history; and it is God's own path of *becoming* the actual true God. At the end of this path, Schelling continues to picture the *hen kai pan*: a blissful all-oneness eschatologically joining God, nature, and humanity.

In the chapters that follow, I develop a reading of Schelling's post-1809 attempts at a system as emerging from the crisis of the post-Copernican universe: a crisis that coincides with the post-Enlightenment crisis of divine transcendence and with the birth of idealist philosophy of history. During these decades, his philosophical-theological narrative turns into a visionary *post-Copernican cosmic and theodical epic*: a narrativization of the genesis of the universe and humanity as divine despite the visible contingency and unblissfulness of universal reality.[1] With all its theosophical and Gnostic undertones, this epic continues to grapple with the Christian-modern world, the world *in* which, for Schelling, the history of the universe presently culminates and *through* which the ascending path to the absolute future leads. Across his post-1809 thought, Schelling constantly returns to the questions engendered by the crisis of post-Copernican modernity: Is there a cosmic significance to human consciousness and history, placed as humanity is on a peripheral planet within the universal expanse? Can one grasp the human as the consciousness of the universe itself and as located at the ideal center of the universe despite the physical decenteredness? Can universal (natural and human) history still be conceived as exhibiting divine world-governance? Can this unblissful universe really be our non-alienated home? And finally, who are the "we" of humanity's providential destiny, and how can one philosophically assemble

---

1. Zakariya, *A Final Story*, speaks of the modern tradition of scientific epic as a synthetic narrative of universal genesis following "an epic ratio in which a few events structure an immensity of time" (8). Schelling's cosmo-theological narrative is also a natural-philosophical epic of this kind. This epic may further be regarded as Schelling's never-finished attempt to fulfill his own vision of a modern *Epos* that would bring into one nature and history (PK 187).

the oneness of "the human" across the globe in spite of the apparent disunity of humankind? What I find particularly interesting about Schelling's post-1809 thinking of the human is his positioning of humanity as the *universal mediator* that re-mediates the immensity of post-Copernican reality toward universal bliss.

In view of the above problematic, the concept of the center (*Centrum*) comes to the fore in Schelling's post-1809 metaphysics.[2] As I will argue, the dynamic of *cosmic decentering and recentering* constitutes the ever-present background for Schelling's systematic concerns after 1809, as he seeks to establish anew a cosmic theodicy that would legitimate the centrality of human history vis-à-vis the decentered post-Copernican reality. On the basis of the interplay of center and periphery, Schelling continues to envision a *Weltsystem* that would, against all odds, make the history of the universe into a narrative of bliss. Indeed, Schelling insists, reality is decentered and dark, and the human is confined empirically to the peripheral earth. Yet through the light of philosophical science and through kenotic submission to God, reality can, in the end, be ideally recentered in human consciousness, and bliss can be regained. This recentering, however, can arrive only eschatologically at the end of the entire work of universal history. In Schelling's post-1809 thought, the not-yet of the world forecloses even more resolutely any bliss in the now.

If one may speak of Schelling's post-1809 "system" in the singular, it is only as a system narrative that, starting with the *Freedom* essay and the 1810 *Stuttgart Seminars*, Schelling never ceases to develop and revise. He never completes his *opus magnum*, *The Ages of the World* (*Die Weltalter*, started in 1811), which would have presented this system narrative in its totality, and never publishes any major work after 1809, even as he keeps actively drafting his system and lecturing about "the ages of the world" as well as philosophy of mythology and philosophy of revelation. Thus, one can reconstruct Schelling's attempts at the overarching narrative only on the basis of the surviving drafts and lecture notes. Although the details of this narrative keep shifting, its contours remain broadly stable, and I agree with Horst Fuhrmans that, after 1809, Schelling keeps developing what is fundamentally one project: the construction of universal history as the "proof" that, despite the world's fallenness,

---

2. While the notions of center and decentering were present in Schelling's identity philosophy, there decenteredness was mere illusion, and intellectual intuition enacted an immediate recentering of the All.

providence and revelation are at work in it.[3] Methodologically, while much of Schelling scholarship has productively focused on his individual works or the more narrow sub-periods within his post-1809 thought, I believe that a (non-exhaustive) synthetic account of his attempted post-1809 system narrative can provide important insight into the continuity of the problematic with which he grapples.

In the post-1809 Schelling, bliss continues to be at once the absolutely first and absolutely last. Philosophical construction remains for him a construction of reality in view of bliss, even if the character of this construction changes, becoming more kenotic, kairotic, and Christocentric. Philosophy for the post-1809 Schelling constructs universal history as a process of the revelation and actualization of bliss, even as bliss stays transcendent to this process, so that immanence and transcendence coincide only at the end of time. This immanent-transcendent structure generates the normativity and not-yet of universal history, imagined by Schelling as a spiral of fall and ascent, of transgression and redemption, that goes through the natural process and the history of human consciousness. One highly modern feature of Schelling's post-1809 narrative is its openness onto the contingent future, even as he seeks to balance this openness with the necessity of the providential law that propels history toward bliss, or with a theodicy of history *in which historical contingency itself emerges as the ceaseless divine proving ground and tribunal*. This precarious balance between contingency and theodicy, a balance that indexes the crisis out of which Schelling writes, and that fills his metaphysics with anxiety about the future, stands at the heart of the synthetic account of Schelling's system narrative that I undertake here.

Preliminarily, the structure of Schelling's post-1809 system narrative may be introduced via Figure II.1. This narrative describes what I call the universal process or *theo-cosmic process*, since it encompasses the history of both God and the universe. This process begins when the ante-original bliss of divine oneness is broken up by the divine will, whose transgression scatters oneness. This scattering is the universal decentering: with it, the theo-cosmic center is lost, fallen into multiplicity. The Fall of the divine will from heaven—Schelling's speculative spin on the Fall of Lucifer—is the beginning of "the great world-creation" (WA27 177). Schelling's post-1809 theology remains a cosmo-theology, so that he is always performing theology and natural

---

3. See Fuhrmans, *Schellings Philosophie der Weltalter*, 307–308. The continuity of Schelling's post-1809 trajectory has also been recently emphasized in McGrath, *Philosophical Foundations*.

1. Ante-original divine oneness (A = A): the nucleus of the universe

2. Transgression of the divine will and its fall into being (Fall of Lucifer):
de-centering and explosive scattering, the first "bad" *ekstasis*
(=the original cosmic catastrophe, divine madness and cosmic war)

3. The proto-material state of the universe:
the fiery, chaotically rotating proto-All prior to space and time
(=the "great world-creation" as laying the ground for revelation)

4. The dampening of the first fire and the emergence of the orderly natural process,
the first "good" *ekstasis* or first redemption
(=the creation of nature proper, the beginning of revelation in nature)

5. The ascent of nature via the inorganic and organic toward the human,
the human's paradisal oneness with nature and the divine
(=conclusion of the first creation)

6. The Fall of the human will (Fall of Adam):
transgression of the human will, tumult and expulsion from paradise
(=the second creation, the beginning of human history as the history of consciousness)

7. The first chaotic and de-centered state of consciousness,
the emergence of polytheism and the ascending re-collection of divine oneness
(=the mythological process)

8. The historical Christ-event (the light of revelation):
revelation of the true God and the general Christian contradiction to consciousness

9. The Christian-modern trajectory of salvation history:
from initial tumult to the Catholic church to Protestantism to the new "religion of humankind"
(=the process of revelation in the narrow sense)

10. The re-centering of the universe and humanity in God,
absolute bliss and realized pantheism

FIGURE II.1 Schelling's post-1809 system-narrative

philosophy or cosmology simultaneously.[4] Thus, the blissful being of God prior to creation corresponds cosmologically to the nucleus from which the decentered universe emerges in a big bang. From the explosive tumult of this cosmic catastrophe, the universe is born first as a chaotic proto-material (quasi-nebular) state, and then, when this hot proto-matter starts cooling down, as an orderly process of nature in space and time. The natural process is envisioned by Schelling as a movement that, across all star systems in the universe, ascends up the hierarchized ladder (*Stufenfolge*) of nature toward the re-collection of oneness and bliss in the human, this truly "universal being" (DRP 491) that emerges on the earth so as to carry the consciousness of the theo-cosmic process itself. With the creation of the human, the process of nature in the narrow sense, or what Schelling calls "the first creation," ends.

If the process of nature forms the "real" side of the universe, in the human the universe produces its own "ideal" side: consciousness. For the post-1809 Schelling, the human remains the site of the actualized intelligence, mind, or spirit (*Geist*) as that toward which the universe develops. Human history begins with the Fall of Adam, or the first transgression of the human will, which breaks the blissful state of paradisal oneness. The resulting tumult, expelling human consciousness from its being-in-God, follows the same natural-philosophical model as the original cosmic tumult of the divine will: an imbalance and inhibition of forces within oneness, creating the rotatory motion that thrusts the will onto the periphery. The oneness of consciousness is thereby scattered, and the history of humanity, too, is a re-collection (in consciousness) and revelation (to consciousness) of the lost oneness, and of true (Christian) monotheism. The Fall of Adam is the beginning of a second creation and a "new world," which "elevates itself above nature" (GPP 467, DNP 390): the history of spirit, recapitulating cosmic history within consciousness.

---

4. I agree with Grant's *Philosophies of Nature* that *Naturphilosophie* remains the ground of Schelling's post-1809 thought. Yet the latter cannot be reduced to *Naturphilosophie*: Schelling is non-reductively performing at once natural philosophy *and* theology. The binary of theology *versus* natural philosophy fails to apply to Schelling, who continues the early-modern tradition of natural philosophy qua cosmo-theology. This binary is a product of a secularist framework, even if one employs it to affirm the theological against the natural-philosophical. Furthermore, one should distinguish between *Naturphilosophie* in the narrow and a broader sense. Narrowly understood, it is limited to what Schelling calls "nature proper," i.e., the orderly natural process (moments 4–5 in Figure II.1). In the broader sense, the intradivine dynamic (moments 1–3) and the history of human consciousness (moments 6–10) are also grasped by Schelling in natural-philosophical terms, so that *Naturphilosophie* forms the ground of the whole system narrative. It is just that ground (*Grund*) does not exhaust in Schelling that which it grounds. *Naturphilosophie* can ground theology without the latter being reducible to it.

The historical emergence of Christianity remains for Schelling central to human history. Even though the entire theo-cosmic process is that of divine revelation in the broad sense (as the revelation of oneness within multiplicity and light within darkness), and even though this process stands from the outset under the sign of Christ as the divine potency of mediation and redemption, it is with the historical Christ-event that this overarching process and the promise of all-reconciliation are revealed *to* human consciousness. At the conclusion of salvation history, humanity ought to recenter not only itself, but the whole universal reality in bliss: such is Schelling's view of the human vocation. The attainment of absolute bliss is to constitute the highest level (*Stufe*) of oneness, consciously achieved. This all-oneness will coincide with the illumination of universal darkness, and with the actualization of the totality of possibility concealed within ante-original divine being: the complete, exhaustive revelation of God. For Schelling, God himself longs for bliss as what is "above God" (WAII 16/73) and seeks to actualize it, doing so through the highest creative act: the creation of the world as God's self-splitting into what is other than himself, allowing God to fully express his being.

Although I have simplified it into a linear succession in Figure II.1, the process of universal history in Schelling is, as mentioned, a spiral-like movement directed toward the lost theo-cosmic center, reiterating at each level, or with every full turn of the spiral, the downward movement of the Fall and the upward movement of redemption. In what follows, I reconstruct this overarching process across Schelling's post-1809 texts, including his early *Ages of the World* drafts; his 1821 lecture course entitled *Initia Philosophiae Universae*; his further lectures on the ages of the world, philosophy of mythology, and philosophy of revelation; as well as his last manuscript, *Presentation of the Purely Rational Philosophy*, which traces the dissolution in bliss of dirempted reason and legitimates anew the place of modernity vis-à-vis Christianity. To advance his vision of universal history as what philosophy must construct, Schelling needs first to theorize the connection between the fallen human condition and the true method of philosophy as what can lead humanity out of its fallenness. It is, thus, to this condition and this method that we now turn.

4
Universal Ekstasis; *or,* Fallenness and Method

WHAT IS FOR Schelling the human condition out of which the task and method of true philosophy arise? In this chapter, I outline his post-1809 account of philosophical construction as responding to the unblissful post-lapsarian condition of human consciousness, and to the modern crisis of universal reality. In this condition, identified by Schelling with the self-assertion of the human will against the divine, the human *inverts* the true relation between the particular and universal. This inversion opens up an abyss within the subject and within nature, plunging them into a state of darkness and decenteredness. Out of this abyss, the self-assertive subject strives in vain to reach heaven or bliss. Modernity at once exacerbates this inverted condition and opens the possibility of a re-inversion through a redemptive submission of human consciousness to the universal. In his thinking of this re-inversion, Schelling continues to position bliss as antagonistic to the modern world while looking for a path to bliss that would lead at once *through* and *out of* the modern condition. At the same time, the (quintessentially modern) threat of universal contingency, I suggest, permeates Schelling's post-1809 thinking of God and history, and his philosophical theodicy during this period seeks most of all to justify history as the arena of divine revelation and providence in spite of the contingency and darkness of post-Copernican reality.

4.1. Decentering: The Fall of Adam and the Inverted World (of Modernity)

Let us assume, with Schelling, the human in its ante-original paradisal condition on the earth. In this condition, the human's blissful being, reposing in a oneness with the divine, has as such no transition to history. As always in Schelling, only a transgression or Fall can originate history, and this holds also for the history of human consciousness. Not unlike for Kant, the history of consciousness begins for Schelling with the Fall of Adam, justified as the "fallen" beginning that is meant providentially to lead to the development of human freedom, rationality, and knowledge of the divine. In the 1821 lectures devoted to the task of philosophy, the Fall of Adam is configured as human consciousness's "fall into error" (IPU 204, 260), which is, however, theodically necessary, since truth can be revealed only by contrast with error, and by going through error and recognizing it *as* error. "There is," Schelling reiterates in his philosophy of revelation, "but one truth: namely, one that has achieved victory over error" (UPO 7). The entire history of consciousness, going through the pagan epoch of mythology and then the Christian-modern trajectory of revelation, forms such a gradual triumph of the true over the false, the divine over the fallen. The Fall of Adam is, at the same time, the fall of consciousness into decenteredness, darkness, and evil ("error," Schelling writes, belongs to the "category of evil" [*Bösen*; IPU 258]): into a state of disorder and confusion (*Verwirrung*), which reign during the deepest times of human history. How does the human descend into this condition? And how can philosophy not merely explain or theodically justify the Fall of Adam but help to convert disorder into the true order of consciousness—to "bring the confused [*das Verworrene*] into the orderly again" (IPU 205)?

4.1.1. The *Ekstasis* of the Fall and the Expulsion from Bliss

Schelling's post-1809 view of the human as the cosmic or universal being stays essentially the same as in the identity philosophy. According to this Romantic view, the theo-cosmic process aims from the beginning at the creation of human intelligence, the "ideal" pinnacle of nature, which finally emerges on this particular planet, the earth, out of all the countless planets and star systems. This does not necessarily have to be understood teleologically in the strong sense: it may be that, looking retrospectively at the evolution of the universe, we can trace the way it has led to human intelligence due to the forces that have been at work in the universe since the beginning. The fact that human intelligence exists means that the universe has evolved to have an "ideal" dimension, and thus that the possibility of this dimension has been inherent in the universal process from the outset. For Schelling, the human is the actualization of the capacity for consciousness that has always been a potential part of the universe. Mind is no less an essential part of the genesis of the universe than physical nature.[1] From gravity to light to organism runs the one continuous genesis of the cognizing subject: the human (GPP 197). *In potentia*, even prior to its actual emergence, the human had been "providentially" determined to be the site, ground (*Grund*), or carrier (*das Tragende*) of universal self-consciousness. Theologically, in the human, the universe becomes conscious of itself as divine creation, and God of himself as God the creator.

The paradisal state of the human is the primordial oneness (*Ur-Einheit*) and consciousness (*Urbewusstsein*), in which divine freedom or "eternal freedom" rests in itself and the human rests at its center. There is here no opposition of forces, only their perfect indistinction. Adamic consciousness lets itself be immediately filled by the divine and, accordingly, *simply is* divine. God, too, here *is* the human.[2] Human consciousness is the "absolute center" and transparent "quiet inner [ground]" that underlies eternal freedom in its self-identity and self-knowledge (IPU 209, 213).

While this state may be blissfully without contradiction, one may discern in it, Schelling believes, a meta-contradiction if one looks back at this state from the standpoint of history. This contradiction concerns the status of the human as the self-consciousness of God. Adam serves as the carrier of this self-consciousness, yet he does not reflectively *know* or has no consciousness of himself as such. Adamic consciousness is "quiet" because it is dormant, "not knowing," and "inactive" (IPU 221). Adam has not tasted from the Tree of Knowledge and does not act freely in a conscious way. His is an unconscious consciousness, unaware even of God as something other, since in bliss there is no reflection. From the perspective of human history and divine transcendence alike, this state cannot but appear as something low and undeveloped. Due to this inner contradiction, Schelling writes, there appears an "unavoidable inner strife" within primordial oneness, in which the will of

---

1. I speak here of "consciousness," "intelligence," and "mind" interchangeably, since for Schelling these terms coincide in the human.

2. This interpenetration rests on Schelling's post-1809 theory of the copula. To say that "God *is* the human" is not to postulate a reductive identity, but to say that human consciousness serves as the "material" carrier or ground of the divine. The human is the *hypokeimenon* or *subiectum*, that which "underlies" paradisal oneness and God's or eternal freedom's self-knowledge within this oneness. See, e.g., IPU 221, 257.

the ground (i.e., human will) senses the contradiction within itself and asserts itself as the *will to know* (IPU 257). In theological terms, this is the original conflict between the human and God, in which the human shows for the first time *its own* will to knowledge, and posits itself as different from God—and thus God as different from the human.

This strife is unavoidable, writes Schelling, "because human consciousness cannot be content with remaining the quiet inner [ground] or mere carrier of eternal consciousness." This does not, he hastens to add, mean that the transgression was "forced" and not free—however, it was still "necessary and inevitable" (IPU 257). From the outset, human reason cannot but choose to assert itself, and so to transgress: a typical theodical conjunction, going back at least to Augustine, of freedom and "higher" providential necessity within original sin. Human reason wants to become autonomous (*eigenmächtig*; IPU 257). The human seeks, from God's perspective, to become "like one of us" through knowledge (Genesis 3:22). "Before the Fall," writes Schelling, "Adam was a perfect image of God, an *alter Deus*." However, he could be such an image only as long as he did not seek to *actually* be "as God," or to rival God by becoming the one who knows (IPU 506–507)—which is what happens when the human attempts to "make eternal freedom into the object" that would be cognized *by* the human (IPU 209). To put this in less theological terms, the human capacity for intelligence starts to mobilize and organize itself in a such a way as to cognize the reality of which it is a part, and to become a developed, self-conscious intelligence. From a Blumenbergian perspective, this conception of the Fall is highly modern: Adam's transgression against divine oneness is the first self-assertion of reason, in which reason opposes itself at once to pre-given ("divine") prescriptions imposed from above, and to the surrounding "objective" reality. In its self-assertion and will to knowledge, human consciousness makes itself into the relative center of cognition and decision-making, and into the judge of what is true. With that, however, prelapsarian creation is made unstable.

This instability is grasped by Schelling in natural-philosophical terms: in terms of a dynamic of forces. Within the ur-consciousness, there is a perfect indifference between the will (*Wollen*) and the capacity (*Können*), or the attractive and the repulsive force. This indifference constitutes the divine "bliss of knowledge" (IPU 189), wherein knowledge is one with non-knowledge. "Eternal power" coincides here with "eternal magic," or the power of the absolutely real within consciousness. The human is (one with) this magic, yet it is not the human's own. The will *to appropriate the power of eternal magic*, to make it his own, is what causes the Fall from bliss. Here Adam behaves as the modern subject of self-assertion who seeks to master and appropriate reality, and whose aporias of striving were central already to Schelling's 1795 metaphysics.

The capacity (*Können*) is the repulsive force because to have power over something, or to have the capability to do something, is to be able to do or *not* do it, and thus not to be bound to it, to keep it at a distance. By contrast, the will is the attractive force because to will something is to be compelled by it and *attract* it (IPU 188–189). Thus, within ante-original bliss, the resting capacity coincides with the resting, non-willing will. With the activation of the human will, however, the human starts to "attract" divine reality so as to make itself into its center—"to turn its own self into the subject vis-à-vis eternal freedom" (IPU 207). Intelligence becomes what it is by gathering and rearranging reality around itself. The beginning of sin and evil is an act of self-assertion qua inversion (*Umkehrung*) or perversion (*Verkehrung*), in which what is supposed to be the ground of divine reality subordinates this reality to itself and claims to be the subject of knowledge. In natural-philosophical terms, this constitutes the first catastrophe (*Katastrophe*) within consciousness (GPP 481, UPO 14, 181), in which the underground force, erupting suddenly out of the human as what used to be the quiet ground, counteracts or inhibits (*hemmt*) divine oneness.

Where there is inhibition, the system is no longer at rest but starts rotating (IPU 266). The strife between the human and the divine within the ur-consciousness generates the spinning or rotatory motion (*rotatorische Bewegung*) and vortex-like turmoil (*Umtrieb*) that grow wilder until the paradisal oneness cannot hold. This vortex reaches a critical point (a point of *krisis* as division or separation), and consciousness explodes, resolving the built-up tension by separating the human from the divine: a fiery cosmic explosion (*Zersprengung, Explosion*) and discharge (*Entladung*), yet within consciousness. "Eternal freedom cannot tolerate" the pretension of human self-assertion, expelling human consciousness from the divine center (IPU 228). Consciousness "becomes peripheral" (IPU 197, 209–210), finding itself in a state of scatteredness and confusion due to the loss of the center. The human, as one who "wanted to make itself into the knower of eternal freedom *within* the latter, is thrown out of it and turned into one who does not know anything" (IPU 219). This unknowing is a lack, an absence, a cosmic void of endless longing, which from now on underlies the human will.

If the being of the ur-consciousness has the form $A = A$, then the rebellious human will in its opposition to the divine, and thus as non-divine, is what Schelling designates as B. The reign of B—of original sin, pride, desire, tumult, disorder—is the first state of human consciousness following the Fall. In this perverted state, B in its self-assertion seeks to subordinate divine oneness to itself. This disorder is due not least to the fact that, while human consciousness has already in truth become peripheral and decentered, it still regards itself as the center and the true subject of knowledge, and still remembers the bliss and magic it glimpsed and sought to appropriate. The human will wants to immediately *be* the All by possessing it. Yet the tragedy of the will and the irony of its condition is that, with the very desire for possession and appropriation, the one immediate All is lost. Human consciousness finds itself amid multiplicity, in a scattered postlapsarian state that is alien to the oneness that consciousness used to enjoy: in the first state of alienation. This mental state is that of the deepest past of human history, but it persists to this day within the depths of our will, underlying the aporias of self-assertion. In this manner, Schelling, like Kant, interprets the expulsion from paradise as consciousness's being thrown into a hostile world over and against which consciousness must assert itself so as to learn to cognize on its own and to orient itself consciously in an alien reality.

The forceful expulsion of the human from the center carries for Schelling a further name: *ekstasis*. This term, not to be simply equated with "ecstasy," has first and foremost a technical sense: it names the operation of dis-placement or dis-location (*ek-stasis*), which is not necessarily rapturous or blissful. "That earlier act," Schelling writes, "through which the human made eternal freedom, which he was supposed to *be*, into the object for himself, was ... an *ekstasis*, in which the center was thrust onto the periphery." The Fall is not the only kind of *ekstasis* possible. "Each dis-location [*Ent-setzung*] and removal from a certain place [*Stelle*] is an *ekstasis*." *Ekstasis*, *Entsetzung*, and *Entstellung* are thus synonymous. The universe is ecstatic, since it is decentered yet strives to regain centeredness; and human consciousness is ecstatic in the same sense. Furthermore, if something is removed from "a position that is proper to it," it is an *ekstasis* "in the bad sense." On the contrary, if something is returned to its proper place, it is a "good" kind of *ekstasis* (IPU 209, UPO 29). Only the good *ekstasis* is blissful. The Fall is a bad kind of *ekstasis*, unlike the future recentering of the human within the divine. The dynamic between the "bad" and "good" *ekstasis*, or between the Fall and redemptive restoration, decentering and recentering, inversion and re-inversion, defines the overarching movement of Schelling's post-1809 metaphysics, even where he does not use the term *ekstasis*.

4.1.2. The Unblissful Present

Disoriented, dislocated, and turned into *one who does not know*, the human has to begin its path to knowledge anew, mediated by the not-yet of the world. The human—so goes Schelling's favorite Platonic thought—carries within itself a memory of the lost bliss, obscured by the alienated world and the rigidity of selfhood. "A dark memory of having at one point been the beginning, the power, the absolute center of all things stirs evidently within the human" (IPU 197). However obscured, this core of bliss remains operative in the dark ground of subjectivity, driving the will to know, and to re-collect reality into oneness. "Nothing remains for him except the dark memory of what he used to be, that is, the *thought, remembrance* thereof—and with that, the striving for recollection begins" (IPU 217). Thought (*Denken*), Schelling claims, is rooted in remembrance (*Gedenken*) and in the longing to know as God knows: to have one's being immediately coincide with one's cognition (an A = A again), to regain immediacy and repose. Modern rational knowledge and science, too, continue for the post-1809 Schelling to be aimed at merging into one immediate cognition, wherein oneness with the power of the absolutely real would be restored in a conscious manner. The modern obsession with re-mediating and controlling the entirety of reality indexes, in this analytic, a deeper longing for oneness, even if modernity's path to this oneness is presently perverted. In the human, and in the external nature that the human cognizes, ur-oneness "seeks constantly to restore itself" out of the "forced state" of the universe as reflected in the mind (IPU 224). The goal of modern knowledge is to overcome alienation from within: to develop rationality to such a degree that it dissolves in bliss, to restore the garden of paradise. This is the goal to which, for Schelling, "the light of science" (IPU 213) must lead.

The path to this end-bliss is dark, toilsome, and treacherous. The condition of the present is full of pain (*Schmerz*; IPU 260). The human is immersed in the erroneous approach to knowledge, which removes the human from its own essence and the essence of nature. Postlapsarian reality restages the general Christian contradiction, the threefold structure of alienation cutting through nature, the human, and the divine. The Fall of Adam is a *krisis* as division (*Scheidung*): the human "divides the natural within itself," that is, finite selfhood, "from the supernatural," that is, from eternal freedom, God, or "the absolute subject" (IPU 204). Thereby the human also divides eternal freedom into what is repressed (*verdrängt*; IPU 267) or obscured (*verdunkelt*; IPU 213) within nature and within the human. The inner subjectivity of nature, originally one with the divine, becomes mere object, "fully external" and "alien," inhuman, estranged from its essence and telos (GPP 471). As a result, nature, the human, and eternal freedom are all estranged from each other and from themselves (a condition of utter *Selbstentfremdung*; IPU 199). The post-1809 Schelling, too, identifies this structure of general alienation with the universal condition of nature and human consciousness—a fact that continues to mark his metaphysics as Christian-modern in character. The Copernican revolution in astronomy, too, is for him an integral part of the Christian-modern trajectory because it *scientifically reveals* to human consciousness the condition of universal fallenness and decenteredness out of which the path to bliss must ascend.

Within paradisal oneness, human consciousness was where all the rays or threads of nature met. Now that human consciousness has abandoned its central position, these threads are scattered and tangled, and consciousness cannot disentangle them. The light of oneness is "extinguished," having "sunk into forgetfulness" (IPU 212), and the dark ground encloses bliss within its depths. The whole of nature is decentered through the Fall of Adam, and this is the human's fault.[3] One must not "cast onto nature . . . that of which the human alone is guilty." Nature is but the object of human transgression and the unwilling carrier of human guilt (*Schuld*; IPU 260). There is, in fact, an original transgression or sinfulness inscribed for Schelling in nature as such, too; however, in having produced the human, nature was supposed to have redeemed its fallenness, since the human was meant to be the one who would "ideally" keep the universe together and serve as the ground for the self-cognition of the divine. However, the human betrayed its central theo-cosmic position. Now, without the human as its crowning element and organ of self-cognition, nature cannot (re)cognize and (re)discover its own divine essence. A veil of melancholy (*Schwermut*) and grief hangs over postlapsarian nature. In modernity especially, "The human has ceased to be the soul of the entire [theo-cosmic] movement, and so nature itself appears as a whole that has been severed from its principles, or as the *ruin* of the whole" (GPP 471).

---

3. In positioning Adam's Fall as cosmic in scope, Schelling also transforms the Platonic tradition of cosmic anthropology as well as the Kabbalistic idea of *Adam Kadmon*. See Schmidt-Biggemann, *Philosophia Perennis*. Cf. Scholem, *Major Trends*, 275: "Adam's fall again destroyed the harmony, hurled all the worlds from their pedestals, and again sent the Shekhinah [i.e., divine presence] into exile." Importantly, Luther holds a related view of Adam's Fall as the second creation through which all of nature turns sinful and "the entire structure of creation and the cosmos [is] altered" (Pelikan, "Cosmos and Creation," 467). Prior to Adam's Fall, in Luther's view, the sun shone brighter, there was nothing poisonous in nature, and roses did not yet have thorns.

Throughout the universe, nature tries to raise itself to eternal freedom again, yet in vain. The universe keeps destroying old forms and worlds and producing new ones, but "There is no progress therein." "Each form is destroyed anew, but what takes its place? Only the same form again" (IPU 193). Without the human, nature flounders unblissfully; all it produces is foam on the surface of the cosmic sea (*Meer*). Eternal magic still glows within nature, but its purpose, its "eternal wisdom," is lost. Despite its productivity, nature stands still (*Stillstand*), imprisoned (*gefangen*) in a cyclical movement in which there is "nothing new" (IPU 193). "The regular course of the celestial bodies and the ever-repeated circle of universal phenomena indicate this kind of standing still" (IPU 191). What Schelling terms "eternal wisdom" may be understood, beside its other connotations, as the providential world-plan (*Weltplan*; GPP 355) inscribed in creation, according to which the universal process was meant to attain self-consciousness in the human.[4] The human was supposed to be the fulfillment of the purpose of nature, the site of eternal freedom's "coming-to-itself," and thus of "actualized wisdom," or divine self-cognition within the accomplished plan of creation. By falling and casting nature downward again, the human thwarts this plan, and, as a result, wisdom keeps spinning and looping, so that, in the derangement of the intended world-plan, nature "keeps producing its wonders without purpose . . . in a vain busyness" (IPU 263).

Schelling's claim that there is presently no newness in the process of nature should not be taken to mean that nature was never capable of producing anything new. In the original production of organic life and then the human mind, nature did attain to newness. However, having peaked in the human, nature cannot produce anything new *anymore*. For Schelling, nature as "the first creation" has been essentially completed; only the past of nature, not its present, may be characterized as world-historical. "The second creation," and thus salvation history, now plays out in the arena of human history alone: this is the point at which Schelling's post-1809 metaphysics becomes more anthropocentric or anthropo-theocentric than it was earlier.

In embracing this position, Schelling excludes the possibility that the universe may produce new consciousness elsewhere: only the human is the realized universal consciousness. It is important not to dismiss Schelling's intensified theo-cosmic anthropocentrism, but to see it as part of the movement of his

---

4. "Wisdom" is what "knows everything in its interconnectedness, grasping beginning, middle, and end" (GPP 450–451). This is the all-encompassing, all-coherent knowledge for which philosophy, as love of wisdom, strives.

time: he thereby contributes to the broader nineteenth-century tendency to turn nature into mere background for human history.[5] There are what may be called a "real" and an "ideal" aspect to Schelling's reduction of nature to a cyclical temporality that cannot produce true futurity. The "real" aspect is that the human *is* the conscious natural being that the universe, after many efforts, produces so as to cognize itself. If the human loses this purpose, the telos of nature is *really* lost with it, and the natural process is rendered futile. The "ideal" (or transcendental) aspect is that nature simply cannot appear as blissful to a consciousness that is dirempted, confused, and unblissful. As Schelling puts it, "The eternal freedom that is repressed within nature is in agreement with the eternal freedom that is bound [*gefesselt*] within the human" (IPU 264). To rediscover order and wisdom in nature, consciousness must restore them to itself; and for this reason, too, the future for Schelling depends decisively on the human, and on whether the human will live up to its theo-cosmic destiny of reconciling the universe. This may explain the late Schelling's increasing focus on human history as the history of consciousness, and of nature and God in consciousness, a focus evident in his almost exclusive attention to philosophy of mythology and philosophy of revelation during the final two decades of his life.

Development in the universe, writes Schelling in his last manuscript, *Presentation of the Purely Rational Philosophy*, starts "from what is distant," or from the entire immeasurable universal expanse, until it "narrows down" to the human, which is "the goal and for whose sake everything is." "The wider the basis above which the human elevates itself, the brighter its uniqueness shines" (DRP 494). The universal process develops toward ever-higher differentiation and complexity, which become increasingly localized, and humanity—not just the way it is but the way it ought to be—is the pinnacle of this process. Referencing Kant's famous passage on the starry skies and restaging Kant's move,[6] Schelling opposes the higher, ideal centrality of the human to the physical universe, asserting the human as the "universal being" despite its physical decenteredness. In fact, the farther other cosmic worlds are removed from our solar system, the lower they are in terms of development.[7] Not the beings "that are supposed to inhabit distant stars," but the

---

5. On this tendency, see Chakrabarty, "Climate of History."

6. See Kant, *Critique of Practical Reason*, 129.

7. Such is Schelling's view already in his notes to the *First Outline*, where he dismisses faraway galactic nebulae as belonging to the past of the universe or "nearing their collapse" (EE 320/93). *The present* is for Schelling concentrated in our solar system.

human is the one who has separated the merely "material" from "the intelligible world," and who is capable of inhabiting the universal as its true home (*Heimat*). As such, the human must be measured "not against a part [of the universe], or the particular celestial body it inhabits, but against the whole." Nor must (adds Schelling in a proleptic critique of the imperative to colonize outer space) the human "expand over other celestial bodies" to fulfill its universal telos. This entire universe that is "so alien and feels so distant" must fill the human, rather, with the sense of the human's own cosmic purpose, which consists in illumining the dark depths of reality with the light of science and in restoring "the lost central position" (DRP 491).

Yet the human presently remains fallen into error, continuing to assert its finite selfhood as the true subject of knowledge. Instead of recognizing the wisdom of the created order and fulfilling its task within it, the human opposes itself to divine reality, subordinating this reality to itself. The human forgets that the only reason it is capable of knowledge is due to its embeddedness in the universal (divine and natural) order. It inverts the order of priority between its self-assertion and the universal order, and it is in this inversion that evil and transgression consist. If error belongs for Schelling to "the category of evil," it is because evil is an invertedness in which the particular refuses to serve as the ground or carrier of the universal but instead suppresses the latter and turns it into its own ground, the ground of self-assertion. The human's fallen condition "emerged because the human broke itself off from universal life and sunk into the particular," subordinating the universal *to* the particular—an original sin for which this condition is the punishment (*Strafe*; GPP 482–483). Evil, in other words, has for Schelling no essence or substance of its own. It is parasitic on its oneness with the universal or divine, on which its self-assertion feeds. Particularity as the principle of (the possibility of) evil is by itself not evil. In fact, it is even good *if* it is subordinated to the universal or recognizes its place within the goodness of the world-order. It is only insofar as particular selfhood raises itself against divine order that its potential for evil is actualized. From 1809 onward, this conception of evil as a self-assertive inversion is fundamental for Schelling. The distinction between good and evil maps onto that between center and periphery: if the particular serves as the ground for the divine or universal, it is centered in the universal; if, however, it asserts itself against the universal, it becomes peripheral and perverted.

Schelling's reduction of nature to the eternally same does not imply that he agrees with the positioning of nature as mere object for human self-assertion. Eternal freedom or the absolute subject works in and through nature, and Schelling continues to critique the view of the natural world as something non-subjective. This view, culminating in the modern neglect of living nature, is the consequence of human self-assertion. Within both nature and the human, self-assertion "turns [eternal freedom] into unfreedom, and yet pursues it as freedom" (IPU 209): a typical Schellingian critique of the modern absolutization of "finite" freedom as the I's autonomy from the not-I. To the external repression of bliss in nature, there corresponds its internal repression in consciousness. This puts a darker, more Romantic spin on the Kantian duality of the ideal realm within and physical realm without. Subject and object alike rest on a dark abyss that is perpetuated by self-assertion. Repressed by the world of self-assertion, the essence of nature turns warped, even "monstrous," mirroring the monstrosity of self-assertion in its inhibition of divine light: in the darkness, monsters dwell (IPU 248). Even as the human is fascinated by this abyss, not least because it resonates with the abyss within its soul, "Nature soon teaches the human through painful experience to turn away, shuddering, from this abyss" (IPU 264). And so the human closes its eyes to the abyss while building the world of self-assertion on top of it. However, as long as this warped abyss persists, the human cannot reach stability, because nature is resentful of the human, "coldly and mercilessly trampling everything human, and annihilating the human together with its works" (IPU 264). Nature flees humanity's appropriative grasp, and its magic turns deceptive: "It shows itself to the human . . . as a true Maya, or she who deceives." *Maya*, Schelling points out, "is a word that is related to *magic*" and means "false, deceptive magic" (IPU 264). Nature turns fugitive—a terrain of flight from self-assertion that is antagonistic to the efforts of the self-assertive subject.

Only the simultaneous emancipation of nature and the human can lead to absolute bliss. Nature's cruelty to the human, this mirror image of the human's cruelty to nature, is not only punishment. It is a wake-up call. For Schelling, it is as though nature were saying to the human: this is my false condition, the reign of falsehood you created. Out of universal darkness, "Everything calls on the human" to awaken from error (IPU 267). "In the human alone, there remains the opening" through which the bad *ekstasis* of universal decenteredness can be corrected, and "That is why eternal wisdom is searching for the human" (IPU 191) so that the world-plan can be fulfilled. Since nature comes to self-consciousness and self-knowledge only in the human, as long as the human remains decentered and without true self-knowledge, so does the universe. Human consciousness thus ought to recognize itself as the inner center of a creation made whole. To this end, however, the subject must first learn to face its abyss—the abyss of its own past—and to recognize and follow the longing for bliss concealed therein.

4.1.3. Heaven as Goal: Longing for the Re-inversion

The abyss of fallenness persists within human history as within every individual. Schelling configures the pre-Christian world ("the entirety of paganism") as an epoch of darkness and error emerging in the aftermath of the Fall of Adam—a shattering of human consciousness, and of humankind itself. Paganism was "the consequence of an immense and frightful explosion that ruptured the whole well-assembled edifice of the original human [being] and scattered its colossal debris" (IPU 259). Out of the dark ruins of the Fall, the movement of ancient mythology proceeds as the re-collection of the light of truth, which finally emerges in Christianity and which modernity inherits. To this day, however, major parts of humanity persist in darkness and error. "Whoever wants to learn the magnitude that error can reach," Schelling states, "must look for it not in those times or among those peoples where public faith, civil laws, and the people's rationality are already developed to a degree that is sufficient to hold error back or to partly prevent it" ("partly," because in the present condition error cannot be completely exorcised). "One must look for it," rather, "among the peoples and times in which error *reigns*" (IPU 259). These lines, written in 1821, show that Schelling continues during this time to view European modernity as the normative standard of rationality and progress at the present stage of history, hierarchizing humanity across its past and present. Despite his view that the entire current state of humanity is fallen, Schelling cannot help but denigrate the "wilder" peoples that do not live up to the European ideal of rational self-legislation and public order, relegating them to that in the present which remains stuck in the past. For Schelling, the dark and monstrous abyss persists outwardly in those who are less than rational, less "civilized" or "developed." Over and against universal darkness, the Christian-European subject is the one who, even in its still-fallen state, carries the movement of universal recentering, and on whom—on whose rational institutions as well as religion, philosophy, and science—the future depends.

At the same time, the dark abyss persists for Schelling inwardly in each and every human, too, no matter how rational. "In every human consciousness, there takes place again the same attraction" that causes the Fall of Adam: the force of the will to know, which makes the subject assert itself as the true subject of knowledge, turning all of reality into object. In this manner, original sin persists within every consciousness. This means, Schelling continues, that "everyone finds themselves by nature in that inner tumultuous movement," even if "the majority of humans wander through their lives in an oblivious state" (IPU 257–258). In most people, this tension fails to reach the point of *krisis* and stays unclarified and unreflected (IPU 258). Still, in everyone, there is a vague yet "constant wrestling for clarity" (IPU 222), which the more rational person can resolve consciously toward the universal. It is perhaps for the better, Schelling muses, that most people exist in a state of "beneficial stupefaction" without being torn apart by their doubt and struggle (IPU 258), for to be able to deal with inner tumult requires purpose and discipline. Yet this tumult, together with a faint memory of bliss, underlies everything humans do, and everyone longs to be free from unrest.

Schelling's post-1809 analytic of the human adds *abyssal depth* to his earlier framework of the subject's striving. It is still the same subject that we encountered in Schelling's 1795 metaphysics: the one seeking to "attract" or turn into object the entirety of reality, so as to regain oneness. Yet the sense of the inner void now intensifies and, as though in parallel to the growing immensity of the universe and the increasing insatiability of capitalist modernity, the subject's appetite, too, becomes for Schelling cosmically endless. To the post-Copernican void that generates and consumes cosmic worlds, there corresponds the void of desire within the subject, who endlessly consumes objects only to crave new ones—so that every attempt to rest, to be content, is doomed in advance, and "not to will" anything becomes "what is the hardest and, as it were, unbearable for the human" (IPU 510). Bliss is the eternal *now*, but one cannot attract or seize it, master or possess it without thereby foreclosing it. In attempting to seize heaven, the subject loses it and is forced to live and strive in the world. I want to quote the respective passage in full, since it not only returns us to Schelling's image of the two paths to bliss (the path of possession and the path of purification) but also conveys well the universal distance (*Ferne*) and emptiness that dwell within the Schellingian subject:

> Only the will that rests is heaven for the human. Everyone searches for this heaven, not only one who persists or endures in the blazing and all-consuming purity of the non-willing will—but also one who blindly succumbs to all cravings, because he, too, searches solely for a state in which he would not have to will anything anymore since he would possess everything he could ever want. This state, however, immediately escapes him, and the more zealously he pursues it the more distant it grows. The will, once it has become active, is the unfillable

void [*Leere*], the ever-gaping depth, insatiable as hell itself. (IPU 509–510)

"Heaven," Schelling reiterates, is "the will in a state of rest, of complete serenity" or letting-be (*Gelassenheit*; IPU 509).[8] In this, we may recognize the state of absolute freedom or bliss.

If "hell consists in nothing other than the constant searching for heaven yet never being capable of finding it," and if "one's will is one's hell" (IPU 509), then we might say that modernity is the epoch of hell par excellence. It is the world of an alienated self-assertive will, a will that inhabits an endless void and digs up the dark geo-cosmic depths of the earth so as to fill the void within itself. Within the structure of self-assertion, all desire is fleeting except the desire *to* desire endlessly. The contradiction of modernity that emerges from this analytic is that modernity is at once the highest rational epoch that is capable of forming the idea of the universal and the epoch of the highest invertedness ("the frightful perversity of our times"; WAII 103/165) that subordinates God and nature to human selfhood. No amount of civil law and public order can hold back the endless vortex of appropriation and desire in which the modern subject exists. Contra Schelling, who sees in rational law that which helps to overcome the chaos of self-assertive desire, an irreducible ambivalence of modernity consists precisely in the fact that its civil and legal rationality codifies a system of insatiable possession and consumption, through which alienation from nature and the dark depths on which this alienation is premised are continuously reproduced and intensified.

The Schellingian subject is a Faustian subject, searching and longing without rest and turning inner cosmic turmoil into the motor of striving. Schelling further diagnoses the modern striving for fulfillment through mastery and possession as underlying the three "corruptions of a higher idea" that, in his account, are central to modernity (GPP 473):

1. *Corrupted magic*, or the desire to "influence" nature at the subject's whim.
2. *Corrupted alchemy*, or the craving simultaneously for possession and rebirth (*Wiedergeburt*), symbolized by the image of turning "common metals into noble ones."

---

8. *Gelassenheit*—a mystical term going back, via Boehme, to Meister Eckhart—is connected by Schelling to the verb *lassen*, "to let (be)." See, e.g., IPU 279. Cf. SA 33: "in a complete letting-oneself-be or, which is the same, a perfect *Gelassenheit*." *Gelassenheit* in the post-1809 Schelling is a synonym for bliss as an absolute letting-be.

3. *Corrupted immortality*, or the wish to infinitely extend one's lifespan, "to rejuvenate the human body and reach an indefinite longevity" as a way of becoming "free from nature"—an obsession that runs throughout modernity and reappears in today's transhumanism.[9]

For Schelling, in its desire for reality manipulation and eternal youth, the subject in truth seeks redemption and eternal freedom, and is driven by the dark memory of the higher, yet in an empty and inverted manner (GPP 473). Corruption of the subject and of nature are co-imbricated with the fantasy of becoming free from nature. As Schelling puts it in his critique of modern philosophy, "Thought that separates itself from nature is equally incapable of reaching heaven and of touching the earth" (GPP 253). As a result, through its separation from nature and the appetite of its self-assertion, the subject is doomed to annihilate whatever it attains and thus, ironically, to inhabit with the rest of nature the cosmic ruins and cycle of destruction. And if absolute freedom means the freedom not to be bound by the unblissful circularity of desire—the freedom not to be chained to the world, the freedom to be nothing, "not to *have* to be anything" (IPU 281)—then nature and the human are, in this fallen reality, equally unfree.

Building on this Schellingian analytic, one might say that modernity inhabits a universe that is cyclical and monotonous in its very generation of newness: new cosmic worlds, new worlds of desire. The ever-increasing acceleration of modernity—of desire, production, consumption—can be understood, from this perspective, as the longing to finally *break through* the cycle toward eternal freedom, non-alienation, and non-will. As long as self-assertion persists, however, this longing only accelerates the rotatory motion within this vicious circle, creating the vortex that modernity inhabits as an epoch of an ever-intensifying, ever-more-explosive crisis that never reaches the clarifying *krisis* that would recenter it in bliss and repose. The modern freedom of self-assertion is an endless compulsion that oscillates ceaselessly between the centripetal and the centrifugal, running in circles around the absent center.

As the one responsible for the unblissful condition of reality, the human subject continues in the post-1809 Schelling to be the unfortunate demiurgic

---

9. These "corruptions" broadly coincide with what Eliphas Lévi calls "the dream of the alchemists": "to be always rich, ever young, and never die" (Lévi, *Doctrine and Ritual*, 280), which places alchemy thus understood at the basis of what Schelling views as modernity's corruption.

subject of self-assertion, creating and upholding this fallen world. Schelling speaks relatedly of the "demiurgic principle," which serves as the basis for the unity of God and his creation, and which is given over to human consciousness "for safekeeping" in its paradisal condition (UPO 392). In the Fall of Adam (*Abfall des Menschen*; UPO 396), the human "activates this principle again," separating it from divine oneness (UPO 392). Adamic consciousness, as we will further see in Chapter 6, has for Schelling a demiurgic role. To become "as God" is for the human to become the demiurge: a modern Gnostic image that persists across Schelling's philosophical trajectory. In the Fall of the human, all-oneness is suppressed, being is alienated (*entfremdet*) from God, and Christ as the Logos that mediates between particular being and universality ("the mediating potency") is separated from the Father and forced into the service of human self-assertion, or subjected to "the violent force [*Gewalt*] of the human" (UPO 392, 396–397). Through human fault (*Schuld*), the "Son of God" becomes "Son of Man," signaling the fact that the divine Logos of creation is now decentered and claimed by the human. The human "usurps the exclusively divine privilege to summon the beginning of creation out of its inwardness again," becoming the usurper-demiurge of the second creation. Creation is to be re-enacted and its mystery (*Mysterium*) unveiled only so that the human can cognize all of reality *for itself*: the ultimate presumption of human self-assertion (UPO 392).

In a theodical ambivalence that is typical for him, Schelling at once condemns the human demiurgic will to know and theodically justifies Adam's transgression as necessary for the development of freedom and rationality, *so that* human consciousness can return to a oneness with nature and the divine, and so that this oneness can be "restored at a higher level [*Stufe*]" and with "the highest conscious clarity" (IPU 247–248). For Schelling, this marks the overcoming of the modern demiurgic condition and the salvific return of reality to God. Then the human will finally "*cognize* what it was like to be in God" (GPP 313). Only "the higher knowledge" can liberate (*befreien*) us from the pain of our alienated present (IPU 260): a Platonic-Gnostic motif that is, however, directed by Schelling toward an overcoming of the Gnostic condition of modernity. "All that is needed is a new inversion" or turning (*Wiederumwendung*), in which "the natural" within the human (i.e., particular selfhood) and "the supernatural" (i.e., the universal) would become one in a conscious manner (IPU 260). For Schelling, there is only one operation that can lead out of modern diremption: the act of *giving up* self-assertion, of submission to the divine. However, this submission must be conscious,

Schelling insists, thereby denigrating paradisal bliss and inscribing it in the ascending development of consciousness.

Modernity is for Schelling a necessary stage in the ascent toward the highest. Modern science and philosophy make it possible to grasp nature and human consciousness as two equally lawful and universal unities, and to develop a meta-standpoint from which natural history and human history can be grasped as governed by universal laws. This, in turn, makes possible the meta-standpoint of a unified universal history, a standpoint that is quintessentially modern in character, even if Schelling also critiques the abstractness and negativity of modern thought. Since for Schelling autonomous consciousness and fallenness are entwined and since history, in his conception, follows a polar logic in which unity is reached through opposition, it is no wonder that he positions the age of fallenness that is modernity as that through which the development of consciousness must necessarily pass so as to reach its peak. The depths of universal fallenness, the "frightful perversity of our times," is that out of which the universal task of philosophy arises. Modernity is an epoch whose mission is to develop abstract thought and the capacity for consciousness to their utmost "negative" limit, so that consciousness can be re-inverted into the "positive" cognition of the human as one with God and nature within the one lawful process of divine revelation. For Schelling, true ("positive") philosophy of divine being is subsequent upon the diremipted rational ("negative") philosophy that emerges from the general Christian contradiction and must be re-subordinated to the promise of reconciliation (see Chapter 6). This re-subordination—the *ekstasis* of recentering in God—is the task of the more blissful epoch that true philosophy heralds, redeeming modernity by re-inverting it and directing it toward the higher.

In order to enter on the path of true knowledge, there is one crucial step that modern consciousness must take. Grasping the one divine order within nature and within itself, human consciousness must recognize the error (the original sin) of severing itself from its own rootedness in this order. The human needs to realize that it is but a part, even if a crucial conscious part, of a universal reality that precedes and exceeds it, to cognize its own embeddedness in the theo-cosmic process, and to rationally identify with this embeddedness as the human's own structural condition. To do so is to reconnect with "the inner history of nature" as divine history (GPP 471–472), to respond to the wake-up call of nature and to abandon self-assertion (GPP 474). One may also put it the following way: for Schelling, human intelligence is that through which the universe cognizes itself. However, the human in its self-assertion falsely considers its selfhood, and not the universe (or, theologically, God as the absolute subject), to be the true subject of knowledge. The human regards its mind as autonomous, without realizing that it is a dimension of the universe. Thereby, the human neglects the real conditions of its own intelligence, to which the universe gives rise, and without which the origin and purpose of intelligence remain incomprehensible and perverted. These real conditions, this groundedness of intelligence in the universe as a real-ideal whole, must be reincorporated into human cognition if it is to become true cognition. Universality must be restored *to* the universe, and the human must abandon its self-assertive pride and grasp itself as the carrier of the universe's self-cognition (itself arguably a hubristic position, which Schelling, however, associates with humility and the giving up of one's selfhood). This would amount to the redemptive re-inversion of the "bad" inversion of the Fall, opening onto an epoch at the end of which the human will be reinstated at the center—in other words, as the highest "ideal" organ of the universe within the restored immediacy and all-transparency of knowledge: a heaven regained.

4.2. Kenosis and Construction: The Method of Philosophy

For Schelling, the practice of true philosophy is that of re-subordinating consciousness to the theo-cosmic process as the movement of the absolute subject. Through this recentering in the divine, the philosopher becomes capable of constructing universal history, including humanity's place in the universe, and pointing the way toward the absolute future. In this subchapter, on the basis of Schelling's *Initia* lectures, in which he provides a detailed elaboration of his post-1809 vision of philosophical construction, I single out *five fundamental operations* that, taken in their unity, constitute the true philosophical method as Schelling envisions it during this period. For him, true philosophy is rooted in a kind of spiritual exercise or spiritual struggle, a practice of de-subjectivation or the loss of self, and an art of turning[10] that provides a way *upward* out of the fallenness of modernity while remaining rational and reflection-based and while constructing universal history with a view to bliss.

---

10. To borrow an expression from Plato's *Republic*, which speaks of "an art . . . of turning the soul around," in which the soul turns its gaze away from darkness and upward, so as to see the light of truth (518c–d).

4.2.1. First Operation: Purification (from the Confusion of the World)

Purification is not so much part of the philosophical method itself as the necessary initiation practice (cf. already UV 472–473). By nature, everyone "finds themselves within knowledge," even those who do not seek knowledge consciously. Yet this knowledge is erroneous. It is "the same knowledge into which the human displaces itself by making itself into the knowing subject over and against eternal freedom": the knowledge reached through the bad *ekstasis* of self-assertion. Our "natural knowledge" is a distortion or displacement (*Entstellung*). Therefore, "those who approach philosophy without having purified themselves or who are, so to speak, covered in the impurity of this [natural] knowledge inevitably find themselves in a state of an even greater confusion" (IPU 259–260). The contrast between the standpoint of philosophy and that of phenomenal knowledge, inherited from the identity philosophy, entails a spiritual practice of de-subjectivation, preparing one for entry into *gnosis*.

"Only to one who is pure does the pure reveal itself" (IPU 265). With these words, Schelling concludes Lecture 11 in the manuscript of *Initia*. The structure of these lectures itself reflects Schelling's emphasis on method: Lectures 1 to 11 are devoted to the essence of philosophy and to guiding the listeners toward the necessity of giving up their natural knowledge so as to glimpse divine bliss and to be able to construct the movement of eternal freedom. Following this, the subsequent lectures construct divine being and the theo-cosmic process. Near the end of Lecture 11, Schelling summarizes the entry point into philosophy as follows: "Everything, accordingly, demands that one give up one's knowledge and reach the point of division" or *krisis*, "through which one not only can, for the first time, glimpse oneself in complete freedom but also can face eternal freedom in its ante-original purity" (IPU 264). To enter philosophy is to glimpse the heaven that the subject in its self-assertion tries to yet cannot reach; it is to be displaced, in a good *ekstasis*, to a vision of bliss.[11] The task of the philosopher is to be able to face the bliss of divinity (to have it *gegenüber* oneself; IPU 264) and not be consumed by it: purity facing purity.

---

11. It is at this point that *ekstasis* reoccupies the function that intellectual intuition used to have in the identity philosophy (as Schelling himself suggests; IPU 202). However, unlike intellectual intuition, *ekstasis* is tied to a decentered vision of reality. One could put it the following way: bliss remains for the post-1809 Schelling the same (non-relational and a-worldly), yet his metaphysics of finitude changes, and the logic of accessing bliss *out of* the unblissful reality changes, too. Cf. additionally Hühn, *Fichte und Schelling*, 206–212.

While the philosopher could at this point become immediately one with the divine in a bliss of mystical seeing (*Schauen*), this is not what Schelling wants. Philosophy is for him tied to the structure of twoness, since the possibility of the world is thinkable only through twoness, not oneness. Accordingly, twoness must be maintained, and philosophical method must be based on reflective thought, albeit the kind that would be free of self-assertion. This is the hardest challenge for the philosopher: to maintain reflection even in the face of bliss.

4.2.2. Second and Third Operations: Self-Emptying and Self-Sacrifice (or the Event of Christ)

Self-emptying and self-sacrifice, which enact de-subjectivation and the giving up of self-assertion, are conjoined by Schelling while standing in tension. Self-emptying is the culmination of purification, an absolute purity that coincides with the emptying out of one's will. It is what Schelling calls the hardest: not to will. To empty one's selfhood is to "leave everything, give up everything, not only what is external but also *oneself*—indeed, especially *oneself*" (IPU 203). Since life equals ceaseless striving, self-emptying is the death (*Absterben*) of finite subjectivity, a becoming indifferent to life. The subject turns here into a non-subject, absolutely dispossessed. As leading up to this operation, purification is a practice of spiritual death.[12] To remain at the standpoint enacted by self-emptying would be to remain in bliss. But then at this standpoint of absolute oneness, there would be, in a familiar manner (cf. Chapter 2), no need for philosophy at all.

Hence, Schelling needs to inscribe self-emptying in a further operation from which the process of philosophy could begin. To that end, he reconfigures self-emptying as an inner crisis of self-surrender or self-renunciation (*Selbstentsagung*) *toward* the higher. Philosophy begins through a *krisis* in the threefold sense of the Greek term: as the division between the finite and the absolute subject, as the subject's judgment over its own fallen self and false knowledge (*krisis* as *Urteil*), and in the medical sense of *krisis* as the critical turning point from sickness to recovery—a point that also coincides, in theological terms, with the moment of conversion, of turning from the darkness of fallen selfhood to the light of the divine. Philosophy

---

12. This death is further associated by Schelling with Plato, and with the Christian logics of diminution and spiritual rebirth: "Whoever wants to gain life must first lose it" (IPU 684–685).

becomes possible as the subject not simply empties itself out but, "horrified" by the depth of its error (IPU 248), sacrifices itself to the absolute subject, who receives the subject's finite selfhood as the ground for unfolding the process of the absolute subject's own self-knowledge or coming-to-itself. In this way, the absolute subject (or the theo-cosmic process itself) becomes the subject of knowledge. "In philosophy," Schelling insists, "it is not the human who knows" (IPU 262). Through human consciousness, the theo-cosmic Logos articulates or constructs itself. As empty, consciousness becomes perfectly receptive, prostrating itself before the movement of the absolute so that the absolute can move through it. "One must remove *one's self* from the position of the subject—displace oneself—in order to make room for the true subject" (IPU 248). At work in this operation is a logic of position or place (*Stelle, Ort*). Self-emptying occurs for the purpose of removing oneself from the unjustly occupied place of the true subject, and of occupying the right place of submission to the higher: *ekstasis* in the good sense again (IPU 203).[13] The invertedness of self-assertion, in which the universal is subordinated to the particularity of selfhood, is thereby re-inverted.

This moment of transcendence, of self-surrender *to* or *for* the higher subject, is what makes the operation of self-sacrifice distinct from sheer self-emptying and from bliss as a state that refuses the division between lower and higher or the logics of reward and telos. Considered immanently, bliss is not for the sake of anything and does not engender transcendence or sacrifice. "Whoever truly wants to philosophize must be rid of all hope, all desire, all longing; he must will nothing, know nothing, feel naked and poor," asserts Schelling—and taken on its own, this is a description of the state of bliss. And yet, Schelling continues, the philosopher must "surrender everything *so as* to gain everything" (IPU 620). Or, in a formulation quoted earlier, one empties oneself "*in order to* make room for the true subject" (emphasis added). Through these formulations, the logics of telos, transcendence, hierarchy, and reward re-enter and supersede immanent bliss. This double operation of self-emptying and self-sacrifice enacts the Pauline-Christian logic of diminution and restages the sacrificial kenosis of Christ in his choice to submit in death to the will of the Father. As Paul writes in the Epistle to the Philippians, Christ "emptied himself [*ekenosen heauton*]" by "humbl[ing]

---

13. The idea of self-emptying *toward* the absolute subject is further configured in Schelling's lectures from the 1830s onward in terms of will: one must renounce one's finite will so as to *will* God as the absolutely first. This willing is the first operation of true philosophy (see, e.g., GPP 462–463, DRP 567).

himself and bec[oming] obedient to the point of death—even death on a cross." And "therefore God also highly exalted him" (2:5–9).

For Schelling, the kenosis of Christ involves precisely the combination of self-emptying and self-sacrifice to the absolute subject.[14] In his philosophy of revelation, Schelling highlights the obedience of Christ in his self-surrender to the Father. One may speak of the bliss of Christ as the immediate coincidence in him of the particular and the universal that is enacted by his self-emptying—but, again, this bliss is inscribed in the logics of sacrifice and of mediation between lower and higher, absent in bliss as such. Through Christ's sacrifice, the fallen being is re-subordinated (*unterworfen*) to God, and finitude's position in the infinite is restored (UPO 391–393). At this point, we transition world-historically from the epoch of pagan mythology to the revelation of the one true God in and through human consciousness. As we remember, the event of Christ for Schelling inaugurates but does not complete this process; Christianity functions within a structure of promise and the not-yet. "Christianity is yet by no means fully actualized [*verwirklicht*]" (UPO 383). The obstacle to its universal actualization is self-assertion, which maintains the reality of fallenness. True philosophy, as Christian in character, must guide the human toward overcoming this obstacle.

The kenosis of Christ and its restaging in philosophy thus mark structurally the inversion of inversion, or the revelation of the divine truth that previously lay hidden in darkness. As illumining universal darkness with the light of science, philosophy takes up the task of revelation and true enlightenment. This, too, means that philosophy cannot be claimed by the human as its own (merely human) knowledge, since that would amount to subordinating revelation to human self-assertion. Philosophy is divine and cosmic, not just human. Schelling employs the phrase "human philosophy" as secondary in relation to philosophy as more than human. "The goal of the entirety of philosophy," he writes, "consists in the coming-to-itself of the absolute subject, so that it can cognize itself in us." This goal is what eternal wisdom has been looking for since the origin of the universe. "In human philosophy, then," Schelling continues, "we are dealing with *the same* self-cognition of eternal freedom" (IPU 249). Cosmologically, the universe has since its origin striven

---

14. Dubilet, *Self-Emptying Subject*, presents an important recent attempt to theorize an Eckhartian kenosis without sacrifice or telos ("without a why"). As containing the dimension of bliss, Schellingian kenosis is likewise without a why, yet it succumbs to the ambivalence that has haunted the concept of kenosis since the original Pauline model, namely, the tension between "without a why" and "for the sake of."

toward the revelation of oneness and toward the intelligence *to* which this oneness would be revealed. The universe itself seeks wisdom as the coming-to-itself of eternal freedom, and therefore philosophy (as love of wisdom) constitutes an inherent dimension of the universal process.

As Schelling likes to emphasize, Christ is the Logos that used to be originally one with God, and what Christianity discloses as the structure of the general Christian contradiction is a theo-cosmic truth that can be traced back to "the foundation of the universe" (UPO 169, POI 142, 329). In Chapter 5, we will consider in more detail Schelling's post-1809 doctrine of world-creation. For now, it is important to emphasize that, as the mediating potency, "Christ" names for Schelling the operation of *mediating what is fallen toward the higher, or toward the universal, through which fallenness is redeemed:* the generic operation that "ecstatically" re-subordinates the particular to the movement of the universal, thereby inscribing the particular into the overarching salvation history. One may speak in Schelling of the cosmic Christ as the persistence of this generic operation across universal history until, in the historical Christ-event, it becomes exoteric, or disclosed to human consciousness. As Schelling notes, the entire content of Christianity consists in the revelation of Christ, including as operative before Christianity (UPO 391).[15] With the revelation of this movement of *universal fallenness and redemption* to human consciousness, the general Christian contradiction emerges as the contradiction in consciousness between the fallen state of reality and the promise of its reconciliation at the end of time. This contradiction entails alienation from natural reality but also allows one to abstract fully from one's particular, "natural" self and to be *in* the world yet not *of* the world: a liberation of human consciousness, which reaches its pinnacle in modern philosophy and science and which in turn makes possible the new inversion in which the particular is subordinated to universality or turned into the ground of universality's unveiling.

Total abstraction from one's particularity, or from the self-assertive I, is what underlies the method of true philosophy for Schelling, and the act of Christ thus forms for him the conceptual model of salvation.[16] To construct true universality, philosophy must inhabit the Christ-event and has always cosmically inhabited it. Grasping the philosophical significance of Christ in

---

15. This point is also central to the accounts of Schelling's Christology that I seek to complement here: Danz, *Die philosophische Christologie Schellings*; McGrath, *Philosophical Foundations*; and Tritten, *Beyond Presence*.

16. One may recognize in this a mutation of Schelling's natural-philosophical idea of "depotentiation" as an abstraction from the I so as to construct the movement of nature.

Schelling is also important for understanding why he values modern rational thought despite its alienated character. Modern philosophy develops, from within an intensification of the general Christian contradiction, the standpoint of universality as the highest standpoint—even if, until Schelling himself, philosophy could not grasp the true character and significance of this standpoint. Moreover, modern natural philosophy, too, premised as it is on the Copernican revolution as disclosing scientifically the universal condition of decenteredness, only reconfirms for Schelling the Christian doctrine of fallenness or the general Christian contradiction as the true structure of universal reality (of "the world" as such). As remaining for Schelling within and confirming scientifically the general Christian contradiction, the Copernican revolution intensifies the sense of alienation from nature, but also makes it possible for consciousness to recognize alienation and decenteredness as the real condition of the universe out of which salvation history must lead.[17] In this manner, Schelling diagnoses modern philosophical universalism, and modern natural philosophy in particular, as the continuation of Christian universalism by other means.

4.2.3. Fourth Operation: Polar Construction (or, Wrestling with God)

In submitting kenotically to the absolute subject, the philosopher lets the movement of eternal freedom take over her will. Based on this, one might expect Schelling to configure philosophy as a radical passivity, leap of faith, or mystical oneness. In such concepts, however, there is no reflection, whereas philosophy for Schelling requires reflection and mediation. As always, philosophy is premised for him on a simultaneous vision of oneness and twoness, which would allow the philosopher to construct the world-process with a view to bliss. At the beginning of philosophy, there is the self-emptied philosopher facing eternal freedom in its purity. From this point onward, philosophy traces eternal freedom's inner logic and its transition into the theo-cosmic

---

17. This dimension of the Copernican revolution is further evident in Schelling's embrace of Kepler (against Newton) as constructing the universe through the joint forces of fallenness (gravity) and redemption (love); see, e.g., WAE 269–270/246–247, IPU 567–568. Moreover, the decentered universe carries for Schelling a Christian lesson of humility. Divine providence is at work in the fact that "the human habitat is not one of those proud lights in the sky, but the lowly earth, for here too applies: to the humble he gives grace" (DRP 494). Thereby, too, Schelling inscribes the decenteredness disclosed in the Copernican revolution into universal salvation history.

process, while always keeping ante-original bliss in view—as the bliss that is lost within the process yet is to be regained at the end. For the philosopher to conceptually construct this process, she must retain a distance from it so as to reflect upon each moment, or step, through which eternal freedom passes and to pass judgment on this moment's true significance and place within the whole. "Our knowledge," writes Schelling, "must be generated piecemeal, with proper divisions and gradations [*Abstufungen*], and this cannot happen without *reflection*" (IPU 252).

For Schelling, true philosophical reflection is not finite reflection as the structure of subject-object division. It is, instead, a kind of *meta-reflection or polarity*, in which the philosopher acts as the grounding force vis-à-vis the movement of universality, in order for this movement, or the theo-cosmic process, to cognize itself within the philosopher's consciousness as its ground or site. Throughout, the philosopher's reflection and judgment should be understood not as "her own," or as belonging to her in her finitude, but as the reflection and judgment of the absolute subject upon its own orderly movement. Theologically, this is divine self-cognition; cosmologically, the self-cognition of the universe; and anthropologically, the cognition by the human of its own place within a universal history that precedes and exceeds it.

Philosophical construction is polar construction: it moves between two poles (*Pole*). As usual, Schelling designates these as A and B. One pole (A) is the absolute subject and the other (B) is the philosopher's consciousness; between them, the dynamic of true knowledge plays out. In the beginning, they stand in opposition. A is the universality that, however, lacks actuality, or groundedness in actual consciousness. It is, so to speak, the conceptual logic of the theo-cosmic process that has not yet become actual and self-reflective, or has not come to itself. B, accordingly, is the philosopher's consciousness as that which does not yet know (*das Nichtwissende*), but which must become the real carrier of knowledge. What emerges in the *krisis* with which philosophy begins is a "free thinking" that is emptied of all content: an ecstasy of *unknowing*, "the bliss of non-knowledge" (IPU 222), the absolute freedom to know nothing and be nothing. This unknowing is, however, there not for its own sake, but for the sake of a higher knowledge. Free thinking is an absolute depotentiation, since this depotentiation alone can make room in human consciousness for the theo-cosmic process. Only in this manner can universal darkness start to be illuminated. Through this "inner division and liberation, the light of science must rise for us" (IPU 213). What follows this division between A and B is the quasi-chemical process of their interfusion or transmutation (*Umwandlung, Umgestaltung, Verwandlung*; IPU 212–213) into a higher oneness.

The opposition between the divine as closed off unto itself and human consciousness as external to it restages, in a specific manner, the human expulsion from divine oneness in the Fall of Adam. A and B, Schelling notes, are the same "elements" that were separated in the tearing apart of the urconsciousness (IPU 246). However, this is an *inverted* restaging, in which human consciousness does not persist in self-assertion but gives it up, recognizing that *I myself do not know*. As such, philosophy restages the Fall of Adam as an act of redemption and repentance. In this regard, philosophical unknowing is for Schelling at once kenotic and Socratic. As Schelling sees it, when Socrates says, "I know only that I do not know," he points to the beginning of philosophy in kenosis and to the divine force of truth as what "generates knowledge" in a way that exceeds the finite self—a generation that unfolds in the dialectical art of conversation (*Unterredungskunst*) between the philosopher and the divine principle (IPU 226). As the "brightest phenomenon of all antiquity" (IPU 226), Socrates confirms that the kenotic Christ-operation is at work in paganism even before the historical Christ-event: an idea that is Christian-supersessionist in character, and that connects to Schelling's broader supersessionism to be analyzed in Chapter 6.

The process of philosophy as it plays out dialectically between A and B is not a smooth emanative unfolding; it is an *agon* or struggle. In his characteristic natural-philosophical manner, Schelling grasps it as an opposition of forces in which B (consciousness) is the particularizing force that *counteracts* the movement of A (the force of the divine subject) so as to slow it down and to hold each particular moment of the theo-cosmic process within consciousness in proper order and succession. In a double vision, just as the philosopher lets A run through her consciousness, she must also reflect upon each step in this process while understanding that it is eternal freedom's and not her own movement: an art (*Kunst*) of which philosopher must become the master (*Meister*). A is the "driving, accelerating force," and B is "the halting, retarding, reflecting force" (IPU 246). The philosopher's skill consists in balancing the two forces within herself while holding them in tension. "Reflection," Schelling emphasizes, consists in "holding the poles apart" or maintaining the meta-structure of twoness and in skillfully controlling "the reflecting force that inhibits the movement [of eternal freedom in consciousness] by constantly contradicting it" (IPU 252). Thereby, the philosopher reflectively reconstructs this movement and *gives being* to knowledge by providing the site—her consciousness—where the absolute subject's self-cognition becomes actual. "In philosophy," as we remember, "it is not the human that knows." "Rather," Schelling continues, "the human is what counteracts [*widerstrebt*] the true generative subject of knowledge, halting it" and reflecting upon it (IPU 262).

While this reflection is not the philosopher's own but the self-reflection of the absolute subject in and through her, the force with which she counteracts the absolute subject *is* her own. The philosopher wrestles with the absolute, trying to inhibit it, and "this inhibition is what demonstrates the philosopher's own force." This inhibiting force must ensure that no moment or stage of the theo-cosmic process is overlooked. Every moment must be *assigned its proper place and time*, so that nothing is grasped out of order. All the points (*Punkte*) through which the world-process goes must be reflected upon and justified as necessary (IPU 213). "Each moment of this movement and [the philosopher's] knowledge of this moment are, in every instance, one" (IPU 225). The rational-mystical conjunction of kenosis and construction thus generates, as the result of the philosopher's wrestling with the absolute, a kind of immediate, transparent, almost automated thinking, in which it is not the self that thinks but the theo-cosmic process itself that passes through and is reflected in consciousness, step after step. Philosophy, Schelling writes, proceeds stage by stage or level by level (*stufenmäßig*; IPU 253), constructing an orderly ladder (*Stufenfolge*) of the ascending universal process. In this, the Schellingian philosopher's task is never to change or intervene in the world, but to reveal and submit to the true (divine) world-order so as to construct it philosophically: a point we should remember for later.

This wrestling takes so much skill and effort because it involves the holding down of the infinite within a consciousness that is finite. A is the infinite force of "the concept [*Begriff*] itself," or the driving force of the absolute concept—the concept that is only "mine" to the extent that I can hold or grasp it within my consciousness. It is "a concept that is stronger than me, a living, propulsive concept" (IPU 224). One must resist the force of the infinite so that it does not overwhelm one's consciousness and so that one can gain knowledge and not come away defeated. The challenge is to wrestle with the absolute to make it reveal itself to the philosopher piecemeal in a way that consciousness can accommodate. The philosopher must keep the absolute subject in tension so that the absolute subject can *articulate* itself in and through her consciousness.

To frame philosophy this way is to configure it as a spiritual trial in the tradition of the struggle or contest (*Anfechtung*) with God in prayer: a struggle modeled upon the biblical episode of Jacob's struggle in the night with a mysterious stranger who might have been God himself.[18] Purification and self-emptying, through which one learns to hold the forces of the world at bay and to remain serene amid the vortex, prepare one for this decisive trial—for wielding the force that aims to wrest knowledge from God. This contest with the divine is distinguished from mystical vision insofar as it is aimed at reflective or conscious understanding. It "concerns the desire to apprehend God fully," as Alister McGrath describes it.[19] "For you have struggled with God and with men, and have prevailed" (Genesis 32:28), as the line addressed to Jacob goes, who has seen God "face to face" (32:30), or to whom the light of the divine Logos has been revealed. For Boehme, whose reading of this scene bears strong resemblance to Schelling's, this struggle "stands wholly in the figure of Christ" as the divine Word.[20] The biblical Jacob identified his will with the divine, "took the Word of promise in him, and said, *I will not let thee go until thou dost bless me*, and wrestled the whole night with the Word of power, until he obtained victory; so that the promised Word gave itself to him as his own."[21] For Schelling, in this manner, the philosopher accesses the universal Logos obscured by self-assertion. The night of this struggle is an inner crisis and divine trial, followed by the clarifying *krisis*. Only the kenotic combination of wrestling with God while letting go of one's self-assertion and submitting to the divine can let the theo-cosmic Logos occupy the place of one's "own" knowledge, while avoiding the fall into hubris and error.

In more technical terms, the attainment of a fully differentiated, self-reflective oneness of A and B is for Schelling a bidirectional process: A and B must infuse each other, A → B and B → A. In theological terms, God must recognize himself in human consciousness and recognize human consciousness as the site of his own self-cognition; and consciousness must recognize its own ante-original oneness with God.

B → A: On the one hand, B gives itself over or "elevates itself to A" (IPU 219) so as, from within its unity with A or as filled with A's movement, to affirm itself as A's real ground, thus restoring to itself the position that it used to have within paradisal oneness. In other words, the philosopher's consciousness surrenders itself to the absolute subject so as to ground the latter's movement in itself. The philosopher's activity is also reflective in the sense that it

---

18. See Genesis 32:24–31. On this tradition, see Podmore, *Struggling with God*.
19. McGrath, *Christian Spirituality*, 95.
20. Boehme, *Mysterium Magnum*, vol. 2, 567.
21. Boehme, *Mysterium Magnum*, vol. 1, 345. Translation slightly modified.

holds up a mirror to eternal freedom in which the latter sees itself at every step of its own movement. In this meta-reflection, I not only become a vessel for the universal subject but remain conscious of myself *as* vessel, reflecting (on) the movement of the absolute within myself.[22] With regard to this movement, the philosopher must become "a calm observing *witness.*" To ground this movement is to *be* (one with) it: to provide being (*Sein*) to the absolute (IPU 225), to serve as its material carrier (*Materie*; IPU 220).

$A \rightarrow B$: From the opposing end or pole, A enters B and fills it or discloses itself to B so as, from within B, to regain itself as now actualized in B. A cognizes itself in B and recognizes B as what was meant to be A's prelapsarian ground. In this way, A accepts B or embeds it in itself, makes B "inner to itself again," recognizing B as its paradisal "inner [ground]" (IPU 219–221). By making room for the movement of A within itself, consciousness proves to A that it is, indeed, the destined site of A's coming-to-itself.

Thereby, the alienation of A and B is overcome in the reconstituted $A = A$. The philosopher's consciousness recenters itself by cognizing its own theo-cosmic conditions of possibility and incorporating them into itself, thus embedding itself in universal reality—an act through which universal reality, so to speak, recognizes this intelligence as "its own" intelligence. A and B reflect each other perfectly within a new wholeness, and the philosopher becomes the absolute subject's conscious carrier (IPU 247), restoring what the *Freedom* essay calls the position of reason as the "calm site" of eternal wisdom (FS 178/76).[23] Philosophy is an art of polarity and tension through which reconciliation, clarity, and the absence of tension (*Spannungslosigkeit*; IPU 210) are achieved. A becomes transparent (*durchsichtig*) to itself in B, and what used to be "dark [*finstere*] matter" becomes the carrier of light (IPU 220; cf. EIP 59).

In this manner, the philosopher's transfigured state prefigures the blissful state of humanity at the end of time. The philosopher's *ekstasis* of recentering toward a meta-standpoint *in* the absolute, from which she can construct the entire system of times including the absolute future, serves a prophetic or divinatory function. Philosophy discerns, out of the present, deep processes of crisis and salvation, of fallenness and redemption, proclaiming a universal future that is not here yet. In tracing the self-articulation of the theo-cosmic

---

22. Cf. Whistler, "Silvering," for a related reading of Schelling's vision of the philosopher as a speculative mirror of the absolute.

23. In his *Confessions*, Augustine likewise speaks of the Sabbath as the state where we "rest in God" and God "rest[s] in us" (157). Cf. also *City of God*, 800 (XVII.12).

process, philosophy also articulates the normative position of humanity therein, which humanity is yet to fully actualize.

4.2.4. Fifth Operation: Anamnesis (or, Re-collecting Fragments of Bliss)

Although I am considering it last, Schelling regards anamnesis or recollection (*Erinnerung*) as one with the movement of philosophy from the outset. As previously mentioned, for Schelling, to *think* is to *remember*. "All science is a recollection" or remembering (WA11 16/73) through which the philosopher re-collects into oneness the fragments of bliss. Scared away by self-assertion, eternal freedom takes flight (*Flucht*) into darkness (IPU 222). However, traces of light—"darkly felt traces of the original truth" (IPU 259)—remain, even as they become dispersed in the explosion of the Fall. A memory of paradisal bliss persists within the human and must be brought to the surface in the *krisis* from which philosophy begins. What is externally repressed must again become inner (*innerlich*) to eternal freedom. This (broadly Platonic) anamnesis is that to which the universe calls the human, and that which the philosopher enacts—again, as a prefiguration of the absolute state in which humanity will have re-collected universal reality in bliss.

In this manner, philosophy responds to what Hans Jonas terms the Gnostic feeling of "awakened homesickness,"[24] which generates the longing for the bliss that, from within the structure of fallenness, appears as the lost paradisal oneness. Schelling grasps post-Copernican cosmic alienation as the inner turmoil and the desire to be at home in this alien universe within all humans (not just the philosopher). However, as capable of facing purity and articulating the universal process *as* divine, the philosopher is the only one who can discern and follow the divine light as reflected in the light of science. Philosophy qua recollection is the restoration of the divine order that promises universally an end to alienation.

4.2.5. History and the Restoration of Justice: Philosophy as "Proof" of the Divine

The new age to which the re-inversion prophetically announced by philosophy leads is the age of the restoration of "the right and true relation" and

---

24. Jonas, *Gnostic Religion*, 50.

"order of things," the order of absolute justice (*Gerechtigkeit*; DRP 491). For the post-1809 Schelling, to employ Schiller's famous expression, the sense that "world history is the world tribunal" intensifies.[25] "Justice" names for Schelling the idea, central to his thought, that *everything and everyone is given their due* by the world-process: that every possibility that is actualized within this process is assigned its rightful place, or that all is revealed for what it is by the light of divine judgment (*krisis* as *Urteil*), which separates the good from the bad, the true from the erroneous, and the higher from the lower. The world-process metes out punishment, insofar as it expels from the divine that which opposes it, as Adam is expelled from paradise. It also pardons and redeems, insofar as one (re)submits to the higher and becomes part of the movement of salvation, as one does when giving up one's self-assertion.

No less important, the world-process for Schelling abolishes oppression and enacts universal liberation—and in Chapter 5, I will theorize the movement of universal history in Schelling as a cosmic revolution leading to the restoration of justice. Schelling's affect is to rejoice at the prospect of divine judgment, perceived as the righting of wrongs and the end to oppression. To this messianic sentiment, he further adds the Gnostic-apocalyptic view of liberation as the liberation from the world itself in its unblissfulness. One awaits divine judgment with joy, not because one believes oneself to be righteous, but because one knows the world to be *structurally* inverted and wrong, and eagerly anticipates its end: the end toward which the world-process itself is directed. The world of self-assertion is a structure of oppression: of the repression of what is essential by what is external and particular—the structure that demands its own abolition. The re-inversion that Schelling proclaims is the inversion of the world's invertedness, leading to an apocalyptic unveiling in which bliss is revealed. The last is to become the first, which is to say, what self-assertion unjustly subordinates to itself is to be liberated and positioned as the true subject above it. And the inner is to become the outer, which is to say, what is concealed (*verborgen*) is to become revealed (*offenbar*).[26] This re-inversion is the path to absolute bliss. There is, in the end, nothing to be

---

25. "Weltgeschichte ist Weltgericht": this verse from Schiller's poem "Resignation" (1786) constitutes a proleptic precis of the German idealist theodicy of history.

26. The new inversion is "the turning outward of what was inner and the turning inward of what was outer" (WAE 233/215), or "the turning outward of what was concealed and the turning inward of what was externally visible [*offenbar*]" (WA14 227/18), where what used to be external becomes the inner ground of what used to be repressed underneath externality. Christianity, for Schelling, is where this structure of re-inversion is revealed to consciousness, marking Christianity's persisting universal significance.

afraid of, *as long as one submits to the divine*—and Schelling's flirting with the doctrine of *apokatastasis panton*, or universal restoration, is characteristic in this regard (SPV 185). Everything can be redeemed, and will be redeemed, *if* the true order of things is restored.

This conditional, this "if," merits additional emphasis. In the post-1809 Schelling, the sense of the contingency of reality—across natural and human history—comes to the fore. Philosophical construction is for him *historical* construction, and the contingency of history plays an important role in his understanding of what it means for philosophy to construct historically. Of course, Schelling asserts that the Christian-providential world-plan is always at work throughout history and that, while natural and human history are replete with events that could have turned out otherwise, the philosopher can discern the workings of providence even in these contingent events. The Fall of Adam is a typical example here: it is contingent, since it would not have happened if not for the human will's free decision to transgress; yet the philosopher discerns in it a "higher" theodical necessity, a divine plan, dispensation, or *oikonomia* according to which the Fall serves the purpose of the development of human consciousness into a knowing carrier of the divine. However, especially when it comes to the construction of the *future* of universal history, philosophical construction can only go so far. The ineliminable contingency of the future limits what the philosopher can see from the meta-standpoint of the system of times.

To understand this, one needs to grasp the meaning of Schelling's claim that philosophical construction is the "proof" of God and divine world-governance, and thus proof of providence in history (an idea that is pivotal for what Schelling calls his "positive philosophy"). "Eternal freedom itself," he writes, "cognizes itself in us," and thus "the entire science is its [i.e., divine freedom's] proof of itself" (IPU 192). "The entire movement" that philosophy constructs, the theo-cosmic process, "is but eternal freedom's proof of itself or exhibition of itself" (IPU 188; cf. UPO 71–72, GPP 466, POP 147). One may observe an ambivalence in Schelling's formulations: is it philosophical construction that is the proof, or is it the movement of universal history itself? The assumption here is that the philosopher constructs the past, present, and future in a way that coincides with the actual movement of history, discerning *within* this movement divine judgment and the realization of eternal freedom. Every ascent and descent, every significant turn of events within the movement of history, is discerned and judged in philosophical construction and assigned its place within the unfolding of the providential world-plan toward the absolute future.

The future, however, has not actually taken place yet, and Schelling insists throughout his post-1809 writings and lectures that the path humanity is yet to traverse remains long and uncertain. Schellingian construction is kairotic: the philosopher discerns the decisive turning points in the history of salvation (what the New Testament calls *kairoi*, the salvific "points of time") that have already taken place, such as the event of Christ, and she can prophesy a new turning point and glimpse it as imminently coming—yet she cannot *know* the future.[27] This explains the brevity with which Schelling always sketches the historical path to the absolute future, since it can be fulfilled only empirically. "The final period [of history]," he asserts, "is just as far beyond the spiritual horizon of our vision as ... the farthest nebulae, whose structure can no longer be discerned with the telescope" (SPV 184/243): the immensity of time is decentered and dark, too, like the universal expanse. Thereby, theologically, a pious distance to the divine is maintained, with the philosopher refusing to claim omniscience; and ontologically, the contingency of reality is acknowledged. The philosopher can construct the universal law or *ought* that governs the world-process, and she can have faith in the absolute future and in the providence that steers the world—but she cannot a priori predict the turns of history.

The absolute future is thus philosophically constructed as universal history's prophesied completion, yet *only the empirical course of history and actual attainment of the absolute future can serve as the proof of this future*, and thereby as the proof that history is the history of revelation and salvation. "For positive philosophy, a future is opened, which will likewise consist in nothing but a progressive proof" (POP 147): this is what the philosopher must have faith in. The future embodies the gap between empirical history and philosophical construction, a gap that cannot be closed as long as the not-yet of the world persists. One aspect that makes Schelling's post-1809 philosophy of history, for all of its Christian piety, so radical is that, in his vision of philosophical construction, the fate of the divine itself hangs in the philosophical air and lacks solid historical ground until history reaches the destination that philosophy announces for it. *Once* the absolute future has been reached, and only at this endpoint, world history will have been "empirically" (a posteriori)

---

27. Cf. Cullmann, *Christ and Time*, 39–40: "*Kairos* [is] a point of time that has a special place in the execution of God's plan of salvation.... To men, even to the disciples, it is not granted to know the date of the still future *kairoi*"—just as it is not granted to the Schellingian philosopher. Prophecy, as inhabiting the standpoint of the end time, is thus distinct from prediction.

or "historically" justified as having led to bliss.[28] Philosophy justifies the world-process as the path to salvation; yet, there remains the danger that history might *not* actually follow this path. The human might continue to persist in self-assertion, forestalling the re-inversion that true philosophy proclaims. The world remains a problem for Schelling due not only to its fallenness but also to its contingency. This, too, is why divine judgment brings joy: it delivers the subject from the contingency, uncertainty, and doubt inherent in the inhabitation of post-Copernican reality and in the present state of humanity on the earth.

Contingency is extended by Schelling to the divine being. "I am not allowed," he notes, "to exclude the possibility for the [divine] essence *not* to be; on the contrary, I *must* posit this possibility." But since it is God, in order to think of him *as* God, I must also posit this possibility as *overcome or mastered* by him (GPP 462). "Only *that* God who has a world of which he is the master [*beherrscht*] is actually God," Schelling asserts; "only *that* God is the actual God who possesses due sovereignty [*Herrschaft*] and glory [*Herrlichkeit*]" (UPO 107). And since "There is no glory in the absence of that which has been mastered" (UPO 185), the world is necessary as that through which God proves himself to be the Lord in actuality, triumphing over the possibility of his own nonbeing. Schelling thus inscribes the logic of *world-mastery*—of domination, lordship, or sovereignty—into his positive concept of God.

How can God begin this path to his triumph over his own nonbeing? Only by exiting his bliss and revealing himself in and through creation, or (since Schelling understands creation as continuous world-steering) in and through universal history. This also provides a new answer to the question *Why must this world be?* It must be, answers Schelling's positive philosophy, for the sake of divine revelation. Only through the divine act or deed (*Tat*), and through world history as the consequence (*Folge*) of this deed and its progressive unfolding, can God be grasped in the positive manner as the living (*bewegliche*) God of creation and revelation. "I am," says the Schellingian God, "who I will be," or "I will be who I want to be" (GPP 444, WA27 137, EIP 104; cf. Exodus 3:14).

To save (*erreten*) God from nonbeing, hiddenness, and concealment is what philosophy must do (GPP 464): to overcome the *deus absconditus* of

---

28. Schelling speaks in this regard of true philosophy as a "progressive empiricism" or "progressive science" (GPP 245–247, 433, 461, PO1 130; cf. IPU 189, 253).

modernity, to let the divine emerge from within fallen modern reality, and thus to overcome Gnosticism, this time completely. To that end, philosophy leads God through what is other than him, that is, finite being, so that he can be shown to have overcome the resistance of being and emerged as the Lord of being (GPP 468). Only at the end of history, via the trial of the world, can God the creator "prove" that he is one with the God of salvation (reconciling the Gnostic divide within God), and that it is ultimately for the better that the world is there despite its unblissfulness.

Nothing less than God's character as the true God is at stake here: if God fails to become the world-mastering God, he will be no more than a failed Gnostic demiurge, and his creation, too, will be irredeemable and illegitimate. Via the transcendent God, Schelling here mediates the same theodical problem of world-legitimation that we saw in his earlier thought. The historical process as rationally constructed by philosophy is "divine" in the additional sense that God himself stands in it on trial: a theodicy of history in which not finite human reason judges God, but God, through self-emptied human reason, judges and acquits himself. "Insofar as this process necessarily coincides with the being that we have before us in experience"—note the emphasis on the coincidence of construction with the empirical—"the being of the positive [divine] essence becomes a posteriori proven" (GPP 466).[29] Then "There can be no doubt that God is the Lord," "the master of the completed creation" (GPP 470, UPO 211). "God is strong enough to withstand the danger of scatteredness and to emerge victorious from it," Schelling assures us (GPP 470). The fact that he needs to assure us of that, however, signals that the *danger* of God being lost to the contingency of universal reality, and deep doubt about God's actuality and legitimacy (GPP 472), are inscribed in the critical moment of modernity out of which Schelling thinks and writes.

---

29. One may regard this as a mutation of the emphasis on the empirical verification of philosophical construction in Schelling's early *Naturphilosophie*. Cf. Nassar, *Romantic Absolute*, 209.

5
Universal Spiral

THIS CHAPTER TRACES the underlying logics of Schelling's post-Copernican theo-cosmic epic as it is narrated in his post-1809 thought. This narrative begins long before the emergence of the human—within the depths of divine being prior to God's transition to otherness and the world. This transition to otherness, or the divine will's own Fall from bliss into decentered being, forms for Schelling the beginning of creation: the original cosmic explosion. Following this explosion, the movement of universal history begins, which I theorize here as a movement of *cosmic revolution* leading to universal liberation and the restoration of justice. Universal history in Schelling is a process of turning and re-turning, one that is at once circular and ascending, so that the *figure* of history is an ascending spiral of spirals. The world-historical process begins at the origin of the universe, runs through all star systems including our solar system, ascends from inorganic to organic to human nature—and is then reiterated in the history of human consciousness as the ascent toward a state of absolute non-alienation and recenteredness that is still far-off in the future. Whereas in the Hegelian dialectic the basic operation is the negation of negation, in the post-1809 Schelling, as I will further argue in this chapter, *the re-inversion of inversion* is the operation that underwrites the universal ascent.

The *rhythm* of this universal ascent, I want to suggest, is the two-part movement of Fall and redemption, in which fallenness is identified with opposing the higher or the divine, or asserting oneself *against* the higher, and redemption with kenosis as the Christ-operation of re-inversion, self-emptying, and free submission to the higher. The Fall is a downward turning, which is followed by redemption as an upward turning and the attainment of a higher level of the universal process, a level at which the conjunction of Fall and redemption is restaged, and so over and over again at every level (*Stufe*) of the ladder (*Stufenfolge*) of universal history. Finally, the *center* around which and toward which the universal spiral revolves is the human as one with nature and God at the end of time: what Schelling calls the realized pantheism, absolute bliss, or all-oneness.

The three major sections within this chapter focus on the different dimensions of Schelling's construction of this overarching process. Section 5.1 demonstrates Schelling's continuing post-1809 emphasis on bliss as the absolutely first and absolutely real, and on the absence of transition from bliss to creation. It also provides an outline of universal history in Schelling as unfolding within the tension between cosmic war and the promised divine Sabbath. Section 5.2 traces Schelling's conception of the divine law (*Gesetz*), revealing the theodical nature of his philosophical construction of history. In Schelling, the law acts as the gatekeeper to bliss, deferring it indefinitely while tempting one to transgress, so that the process of divine judgment and the division between good and evil can be upheld. Section 5.3 then focuses on the figure of the cosmic revolution itself and its underlying logics (including those of transcendence, hierarchy, and place-assigning justice), as well as the relation between cosmic and political revolution. The figure of the ascending universal spiral, I suggest, allows one to better understand Schelling's political thought. During this period, as is well known, Schelling is a conservative who opposes the democratic revolutions of the nineteenth century. At the same time, as Manfred Frank has argued, there are elements in Schelling's philosophy that mark his affinity with early socialism.[1] I concur with Frank on this point, arguing that both the more conservative and the more radical elements in Schelling's post-1809 thought—both, so to speak, the "right" and the "left" Schelling—emerge from his vision of the structure, movement, and rhythm of universal history.

5.1. God's Own Shelter from the World: Cosmic War and Cosmic Peace

All movement is but a searching for rest.
—SCHELLING (PO2 13)

Schelling's post-1809 metaphysics remains a metaphysics of bliss and the world in their antagonistic entanglement, and he continues during these years

---

1. See Frank, "Einleitung des Herausgebers" and "Schelling, Marx und Geschichtsphilosophie."

to configure the beginning of world-creation as a Fall from bliss. The first theo-cosmic act of transgression, a transgression inscribed in the Schellingian universe or world (*Welt*) as a whole, is enacted by the divine will itself. God breaks up or splits his ante-original blissful oneness, so as to reveal himself—to reveal this oneness—out of multiplicity, decenteredness, and scatteredness. Thus, the still-ongoing process of creation equals that of God's revelation and explication, his self-expression in nature and human consciousness: "the development of a living, actual [divine] being exhibiting itself in science," that is, in philosophical construction (WA11 3/56). This vision of God's becoming actual over the course of universal history remains fundamental for Schelling throughout his post-1809 writings and lectures, even as he continues to position bliss as something that precedes and exceeds this process.

5.1.1. Unprethinkable Bliss, or, An Idle Divinity Prior to God

Disclosed in the philosophical self-emptying is a purity (*Lauterkeit*) that precedes all thinking and articulation. "In this *ekstasis*," Schelling writes, "eternal freedom arises for us, yet as a concept that is so pure that it stands above everything—as the ungraspable itself." "Our dialectical capacity," he continues, immediately seeks to draw distinctions in order "to pin down this pure freedom" and unfold it, so that philosophical construction can begin. Considered immanently, however, this purity precedes any transition to dialectical movement and cannot be grasped as anything. It is a "pure nothingness" that coincides with pure being, and to which dialectical terms do not apply (IPU 268–269).

"Purity" is a key term that, after 1809, becomes in Schelling synonymous with "bliss" as part of a terminological nexus that expresses the one state of bliss in its various aspects and that further includes heaven (*Himmel*), serenity or letting-be (*Gelassenheit*), joy (*Wonne*), and divinity (*Gottheit*). In the post-1809 Schelling, the function of bliss stays the same as in his earlier thought: it is the non-processual and nonproductive state that must be thought of as preceding and refusing the possibility of the world. Accordingly, the problem of (the possibility of) "exiting" this state or transitioning from bliss to creation remains for Schelling the pivotal, indeed, "first question of human thinking" (IPU 268; cf. WA11 17/74).

"How do we even begin to describe this purity," this "primordial essence" or "divinity"? Schelling asks, implying that bliss cannot be articulated in finite categories (WA11 15/72). All binary logics are ungrounded within the sheer nakedness (*Bloßheit*) of bliss. The state of bliss is an indifference

(*Indifferenz, Gleichgültigkeit*) that precedes the very possibility of distinguishing between oneness and twoness. As absolute indifference, bliss equals absolute freedom: the "unadulterated purest freedom," which "wills nothing and desires no cause, to which all things are equal, and which is unmoved by anything" (WA11 15/71). "Heaven," as we remember, is the resting will; and "only that will is absolutely free," Schelling reiterates, "which wills nothing" and "is as nothing" (EIP 109). The non-willing will "burns with a calm fire" that is so powerful that, if let loose, it would "consume" all being (IPU 377). The blissful being of such a non-will is a state of "pure delight," "grace, love, and simplicity," "serene joy," and "calm innermostness [*Innigkeit*]," which has no need to develop or go outside itself, and which "revels in not being" (WA11 15–16/71–73; cf. GPP 313: "freedom from being is joy").[2] It is the Eckhartian "simple silence" and "quiet desert, into which distinction never gazes."[3] *To be as nothing, to be as one who is absolutely free from being*: such is the formula of the state of bliss in the post-1809 Schelling.

The blissful being glimpsed by the philosopher is ante-original divine oneness, or the being of eternal freedom in its purity: the being of God prior to creation, and prior to any act of will, any division or decision. While Schelling's post-1809 philosophical monotheism is a construction of the living God or God the creator, bliss constitutes the non-processual and impersonal core of the divine. Terminologically, this is sometimes expressed by Schelling as the distinction between divinity (*Gottheit*) and God (*Gott*), which I adopt in what follows. Whereas God is the one who becomes actual through the world-process, divinity is the non-processual essence of the divine, or that within God which can never become part of or transition to the universal process. To theorize this distinction, Schelling refers again to the distinction between "essence" and "form." In God prior to creation, divinity or bliss is his *essence*, or what in Chapter 3 I called the pure "=," whereas the *form* of divine being is A = A. (The essence of absolute identity, in other words, exists in the form of what is identical with itself; the form is divinity's clothing or garment of light, the primordial divine name or form of articulation.) In the form of

---

2. Schelling's use of mystical terminology is deliberate. In his 1827/28 lectures, Meister Eckhart, Johannes Tauler, Henry Suso, Jan van Ruysbroek, and "all the mystics of old" are named as adherents of the idea of divinity thus understood (WA27 162). The post-1809 Schelling continues in part to adhere to the heretical and mystical antagonistic tendency that undoes the world and its creator, de-creating the world in bliss. However, as we will see, he ultimately decides in favor of the world and its creator-God, and hence against mysticism as an immanent dwelling in and with the divine non-will.

3. Eckhart, *Essential Sermons*, 198.

his being, God is articulated as triune: within A = A, one may distinguish the subject or selfhood (Father), the object or carrier of selfhood (Son), and the copula (Spirit). Thereby, Schelling reconfigures the form of self-identity in a Trinitarian manner. In God's ante-original state of bliss, however, this distinction is purely virtual, since the divine persons or powers (potencies) are here immediately dissolved into absolute oneness. What the triune oneness of A = A expresses is an essential bliss that, as such, precedes God himself: the innermost essence, which the ante-original form of divine being at once envelops or clothes and expresses or articulates.

This bliss is the "inaccessible light," the hidden light in which the unclothed divine essence dwells (WA27 162; cf. already STI 302/211), the spark of divinity that is not proper even to God. *Wherever* there is a state of bliss, this spark is what it expresses. *Whoever* is in bliss is one with this inaccessible light where being and nonbeing coincide. To be in bliss is to be as nothing, not even as God. This purity, Schelling writes, is "not God." "In the human, it is the true humanity [*Menschheit*]"—note the identification of human bliss with what is not properly human—"and in God the true divinity." "We have dared," he continues, "to posit this simplicity of the essence above God" (WA11 16/73). In God, in the human, and in nature bliss is concealed underneath or within their form of being and constitutes the innermost essence, the divine spark that does not belong to any of them. To be in bliss, to express this spark or be one with it—"to be as though one were not," to be the non-willing will—is "the highest" in God as well as "in the human and everywhere": "the highest bliss of which all being is capable" (IPU 278, GPP 313). Just as "the divinity of God consists in willing nothing" (EIP 108–109), so the essentiality of the human consists in the same non-will—as does the essentiality of nature, the absolute rest for which nature longs as its own essence. To be blissful is to be as an A = A that immediately dissolves in the pure "=." To pure essence, Schelling emphasizes, there corresponds pure, utterly "non-objectified being" (IPU 270). The state of bliss is a state of oneness, yet it is oneness as none-ness: to be in bliss is to be as nothing and no one, to give up one's particularity or selfhood, to be "naked and poor" (IPU 620) and "without quality [*eigenschaftslos*]" (WA11 15/71–72, WA27 162). Across universal reality, bliss carves out a shelter of nonbeing and non-will in all that wills and strives, a shelter where God and all reality can rest "unburdened [*unbelastet*] by the substance of the world," as Schelling characterizes the absolutely first (GPP 392–393).

Bliss remains, in Schelling's post-1809 thought, a crucial residue of the identity philosophy: the bliss of God, of the human, and of nature is the one bliss-in-common.[4] This bliss is what the philosopher glimpses in her self-emptying and what makes the philosopher "abandon everything finite," "abandon all being and even God, since God, too, is a concept that implies being" (IPU 684). Absolute freedom is the freedom to be nothing. To glimpse the essence is to glimpse the *shared nothingness* at the heart of all being: "the three potencies in their common nothingness" (EIP 90). The fact that bliss qua essence precedes any form of being is crucial, since this implies that there is only one essence of bliss that every A = A, every *simply being what one is*, expresses—an essence that is non-appropriable and non-objectifiable. There is nothing possessive in bliss, so that even to speak of the bliss *of* God or *of* the human is, strictly speaking, inappropriate. In this manner, bliss continues to cut across and dissolve the divisions of the world, persisting as the pantheistic core of Schelling's thought.

To speak of divinity is thus not to speak of the personal God of revelation. Divinity cares not for revealing itself or creating the world. Divinity as what is above God is what Schelling calls "the tranquil God" (*der stille Gott*; WA27 163) or hidden God, "God within himself" (WA27 150). Unlike God the creator, divinity or the hidden God is idle and does not care to go outside itself. In its absolute freedom, divinity is non-relational and "fully intransitive" (GPP 435, 440). It is, Schelling maintains, "outside all relation to the world," "completely free from the world," and has "no relation to creation" (GPP 379–380, 388). Only such non-relationality and absolute freedom from the world can be called the highest (GPP 379). To be transposed ecstatically to this highest standpoint is to completely annihilate the world: to *not* think the world, to preclude its very possibility (GPP 380), and thus to *not* think God the creator either. To retreat from his being into divinity is bliss for God himself: the "heaven where God dwells" and "eternally" loses himself in his essential *Mysterium*, in a "loss of self" that equals "the absolute in-itself" (WAF2 156, 178). If the personal God is a "he," then divinity is neither a "he" nor "she" (despite *Gottheit* and *Seligkeit* being feminine nouns in German), but "a sheer it" (*ein bloßes Es*; WA27 163): a pronoun that signals the nonbinary character of bliss. The hidden God is an "it," an impersonal God.

Impersonality, indifference, non-relation, non-will: these are the characteristics of heaven or bliss and of absolute freedom from the world, even for God. As long as one *is* (and this holds for God too), one feels the incessant pressure of "development," "progress," "revelation," "necessity," of all the burdensome

---

4. Cf. Eckhart, *Essential Sermons*, 195: "Just as all angels in the primal purity are all one angel, so are all blades of grass one in the primal purity, and all things are one."

not-yets of being. "All being strives to reveal itself," Schelling notes, "and hence strives toward development; everything that is carries within itself the sting of progress and self-expansion, of wanting to express its infinity" (WA11 14/70). That is why, he observes, "already in ancient times one sensed the unblissfulness of being" (EIP 102). "One note resonates through all the higher and better teachings," he relatedly asserts, and it is the note of bliss: the intuition that there is "a deeper state of essence," an "unconditioned state that is above being" (WA11 14/70) where nothingness and anonymity reign.

The Christian God, however, is a personal God, who creates and lawfully governs the world and who reveals himself.[5] This God is, as Schelling calls him, God in the "positive" sense, not the "negative" God (WA27 163). Considered positively, he is the relational God, and Schelling speaks in this regard of God's relativity (*Relativität*) or relationality (*Beziehung*; WA27 152–153). Unlike divinity, God stands in a relation to the world that he creates, over which he lords, and through which he becomes the actual God (UPO 107). For all of Schelling's talk about God's freedom, as positive and actual, God *needs* the world or is bound to the world through his very character as the positive God, so that one may speak of "God" in the post-1809 Schelling as already part of the logic of the world, or of world-creation and world-mastery. "God" and "world" are reciprocally determined. Only divinity remains absolutely a-worldly. God needs the world not in the sense that he *has* to create it, but in the sense that, without having created it, he cannot be "positively" God. Can the ur-being even be called a God, not to mention the one true God, unless he creates and governs the world? It is "the great fact of the world" (GPP 273) that prompts Schelling's focus on the positive God. As always in Schelling, the problem is why the world is even there, and the positive God is at once a function of and an answer to this problem. The world is there not for the sake of the world itself as a structure of invertedness and unblissfulness; it is there so that God can reveal himself as God in the positive sense and can be proven to be the one true God who triumphs over nonbeing. Nothing can be further removed than this God from the idle, hidden, nonproductive divinity. An absolute distance, without transition, separates the positive from the hidden God.

---

5. God is "personal" for Schelling not so much in the subjective sense as in the sense of being the ur-personality, the first triune A = A, the prototype of all will, as well as one who can be held accountable for his actions within a "lawful order" (DRP 536). In God's case, his actions as a person are subject to his own divine law. It is thus God as a person to whom the question of theodicy is addressed. This does not, of course, mean that Schelling's understanding of the personal God excludes the subjective aspect (e.g., in faith).

The fact that there is no transition between divinity and the positive God, or between divinity and the world, is a problem for philosophical construction as the construction of the theo-cosmic process. Considered immanently, divinity in its bliss does not proceed to any processuality. Construction thus begins with what is without transition to the movement that the philosopher must construct: it begins, as it were, prior to itself. Before one can approach this zero point with any thought-categories, Schelling says, it is *already there*. Instead of "the unconditioned," Schelling now calls it "the unprethinkable" (*Unvordenkliche*), that is, that which has no origin in thought and which thought cannot anticipate. Just as it precedes all active thought, so too it precedes all active will, while being absolutely first with regard to both—as the non-willing will in its pure being (UPO 638). This blissful being, which in its A = A dissolves into the nothingness of the essence, is "what is always ahead of all thinking," or what "must be presupposed before everything." It immediately "posits itself" before we can posit it, Schelling asserts, using the same language that he used to describe the unconditioned in 1795. "Prior to any positing, it is already the presupposed [*voraus Gesetzte*], or what is already there before we begin thinking." Our thinking cannot but arrive belatedly with regard to this purity, which precedes and exceeds it. "No matter how early we arrive," this purity "has already assumed the place of the unconditioned" (WAE 214/196; cf. IPU 283). This blissful (non)being is precisely the non-objectifiable being or nothingness-in-common that is revealed equally in the bliss of God, the human, and nature. The distance between the unprethinkable and the thinkable is the same absolute distance as that between the salvific hidden God or divinity and the positive God. How can philosophical construction bridge this distance? How can it re-mediate non-processual bliss into the theo-cosmic process?

5.1.2. The Divine Will and the Breaking of (the Form of) Oneness

The absolute distance within the divine reintroduces the Gnostic split between the salvific hidden God and God the creator, so that the specter of Gnosticism continues to haunt Schelling's thought. In the same stroke, this split inscribes in the divine from the outset the structure of the general Christian contradiction as God's alienation from his salvific essence.[6] *Relation*

---

6. To emphasize: God's self-alienation and the structure of the general Christian contradiction are for Schelling there already at the origin of the theo-cosmic process. What happens in

to the world is what alienates God from himself. Starting from Schelling's 1795 metaphysics, the question of why the world is there is entangled with another question: How is the possibility of the world thinkable? Since the absolutely first remains for Schelling without transition to the world, the latter question is equivalent to asking: *How is transition thinkable from what is absolutely intransitive?* Theologically, this is in turn the same as to ask: How to think the oneness of God across the absolute distance that separates him as creator from his blissful essence? How does the negative God become the positive God, so that the two are reconciled? Only in this manner can the Gnostic divide between the God of salvation and the God of creation be overcome.

For Schelling, God's self-alienation can be reconciled only through the history of salvation, or through the theo-cosmic process. Universal history alone can mediate the absolute distance. Only the absolute bliss at the end of the world can reconcile the bliss of divinity and the work of creation. This is why it is so important for Schelling to uphold the not-yet of history: it is salvific and reconciliatory for God himself. If bliss were to be enacted *right now* in an immediate annihilation of the world, disregarding the not-yet, God would not have proven himself to have mastered the world. Instead, in this scenario, the bliss of divinity would be directed, antagonistically and Gnostically, *against* the world, and *against* the God of world-creation and world-governance. And so the orderly not-yet must be maintained, so that bliss can emerge gradually as all-reconciliation from within history. To reconcile the world is to reconcile God as well. The positive God must subordinate the bliss of the hidden God to his own purposes: to the goal of creation and revelation. If Schelling positions, in an anti-Gnostic theodical manner, the positive God *above* the hidden God, despite proclaiming bliss to be the highest, it is because only the inscription of bliss in the world-process (as a process directed providentially toward bliss) can justify this process, and justify God the creator and world-steerer as the salvific God.

In order to subordinate the hidden God to the positive God, Schelling must claim that the will of the positive God—the will to creation and revelation—coincides with the non-will of the hidden God. The ultimate proof of this coincidence can be only universal history as leading to the universal restoration of the bliss of the non-will. In order to think universal history, however, the transition from oneness to actual difference, or from $A = A$ to $A = B$, must first be made thinkable. Since ante-original divine bliss is "fully intransitive,"

Christianity is the revelation of this structure as the true structure of reality (and the revelation of the promise of reconciliation inherent therein) to human consciousness.

and yet the world is there, there must have been an original break, a shattering of blissful oneness, through which "transitivity" was enacted (GPP 435). In order to maintain the unity of the hidden and the positive God, Schelling must configure this original break as enacted *by* God himself: after all, no one except God can bridge the absolute distance within the divine—and if philosophical construction can bridge this gap, it is only because God himself does so in a divine act that the philosopher reconstructs.

Therefore, in his post-1809 metaphysics, Schelling grasps this break or division (*Scheidung*) as a divine decision (*Entscheidung*) or the act of God's will, which exits its idle inoperative state and becomes active or operative (*wirkend*; IPU 278). God himself groundlessly or freely—that is, in a way that cannot be derived a priori from ante-original oneness—exits the heaven in which he dwells as the hidden God. God abandons his divinity and breaks the oneness of his being, transitioning to what is non-divine, since it is only within the structural opposition between the divine and the non-divine that world-creation can function. The beginning of creation is thus a transition from the form of oneness to the form of twoness or brokenness (*Gebrochenheit*; WA27 176).

It is the very concept of the will that, in the post-1809 Schelling, mediates between the non-willing will and the will to creation. To understand this, let us return to Schelling's distinction between essence and form. The essence of the non-willing will is absolute freedom or bliss, and the form of its "purest being" is oneness or non-twoness (*Nichtgezweitheit, Ungezweitheit*): an A = A (IPU 278–279, 308). The prefix *non-* signals that, in this absolute being, there is no actual doubling, only a virtual distinction between the left A (Father, or divine selfhood) and the right A (Son, or divine being), whose oneness is their immediate dissolution in bliss, or in the state of a "general ecstasy [*Ekstase*]" or "rapture" (IPU 405, 744). Theologically, this is the immanent Trinity: the will of the Father in its inoperativity is one with the Son as this will's pure being, and Spirit is their reciprocal letting-be (*Gelassenheit*; cf. IPU 279). To will something, as we remember, is to attract and appropriate it. In this blissful state, however, the Father's non-willing will does not attract being but simply *lets it be*. Cosmologically, one may envision here the nucleus of the universe prior to the big bang: an A = A in which the attractive force (the force of selfhood) and the expansive force (the force of being) exist in a state of perfect indifference. What is theologically a *will* is natural-philosophically a *force*. Divine being is the ur-being cosmologically, too, precisely as the "divine" nucleus prior to the emergence of the universe, and as the perfect balance of forces, an A = A, which every finite being strives to regain out of fallenness.

This divine nucleus is at once a nothing or no-thing, a completely non-objectifiable utopic nonbeing preceding even the possibility of space and time, and absolute being or "being in itself" (cf. IPU 279), containing in an undifferentiated manner what will become the All. In this "inseparable all-oneness," this ante-original *hen kai pan*, the very distinction between *pan* (all) and *hen* (one) is yet virtual (GPP 440, IPU 423, 744). Likewise, the same forces that exist here in a state of indifference and indistinction (in which the divine nucleus simply rests within itself) are the forces that will be at work in creation.

The non-willing will has thus a form of being in which the will's attractive force is dormant. This point is crucial: this will is inoperative; however, it has the power to become operative. To say "Eternal freedom is the will that wills nothing" is to express an ambivalence inherent in the concept of will. It presently wills nothing—however, as *will*, it has the capacity to become active. Instead of willing nothing, the "fatherly will" (WA27 161) can start to will something (namely, objective being). This transition from the inoperative to the operative requires no ground, expressing the fact of divine freedom. Absolute freedom is the power not to be bound to the world, "persist[ing] within pure capacity" (IPU 377). Yet this capacity is "the capacity to be *or* not to be," and thus "to split itself" (*sich zweien*; IPU 283). God has "the freedom to break this form [of A = A]," to burst open his oneness (GPP 438–439). What is absolutely free is what "can act or not act," and what can "positively" exit itself in an enactment of the divine "I will be who I *want* to be" (GPP 444). In other words, as Schelling insists, the possibility of this transition and self-shattering rests within the non-willing will and can be grasped only retroactively as the first act of will (GPP 440). "If God is A," Schelling writes, "then in his [activated] will he is an other, no longer an A = A or absolute self-equality, but an A = B" (WA27 163).

"B" is Schelling's designation for the non-divine, or what is other than divine being. The beginning of creation is thus configured by him as the self-othering of God through the activation of the divine will, which asserts itself *against* divine oneness: the first act of transgression. The non-willing will is thereby turned demiurgic, and divinity itself, Schelling postulates, becomes God the creator. This postulation, however, remains precarious, since it positions God against the bliss of divinity. The creator God is the one who ruins bliss, the de facto demiurge of this unblissful world, who can be reconciled with his divinity only once history reaches its absolute destination. Despite Schelling's insistence that the demiurgic will is the same as the non-willing will, he inscribes duality and transgression in the act of creation, and in the universe and universal history.

5.1.3. The Fall of the Will: Divine Madness and Cosmic War

Let us summarize the theological and cosmological dimensions of the activation of the divine will as what launches "the great world-creation." Theologically, to affirm himself as the positive God, God must face a being (i.e., the being of the world) in which he would reveal and cognize himself *as* God. All revelation, as Schelling likes to emphasize, is *per contrarium* or through the opposite (FS 144/42, EIP 114). Hence, God needs a being that is non-divine (B) to reveal himself as God. Similarly, in order to cognize himself and be cognized as the positive God—and God's "is the will to make himself cognizable" (EIP 105)—he needs to establish a structure of reflection or opposition. "The positive concept of God," Schelling reiterates, "is that he is the freedom to will, and thereby to posit himself as unequal to himself" (WA27 163): to transition into being. He can, however, posit otherness only by *breaking himself apart*, releasing out of himself that over which he could lord: the world. This is what Schelling often depicts as the act of divine contraction, a divine *tsimtsum*.[7] God negates himself, and since what he is *not* is multiplicity and scattering (non-oneness), God now functions as the oneness *opposed* to multiplicity: a divine center-point that persists amid the decentered and dispersed reality. There is the first negation (*Verneinung*) of oneness, creating the scatteredness of being, but this negation is posited solely to create the polar structure within which the theo-cosmic movement is to unfold as "the overcoming of this negation" (WA14 224–225/16).

Cosmologically, the self-assertion of the divine will is the activation of the contracting or attractive force, which inhibits the balance of the divine nucleus. In order to think the transition from A = A to the possibility of creation—as the possibility for the nucleus to explode into a universe—one must think differentiation and tension within oneness. Since one cannot a priori derive imbalance from the state of balance, one can conceive of this imbalance only as a contingent or groundless event, for which no reason can

---

7. See Bielik-Robson, "God of Luria," and Wolfson, *Heidegger and Kabbalah*, who also explores further resonances between Schelling and Kabbalah. The ambivalence in the post-1809 Schelling regarding the question of whether the first chaotic proto-state following the divine contraction takes place still within or (more theistically) outside God is likewise characteristic of the Lurianic doctrine of *tsimtsum*; cf. Scholem, *Major Trends*, 263–264.

be given. From this perspective, too, the getting out of balance of forces is a "free" event, an act of divine freedom—where freedom indexes what cannot be derived with a priori necessity. We know a posteriori, based on the fact of the world, that this event took place, since otherwise the nucleus would have remained stable and the universe would not exist. But we can give no a priori explanation for why it happened (in theological terms: divine freedom is unfathomable). In Schelling's post-Copernican cosmo-theology, the creation of the universe is the original cosmic contingency.

The natural-philosophical model that Schelling uses to describe the Fall of the divine will is the same that we saw in his account of the Fall of Adam. The attractive force opposes itself to the whole, and this inhibition creates a turmoil within oneness, the rotatory motion that tears oneness apart, resulting in the cosmic explosion and scattering. The similarity with the Fall of Adam is not coincidental: the latter restages within human consciousness this first theo-cosmic Fall. The divine Fall is the original transgressive act of self-assertion, in which "the fatherly will"—that, divine selfhood, egoism (*Egoismus*), or selfishness (*Selbstischkeit*)—disrupts its ante-original oneness with the Son or divine love (*Liebe*; WA27 161). In this act, divine egoism is let loose.

This divine Fall may be understood as Schelling's speculative spin on the war in heaven and the Fall of Lucifer. B, the fallen divine will, is the Luciferian will, the fire of egoism and pride, which perverts the fire of bliss. Lucifer is to be viewed here as the "fallen" divine principle of selfhood, which opposes itself to divine being or rebels against it. The war in heaven is the first contradiction (*Widerspruch*; EIP 105, WA27 177), "a violence that blindly breaks up oneness" (WA14 220/13), a "conflict between an outward and an inward movement" (EIP 119), or between the centrifugal and the centripetal force. In his Fall, Lucifer is expelled from the heavenly center and turned into B: the divine will "sinks down" or "falls into being" (IPU 477, 482, 776, DNP 308).

The first transgression creates the opposite of heaven: the blind decentered depths burning with a dark fire in which the fallen divine will now dwells. Metaphysically, B is the principle of non-oneness, of multiplicity and scatteredness. Theologically, Lucifer is also Satan, and B is the principle of hell, of perverted or inverted being, and thus of (pre-human) original sin, which human consciousness reactivates in the Fall of Adam.[8] Although one

---

8. This also makes Satan or B as the principle of evil into an instrument of divine providence, who opposes God yet, in this opposition, takes the blame for transgression (theodically exonerating God from direct responsibility for evil) and serves God's own goal of creation and revelation. Satan functions both against and *within* divine order—and Schelling joins the

should not for Schelling ascribe direct responsibility for sin and evil to God, one may still speak here of sin (*Sünde*) "by analogy" as "the transition from unbound being to one that is bound" (IPU 453, 758): to unfree, fallen being. Cosmologically, one needs to picture here a hot, vortex-like proto-material state at the origin of the universe, a state in which there is yet no division between darkness and light, and in which no orderly material being has yet formed (no galaxies, stars, or planets): a vision that may be taken to speculatively recast the nebular hypothesis of Kant and Laplace. In this state, there is only an unceasing swirling and "oscillation" that cannot become recentered or regain stability. It is the embodiment of decenteredness and inconstancy (*Wechsel*) as such, the chaos preceding orderly creation (EIP 118).

This shows how Gnostic Schelling's doctrine of creation really is: the first decision functions as a divine violence, and not what one might imagine as a benevolent act of creation. Bliss was an absolute peace (*Friede*), but this peace is lost (WA14 219/12). "Where there used to be oneness and repose," the self-assertive will creates "war and discord" (GPP 447). Looking at the negativity and strife evident in the formations of nature, "Is there anyone who would believe," Schelling asks, "that everything in nature has been formed peacefully?" (GPP 472). In this decentered universe, "Everything begins [with] a great dissonance," and this dissonance continues to underlie universal reality, so that "the fundamental tone of all life" remains inconsonant (WA27 163). Since its inception, the world has been at war: The universe that Schellingian God creates is disharmonious and unblissful, and in this continuing disharmony that the modern subject continues to inhabit, we hear an echo of the cosmic war that made the universe the way it is.

To configure creation in this manner is to introduce a double-facedness and derangement into God, a kind of "intradivine demonism,"[9] since Lucifer or B at once is and is not God. In this split state, God exists as though in a condition of blindness and madness, a deranged self-sundering. As B, God is a will that rebels against himself, seeking not to be subordinated to the divine center, an operative "will without telos, without limit," a pure expansive or scattering force, "and thus a will that is blind" (WA27 163). Here the absolute divine I turns into the absolute not-I. Breaking divine oneness, B expands in a way that is unconscious and unlimited (WA27 139), driving God out of himself or,

---

tradition of simultaneously othering and instrumentalizing the Devil. See Kotsko, *Prince of This World*.

9. Balthasar, *Der deutsche Idealismus*, 238.

so to speak, out of his mind. This expansive force, which generates what will become the material expanse of the universe, makes God decentered, at odds with himself. In his swirling fiery frenzy, "God is B," Schelling says, "in the same way that Hamlet is a madman: that is, he both is and is not mad" (WA27 163).[10]

To say that God both is and is not mad serves a theodical purpose: to exonerate God from the accusation of being a deranged demiurge. God lets his fatherly will loose not because he has truly gone mad but because this will is to become the ground of the process of creation and revelation (or, cosmologically, the first proto-material state from which the universe is to develop). The first self-assertion of the divine will is an act of transgression, yet also the first necessary step in God's own self-assertion as one who is to become God in the positive sense (WA27 148). B is merely the instrument or means (*Mittel*) that he employs, the material (*Stoff*) for the realization of his creative vision, the egoism that in all nature serves as the basis (*Basis*) for the higher—and what seems like madness is in truth part of the providential world-plan (EIP 107, SPV 185; on the lower as *Mittel* see also GPP 196). If "the Father takes on an alien being," it is only so as "to make this alien being into matter as that which is independent from the Father," and on the basis of which the world is created for the purpose of divine revelation (WA27 179). Here Schelling continues to tread the line between Gnosticism and Christianity. B is the unblissful demiurge who separates the forces within ante-original oneness, turning them into the "cosmic, demiurgic potencies" (WA27 144–145). However, this demiurgic agent unwittingly serves God's own salvific goal, and B's will is, in truth, one with the divine providential will, even if B in its self-assertion does not realize it. B may be blind and unaware of its higher purpose, yet divine providence is already at work in it.

To emphasize the subordination of B to the providential world-plan, Schelling claims that God only pretends to be mad, even if he temporarily becomes self-split and deranged within this pretense (which may be Schelling's way of seeing Hamlet's madness in the play, too). For God in his creative vision, this is a kind of stage play as well, an overarching "divine irony [*Ironie*]" and *Verstellung*, a term meaning "pretense," "play-acting," and "disguise," but also "misalignment" or "mis-placement" (*Ver-Stellung*). The beginning of

---

10. When Schelling writes that "madness is the condition of hell" (SPV 174/238), he means precisely this divine madness that splits God between A and B. Madness in Schelling is, to borrow Benjamin Norris's turn of phrase, a "rational madness" (*Schelling and Spinoza*, 470), a structure of inverted sundering, of the self-assertion of spirit "in separation ... from God" (SPV 162/233), of B as independent from A—which is the prerequisite of the structure of reflection.

creation is a divine *Verstellung* as *Entstellung* or displacement, a "bad" *ekstasis*, the Fall from center into periphery (EIP 107). God becomes "the externally disguised and inverted God," yet "internally" B remains divine: it is just that its divine essence is now repressed in the depths of fallen being. Still, this essence continues to be operative in these depths as the universal longing for the restoration of bliss, a longing from which not even hell is free. In this manner, the divine persists underneath the shell (*Hülle*) of fallenness and can be revealed by contrast with this fallenness, or through an overcoming of B—the overcoming in which the entire ascending world-process consists (GPP 464–466). God's becoming God and his cognition of himself *as* God require the staging of what is counter-divine—of the original theo-cosmic insurrection—so that, in the end, God can triumph over it. Just as in the Fall of Adam human consciousness loses its bliss so as to develop a "higher" knowledge of the divine, so the Fall of Lucifer serves the purpose of the development of "divine consciousness" (FS 170/68). Within ante-original oneness, Schelling says, "eternal freedom is freedom, but does not know or will itself as such"; it is yet "without consciousness" (IPU 745; cf. 433–434, 750). The Fall, accordingly, is theodically justified and *must* happen if knowledge is to develop—and this pertains both to the Fall of Lucifer and to the Fall of Adam, which are part of one overarching theo-cosmic process. In this process, as philosophy constructs it, the Fall of Lucifer creates the first state of the universe as the ground for the ascending natural process, a process in which the human emerges as the conscious being that is supposed to be the carrier of divine self-consciousness. The Fall of Adam too, as we know, is directed at this highest providential goal.

Transforming an identity-philosophical motif, Schelling declares B, this divine pretense, to be but a semblance, illusion, or appearance (*Schein*), the "seeming will" and "seeming being" of the non-divine (EIP 110, GPP 465). B is what Schelling sometimes calls the *Unwille* or *Unsein*, that is, a will or being that is there solely the purpose of something higher (EIP 108, GPP 356). "*Beginning*," he emphasizes, "takes place only where that *is* which immediately ought *not* to be for its own sake," but only for the sake of the higher—that is, B is posited not for its own sake but for the sake of revelation (WA27 163; cf. GPP 335, 465). God's self-alienation is both an actual splitting and a seeming one, since the essence of B remains divine. This seeming will, or God's madness and self-displacement, must be thought of as subordinated to his "true will" (EIP 110, 114–115), to eternal wisdom in its providential *oikonomia*. How can universal bliss be revealed if not by transfiguring what is universally unblissful? And how can cosmic peace be made desirable if not through the universal longing for the cessation of the cosmic war? The divine decision is, perversely, a decision for war for the sake of peace. To justify this decision and the unblissfulness it brings is the central task of Schelling's providential-theodical construction of universal history, a construction that reflects his grappling with the present state of the world as a state of war, negativity, and division, and that legitimates this state as necessary for the attainment of the absolute future.

5.1.4. When Will God Rest?

In sum, the blind expansionism of B is the scattering of oneness that is required for independent material being to become possible. Throughout the theo-cosmic process, B remains the dark substrate of the universe and the carrier of the universal ascent to bliss as the re-collection of oneness from scatteredness, so that the entire history is the metamorphosis of the *one and the same* will (GPP 287). There is no substantial or essential dualism between A and B but only a relative one, which is overcome through the world-process. Hence Schelling's post-1809 thought is permeated by a tension between the apparent theism and the essential, concealed, abyssal pantheism of bliss. The world-process is but a metamorphosis of the divine that splits itself, or (cosmologically) the material splitting and expansive unfolding of the cosmic nucleus, so that the world in the post-1809 Schelling appears as an intra-divine tear or gap: the structure of self-alienation and its promised reconciliation that *is* the world.[11] The drive toward oneness that propels the world-process, too, is a longing that emerges from the innermost depths of the fallen reality that remains essentially divine. The state of absolute bliss at the end of time, Schelling asserts, "is still B: B posited as A, B transformed into A" (GPP 287). In this we may recognize the vision of a chemical interfusion of A and B toward all-transparency, a gradual transfiguration of B's darkness into the transparent A = A as the revelation of B's concealed divine essence. B may be inverted, but this inversion is there so it can be re-inverted, or transformed into the ground of divine revelation and self-cognition.

The world is not merely a material prison, in which bliss is repressed by self-assertion, but also the providential vessel of divine revelation, to be overflown with bliss at the end of time. For, Schelling asks, "What is the suffering inherent in this path compared to the overflowing bliss, in which the

---

11. This is, again, the structure of the general Christian contradiction.

great originator of life brings back unto itself what is alienated from him?" (GPP 313). In this rhetorical question, Schelling's post-1809 theodicy of universal history is encapsulated, in which pain, suffering, and fallenness are legitimated as the path to the allegedly higher state. "Suffering is universally, in the human but also in God the creator, the way to glory" (WAII 40/99): we should remember this (Christocentric) formula, since it is through this logic that the unblissful present is justified for the sake of an ostensibly more blissful future.

Until this indefinite future comes, however, there is only the divine work on and of the world, through which God is to become the actual God. God cannot rest until the work of creation is complete—work leading out of the dark fallen depths toward the recentering of reality in bliss. As B falls away from A, A cannot but become the force of oneness that *counteracts* the expansive force, and this dynamic opposition of forces (captured by A = B as the formula of finitude) is what constitutes the materiality of the universe. As Schelling puts it, divine being, which is "contingently prevented" by B from remaining "pure and infinite," as a result of this "has to strive to restore itself" to the form of oneness (GPP 446).

The notion of finitude as an inversion or turning (*Umkehrung* or *Umwendung*) of ante-original oneness is important for understanding Schelling's conceptualization of A and B as universal forces. Namely, within divine oneness, the fatherly will was the attractive force, or the force of divine selfhood as what held this oneness together. In the rotatory motion that emerges with this will's activation, the will as B is expelled outward and downward from heaven, or outside divine oneness, becoming the force of expansive scattering. By contrast, A—divine Love or the Son—becomes now the force that re-collects or gathers scatteredness into a unity, seeking to reconstitute the lost oneness (A = A).[12] If B is self-assertion and fallenness exemplified, then A (the Son, Love, or cosmic Christ) is the operativity of redemption that, out of fallenness, directs being upward. Theologically, this cosmic interplay of

---

12. In technical terms, within A = A, the left A (divine non-will) is the *Seinkönnende* (i.e., what *can* attract being but does not do so), and the right A is the *Seinmüssende*, the necessary divine being. The copula is the wholeness or spirit as the divine ideal or norm, and thus the *Seinsollende* ("what ought to be"). Within the falling away of B, however, the order of these potencies is reversed, and they become differentiated and operative. B becomes the *Seinkönnende* (potential being): the ground of all being. A^2 becomes the principle that mediates B, the *Seinmüssende* (since it *cannot but* impose the form of oneness, shaping B into material being); and A^3 becomes the principle of wholeness as the telos toward which this mediation is directed, the *Seinsollende*. Out of fallenness, A strives to restore itself to oneness, and the potencies structure this striving.

forces is the interplay of fallenness and redemption, and later I will return to this conjunction, which is placed by Schelling at the origin of the world.

The process of an ascending re-collection of the All as that which, out of all the differentiation it undergoes, in the end reveals oneness again is the universal process as philosophy constructs it. In addition to ascent and re-collection, this process combines several further logics that are reiterated across Schelling's post-1809 writings and lectures and that are worth enumerating. The first of these is the logic of *revelation*: through and out of scatteredness, divine oneness is revealed. The second is that of *illumination*: the dark depths of being are transfigured (*verklärt*) step by step as the ladder of nature ascends via inorganic and organic being to human consciousness, and as consciousness in turn develops so as to illumine these depths with the light of science. The path of universal history goes "from darkness back to light" (WA14 289/66). "Out of darkness," God is to emerge as all-triumphant, "like the sun from behind the clouds" (IPU 765). At the end of this process, which is also the process of *salvation* from fallenness (the third logic), the will becomes the quiet transparent carrier of the divine, reality becomes all-blissful, and "even hell is no more" (SPV 184/243). At this point, B *as* B (or Satan as the opponent and instrument of God) ceases to exist, "self-annihilating" in the "final *krisis*" or the Last Judgment (FS 168/66). In this realized all-oneness (GPP 373), "God is actually All in All," "pantheism is true," and "everything is subordinated to absolute identity again" (SPV 182–187/242–243; cf. 1 Cor 15:28): a state in which being is one with the mind that inhabits it, and A = A is restored in a self-conscious, self-transparent manner.

As the language of God's becoming the actual God suggests, the process of revelation is also that of *actualization* (the fourth logic). "This time," says *Initia*, "is with regard to us the future: the time when time will be no more . . . the time of a completely actualized eternity" (IPU 577)—or, which is the same, the time "when God has been fully actualized" (FS 168/66). Universal history is the actualization of the positive God and of his creative world-plan.[13] At the same time, it is the actualization of the totality of possibility contained within the "divine" nucleus prior to the big bang. Within ante-original A = A, all possible forms of being are virtually contained in an enveloped (*eingewickelte* or *involvierte*; IPU 435) manner. The Fall of B makes possible the universe of space-time in which every possible finite being (A = B) unfolds out of the nucleus toward the reconstituted A = A, wherein all possibilities will have been

---

13. See also Fuhrmans, *Schellings Philosophie der Weltalter*, 294–308.

actualized.[14] To say that God actualizes himself through world-creation also implies that he actualizes his creative vision, or the ideas within the divine mind, in something other than himself (cf. GPP 448–449). In this manner, God's "theistic" actualization as God the creator coincides with the *explicatio* of divine being: the bringing of the totality of divine possibility to light.

The imperative of the complete exhaustion of possibility is crucial for Schelling's understanding of the end-state of the universe: the realized *hen kai pan* as the completion of creation, where no possibility is left unrealized or unrevealed. In this state, the highest possible differentiation or complexity coincides with the highest oneness. Both theologically and cosmologically, *no further work* is here possible. Absolute bliss marks "the seventh day," "the great Sabbath, God's rest from his work" (*Arbeit*; IPU 578). As long as there is work, there is no bliss; and yet, in a way that is characteristic of the re-mediation of bliss by the world, the work of universal history is justified as serving the purpose of the *cessation* of work. Through work, universal bliss and cosmic Sabbath are supposed to be actualized, and the essence of "inactivity and inoperativity" restored once divine light has "overwhelmingly illumined and triumphed over everything" (IPU 486). The promise of blissful repose is what upholds the not-yet of creation as well as the Christian order of time that—in the form of the seven-day week and the Christ-event, and of the kairotic deferral of the end of the world—Schelling imposes on universal history.

God's "positive" status as God the creator must be earned, actualized, produced through work. As any mature individual, Schelling's God rests only after his work has been completed. The positive God cannot be accused of indolence, this central vice of which divinity, the hidden God, is guilty. God's own bliss is thereby inscribed in the temporality of the work week and the imperatives of development and reward. A theodical tension is here revealed again: bliss threatens to delegitimate the very imperative of work; and so bliss in its immediacy must be cordoned off and portioned out, subjected to the logics of not-yet, worthiness, and reward. God wants to rest, too, seeking to return to the bliss of divinity. He wants, perhaps, to lie on water and look at the sky, to retreat into non-will, doing nothing, and being nothing, to become

---

14. The role of form for philosophical construction in the post-1809 Schelling thus remains similar to the identity philosophy. We have before us the empirical, unblissful world. *Form* is what allows the philosopher to re-mediate this unblissful finite being as A = B, and thus as what has fallen away from A = A and strives to return to it in a lawful manner, which the philosopher reconstructs.

anonymous, to no longer have to carry the infinite burden of the names "God," "Father," "Lord." Yet, until his work is completed, he is prevented from doing so and cannot retreat into his essence as his shelter from the world.

Like the human and the natural subject, Schelling's divine subject, too, is highly modern. The divine I is the subject of demiurgic production and ceaseless work, who becomes the true subject only *through* striving and work, who is subjected to the curse of production, yet who seeks bliss as an absolute freedom from the world as the subject-object (God–not-God) structure to which he is confined. Schelling's post-1809 theo-cosmic narrative continues to grapple with the modern problem of the *production of bliss* out of the alienated structure of reality, and thus with the problem of modernity as a demiurgic and salvific epoch. In the Schellingian schema, the will (be it divine or human) is at once the demiurge of this fallen world *and* the carrier of salvation. This salvation is to be attained through the work on the world whose end is deferred into an indefinite future, serving but to reproduce the structure of alienation in the present. To reconcile this divide within the (divine or human) subject between himself as demiurgic and as salvific, the world that the subject demiurgically creates must itself be legitimated as the path to bliss. Schelling's post-1809 tale of two Gods, in which the will doubles into the salvific non-willing and the demiurgic will, is thus a tale that refracts the doubling at the heart of modernity, the doubling that is part of the broader Christian-modern antagonistic entanglement between bliss and the world.

Only bliss can break the cycle of work. However, in a theodical sleight of hand that is constitutive of the Christian-modern world, the promise of bliss becomes that through which the world of work is reproduced and legitimated. In a familiar cruel optimism, the (divine, natural, human) subject is endlessly drawn back into work through the promise of the future cessation of work that would bring fulfillment and repose. Despite the repeated promise of the positive arrival of bliss, divine, natural, and human history turns de facto into an unceasing postlapsarian toil: God's work of creation and self-actualization, nature's striving to break through to eternal freedom, and the toil and effort (*Bemühen*) of the human to recenter itself in the divine (IPU 213).

Why cannot God rest? Why must the world be? This problem is evident in the question Schelling raises in the *Freedom* essay: "Will the evil ever end, and how? Does creation even have an end goal, and if it does, why is this goal not reached immediately, why is perfection not there from the beginning?" Like all questions of theodicy, this one is permeated with anxiety about the negativity of the world; and like with all theodical questions, there is ultimately but one, essentially circular answer: *because this is the way it must be.* "There is no answer to that question, except the one already given": namely, that God, like all being, must go through the proper process to become what he is (FS 168/66). Everywhere, again, suffering is the way to glory and bliss. Philosophy constructs the not-yet of the world so as to show this not-yet's necessity and to direct the world toward its promised next stage. The speculative philosopher must become one with the providential and salvific movement of the world, not interrupt or change it. Due world-process must be upheld: this is the law.

5.2. Bliss before the Law

For Schelling, the cosmic war is a just war. The activation of the will generates a tumult in divine oneness, resulting in the divine decision as self-splitting. Crisis in the sense of tumult generates a *krisis* as division and judgment: "the judgment that slices"[15] and that expels B from heaven. The justice and judgment inherent in the first Fall are dramatized by Schelling in *Initia* as a scene that plays out between the divine law (*Gesetz*) and the will. The purpose of this scene is "to glimpse in more detail" how the inoperative will "is brought to transition to actual being" (IPU 489), or how egoism awakens in the will, disturbing "the complete oneness of being and essence prior to the decision" (IPU 770).[16]

In this scene, analyzed below, Schelling continues to be concerned with the theodical question: Why did the divine Fall, despite being free or contingent, *have* to take place from the "higher" standpoint of providence? What can justify the original transgression? Throughout his post-1809 thought, he interweaves Augustinian, Leibnizian, and Kantian-Enlightenment theodical motifs to create an all-encompassing philosophical legitimation of the world, the God who creates it, the theo-cosmic Fall through which it emerges, and thus also the Fall of Adam as the restaging of this theo-cosmic Fall at the origin of human history.

It has sometimes been observed that Schelling's project of theodicy, understood in the narrow sense as the exoneration or disburdening of God the creator, ultimately *fails*: despite Schelling's efforts, his positive God ends up burdened with the transgression inscribed in the world or universe.[17] This

---

15. To quote François Hartog's description of *krisis* in *Chronos*, x.

16. In my reading of *Initia*, I draw both on Schelling's manuscript and the lecture notes published as part of the same volume of the historical-critical edition (HKA II/10).

17. See, e.g., Hermanni, *Die letzte Entlastung*, 261, and Caputo, *Specters of God*, 114.

much may be true; however, it is not only a question of the "success" or "failure" of Schelling's theodicy, but of its stakes. I would suggest that what matters the most for Schelling, in his Christian-modern anxiety about the contingency of history and the unblissfulness of the world, is not the disburdening of God, but the *legitimation of world history* as providential in its origin and course, as a divine tribunal that assigns to everything its rightful place, and as a movement of Fall and redemption that ascends out of the cosmic depths of suffering to absolute bliss. His post-1809 theodicy is no longer one of a "static" God. It is a processual post-Kantian theodicy of universal history, whose purpose is to discern the law that governs historical development. Schelling's theodical construction of history emerges from the dark decentered depths of universal reality and carries with it the promise of an all-reconciled future. In this theodicy, what takes the center stage is not the *disburdening* of God and history but the legitimation of the endless *burden* of history—the burden of this negative world, of the alienated subjectivity that lives and strives in the world, and of the uncertain path to bliss yet to be traversed. If God is in the end acquitted in Schelling's theodical construction too, it is because he likewise has this historical burden to bear.

5.2.1. The Temptation of Temptation: A Prologue in Heaven

The scene in *Initia* between the divine law and the will plays out as follows. The law "says to the pure will: do not be presumptuous of your freedom," do not overstep it—which the non-willing will would do if it were to disturb the divine repose by becoming operative. "Do not lust after being," commands the law (IPU 428, 447).[18] This command may be regarded as ironic in the Schellingian sense of "divine irony": namely, it has the inverse intention and effect compared to its literal meaning. By telling the will not to transgress, the law *tempts* it into transgression. Before the law voices this command, the will in its indifference has no care for being. But now something awakens within the will: the first distinction. The will becomes aware of its freedom, of the possibility of being otherwise than it is, of desire, of transgressing the divine law—a transgression that would consist in appropriating divine being with all the possibilities contained therein. The divine law is for Schelling the law of *simply being what one is* reconfigured as *not overstepping one's bounds*, and thus

---

18. Schelling's allusion here is to Paul's Epistle to the Romans 7:7: "Is the law sin? God forbid. Nay, I had not known sin, but by the law: for I had not known lust, except the law had said: Thou shalt not covet."

as *knowing one's place* ("overstepping," *Übertretung*, means "transgression" in German, and Schelling plays on this connection). What the law commands is A = A as the normative ideal.

The law is thus a divine normativity that introduces an ought (*Sollen*), demand (*Forderung*), or imperative (*Imperativ*) into ante-original blissful being, and with that the distinction between what ought and what ought not to be. By articulating the difference between right and wrong, the law announces the (at first purely virtual) duality of obedience and transgression. The will is "revealed to itself as what can attract *or* not attract being" (IPU 428). It is confronted with an "either/or" (IPU 426) and with the option to *enact freedom as its own* in a transgressive manner, to assert itself, to oppose itself as subject to being as object, to choose evil over good (a distinction that is thereby made, virtually, for the first time), to "usurp freedom" (IPU 770; cf. 454). Absolute identity precedes the possibility of the good/evil binary (FS 173). Only with the either/or does the possibility of good and evil appear.

This either/or nearly throws the will off balance (IPU 507, 771). The will has not yet overstepped its bounds. However, the possibility of usurping freedom arouses something within the will. (*Der Wille* is a masculine noun in German, *die Freiheit* is feminine, and *das Gesetz* is neutral; and this gender dynamic is utilized by Schelling.) By prohibiting desire, the law reveals the possibility of desire to the will and presents freedom *as* something desirable and objectifiable, something to be appropriated. The law says: do not take freedom forcefully for yourself—even as the law, in the same stroke, presents to the will a tempting, attractive image (*anzügliches Bild*; IPU 770) of freedom in her infinite possibility or fertility, "an image of endless freedom and therefore of endless possibility" (IPU 507). Freedom appears here as a beautiful woman whom the "fatherly will" could possess, and who does not yet even know herself as an object of desire, lacking all objectivity. Where there was only the nonbinary "it" of divinity, there is now a gendered binary opposition. And where there was divine fullness as an absolute freedom from want or desire, there is now a structure of attraction, of desire as lack (*Mangel*; IPU 496–497, 507, 770).

This is the original temptation: the first bait (*Lockspeise*; IPU 770), arousing the egoism of the will. This scene further develops Schelling's question, found in an earlier *Ages of the World* draft, regarding the intransitivity of bliss: "For how should that which is one, perfect, and complete unto itself be tempted [*versucht*], provoked, or baited [*gelockt*] into exiting this state of peace?" (WA14 219/12). "The feminine" becomes "the first temptress of the will" (IPU 770): the proto-Eve, who tempts the will to become operative, to claim infinite freedom for itself. (In Schelling's theo-cosmic epic, the first war is a war over a woman, too.) Through this formulation, however, Schelling shifts onto the feminine the blame for temptation, disburdening the law from blame. This scene is the first theodical trial staged by the divine law, which, as law, wants more than anything to *judge*. And for that, as Schelling sees it, the law needs to tempt. Can the will withstand temptation? Will it choose good or evil, so as to be judged as good or evil?[19]

Underlying this scene of the law's temptation is what Emmanuel Levinas has called the "temptation of temptation" as the paradigm of the Western will. In Levinas's formulation, the highest law of this will goes as follows: "We cannot close ourselves off to any possibility . . . we must enter history with all the traps it sets for the pure." To simply remain in bliss is, in this paradigm, judged as lower than going through temptation and transgression, exploring even the possibility of evil so as to emerge triumphant on the other end. From the perspective of the temptation of temptation (which is Schelling's perspective as well), "There would be no glory in triumphing in innocence."[20] One must traverse fallenness to be redeemed and to reach the highest bliss. The temptation of temptation as that from which not even the divine A = A is free is a theodical paradigm that justifies the Fall from bliss for the sake of the development of endless freedom qua endless possibility. The first free choice, as the choice between good and evil (and for the post-1809 Schelling finite freedom is always freedom for good or evil), is also the first act of actualization—of actualizing the first possibility, and thus launching the world-process as the realization of the totality of possibility contained in the depths (*Tiefe*) of divine being (IPU 497).

5.2.2. The Law and the Binary of Good and Evil

Through temptation, the will faces the first choice. The will is presently nothing, and it can either attempt to become everything or "remain in nonbeing" (IPU 753). The divine Fall is a free or contingent event because it could

---

19. Theodically, Schelling wants to distinguish temptation from efficient cause. The law may tempt the will into transgression, but the direct cause of transgression is the will's own choice to transgress. Schelling here follows Augustine, *City of God*, 505 (XII.6). Furthermore, in ascribing intention (*Absicht, Intention*) and want or desire to the law (see, e.g., IPU 452, 758: "the law wants . . ."), Schelling configures it as the original ("divine") structure of desire, preceding and generating the desire-as-lack within the will. The desire of the law is directed at launching, upholding, and expanding the world-process so that nothing remains unjudged.

20. Levinas, "Temptation of Temptation," 32–33.

also *not* have happened, in which case the first desire would have been subdued by the will in its obedience to the law, and the indifference of forces would have been upheld in "a voluntary self-renunciation" (a description in which we recognize the operation of kenotic submission). However, Schelling continues, "Obviously that did not happen," for in that case there would be no world, only bliss (IPU 755).

The fact that the universe did not have to be, and yet it exists, points in this counterfactual scenario to the contingency of the fact of the world. However, to legitimate the world, Schelling wants to adduce further reasons why, despite this contingency and the world's unblissfulness, it is *for the better* from a providential perspective that the original transgression took place and that bliss was not upheld. "What would have been better with regard to the end goal of the whole, that being should remain internal [to divine oneness] or that it should exit it?" (IPU 757)—Schelling asks, confirming that it was, indeed, better (*besser*) that the will broke up the heavenly oneness (IPU 475, 485, 764). This is not equivalent solely to saying that it is better that there is something rather than nothing. Schelling's "better" is a theodical "better": the Fall, despite being an act of transgression, is "good" because it takes place for the purpose of revelation, of realizing the providential world-plan, and of God's becoming God.

Additionally, even if the will had decided not to transgress, the possibility of transgression would have remained: there could have been no guarantee (*Sicherheit*) that transgression would never occur (IPU 475, 758). This absence of guarantee creates a situation of an even greater, more original anxiety than the anxiety inscribed in the world itself. The law needs the will to decide, paradoxically, in favor of transgression before the will can choose obedience, because the law needs to ensure that the will's obedience is *consciously* free and not itself contingent. For that, the law needs the will to cognize its own freedom. But how can the will really know the full extent of its freedom if it does not actualize a crucial dimension of it, namely, if the possibility of transgression remains concealed? (IPU 476, 760) The paradigm of the temptation of temptation again comes to the fore: all possibility must be explored.

Furthermore, for Schelling, obedience out of the depths of transgression, *obedience that redeems*, is higher than the obedience of one who never transgresses. "For," he explains, "according to the gospel there is more rejoicing in heaven over one sinner that repents than over ninety-nine just persons that need no repentance" (IPU 480, 764). Similarly, the will that goes through "all the sufferings and rejoicings of being" before "sacrificing" itself to the divine achieves a higher joy (IPU 764). The first transgression is a fallenness that carries with it the possibility of redemption, and this makes it theodically necessary and even higher than the non-transgressing will. Thus, Schelling affirms, there "had to be the sinking down [of B] into being," there had to be an actual transgression to be followed by B's re-submission to A, for in this way a higher sacrifice (*Opfer*) to the absolute subject is enacted (IPU 760). In this conjunction of theodicy and sacrifice, we recognize again the kenotic act of Christ as inscribed from the outset in the theo-cosmic process.

"Of course, the law does not directly want sin or transgression," Schelling asserts, borrowing the distinction from Leibnizian theodicy between direct and indirect divine will, or between God wanting transgression for the sake of transgression and "merely" permitting it in his eternal wisdom.[21] "However, if sin and transgression are necessary ... for the revelation of what is concealed," of the plenitude of possibility contained in the depths of divine being, "then the law wants even sin, although not sin in itself but revealed sin, so that everything can be clear, pronounced, and decisive" (IPU 453, 757). This applies equally to the Fall of Lucifer and the Fall of Adam. The law is what judges, and even though it may not directly want sin, it still needs sin to be revealed *as* sin so as to judge it, assigning to B its rightful place outside the divine. Freedom for good or evil is thus imputed to the will so that transgression and guilt can likewise be imputed to it, and so that the will can be judged and punished *as* guilty: the position (of the carrier of guilt) that is necessary for the divine stage play to begin.[22] From the viewpoint of the divine *oikonomia*, just as B is God's seeming (*scheinbare*) will, so the free choice to transgress is a seeming choice: even before it fell, the will had been assigned its position as B in the divine stage play—hence the law's temptation, baiting B into voluntarily taking the place that is "proper" to it. This, too, is the imputation of guilt: in this Schellingian paradigm, you freely *choose* what you already *are*, acting out of your place or role in the overarching providential play. And since you have chosen to transgress, this means you have always been, from the viewpoint of the law, the disorderly, transgressive element (B). Accordingly, you are judged and punished as such.

B's blind fire of pride itself embodies, in its fallenness, divine judgment over Lucifer since, as Schelling likes to claim, to the will that is inverted or perverted

---

21. See Leibniz, *Theodicy*, 138.

22. Nietzsche astutely discerned this theodical ruse behind the Christian-modern paradigm of the freedom of the will: "People were considered 'free' so that they could be judged and punished—so that they could be *guilty*: consequently, every act *had* to be thought of as willed" (*Twilight of the Idols*, 181).

God manifests himself as the fire of wrath, not as love.[23] The divine essence continues to be operative within B's inversion as God's "consuming wrath" (FS 168/66). "With regard to those who are inverted, God is likewise inverted" (GPP 356). What seems like Lucifer's "own" flame of desire is the fire of divine wrath. What is inverted must be judged and punished so as to prompt it to convert (or be re-inverted) back into obedience to the divine. The punishing fire is a cleansing fire, in which all self-assertion is, in the end, destined to be transfigured. The enflaming of B is, again, a *krisis* as the judgment that slices, the severing divine sword. This is the sword that Christ brings, too ("I did not come to bring peace but a sword"; Matthew 10:34). The world-process as the process of revelation, judgment, and actualization unfolds within the duality between the divine and the inverted or counter-divine, or good and evil.

$A = A$ is also the formula of self-consciousness and self-knowledge, the prototypical subject-object or the idea of a self-conscious mind (DNP 304). Accordingly, the providential law is the law of the development of divine consciousness as the fully realized $A = A$: eternal freedom's "fullest coming to itself and becoming conscious of itself" (IPU 761; cf. 480). As demanding conscious obedience, the law triggers the development of the divine will's self-knowledge, which can develop only through transgression. Schelling grapples here with the paradox of rational knowledge in general: to become what it is, intelligence must oppose itself to the being in which intelligence is immersed in its merely potential state, reconfiguring its own relation to the environment as a relation of separation and reflection (even if this process is initially blind or unconscious). Yet, by doing so, intelligence severs its rootedness in the environment or breaks up oneness, appearing as transgressive in its self-assertion. This transgression is, however, necessary for intelligence to develop, to cognize its own conditions of possibility, and to re-incorporate them into itself, restoring oneness and coherence at a "higher" conscious level. Such is the modern epistemological dimension of Schellingian theodicy, a dimension that also explains why, for him, a higher unity of reason with nature and God can be attained only through the structure of original alienation.

Finally, $A = A$ is the formula of good and evil. That is evil or transgressive which asserts itself against $A = A$, and that is good which obeys it. The law wants the will to make the decision, asking the will: *What are you? Do you choose good or evil?*—and, for Schelling, it is for the better that the will chooses evil, since then B can cognize itself *as* evil, recognize the error of its

---

23. Cf. Augustine, *Confessions*, 157.

ways, and resubmit redemptively to the good, which is in turn revealed *as* good by contrast with evil.[24] Evil is at once punished and instrumentalized as part of divine order. The possibility of evil is actualized so that the good can triumph over it, and so that at the end of creation God can pronounce that his creation is good and he is, indeed, the true God. The law thrives on transgression and needs transgression to take place in order to judge it. It is as though the law were saying: *Bliss must not be; the world must be.* Following the first transgression, the world emerges *as a distribution of good and evil directed toward the good*, or toward the overcoming of B by A. As Schelling emphasizes, "Everything serves the law, either willingly or against its will; right and wrong, good and evil—all serve the law" (IPU 769; cf. 457, 494). The overarching theodical violence of the divine law is that there is *no escape* from judgment: even in transgressing the law or rebelling against the divine (as Lucifer does), one is judged as evil and assigned one's proper place outside and below the divine—the position that allows the providential world-process to unfold. Evil and error are a constitutive part of the world, since the path to the absolute future ascends through the binary between evil and good, or fallenness and redemption, and through truth and goodness as "achieving victory" over error and transgression (UPO 7). The structure of judgment or *krisis* and the structure of the world coincide in Schellingian construction: the world *is* the space-time of inescapable judgment.

It is in this sense, too, that true philosophy is for Schelling critical philosophy—and not in the Kantian sense of critique, against which *Initia* polemicizes (IPU 261–262). "Critique" is, like *krisis*, connected etymologically to "separation," "decision," and "judgment"—a connection of which Schelling avails himself. For him, philosophy is "critical" insofar as it re-enacts the divine movement of *krisis*, leading kenotically to what is above the human, and in this manner limiting the pretensions of self-assertive reason. Put differently, Schellingian construction is critical because it traces, out of crisis qua tumult, operations of judgment (*krisis*) through which the crisis is resolved and divine order is restored across history.[25] Only in this manner can the specter of dogmatism, and all the "spirits and ghosts" of uncertainty, be

---

24. This is a theodical idea that can also be traced back to Augustine, who suggests that the good angels could for the first time cognize themselves as good only by contrast with the transgression of the fallen angels; *City of God*, 467 (XI.13), 471 (XI.17). Schelling's notion of transgression as inversion and downward turning is likewise Augustinian; see *City of God*, 498 (XII.1), 504–506 (XII.6).

25. The Christian model for this conjunction of crisis-as-tumult and *krisis* is the turmoil of the Apocalypse followed by the Judgment Day, the cleaving sword of divine law.

exorcised as philosophy attains, step by step, the highest clarity (WA27 138). Thereby, the movement of *krisis* in Schelling inherits and transforms that of Kantian critique, and critical philosophy is reconfigured as a theodicy of universal history.

5.2.3. The Law and the Unfolding of Possibility

The law needs the totality of possibility contained in the depths of divine being to be actualized so it can judge each possibility from the meta-standpoint of A = A. The law, Schelling says, is averse to leaving any possibility concealed (IPU 758). Unless every possibility develops toward decision and transparency, being will contain within its depths a remainder of what is undecided, enfolded (*eingewickelt*), unjudged, and thus opaque and threatening. This darkness must be illuminated by the light of judgment as coinciding with the light of science, so that everything reveals itself for what it is. "Nothing can remain ambiguous" (*zweideutig*; FS 143/41). This makes the law want the world to exist as the widest possible playing field for judgment. The goal of judgment and the goal of revelation coincide within the world-process. Thereby, the law is affirmed by Schelling as "the highest law of the universe" (IPU 746), meting out justice and pronouncing judgment at every turn of universal history as a continuing divine process (*Prozess*), trial (*Probe*), and tribunal (*Gericht*): all the juridical terms central to modern theodical imagination. To construct history from this vantage is to confirm that, as "all voices say of God," "justice and tribunal, division and decision are the foundation of his throne" (DRP 491).

Everything must (lawfully) unfold. Creation carries transgression with it, yet this transgression is what, in keeping with the providential world-plan, leads to the exhaustive actualization of possibility and the maximal diversification of being: the "richest unfolding," the highest "expansion of life" (IPU 486, 766). This vision of the richness of life prompts Schelling's reference to the theodical doctrine of felix culpa, or fortunate sin:

> We may apply here, as it were, in the highest case [i.e., in the case of the divine Fall] what one church father says on a different occasion [i.e., about the Fall of Adam]: happy is the fault [*Schuld*], happy is the transgression that has led to such a rich unfolding, liberation, and redemption of life. (IPU 487)[26]

---

26. Cf. IPU 766: "which has led to such a perfect unfolding of life." Schelling is quoting here a hymn attributed to St. Ambrose, which Leibniz likewise quotes in *Theodicy*, 129.

"From the standpoint of science," Schelling adds, "it is for the better that the oneness [or A = A] demanded by the law is not the initial oneness" but the oneness yet to be attained. For him, philosophical construction is a theodical construction that pits mediation and futurity against the immediacy of bliss, legitimating fallenness as the fortunate fall directed, via the not-yet of the world, at the "highest and distant grounds and goals" (IPU 766–767; cf. 487–489).

The philosopher lets her thought be governed by the same divine law that governs the universe, and in this her standpoint and the standpoint of theodicy coincide. The post-Copernican universe may seem disharmonious and dissonant, yet philosophy reveals even discord and cosmic war to be necessary for the attainment of higher harmony. "Knowledge is coherence [*Cohaerenz*]," Schelling insists, and this is a theodical statement. The success of theodicy hinges on demonstrating that universal reality coheres—and philosophy upholds the coherence of the world by showing that, even though the universe seems disorderly and contingent, one can discern in it a lawfulness due to which it forms a single movement that can be scientifically grasped (IPU 263). Even apparent detours, such as the faraway cosmic worlds that, as we remember, represent for Schelling a dead end because they have not developed toward intelligence—even these must be constructed not as mere digressions, but as part of actualizing the fullest expanse of possibility. Across this expanse, all possible stages and directions must be explored and all levels of the universal *Stufenfolge* traversed, so as to create the widest basis for the emergence of what is the highest (i.e., human intelligence). The law ensures that everything is at once differentiated or brought to light, assigned its place, and subordinated to a higher movement.

Yet let us forget for a moment about the law with its ceaseless division (into good and evil), hierarchization (of higher versus lower), and instrumentalization (of lower for the sake of higher), hanging over the Schellingian universe and upholding its unblissful not-yet. When at one point in *Initia* Schelling starts speaking about the endlessly rich universal life and about creation as the "infinite multiplication" and "diversification of the one," do we not hear in this the continuing echo of his identity philosophy? "The [universal] life that is multiplied an infinite number of times," Schelling writes, is immediately "reflected" in the mind of "each individual as a center unto himself" and in humanity as a whole as consisting of "countless [such] centers": the plenum of the real that is one with the plenum of the ideal (IPU 766; cf. 487). Here Schelling suddenly re-visions the universe again as the common being of the All, a garden that requires no redemption.

The very "endless dissonances" generate, *right now*, "an endless consonance" (IPU 487). If not for the law that seeks to classify being into lower and higher, into evil and good, every possibility would appear as blissful within this universal weave, where each moment reveals something in which the whole is reflected, and where a multitude of threads shoot through each moment and carry it within one universal being—the universality that this moment inhabits simply by being what it is, so that the particular and the universal immediately coincide. One may view this immediate consonance-in-dissonance, erupting from Schelling's text, as a vision of inhabiting the post-Copernican universe immanently, without judgment or the not-yet. In this vision, each and every moment needs no redemption, not because it knows its place and submits to the higher but simply because it is there, because it realizes some possibility that otherwise would have been left unrealized, because it reveals something that otherwise would have remained concealed. And even if this moment is useless, or if nothing develops from it, the same plenum is reflected in it, and it still shines as brightly as all others with the absolute light of bliss. The negative and the positive, potentiality and actuality, diminution and glorification, damnation and salvation are indifferentiated within this expanse of being whose immediate center is everywhere. All finite being strives and suffers, longs for bliss and fails to attain it, becomes mired in guilt just as it begins to live, ascending and falling ecstatically, over and over again. And yet, amid this very striving, all expresses the bliss that it simply *is*, the infinite manifoldness of creation, the pure "=" that cuts through the divisions of finitude.

At this moment in *Initia*, it is as though theodicy itself breaks through to bliss, so that theodical vision and vision of bliss seem almost to coincide—I say "almost" because this vision is still permeated with the same issues as Schelling's identity philosophy (see Chapter 3), including the issue of theodical indifference, and because the logics of possibility, relationality, and judgment prevent this reality from being truly all-blissful. Still, this is arguably as close as the post-1809 Schelling approaches a vision of reality as bliss-in-common *in the now*. Perhaps here Schelling, without mentioning it, gives us a vision of what he calls realized pantheism—which he, however, in the same stroke defers to the end of time. To see reality as blissful would be to dispense with the law, which needs to maintain binaries so as to be able to judge, and which postpones and pulls apart bliss so as to maintain itself in the center as the universal sorting and mediating mechanism. And so the law says to being: you are not yet the center; you *used to* be the center but you transgressed and will become the center again only following the Last Judgment; for now, you ought to know your place without overstepping it.

In truth, of course, there can be bliss only in the present tense, here and now, in simply being, without any further determination. Yet this is precisely what the law disallows. In this manner, philosophy qua theodicy forecloses bliss just as it momentarily lets it shine through.

5.2.4. The Law and the Two Types of Freedom

Unprethinkable bliss is free from the law: in bliss, there is no imperative or judgment, since judgment is premised on division. There can be no law of bliss, and bliss itself requires no law. The law is Schelling's way of re-mediating the purity of bliss into an *ought*, into $A = A$ as an imperative or norm premised on the binary of good and evil. Conceptually, the law is inscribed not in the divine essence or divinity but in $A = A$ as the form of divine being; this form is what holds the world-process together, too, as the restoration of $A = A$ out of $A = B$. Normativity is revealed by contrast with what does not conform to the norm, and the form of $A = A$ carries with it the possibility of both adherence to $A = A$ and deviation from it. The form articulates bliss (as $A = A$) as well as the falling away from bliss (as $A = B$), mediating between the blissful state of being and the transition to creation. The form inscribes the possibility of the subject-object division and reflection into the being of absolute freedom; and this possibility, even before it is actualized, already marks a departure from bliss. This (at first virtual) departure is the temptation of temptation, the will to will, the ur-possibility of all possibility—which, once introduced into the will by the form of $A = A$ qua the divine law, tempts the will to transgress, to abandon bliss.

The freedom to obey or disobey the law is likewise no longer absolute freedom or bliss. Schelling sometimes obfuscates the distinction between these two types of freedom for theodical purposes, but this distinction is fundamental. The freedom to obey *or* disobey, to follow *or* not follow the law, implies a binary and an ought. Unlike bliss, this freedom is based on an active will, and on a choice that functions within the vision of what ought to be yet is not. As mentioned, this active freedom for Schelling is the freedom for good or evil, the freedom to follow the norm or pervert it, which even as perverted remains governed by the law in its judgment.

This decisive shift in the meaning of freedom—from bliss to the freedom of obedience or disobedience that implies a structure of reflection and judgment—is inscribed in Schelling's statement that "one cannot think freedom without law" (IPU 426). The form of the law is what mediates between these two kinds of freedom, even if bliss as such cannot be mediated. The law is imposed on bliss so that transgression can occur; and already this imposition is a break from bliss. Schelling's Christian-theodical proclamation that the will had the power *not* to fall, and so it was the will's own free choice to sin, is a sleight of hand. To inscribe ante-original blissful being in the form of the law is *to force it to decide* to obey or disobey God, to "awaken" the non-willing will, and to put an end to bliss in its sheer indifference to any binary. Even if the will *decides* for the good, it does so on the terms established by the law, obeying the law as a transcendent authority; yet there is no authority in or for bliss itself. To choose evil is to assert itself, to choose A = B; to choose good is to kenotically "let being be" (IPU 747), to enact A = A. However, the will that decides for the good may be good but it is no longer blissful, since it exists within—and heeds or cares for—the binary of good and evil, and hence (following the Fall of B) for the distribution of good and evil that is the world, subordinated to the transcendent authority of the law. Whenever Schelling claims that the highest is to *choose* to consciously empty oneself toward God, to choose to deliver one's will to the absolute subject, he inscribes bliss in a structure of judgment, transcendence, and sacrifice. In this way, law is forcefully imposed and bliss is foreclosed. Where bliss used to be, there is now a "relentless working of the law" (IPU 476).

The question, *Do you obey the higher A = A, or do you transgress?*, even if one chooses to obey, cannot but reproduce the logic of binary and exclusion—and the threat of transgression as what might disturb the unity of A = A cannot be extinguished as long as the law performs its tribunal. Schelling's example of a just tribunal is symptomatic in this regard:

> The law is . . . what decides everything and sets everything in *krisis*. Each *krisis* is a tribunal, and each tribunal is a *krisis*. When, for instance, the state [*Staat*] or the dignity of [its] laws is attacked from within and the state judges the criminal, this merely exemplifies the continuing organic life of the state, which in this case expels a malign and harmful matter. (IPU 757; cf. 453)

Schelling's model here is that of an "organic" A = A that judges what or who stays inside or gets expelled according to the law that *A = A is what ought to be*—that is, that society ought to be defended from any transgressor. Only in this manner can A = A remain healthy and whole. But even if no one transgresses, the possibility of transgression remains—there is, again, no guarantee that transgression will not occur at a future point—and so the law stays vigilant and the tribunal remains ceaseless. The specter of exclusion haunts the whole, breaking it down into the dichotomy of those who obey and those who (may) disobey, those who are included and those who are excluded (even if the latter set is presently empty). Even one's remaining within A = A is mediated by the law and its binary logics. Life in the state is a life of judgment, not bliss, and the same goes for divine world-governance.

It is therefore crucial to distinguish between bliss as such and the manner in which the blissful being of oneness appears in the eyes of the law. The law, as needing to make distinctions in order to be able to morally judge, cannot but be annoyed at the immediacy and indifference of bliss, which does not care to choose or to develop. Accordingly, from the standpoint of the law, indifference as absence of care is configured as *indecision* in the face of the law (IPU 426). The law disparages the rapturous being-in-bliss as a "childish" state of innocence (*Unschuld*) and uninvolvement (*Unbefangenheit*) (IPU 425, 441, 745, 752). "We are speaking, as it were, in the name of the law," Schelling proclaims, "[when we say] that the [blissful] being of eternal freedom . . . cannot and must not remain" (IPU 436). *The philosopher is a theodician who speaks in the name of the law and justifies transgression*; the foreclosure of bliss could not be made clearer. Schelling's simultaneous Romantic positioning of the child as a model of bliss and Enlightenment denigration of what is too childish is characteristic of the tension between bliss and theodicy in his thought and in modernity more broadly. It is as though the law were baiting God himself by telling him: in your bliss, you are not a mature God yet, you are but a God-child; how can you obey your own law if you do not do so consciously? This is a motif of rational theodicy, too: God *answers* to the law—not in his unprethinkable bliss, but as God the creator. He starts to perceive his blissful being as a lack, viewing himself as one who must develop into a positive, "adult" God. And so, again, God cannot hide from the law in his shelter of bliss.

Schelling's theodical construction highlights the ambivalence in his post-1809 thinking of bliss. He may call bliss the highest, yet he likewise calls the law what is the highest in the universe. Thereby, he proves himself to be a good Christian (the highest is to obey the divine law) and a good German idealist (for whom normativity and will are higher than indifference and non-will). This oscillation between the absolute freedom of bliss and "worldly" freedom reflects Schelling's continuing spiritual investment at once in bliss and in the world, and the aporetic attempt to bring the two together into one system narrative. As a result, A = A as the formula of the law *overwrites* A = A as the formula of bliss, or of *simply being what one is*. Whenever one wants to enter bliss, one encounters the self-appointed divine gatekeeper, the law. And before the law there is no bliss.

In Schelling, only the promise of an absolute bliss at the end of the world can reconcile the two types of freedom: freedom as the bliss of non-will and freedom as reflective choice. This, more than anything, shows how at odds these types of freedom are, seeing that they can coincide only apocalyptically once the world is no more—so that Schelling's very use of the term "freedom" for both is a theodical ruse. The law, as the gatekeeper to bliss, demands that one consciously choose what is good and obey divine providence. Thereby, however, the gate guarded by the law is destined not to open until the end of time, re-mediating bliss into the endless not-yet of the world. The law tempts one to transgress, plunging the will into darkness and perversion in a divine trial—and proclaiming suffering and submission to be universally the way to salvation. In this manner, the law perversely legitimates the negativity of the world-process as the supposed path to a higher bliss. However, this is theodical deceit, for as soon as one is baited into decision, one becomes bound to the structure of division through which the world is reproduced, and bound to accept the not-yet of the world as the way of providence. In truth, there is no "higher" bliss, only the one bliss that has no care for the law.

5.3. Recentering the Human in a Cosmic Revolution

The human is the goal of the world and of all creation.
—JOHANNES KEPLER

The power I sought for man, seemed God's.
—ROBERT BROWNING, *Paracelsus*

In what follows, I focus on the conjunction of Fall and redemption as the two-part rhythm of the Schellingian theo-cosmic process and argue that universal history turns for him in the shape of an ascending spiral, or what I call "cosmic revolution." This spiral unfolds out of the tension between fallenness, on the one hand, and divinity or bliss configured as transcendent telos, on the other. From the abyss of decenteredness, the movement of re-collection ascends step by step, collecting all cosmic worlds and human history—all circles of circles—into an upward spiral whose peak, that is, human consciousness as one with God, is the new center: a heaven regained. As the construction that plunges one into scatteredness and darkness before lifting one redemptively toward light, the course that philosophy constructs is an all-encompassing movement of reversion or turning, of which the "bad" and the "good" *ekstasis* are equally part. This movement is grounded in the revolution of celestial bodies or planetary rotation (*Umlauf*) and amounts to the process of ceaseless *Umkehrung*, *Umwendung*, and *Wiederumwendung*, terms that invoke at once "inversion" or "reversal," "turning," and "revolving motion."

The figure of the spiral allows one to better grasp the logic of the ladder (*Stufenfolge*) of nature in the post-1809 Schelling and to discern the place of modernity and true philosophy within the spiral of history. At the same time, Schelling's vision of the cosmic revolution as a restoration of justice—enacted through humanity as the highest A = A—puts him in proximity to early socialism and reiterates at the meta-level the foundational move of modernity and the project of human self-assertion. Despite his political conservatism, Schelling's Christian metaphysics of history should not, I contend, be reductively understood as anti-modern, even if he positions the cosmic revolution *against* the political revolutions of the nineteenth century.

5.3.1. Cosmic Catastrophe: The First Fall and the First Redemption

The movement of universal history in Schelling at once generates novelty and uncovers what is already there: that is, eternal freedom as repressed in the depths of reality. Novelty coincides here with this breakthrough to absolute freedom and thus with restoration and fulfillment. The movement of *Umwendung* enacts the gradual inversion of inner and outer, in which what is concealed becomes revealed, and what is external—including rigid selfhood—becomes the inner carrier of the absolute. *The German Dictionary of the Brothers Grimm* defines *Umwendung* as, among other things, "circular turning" or "rotation," a usage dating back to the sixteenth century—and what Schelling describes is an all-encompassing cosmic re-turning: a revolution in the cosmic sense.[27] Its movement proceeds downward before re-collecting

---

27. "UMWENDUNG, f.," *Deutsches Wörterbuch von Jacob Grimm und Wilhelm Grimm*, digital edition, Version 01/23, https://www.woerterbuchnetz.de/DWB?lemid = U04409, accessed December 11, 2023. Campe, *Wörterbuch der deutschen Sprache*, vol. 5, 85, defines *Umkehr* as reversal, moral conversion, and return, and *umwenden* as "to turn around oneself so that the lowest becomes the highest or what is in the back becomes what is in the front," and "to proceed again to the place whence one came" (113). Schelling plays with all of these meanings. Relatedly, Frank, *Der unendliche Mangel an Sein*, 253, notes that for Schelling *Umkehr* or *Umkehrung* "is no mere logical problem. One can see how, behind its philosophical meaning,

itself upward, and this cycle is reiterated or "potentiated" at every stage (*Stufe*) of the universal spiral, all the way until the final historical turning as the restorative turn (*Wiederumwendung*) to justice and the true order of things.

Schelling speaks of creation as a *katabolē*, a "throwing down" or "laying down," and in particular the laying down of a foundation of the world. He further translates it as *Niederwerfung*, literally "throwing down" or "downward thrust": the Fall of B as the sinking down into being that provides the ground for what will become the material universe. The scattering of the Fall, Schelling says, is the beginning of the universe (*Universum*) as *universio*, the turning (*versio*) of what is one (*unum*), the inversion or rotation of the one. The "first *universio*" is the rotatory motion, the vortex-like swirl of B that disperses oneness, followed by the "second *universio*" as the beginning of the re-collection of oneness through the submission or prostration (another meaning of *Niederwerfung*) of B before the higher principle of oneness (WA27 176–177; cf. WA14 242/29–30, 265–266/46–47, IPU 528–529, GPP 362–363). The first downward movement is followed by the first upward turn, in which what is fallen prostrates itself before the higher. The first Fall, in other words, is followed by the first redemption.

There is also a political dimension to Schelling's account of the Fall of the divine will as the origin of the cosmic revolution. The Fall of B not only generates a cosmic war but is at the same time the first *Umsturz* (of which the Fall of Adam is a restaging; UPO 57, 181, GPP 467): a term that means a fall but also a coup d'état, the first (Luciferian) rebellion. It is, moreover, the first cosmic catastrophe (*Katastrophe*), likewise recapitulated in the Fall of human consciousness: the wild rotation and explosion of divine oneness. In Greek, *katastrophē* is a compound word made up of *kata* ("downward") and *strephein* ("turning"), the two elements likewise contained in the terms *katabolē* and *universio* that Schelling employs. In his poetics, Aristotle calls this kind of turn *peripeteia*, "a reversal in which a situation turns into its opposite, from fortune to misfortune."[28] Schelling has in mind this dramatic dimension of the Fall, too, when he refers to it as *fortuna adversa* (IPU 518). This first contingency and catastrophe continues to underlie the drama of universal history,

---

there gleams the original sense of 'revolution,' which explains the pathos of Schelling's polemic." On revolution and the spiral in modernity, see also Koselleck, *Begriffsgeschichten*, 240–251. In the identity philosophy, Schelling relatedly opposes the (essentially cosmic) idea of revolution as return to the idea of linear progress; see WS 433 (§313).

28. Horn, *Future as Catastrophe*, 6.

full of twists and turns, of peripeties and reversals, yet following the stage play directed by the divine law.

In Schellingian theodicy, a catastrophe also implies the promise of restoration, of movement toward the higher. In this way, Schelling joins the tradition of Enlightenment theodicy that seeks to inscribe the contingency, disorder, and catastrophic character of post-Copernican reality into a higher rational order, so as to reaffirm the goodness of creation.[29] Leibniz's statement that "disorders [take] place within order" applies likewise to the Schellingian universe.[30] How can B, the fallen divine will, redeem itself and, in its very fallenness, demonstrate the orderly goodness of creation? Such is the first question that Schelling needs to answer so that, amid the tumult of the Fall, order can be maintained and so that the Fall itself can be inscribed in orderly salvation history. Otherwise, Schelling points out, the scattering of the Fall would entail the danger (*Gefahr*) that this disorder may not be contained: that oneness may be lost, dispersed "into infinity," and that no return may be possible (WA27 142). Thereby, Schelling betrays again his own (and modern thought's) anxiety about universal contingency and decentering.

As we know, cosmologically, B is the first proto-material state of the universe following the big bang, the "blind nature" or "first blind life" (WA14 228–229/19–20), the initial postlapsarian state of being. With the Fall, the fire of divine egoism is scattered in a cosmic explosion, "spreading the hidden God as in a radiance" (*Glanz*; WA27 163): the beginning of divine revelation, even if a blind and unconscious one. This state is proto-material, or only "relative matter" (WA27 177), since to speak of material being proper is to speak of a materiality of *something*, of material form, whereas there is yet no stable form in this chaos. B is "non-corporeal"; it is "the will, [or] spiritual, astral, sidereal fire"—the stuff from which stars are to be made. At their core, celestial bodies are for Schelling pre-corporeal: "That which is, properly speaking, astral within a heavenly body is non-corporeal" and "cannot be brought under the three potencies" (WA27 176–177; cf. GPP 362–365, DRP 430). As such, "Heavenly bodies exceed mere forces of nature: they are the works of God,"

---

29. Catastrophe, according to thinkers in this tradition, may appear as a negative event, but it is also something that breaks up the immediate state of reality, forcing reality to unfold the possibilities latent in it. On this idea in Leibniz, see Rossi, *Dark Abyss of Time*, 55–56. See also Chepurin, "Theodicy across Scales."

30. Leibniz, *Protogaea*, quoted in Rossi, *Dark Abyss of Time*, 55.

that is, of B as the fallen (yet essentially divine) fatherly will (IPU 559).[31] In this first state of B, however, stars and planets have not yet appeared. There is here no distinction yet between darkness and light: B's fire is a dark fire of pride, "the fire of blind being" (EIP 119) that does not illuminate. In its falling away, the will keeps spinning and swirling. The first existence "gyrates eternally within itself" in a deranged "circle" (WA14 229/20): an uroboros serpent swallowing itself. It is a *looping circle of circles or vortex of vortices, which fails to stabilize or to open itself onto the higher*, a "rotatory movement that cannot find its beginning or end," and thus "unblissfulness as such" (*Unseligkeit an sich*; UPO 92; cf. IPU 513, 778). Insofar as nature remains caught in the cycle of the eternally same, it remains bound to this original unblissfulness.

This proto-matter already contains in itself the power to generate the world but, subordinated to B as the force of scattering, this power cannot yet re-collect itself, cannot become the "ground for revelation" (WA14 223/16). The hot proto-stuff that Schelling depicts here is the future birthplace of cosmic worlds: the universal hearth (*Herd*; WA14 230/20), the cosmic forge, whose all-consuming yet also (potentially) all-generative fire burns to this day in the depths of nature and of the human. "Precisely that must become the ground for revelation," Schelling writes, "which [originally] negates all revelation" (WA14 223/16), that is, what used to be the non-will of the hidden God, which is thereby subordinated to the will of God the creator. This first negation is B in its darkness, which is there so that it can be clarified by light: as we remember, for Schelling, a beginning is the positing of what ought *not* to be for its own sake.

In more technical terms, to say that the first nature is the all-generative proto-being that will become the material ground of the universe is to suggest that it contains within itself the potencies of finitude, the powers or *elohim* that are to shape creation (WA27 144–145). These are grasped by the post-1809 Schelling as the persons of the Trinity turned, with the Fall of B, into the cosmic demiurgic potencies whose purpose is to structure the world. This theological framing aside, they are the same potencies that we encountered in Schelling's identity philosophy: A = B (gravity), A^2 (light),

---

31. Cf. WA14 331/98: "They are works of God, works of wrath, of the fatherly force, which is the oldest force of all." The fire of the stars is not the fire of bliss. It is the "pure, untransmuted B" (EIP 128), not yet subdued or bound (*gebunden*; UPO 631): the Luciferian radiance of the fallen will. "Radiance" or "shining" is another meaning of *Schein*, and Schelling's speaking of B as "astral" or "sidereal" is also an allusion to Lucifer's traditional titles *morning star* and *shining one*.

and A³ (wholeness or oneness-in-differentiation, which he now calls "spirit"). Within ante-original oneness, these potencies are the three aspects of the divine A = A. Within fallenness, they become unbalanced and start falling apart (*auseinandergehen*), caught up in B's vortex. The first state of the cosmic war is also that of an unresolved "conflict of the potencies" (IPU 785). Cosmologically, this marks B precisely as the chaotic proto-material state of indistinction because an orderly interplay of the potencies in their separate functions, which is necessary for the emergence of stable material being, is yet absent here.

Theologically—and this is Schelling's post-1809 spin on the logic of illusion (*Schein*)—B falls because it asserts itself as the true subject and wants *to be the All*, to be as God. In its egoism, B believes itself to be all-powerful, and even as it becomes "peripheral," "merely an illusion and shadow" of the divine, it continues mistakenly to conceive of itself as the divine center and all-oneness (IPU 537, 781, 785). In this way, B finds itself in a state of self-deception (*Täuschung, Selbstbetrug*) and self-infatuation (*Blendung, Betörung*; IPU 507, 511, 775, 779).[32] Lucifer's tragedy is that his role is that of God's seeming or illusory (*scheinbare*) will, yet he mistakenly regards himself as the true will. B insists on itself as the All, persisting in its illusion, and thereby binding the potencies to its swirling motion and precluding the development of the higher (B is *ausschließend* or exclusionary, Schelling writes; IPU 818, DNP 308).

However, this illusion, too, is theodically necessary as part of the providential stage play, and it is important that B should act "*as if* it were there for its own sake" (IPU 779). In regarding itself as the All, the will in its expansion generates what is to become the material expanse of the universe, laying the foundation of creation. Schellingian theodicy justifies the necessity of B's self-assertion, and in that, theodicy rests on illusion and deceit (a theodical as-if), on baiting the will into an erroneous state so that the goals of providence can be achieved. Furthermore, the fallen will as the (scattered or particularized) force of divine selfhood imparts *particular selfhood* to all beings in the universe. B is the seeming will whose true purpose is to spread the fire of the

---

32. Fallenness thus originates in erroneous judgment, an attempted subordination of the universal to the particular and a persistence in ignorance, leading to disorder, derangement, and phantasm—a Gnostic motif, reflected also in Schelling's earlier-quoted dictum that error belongs to "the category of evil." Cf. Pleše, "Evil and Its Sources," 107. In Schelling, we encounter what Pleše calls the "*Leitmotiv* [of] the Gnostic accounts of evil," namely, "the theme of ignorance (*agnosia*) as the symptom of an internal split, of a divided self" originating already within the absolute (132).

hidden God, to share what used to be God's alone—the principle of egoism or selfhood—with finitude. The error of self-assertion creates the basis for the ascent to divine truth. This is a necessary operation, since particular selfhood is the universal principle of differentiation, a principle on the basis of which the differentiated all-oneness is to be developed, and which is thus essential for actualizing the divine plenitude of possibility. "The force of God through which he [was] closed off unto himself," Schelling writes, "is the same force that is laid down as the ground of revelation" (WA14 243/30): what used to be inner to God (i.e., divine egoism) becomes outer or revealed, whereas divine oneness or love becomes concealed underneath scatteredness. Divine selfhood is the prototype of all finite selfhood: all finite being must be a relative center unto itself, even if it cannot be the absolute center (cf. IPU 568). This is why the Fall is already the first revelation, however blind and deranged: God "reveals" his selfhood to what is to become his orderly creation. B, Schelling writes, is the ground and strength (*Stärke*) of will, the "barbaric principle" without which the universal would remain empty and abstract (WA14 223–224/15–16, 243–244/30–31, 342–343/106), yet which must submit to the universal (not unlike barbarism must, for Schelling, submit to civilization; cf. Chapters 3 and 6). "Strength must precede meekness, sternness must precede gentleness, and wrath must come before love" (WA14 311/83): a statement that is to be understood in a kenotic manner. B must subdue the blind fire of its self-assertion and open itself to divine love.

Schelling continues to configure this first submission of B to the higher—the first act of redemption or the first "good" *ekstasis*—in natural-philosophical as well as theological terms. Cosmologically, Schelling still broadly follows here the nebular hypothesis: out of the first hot swirling state, star systems begin to form as this state begins to cool down. This is the dampening (*Dämpfung*) of the first fire, in which blind desire is transfigured into life-supporting flame. The subdual of B sets the cosmic potencies free to do their demiurgic work, allowing them to generate the system of the revolution of celestial bodies (WA27 176–177, EIP 129, DNP 329) as the foundation of the ascending ladder of nature. "All life," Schelling notes, "has its beginning in a rotatory movement. . . . All life occurs through a movement around its axis," which is then "elevated" into an upward movement (IPU 810).[33] This elevation is precisely the redemptive ascent. If the first *universio* or downward

---

33. This, too, is a cosmological thesis, aligned with both the nebular hypothesis and, e.g., William Herschel's work on the construction of the heavens, in which he ascribes "a rotatory motion [to] a celestial body in its very formation" (quoted in Schaffer, "Great Laboratories,'" 100).

turn is the beginning of "the great world-creation," the dampening of B as the first upward turn is "the creation of nature proper," that is, of the orderly process of nature and the order of creation in the narrow sense (WA27 177). Only starting from this point can the world be properly called a divine creation or creature (*Kreatur*; cf. IPU 799).

Theologically, the fallen will's illusion must be dispelled once its theodical mission has been accomplished. At some point, the will cannot but face its unblissfulness and recognize the fact that it is decentered, inverted, and peripheral (IPU 785, WA27 176–177). It must acknowledge its fallenness and prostrate itself before the divine. It is crucial for Schelling to configure what is essentially a natural-philosophical moment, the cooling down of the swirling proto-All, as a willing kenotic surrender (cf. also DNP 310). B is judged by the law to be the lowest and not the highest, and it submits to this judgment. In this moment of submission—the second *universio*, the new *Umkehrung* as conversion (*Bekehrung* or *conversio*), as Saul's becoming Paul on the road to Damascus as well as the Augustinian *conversio ad Deum*—B is so overwhelmed by the divine light breaking through the darkness of desire that it voluntarily gives up its self-assertion. In a typical theodical conjunction, B's giving up of self-assertion and surrender to the higher is cast by Schelling both as free and as necessary from a providential standpoint and the standpoint of the process of nature. The divine, Schelling writes, is revealed to B as infinitely superior (*überschwenglich*), exceeding B to such an extent that B *cannot but* freely surrender itself, prostrating itself before the higher and becoming the ground for the theo-cosmic process (WA14 233–234/22–23).[34] In this manner, the circular rotatory motion of B is opened upward in the first ascending turn of the universal spiral.

5.3.2. The Fall and Redemption as the Structure of the World-Process

The first conjunction of Fall and redemption is then reiterated across the universal process as Schelling constructs it: across the ladder of nature and

---

34. Augustine likewise applies the model of conversion to the origin of the cosmos in his interpretation of the story of creation from Genesis—a story in which he discerns the redemptive transition from what is dark and formless to the orderly, illumined, and well-formed creation, the turning to God of what is "turned away" from him, or "conversion [as] formation" (*Literal Meaning of Genesis*, vol. 1, 20–25 [I.1–5]). Via Augustine, Schelling's account of the transition from chaos and darkness to the orderly world-process can be understood as his speculative exegesis of Genesis, too. On the transition from tumult to *krisis* ("point of decision") qua conversion, cf. Augustine, *Confessions*, 403.

human consciousness. This process, as mentioned, is a spiral of spirals: each galaxy and star system is a spiral, but the broader processes of inorganic and organic nature are spiral-like, too. Thus, the gradation of inorganic nature is a succession of steps or levels (*Stufen*) through which gravity becomes increasingly permeable to light. The basis of this movement remains stellar and planetary motion, on top of which further turns of the spiral are layered. From a standpoint of the even higher level in this ladder—from the standpoint of organic life—the entire inorganic realm, across the universal expanse, appears as a realm of fallenness, or of the relative preponderance of B over A.

The transition from inorganic to organic nature is, accordingly, also configured by Schelling as a kenotic act of submission: in a "sudden change of heart," B gives up its rigidity, or resistance (*Widerstand*) to light. "B, or the ur-principle of nature," Schelling writes, "makes itself susceptible to, and overcomeable through, the higher potency" (DNP 366). In this manner, the spiral's redemptive upward turn generates the realm of organic life. The emergence of the organic is a re-inversion of what was inverted in the inorganic: "What in inorganic nature is mute," subordinate, and concealed, that is, the freedom of inner life, becomes in the turning toward the organic "what is high and dominating" (UPO 6). This is an operation of conversion, too: "Without such an inner transformation and, so to speak, change of mind on the part of the original blind principle, the progression from inorganic to organic nature would remain incomprehensible" (DNP 366). It is, in other words, a contingent and emergent natural event, which Schelling recasts kenotically as a Christ-event by emphasizing the will's self-prostrating agency both in this event and throughout the *Stufenfolge* of nature, which in its entirety is an ascending metamorphosis of B.[35]

In this *Stufenfolge*, every ascent or upward turn is followed by a relative fall or downward turn (which still remains above the previous *Stufe*), a turning that then leads to a re-turning or an even higher ascent. The goal of the relative fall is always to create the widest possible basis or ground for the subsequent ascending turn. One may consider here the example of plant life as Schelling configures it. Plant life is higher than inorganic nature, yet it is also relatively fallen. To the extent that it is fallen, it is circular: the plant generates the seed, from which another plant grows, and so without end. At the same

---

35. One may see in B Schelling's continuing search for the principle of the *restless freedom* of nature underpinning the entire natural process—a search that is evident already in his 1798 *On the World-Soul*, in which the first proto-matter is identified with ether (see VW 254–257). Cf. WAF1 209 on "pure electric fire" as what runs through the metamorphosis of B.

time, it entails a movement of fall and redemption, in two senses. First, the plant begins its life in the soil and strives toward the sun, reflecting in this the force of love, the longing for ascent inherent in nature. Second, the plant finds its *higher redemptive and providential meaning* within the universal process by serving as the material basis or ground for the development of animal life, which feeds on the plant and breathes the oxygen it generates. Within the plan of eternal wisdom, plant life is meant to create the widest foundation for the emergence and subsistence of the higher. Therefore, plant life is not merely circular: it, too, is a spiral that opens onto the higher through its incorporation in the ascending process of nature and thus in the universal history of revelation and salvation. Each level of this spiraling ladder, moreover, marks the reiteration of the movement of (re-)inversion, of turning and re-turning.

The emergence of the human is the pinnacle and completion of the process of nature or first creation. At this point, we see the human as one with God in the Garden of Eden: the paradisal state of the human with which I began Chapter 4, and whose genesis we have now retraced starting from the origins of the universe. With regard to the human, all of nature appears as a relative realm of fallenness, which the human redeems in the final turning of the natural spiral.

Yet the human then falls, too. Following the Fall of Adam, nature reverts to its unblissful circularity, and the history of salvation now plays out in the arena of human history. This history also starts with B as the explosive scattering of human consciousness—the expulsion from paradise. Out of this scattering, human history ascends as a process that recapitulates in consciousness the process of nature. The first Fall is followed by the first redemption, the first submission of consciousness to the higher, from which the process of mythology or paganism begins as the re-collection of the one God out of scatteredness—the God who is then revealed in Christianity: the revelation that redeems the fallen pagan world. At each stage of the *Stufenfolge* of human consciousness, we have again a relative Fall and a higher redemption as part of one ascending spiral. Thus, the process of Christian revelation proper likewise begins with confusion and scatteredness: the fall of the Roman Empire and the migration period that Schelling terms *turba gentium*, the vortex-like tumult of the peoples (FS 148/46). Following this fall, the first redemption occurs with the rise of the Christian church as the institution to which the tumultuous consciousness submits. After this, salvation history keeps ascending as an orderly process divided into the epochs of Catholicism, Protestantism, and the future religion of love and humanity, which is meant to fulfill the original Christian promise, and to which I will return below. At the summit of this spiral, humanity and nature will be liberated from unblissfulness, and bliss will be regained.

Cosmic revolution in its entirety, across natural and human history, may be viewed as one overarching movement of conversion to the light of truth and the one true God. The two-part rhythm of Fall and redemption as generating kenotically the hierarchized ladder of being, in which the relatively lower exists for the sake of the relatively higher and provides the latter's basis, is essential to this movement. To grasp this rhythm is to grasp the basic structure and operation of Schelling's entire post-1809 metaphysics. The conjunction of Fall and redemption is the same as that of scattering and re-collection, self-assertive pride and kenotic submission, "bad" and "good" *ekstasis*, decentering and recentering, fall into darkness and ascent to light (or transfiguration toward a higher clarity [*Verklärung*]), bondage and liberation, error and its re-subordination to truth, inversion and re-inversion. This conjunction is precisely the cosmic Christ, the Christ-structure or Christ-operation: the Fall as what theodically makes redemption possible, or the Fall and redemption as bound together within the overarching A = A. This two-part Christ-operation is what generates the levels of the *Stufenfolge as* levels, separating one level from another across the universal spiral. To understand Schelling's claim that the historical view of the universe is identical with the Christian view (UPO 5), one needs to grasp this Christ-structure as the logic of the whole theo-cosmic process. The figure of universal ascent qua the iterative movement of Fall and redemption underlies Schelling's theodical re-visioning of the decentered post-Copernican universe. The Christ-event is inscribed in the foundation of universal reality and then, with the historical emergence of Christianity, revealed to human consciousness in the form of the general Christian contradiction and the promise of all-reconciliation at the end of time. For Schelling, there is but one true religion: what we may call the cosmic Christianity.

This Christ-structure or Christ-operation is likewise evident in Schelling's post-1809 doctrine of the cosmic potencies of gravity, light, and spirit. While this doctrine is complex, its broad contours may be outlined as follows. Ontologically, the three potencies (A = B, A^2, A^3) form the three dimensions or steps in the formation of every individual being: it must be a particular material instantiation of a concept, a particular carrier of a certain form (*eidos*), and no individual being is thinkable without matter and form. A = B expresses the material particularity that a being possesses, A^2 the form that this particularity carries, and A^3 the copula between matter and form within it. To impose form on the proto-matter is to create a relatively independent material being (A^3), which is not to be imagined as a separate third substance or force but as the balance or oneness between the particular and the universal, matter and form. In nature or "the real," this oneness is expressed by the stone, the plant, and the human, yet in different ways, so that it is only the human that attains "pure" spirit. In consciousness or "the ideal," this unity is also expressed differently by the different historical forms of human consciousness, for example, the Homeric consciousness or the early Christian consciousness. In this regard, each being reflects or reassembles, to the best of its power, A = A from within the structure of opposition that defines finitude, and the divine A = A remains the prototype of all finite being. Furthermore, to impose form is to actualize a possibility concealed in the depths of the proto-matter or the depths of consciousness; it is to articulate or unfold this possibility, to bring it from darkness to light, to open toward the universal what seeks to close itself off (*sich verschließen*; WA14 319/89). In this manner, A^2 is not only the mediating and illuminating but the articulating and actualizing principle (the divine Light is also the Word, so that revelation and actualization coincide). A^2 may be called the Christ-potency, the Son, which "redeems" particularity or scatteredness by directing it toward the higher: the Christ-operation again.[36] In this manner, Schelling positions Christ as the truly universal mediator—and not only the movement of universal history, but the structure of all being is cast in Christocentric terms.

5.3.3. Transcendence and Hierarchy in the Ladder of History

Schelling's post-1809 turn from Spinozan immanence to transcendence is likewise crucial for the way he envisages the hierarchy of being and the beginning and telos of the universal *Stufenfolge*. His *reconfiguration of bliss as transcendent* is central to the logics of the world in his post-1809 thought. Schelling depicts B's moment of conversion as a ray of transcendence breaking through the darkness of the fallen will's desire.[37] This moment is where the logic of transcendence emerges as such. Within ante-original oneness in

---

36. Cf. Augustine, *Confessions*, 341, on Christ as the mediator between below and above, who "raises up those who submit themselves to him." Cf. *City of God*, 843 (XVIII.18): "the Mediator through Whom we climb from the depths to the heights."

37. This logic of transcendence as what is infinitely above and overwhelms B is present already in the early *Ages of the World* drafts, and in *Initia* Schelling explicitly speaks of the *Überschwengliche* as "transcendent" (e.g., IPU 261, 430).

which the *hen* and the *pan* are undifferentiated, there is yet no transcendence. For this reason, the divine essence is designated by Schelling as A^0, or what is potenceless (*das Potenzlose*), the zero point of divinity. The Fall as the sinking down into being creates the first division between above and below, and thus it is the beginning of transcendence: of heaven *as* heaven in opposition to what is fallen. A^0 emerges (*hervortritt*) for the first time as the eternal freedom that remains "outside and above the potencies" (IPU 455, 784) and therefore outside and above the world.[38]

Importantly, divinity emerges as the zero point only retroactively from the standpoint of the potencies or the standpoint of the world. A^0 is the bliss that has been lost at the beginning of the world-process and emerges here as the transcendent divinity *for us* (for the philosopher) but not for B. As we remember, B still considers itself to be divine all-oneness. The proto-matter is therefore an illusory state for a further reason: it is a seemingly pantheistic state. As Schelling puts it, "A = B wants [here] to be at the same time A^2, A^3 and A^0, to be the totality of the potencies as well as the potenceless eternal freedom." The fallen will "wants to remain the All, to be A^2, A^3 and A^0... and even though it has already become peripheral, it seeks to remain the absolute point and center, or to remain at once periphery, radius, and center" (IPU 784): a contradiction that cannot be resolved until B awakens from its illusion.

Thus, just as we see in this state the "birth pangs of nature" (IPU 786) but not yet the orderly natural process, so, too, we glimpse here the birth of transcendence, which is not yet transcendence as such but a state of all-confusion in which B refuses to acknowledge the distance between itself and God (IPU 782). For Schelling, transcendence proper implies hierarchy and order, and so the first chaotic state cannot break through to transcendence until B assumes its rightful place as what is the lowest, and its blind desire or craving (*Sucht*, *Begehren*) is "softened into a longing [*Sehnsucht*]" for bliss (WA14 239/28). Only once B acknowledges itself as fallen and submits to the divine as what is infinitely above it does transcendence appear as such. This is also the first divine revelation proper, for which B serves as ground: the revelation of "love, calm, and justice" out of "darkness and concealment" (IPU 807–808). Revelation in general occurs "when oneness breaks through and God reveals himself as such, as supernatural" in contrast to darkness (UPO 9–10), and

---

38. Since, raised to the power of zero, any number mathematically equals 1, A^0 may be understood at once as the zero point of divinity and as transcendent oneness, or the One beyond the world.

this formula is just as true of the emergence of Christianity, whose light shines through the error of polytheism, as it is of B's first submission at the origin of the universe. What thereby arises, overcoming the quasi-pantheistic state, is precisely cosmic monotheism or cosmic Christianity, to be revealed to human consciousness in the historical Christ-event.

The emergence of transcendence qua transcendence coincides with the establishment of hierarchy and the theodical logic of rightful place. B is judged by the law to be the lowest, and it submits to this judgment. B recognizes that it is but the "material [*Stoff*] for the actualization" of the higher (WA14 240/28, IPU 787). The hierarchization of being and the instrumentalization of the lower as the ground, material carrier, or basis for the higher are operations reiterated across Schelling's post-1809 writings and lectures. This instrumentalization identifies kenosis not only with the logics of sacrifice and redemption but also with the logic of use: the lower must submit to the higher so it can become *useful* for the goals of providence (and not resist them, generating tumult and disorder). "Only the highest is the measure" of all being, Schelling's dictum goes. The divine law measures and weighs every being, judging it and assigning to it its place within the *Stufenfolge* according to this being's usefulness for and proximity to the highest $A = A$. The lower, Schelling writes, can "connect with" and become part of the higher—and thus become relatively redeemed and assigned its proper place (*Ort*)—only by giving up its self-assertion and submitting to the higher's "guidance" through the part of itself that is capable of receiving such guidance (WA14 240–241/28–29). If the lower *cannot* elevate itself to the higher so as to participate in the universal ascent, it is left behind as a relic of the past. This happens, for instance, with the distant star systems mentioned earlier.[39] At one point, they were useful for the unfolding of the world-process, but now they have nothing to offer.

Crucially, what is higher is higher at once *by nature* and *according to the divine judgment and justice*. These two standpoints coincide in Schelling's construction of the universal process from the perspective of the law. In his naturalized theodicy, natural judgment, that is, the way things naturally are or the proper place they have by nature, is divine judgment, and vice versa. Thus, the plant is lower than the animal by nature since it constitutes an earlier stage of natural development, and this also determines its lower place within the providential world-plan, according to which it exists for the sake

---

39. Or with those peoples that are no longer of use to the movement of history; cf. Chapter 6.

of the animal, which in turn is there for the sake of the human. As Schelling summarizes this ascent, "Inorganic nature is the presupposition of the organic, and this latter in turn the presupposition of the human. Hence, the untrue is the presupposition of the true, the step [*Stufe*] toward the true" (UPO 6). The hierarchy of being is also that of relative error and truth, as well as relative darkness and illumination.[40] What is lower is relatively darker than the higher and is clarified through the *Stufe* that brings being one step closer to transcendent light. While the ladder of nature is a Platonic motif, it is for Schelling not simply pre-given or imposed on nature from above, but emerges *from within* nature out of the dynamic interaction between the potencies, and out of B's free kenotic submission to transcendence, a submission that generates nature's immanent movement of unfolding qua self-transcending, from level to level.

Just how foundational the hierarchized salvific logic of place is for Schelling is likewise evident from his opposition to Newton's abolishment of the division between above and below, and his preference for Kepler's adherence to a vision of cosmic hierarchy. The Newtonian universe, Schelling asserts, is one of fallenness. For Newton, "There is, properly speaking, no up" (WAE 270/247), "only an infinite, groundless below but no above" (IPU 568). As a result, there is no possibility of recentering in the higher; instead, "everything strives downward" (WAE 270/247). Against this fallen vision, Schelling affirms: "There is a true above and true below, a sun and heavens that are above the earth" (IPU 567; cf. WAE 269/246–247).

For his naturalized and hierarchized theodicy to hold, for the distinction between lower and higher to be grounded in nature, Schelling needs to impose hierarchy on the de-hierarchized modern universe. That is why, arguing that, unlike Kepler, Newton perverts the Copernican system (in that Copernicus himself retained the sense of an above), Schelling distinguishes between gravity as the force of self-assertion and love as the "elevating, exalting" force (IPU 566–568). Gravity is what binds the earth to its proper place "below" the sun and makes the earth assert its particularity or "claim its own place in the universe" (WAE 269/246): an idea that reiterates Schelling's earlier vision of the conflict between the earth and the sun (see Chapter 3). By contrast,

---

40. It is at the same time a hierarchy of the *degree of reality*. "Being that has a lower degree of reality functions as [relative] nonbeing"—as mere materiality or potentiality—"with regard to the being that has a higher degree of reality." In turn, this higher being "can itself appear as [relative] nonbeing vis-à-vis a being of an even higher order" (WA14 222/14; cf. IPU 788). Relative nonbeing, Schelling explains, refers to "all that is merely matter or material" for the higher (IPU 787).

love is what attracts the earth to the sun as the higher, or elevates the earth's particularity toward the universal—and the same holds for all things on the earth. The roots of a plant go down into the earth, and this is the work of gravity; but the plant also strives toward the sun, and this is the work of love. Or, if one throws a stone, it falls down because the earth is its proper place.[41]

As Schelling summarizes it, "Just as in the *Stufenfolge* of the animal kingdom the significance of each part of the organism consists in its place within the whole," so everywhere "This thing belongs to this place, and this place belongs to this thing: the thing and the place are one" (IPU 810). Schelling's opposition to de-hierarchization and his insistence that *everything belongs in its place* form a part of his Romantic attempt to overcome cosmic alienation in response to the crisis of cosmic theodicy and of universal reality itself: the reality that, by the early nineteenth century, is increasingly perceived as contingent and inhuman. His turn to Christianity may also be understood as part of this attempt. Schelling seeks to counteract the foreclosure of bliss in modernity by making bliss transcendent now that it cannot be intuited immanently, or by reconfiguring it as the immanent-transcendent telos of universal reality.

To summarize, in Schelling's kenotic configuration of the universal *Stufenfolge*, bliss and the longing for bliss are inscribed in the logics of transcendence, telos, hierarchy, place, and use: logics that are foreign to bliss as such. From this point on, since nature "cannot return to quiet purity, it has to press forward" and upward, striving toward bliss positioned as transcendent (IPU 788). When Schelling claims that divinity as such remains outside the world-process, this does not mean that he adheres to the traditional idea of a supernatural God who remains beyond the material universe. With regard to the world-process, divinity appears as the bliss that has been lost and toward which this process self-transcends from within. In other words, divinity is the *immanent-transcendent normativity* that drives this process onward and upward. When Schelling compares it to Aristotle's unmoved mover (IPU 441), this is not to be understood in the sense of a reified theistic representation of God, which would contradict Schelling's emphasis on God's becoming God.[42] This normativity is immanent insofar as it continues to constitute the

---

41. The universal logic of place is so absolute that, Schelling's example goes, "even if the rest of the earth were annihilated," the stone "would still sink toward the same place": it would still claim the place it would have on the earth because that is its assigned, proper place (WAE 268/245).

42. Lovejoy emphasizes the following tension: "[If] Schelling meant seriously ... that God is ... 'subject to suffering and becoming,' he could not consistently hold to this conception of a transcendent Absolute who does not participate in the world-process.... The two theologies

blissful essence of fallen reality, the essence that generates reality's longing for bliss; and it is transcendent insofar as it is not part of the theo-cosmic process but remains "above" it as the ideal center around and toward which the spiral turns. It is God's own normativity as well, his striving for the Sabbath. This normativity is lawful: its formula (A = A) is the formula of the law that judges all beings based on their approximation of, and contribution to, the overarching ought or telos.

Thus, although Schelling adopts a vision of a ladder of being, this vision is already modern. It is a natural-philosophical vision of a lawful normativity governing universal history and generating the evolving *Stufenfolge* of being through one universal law, a law acting from within the orderly interplay of forces that constitutes being. In the same stroke, it is a Christian-theodical vision that justifies error, darkness, and fallenness by subordinating them to the higher. It is as though the law were saying to each form of being: *the only way in which you can attain what is higher is by becoming useful to the higher, by giving up your self-assertion and offering yourself as the material for the actualization and revelation of the higher. The extent to which you are capable of this determines your place in the universal hierarchy*. In Chapter 6, we will see this logic culminate in Schelling's racialized vision of human history, so that, to use his own examples, when the "lower" South American peoples die out from the contact with the "higher" European principle, or when black Africans are enslaved and transported to the New World, all of this is in keeping with the (at once divine and natural) law. In this manner, the path to bliss is in Schelling hierarchized and racialized.

5.3.4. Divine Geometry: Constructing the Circle of Circles

The turning of the cosmic spiral is a way of creating complexity. The end goal is the highest differentiation coinciding with the highest transparency as the revelation of every possibility contained in the depths of being. In the end, everything will have been unfolded to the fullest. This unfolding is what

---

still subsist side by side; but one of them is a survival, the other is an innovating idea which is on the point of destroying the former" (*Great Chain of Being*, 320). However, Schelling's notion of transcendent divinity is itself modern, insofar as he turns the bliss of divinity into the lawful normativity (A = A) that drives from within the process of nature's development. Lovejoy fails to consider that, following the breaking up of oneness, transcendent divinity does not have a separate being for Schelling. Divinity is nonbeing and non-will; as such, it is *not*. The *nonbeing of what ought to be* is what generates the not-yet of the world-process, the *ought* that steers the universe. Divinity is "supernatural" in the sense that it is not nature, but nature's immanent-transcendent telos.

philosophy constructs starting from ante-original divine oneness—and, as the images of circle and spiral, of cosmic turning and re-turning suggest, this construction in Schelling is geometric. He thereby builds on the early-modern tradition of geometric cosmo-theology going back to Bruno, Kepler, and Boehme.[43] The question *How is the ante-original divine nucleus unfolded into the universe?* is, in this tradition, equivalent to the question *How to construct the universal circle of circles out of the one as the dimensionless divine point?*

Thus, Kepler maintains that God constructs the universe using a straight edge and a compass (the instrument used for inscribing circles or arcs) as his drawing tools.[44] Boehme identifies Christ with the "circumference" through which the threefold divine oneness is articulated, conjuring up the image of a triangle inscribed in a circle.[45] Bruno, for his part, is drawn to the cosmological implications of the compass no less than the image of the universe as a circle of circles.[46] When Schelling speaks of ante-original A = A as the circle coinciding with the point, he echoes Bruno's praise of the circle as a figure of the absolutely one without dimensions, a monad in which "opposites coincide: chord, arc, spike, point, end, nothing, everything . . . right and left, arriving and returning, movement and rest."[47] "The greatest is round and without quality," Schelling likewise reiterates with regard to the divine nucleus (WA11 15/71, WA14 235/24). The blissful divine essence is the "absolute point" and "the inarticulable [*Unaussprechliche*] itself" (IPU 330).

At the same time, Schelling distinguishes a threefoldness within the form of divine being. The Trinitarian analogy is easily discernible in his speaking of the first aspect of A = A as the point (Father), the second as the "radius" emanating from the point (*das Ausstrahlende*; IPU 331–332), the principle of articulation (the Light, Word, or Son), and the third as the circle in its entirety, the aspect of wholeness (Spirit). These dimensions, however, are undifferentiated with ante-original being, which is "without multiplicity," "the

---

43. As observed in Woodard, *Schelling's Naturalism*, 95, Schelling generally prefers geometric over analytic thinking. What has been less explored is the continuing importance of the geometric figure of nature in Schelling's post-1809 thought.

44. See Field, *Kepler's Geometrical Cosmology*, 122. The image harkens back to Proverbs 8:27: "When he prepared the heavens, I was there: when he set a compass upon the face of the depths."

45. See Boehme, *The Clavis; or, An Explanation of some principal Points and Expressions*, 7 (§36), in *Works of Jacob Behmen*, vol. 2.

46. See Eusterschulte, *Analogia entis seu mentis*, and Saiber, *Giordano Bruno*.

47. Quoted in Saiber, *Giordano Bruno*, 136.

circle in itself, the primordial ur-image of the circle," or "the absolutely one as the oneness of periphery, radius, and center" (IPU 332–333, EIP 90). As we may recall, ante-original bliss equals "the three potencies in their common nothingness" (EIP 90), just as the absolute point is at once All and Nothing, "absolute non-time" and non-place (IPU 577). This point is *utopic* in the combined sense of "non-place" and "good place," and the overarching movement of the All is the unfolding of this theo-cosmic utopia.

With the Fall, the dimensions come apart, and the first nature emerges as the tumult of the forces of the point, radius, and periphery (IPU 519). The becoming peripheral of B coincides with the spreading of the point (the fatherly will). In this manner, the *articulation* of the absolute point begins, which is now posited outside itself (cf. EIP 54), and which in its movement generates the first all-encompassing circle within which the material All will be formed. The chaotic tumult of B is circumference without center: decenteredness as such. The first upward turning is the beginning of recentering and of the universal process as the progressive differentiation within the all-encompassing circle, or within the proto-All as containing "the material of the whole" (IPU 793; cf. 529). The transformation of the tumult into an orderly natural process with B's "first submission" to the higher signals "the emergence of the system of the universe," in which "the opposition of center and periphery" arises, and decenteredness is subordinated to recentering (EIP 128, GPP 362). From this moment onward, universal history is constructed through successive turnings and re-turnings of the metaphysical compass.[48]

One may picture this geometric construction of the All as follows. Within the widest all-encompassing circle, further narrower circles are formed that turn into galaxies; within these, star systems are differentiated; within each star system, the yet narrower circles of individual planets; and so on, until the construction reaches each of us, who exist in a community or state (also a relative circle or A = A) and whose life is likewise circular. One's life develops, in this Schellingian schema, from a purely potential oneness (an anthropological point) through an expansive rotational turmoil that ought to settle into an ascending spiral directed at the universal—a spiral that unfolds one's powers or potencies and allows one's particularity to express the universal. In this manner, across the overarching spiral of spirals, every "lower" circle serves as the basis for the "higher" one, expressing oneness with increasing complexity and differentiation. In this process, each being follows the divine A = A as the

---

48. I borrow the expression "metaphysical compass" from Eusterschulte, *Analogia entis seu mentis*, 473.

prototype of all being and the archetype of the circle. When Schelling calls the highest the measure of all things, this has a geometric sense, too: all being deviates from yet seeks elliptically to approximate A = A, to be a circle unto itself—and all being is judged according to the extent of its deviation.

Schelling does not explain how the overarching temporality of the seven days of creation in *Initia* aligns with the construction of the universe as a circle of circles. However, a striking contemporary parallel of using geometric construction as a way to interpret creation can be found in the Romantic painter Philipp Otto Runge's letter from 1803. The absolute point, Runge asserts there, cannot be articulated *as* a point. It can be only glimpsed "momentarily" as the non-place "where all thoughts cease." The point is "pure or abstract black," "the absence of all color," sheer "annihilation." And yet, creation, or the universe in all its color, is but an unfolding of the nothingness of the point: "The *articulated* [*ausgesprochene*] point is what proceeded from God, *the Word*, and all things are made through it." Articulated "light and life" can be grasped in a threefold manner: in mathematics, in color, and in words—and Runge draws a geometric figure in his letter (see Figure 5.1), which represents the

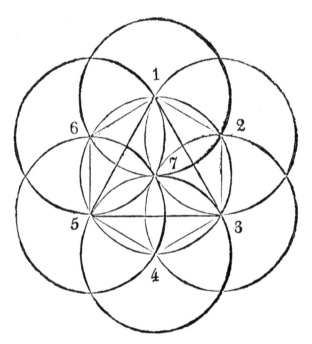

FIGURE 5.1 Runge's construction of the seven days of creation
Staats- und Universitätsbibliothek Hamburg, Scrin A/445: 1

mathematical articulation of creation. God's "Let there be light" marks the first constructed circle (number 1 in the drawing) or "the first day."[49] Every turning of the compass that draws the next circle circumscribes the respective day of creation. Runge's articulation does not simply adhere to the book of Genesis. Like Schelling, he transposes the seven days of creation onto salvation history as a whole. Thus, the fifth day is for him the Fall into sin, while the sixth is the period we inhabit, whose meaning "is not understood, and cannot be understood, until *the* day comes when all will return to light, and that is the seventh day." This final day is the middle circle, into which Runge inscribes the hexagon connecting the centers of each day as well as the triangle as the symbol of the Trinity. "In 7 all is united again: it is the holy of holies, the point become the circle"—or, rather, the circle of circles.[50]

The resulting figure represents the complexity of creation as it is revealed from the perspective of salvation. When at the end of *Initia* Schelling likewise describes each day or epoch of creation as a circle of time, with the Sabbath as the seventh day that concludes the *explicatio* of the divine point and closes the circle of circles (IPU 577–578), one may picture this construction in the manner of Runge's figure. In Schelling's case, furthermore, this figure must be imagined as layered and directed upward, so that circles turn into spirals, and must be overlaid in some way with the spatial construction of the universe and star systems described above.

The layered character of Schellingian construction—what he calls "a manifold of layers [*Schichten*]" within the "system of times" (WAII 11–12/67)—marks it not only as geometric but also as *geological*. Each circle of time is a layer whose darkness increases the lower it is located, or the closer it lies to the chaos of B. "We see," Schelling writes, "a series of times, in which one time follows and covers the preceding one," so that the speculative philosopher must travel downward in a philosophical descent into hell—into the times of deep fallenness—before she can proceed upward in (re)constructing the world. The "multitude of layers that are laid, over and over again, on top of each other" must be traversed, and the "work of thousands of years cleared away in order to finally arrive at the ground" (WAII 12/67).[51] Each layer is full of its respective forms of being, some of which exist to this day, while others

---

49. Runge, *Hinterlassene Schriften*, 40.

50. Ibid., 41. On the sixth day as the present, cf. Augustine, *City of God*, 1182 (XXII.30).

51. The fact that Schelling measures pre-human deep time in thousands of years shows how far he is still removed from the present notion that the universe is billions of years old.

have turned into fossils or "mere monuments of a life long past" (IPU 791; cf. GPP 471), which the speculative philosopher excavates. These dead forms, too, are part of the unfolding of the cosmic fullness of possibility, and their meaning is tied to their respective stage qua layer (*Stufe* as *Schicht*).

In Schelling's geometric construction of the cosmic revolution, nature is the figure (*Figur*) of God, and divinity in its transcendent A^0 remains the absolute zero point unfolded or exhibited by the figurality (*Figürlichkeit*) of the universe (IPU 792–797). In this manner, God geometrically "exhibit[s] himself in his purity and nakedness" (IPU 794). As in Runge, the beginning of nature is in Schelling the transition from what is "without figure" to the "figural," so that the All unfolds as a moving "figure or image of oneness," as "pictorial [*bildliches*] life" (IPU 792). This helps to visualize how Schelling understands transcendence, and why he envisions it as the universal telos rather than a supernatural being in the standard sense. The divine point, Schelling writes, remains in place while the figure of the All unfolds around and toward it: "It persists in the middle [*Mitte*] as A^0" (IPU 794). As B, the divine will goes outside itself into otherness while the essence remains in the middle as what guarantees the oneness of creation, ensuring that all of creation unfurls around the same center.[52] In Runge's figure, this would be the center of the seventh circle: the entire creation is the articulation of this point, yet the point itself remains unmoved, not unlike Aristotle's unmoved mover. The final circle is but the concluding explication of this central point: the bliss of $A = A$ restored in a fully articulated manner.

How much tension can a turn of a spiral hold? In Schellingian construction, it holds the longing and striving of the entire universe and of God's will to revelation. Each turn of the spiral is an operation of judgment and a point of *kairos*, bringing the cosmic revolution closer to the endpoint of bliss. Each turning is also a peripeteia in the Aristotelean sense: geometric cosmic theodicy coincides in Schelling with an aesthetic theodicy of form and figure, and a poetic or dramatic theodicy of the providential stage play. Realized pantheism arrives when every dramatic arc has been traversed and its moral judged. Schelling's universe is explosive and catastrophic, dark and layered, and the ascending spiral has to constantly withstand the tumult of forces and to convert this tumult into an orderly hierarchy. Cosmic construction in Schelling hangs in an infinite geo-cosmic abyss: "The whole creation

---

52. A and B may thus be compared to the two legs of the divine compass, with one remaining in the center and the other circumscribing creation. Cf. Eusterschulte, *Analogia entis seu mentis*, 474–475.

is an elevation out of the deep" (IPU 556, 806). Without the force of love directing this construction upward, "Everything would sink back into chaos" (IPU 811). The dark unruliness (*das Regellose*) that persists below might still "break through again," consuming all "rule, order, and form" (FS 131/29): the threat that the rising spiral-shaped edifice of universal history is meant to subdue. The circle of circles is a tower of order arising, level by level, in a victory wrested from contingency and disorder: the tower of spiritual ascent to heaven, which philosophy constructs. The Schellingian spiral seeks to *contain* a tension of truly apocalyptic proportions, to keep it at bay, and to direct it upward so as to resolve it eschatologically. This spiral tells us: if one but pierces, under the guidance of divine light, through cosmic darkness and attends to the figurality of the All, one can see universal history's orbiting around perfection and bliss, and one can discern balance and justice at work throughout reality. To do so is to glimpse the pure figure of Schellingian theodicy, and of his historical proof of the positive God.

5.3.5. The Religion of Humanity and the Question of Revolution

The unfolding of nature is a progressive revelation of divinity and bliss, and in each natural form, one can glimpse the divine essence. "It is," Schelling says Romantically, "that which shines through in every flower, in every formation of nature—something that is always on the verge of overflowing" the particular form just as it is captured (*gefaßt*) in it as in an image (*Bild* or *Gestalt*; IPU 801, 545). Every being is blissful to the extent that it simply *is*, expressing thereby the unprethinkable being of bliss. Bliss is the essence that exceeds every form; and yet the higher the universal spiral ascends, "the more the form appears as the form or vessel [*Gefäß*] in which the pure essence comes to light." "The intention of all development," of "the entire ladder," is for reality to become such that bliss can immanently inhabit it. Within all being, bliss is what can be glimpsed, yet what "can never be grasped or possessed," the non-appropriable common nothingness and non-will. However, nature conceals and represses bliss just as it reveals it. In nature, eternal freedom still "awaits its liberation" (IPU 544–546, 800–802). Liberation, the end goal of the cosmic revolution, can occur only through the human as "the form [*Gestalt*] in which the heavenly seed is fully unfolded and the essence is brought above all else" (IPU 547). The human is where the natural process culminates, "the end intention of creation" (WA27 172) or "the restored, actualized idea (A = A)" (DNP 389). "The end goal of creation" is "the being in which the divine *restores* itself," and this can occur "only in human consciousness" (GPP 469).

According to its vocation, the human thus stands at the center of Runge's seventh circle as the realized carrier of divinity. From this recentered position, the human can freely oversee the *Stufenfolge* of being—not just to master reality in a Promethean self-assertion, but to deliver reality to God: the last recapitulation of the act of Christ, through which the final redemption of finitude is enacted. Just as A^0 is outside and above the potencies, so the human is A^0 actualized: "to the human there must be conceded a principle outside and above the world." Thanks to this, the human is the only cross-scalar being, capable of traversing, through science, all layers of reality, including the "deepest night" of the universe's formation (WA14 200/xxxvi). In the human, God has "the *co-knower of his path* and of all of his deeds" (GPP 470). Only by the human can the perfect transmutation of inner and outer—the material-spiritual *alchimia* as the completion of nature—be enacted.[53] With this, bliss fills the human and, overflowing, streams down the entire ladder of reality, joining with the bliss concealed in nature and transforming the last remnants of darkness into an all-transparency. Universal reality is thereby transfigured into a blissful being-in-common, the order of space and time is no more, and calm, non-will, and nothingness are restored.[54] Only at this restored central point can the human say: "Now I *know* what it was like to be in God" (GPP 313). The uroboros or world-serpent comes here to rest, having fully unfurled (*aufgerollt*) the implications of the Fall of B and returned to its coiled state (*gekrümmt*; UPO 237), symbolizing that all things generated by divine providence are again resolved into the divine.

The star or celestial body (*Gestirn*) as the first universal creature, and the human as the last, stand respectively at the lowest and the highest level of the universal ladder. Whereas B is purely astral, "The human is astrality fully *overcome*," B transmuted into A, blind being into self-consciousness and self-legislation (DNP 384). For Schelling, the human is higher than the stars; and that is why, for the human recentering that his philosophy envisions, it does not matter that the human is not located physically in the center of the universe. The human emerges on the earth, yet "The human is not specifically a product of the earth but the product of the entire process." Nor is the human *for* the earth: "He is for all the stars, since he is created for the whole universe, or as the end goal of the whole." "It was the destiny of all the potencies in the

---

53. On this sense of *alchimia*, see Paracelsus, *Essential Theoretical Writings*, 211.

54. Cf. GPP 345 and 465 on bringing B back into the state of repose (*Ruhe*), nothingness (*Nichts*), and nonbeing as the goal of the world-process.

universe, of all of its separate moments to be gathered in the human" (DNP 389–390; cf. GPP 360, 470–471). Humanity is "the redeemer of nature" (FS 174/72), and without this central point holding the universe together, the universe falls back into decenteredness. Since the modern subject in its fallenness lacks the consciousness of itself as the theo-cosmic center, the human—the entire humanity, since only in humanity as a whole can the idea be fully actualized (DNP 389)—is yet to recognize itself as such an ideally central being. The goal of true philosophy is therefore to help the human "accept and affirm the position of the universal subject" (GPP 471).

The next turning within the cosmic revolution must thus consist in a revolution in human consciousness: a philosophical revolution. In a short text on French and German philosophy from 1834, Schelling makes his ambition clear: philosophy, he says there, is presently in a state of confusion preceding a new *krisis* (VVC 223), which will entail a judgment pronounced over the false philosophy and the ascent of true philosophy. This coming *krisis* entails also the judgment of the true position of humanity in the universe and the true direction human history ought to follow if the Christian promise is to be fulfilled. For all of the late Schelling's opposition to political revolution, he continues to adhere to a broadly Romantic vision of an apocalyptic battle between false and true philosophy, and of a new epoch to be inaugurated in a revolution of spirit.[55]

A revolution in philosophy is not something abstract: it remains for Schelling a phenomenological revolution in how the human perceives itself and the universe (cf. Chapter 3). A higher knowledge alone can liberate from alienation. Only a revolution in consciousness can decide whether the universe remains estranged or becomes reconciled and whether science continues to treat nature in an objectified manner or grasps it as divine. To enact such a revolution is to go beyond the present human condition: a self-transcending that the human can enact only by delivering itself kenotically to God or the absolute subject.[56] Only once the development of human consciousness is completed and the human rises up to the task of regarding itself as the intelligence *of* the universe, and not as a subject that seeks to appropriate the

---

55. Cf. Schelling's 1795 ambition of "a revolution in philosophy" as a "complete inversion [*Umkehrung*] of its principles" and a liberation from false philosophical systems, these "prisons of human spirit" (VI 77/67).

56. This kenotic self-surrender to the movement of the absolute subject is, I believe, the meaning of Schelling's statements such as "Only through *God himself* can the bond between the spiritual and the natural world be restored" (SPV 148/228).

universe as object, can the universe really cease to be object and cosmic alienation be overcome.

Schelling understands that a phenomenological revolution must develop its corresponding communal and institutional dimensions. For him, the transformation of human consciousness goes hand in hand with the transformation of the way in which humans live together. A new kind of community must emerge, corresponding to the higher level of humanity's development. In his post-1809 thought, Schelling develops the idea of such a community—in theological terms, a new church—that would go beyond the state.[57] The state, with its external coercion (*Zwang*), remains unsatisfactory for Schelling. He sees in it a modern formation that is born from an intensification of alienation and that must not be a-historically absolutized or positioned as the goal of history. The state may be necessary at this historical stage, and it may in an important sense enable modern rational freedom, yet it must be overcome. Accordingly, the state constitutes the (relatively fallen) ground or condition for the higher redemptive turn of history. A more blissful age entails for Schelling, Romantically, a religion of love and a form of communal life in which reality would be inhabited in common, without alienation or domination. The higher oneness of internal and external legislation is precisely what he grasps as the new religion and universal church: "the religion of humankind" (PO2 328), a philosophical religion that will coincide with the immediate science qua magic and fulfill the universal promise of Christianity. The philosophical revolution is a religious revolution, too, marking the completion of the Reformation and the reconciliation of Catholicism ($A = B$, the "ground" and "strength" of Christianity) and Protestantism (A^2) into a higher oneness (A^3).[58] The church of the future is an institution to end all institutions, a form of common life in which the need for external institutions falls away. Outside these broad contours, one cannot describe in detail this blissful common being to come. It can be historically discovered only when or if its conditions are met.

The modern state is viewed by Schelling as a symptom of the crisis that is modernity, a crisis exemplified by the French Revolution as seeking to overcome yet falling back into individual self-assertion and societal fragmentation. Unity, he insists, cannot be established in a purely "external" or "negative"

---

57. On the new church in Schelling, see Kasper, *Das Absolute*, 412–421; Wirth, "Schelling and the Future"; Zöller, "Church and State"; Das, *Political Theology of Schelling*, 18–19, 203–208.

58. See Kasper, *Das Absolute*, 415–417.

manner (cf. SPV 146/227). Schelling's proclamation of an imminent new turning in the cosmic revolution remains idealist insofar as he insists on the revolution and *krisis* in consciousness first and foremost, seeing in the political revolutionary tumult and in the demand for a more democratic constitution an erroneous focus on the external. He refuses to acknowledge that a tumult and turning from below, and a leveling of hierarchy, may also constitute a kairotic event within the universal spiral. His own conceptualization of the cosmic revolution, after all, implies that fallenness and rebellion are part of the path to truth and that the *Umtrieb* arising from below is no less necessary than the order into which it is transfigured. What is perhaps the most "meta" about the idea of the cosmic revolution is that it is a polar movement that encompasses both "Left" and "Right" as the two poles that require and reinforce each other, and in the tension between which history unfolds. Revolt against transcendent authority is, in this polar construction, no less necessary than the vision of freedom as submission to a universal truth that transcends all self-assertion.

This means that Schelling did not have to reject the demands for political revolution. It is just that, for him, the eighteenth century had already been *too much* of a "universal overturning" and descent into self-assertion (*Umsturz* in its political connotations, too; UPO 690), and his own time risked falling irreparably into an abyss if it were to continue turning downward.[59] But the signs of the time could have been interpreted differently had Schelling been less spiritually invested in opposing further disorder. In *Initia*, in fact, he sees contemporary "struggles for political constitutions" as part of the same movement of the age as post-Kantian idealism. The "fundamental view" of the late eighteenth-century moment, he maintains, was the demand for the restoration of freedom at the center. This view marked "the turning point of our time," and thus part of the movement of universal revolution, bringing "great changes" with it. "Internally and scientifically," Fichtean idealism, and "externally," political revolution expressed this turning of the historical spiral. Yet—and this is where Schelling's conservatism comes into view—they "were mistaken in their means" (IPU 767; cf. 488, 493). Self-assertion, be it political or philosophical, cannot accomplish true recentering or attain absolute freedom. Still, for all his critique, Schelling here legitimates revolutionary

---

59. The revolutionary "sickness," writes Schelling in 1848, consists in "intend[ing] to overturn [*umstürzen*] the entire society," intensifying the *Umsturz* and *Selbstsucht* instead of overcoming them (quoted in Schraven, *Philosophie und Revolution*, 45).

thought and agency as a necessary turning point in modernity's striving for bliss.

The possibility of a left Schellingianism, in other words, is not as absurd as it seemed to Engels and Marx. Schelling's critique of the state from the position of a new religion of humanity is not simply anti-modern, either, unless one simplistically equates modernity and secularism or disregards the revolutionary character of Schelling's philosophical religion. His vision of effecting a revolution in human consciousness in which all of nature becomes liberated could not have been possible prior to the post-Enlightenment and post-Revolutionary age. Generally, there are many significant moments that mark the affinity between Schelling and pre-1848 socialism. These moments include his dynamic conception of history as underwritten by the future-oriented will, his emphasis on humanity as the carrier of universal revolution and universal or divine self-consciousness, his Romantic-apocalyptic sense that the time is ripe for the open battle between the true (the liberatory) and the false (the repressive), and his understanding of emancipation as the restoration of justice, the abolition of the state, and an end to alienation, domination, and possession. History in Schelling is, moreover, open to the possibility of inversions and turnings, of contingency and catastrophe, of making manifest what is hidden and elevating what is suppressed. To that one might add his antagonism to the very *structure* of the world as one that is inverted and oppressive. And although we tend to associate "progressive" socialism with critique of religion, and revolution with a singular disruptive event of newness within an arrow of time, in early socialism revolution was widely conceived as a movement that gradually unfolds in history, as the restoration or renewal of humanity, justice, love, and community, and as affined to Christianity and leading to a new religion of humankind.[60] At the time of Schelling's famous 1841 Berlin lectures on the philosophy of revelation, in other words, socialism was not yet secularist. For these reasons, I believe that Manfred Frank is right to conjecture that Schelling wanted to appeal with his Berlin lectures not least to the radical audience.[61]

---

60. It is thus not coincidental that Schelling found his most prominent advocate on the left in Pierre Leroux, an ex-Saint-Simonian who coined the term "socialism" and who advanced a positive religion of humanity to be erected in an overcoming of Christianity—a religion that Leroux opposed to the negativity of the age of critique. See Chepurin et al., *Hegel and Schelling*, vol. 1, 94–98.

61. Frank, "Einleitung," 20–21.

At the same time, two central moments mark Schelling's philosophical construction of universal history as affined to conservative thought. The first is the structure of Fall and redemption as Schelling understands it. Based on his Romantic critique of the "fallen" Enlightenment period for its separation from nature and God, Schelling proclaims that the new turn of history, the re-inversion of invertedness, must be an act of redemption as kenotic surrender to transcendence, identified with the restoration of proper order and hierarchy. He therefore criticizes communism à la Proudhon—which, as we may recall, his own identity-philosophical vision of bliss approached at its most radical—for seeking to abolish "all distinction" and possession (*Eigentum, Besitz*) and to overthrow "all authority and power [*Gewalt*]," thereby threatening to ruin humanity's precarious spiritual ascent (DRP 538).[62] Characteristically, in his 1848 diaries, it is the disorder, noise, and tumult of the revolutionary mob that annoy Schelling the most. For him, this disorder forecloses the possibility of higher spiritual pursuits.[63] The emphasis on order and hierarchy in turn has to do with Schelling's hierarchized natural-philosophical and theological vision of history: the vision of the orderly *Stufenfolge* in which the lower must submit to the higher—including, at the present historical stage, to the state and its law—so as to eliminate its own inherent disorder. What makes Schelling position the cosmic revolution against political revolution is his Christian-modern theodicy of history, in which justice is identified with the judgment of what is higher (so that the lower must prostrate itself before the higher), and with the justification of this submission as necessary for the ascending movement of the universal spiral. Thereby, the path to non-domination and the one common being is hierarchized, leading necessarily *through* domination and submission. For Schelling, justice means not only that everything finds its place and time but also that everything observes its proper place, knowing not to overstep its bounds or cause any further tumult.

This *place-assigning justice*, the logic of justice as what is proper and due, forecloses the one blissful being just as it promises it, or even through the very promise of an absolute future that is not here yet. For Schelling, one must not rush ahead of the orderly not-yet of salvation history. Rebellion against the higher may have its part in this vision of justice too, but only if

---

62. On Proudhon as the target of this critique, see Sandkühler, *Idealismus in praktischer Absicht*, 207.

63. See Schraven, *Philosophie und Revolution*, 137. Scholarship, philosophy, and art are configured by Schelling as the activities demanding the silence that the noise of revolution disrupts.

it acknowledges its wrongness and resubmits to the higher, thereby restoring proper order. This, too, is why disorder and tumult that refuse to surrender to the higher, and that persist immanently in this antagonistic refusal, are something that Schelling cannot accept.

5.4. Conclusion: Human Self-Assertion Restaged at the Meta-level

Schelling's philosophical construction is never simply anti-modern because his goal remains, as it was in 1802, the proclamation of a higher stage of history that would retain the achievements of modern universalism while overcoming inversion and alienation. He never calls for an abandonment of modernity, only its higher potentiation that would fulfill the universal promise of Christianity, the promise within which the modern age, too, continues to function. Even his kenotic vision, for all of its critique of the subject's self-assertion, reiterates the modern existential program of human self-assertion at the meta-level by positioning humanity at the highest, ideally central point of the universe. His vehicular theodicy, in which humanity becomes the privileged carrier of providence and salvation[64]—the carrier on which *everything* depends—is, as I have argued, a product of a highly modern crisis: of the intensified decentered position of the Christian-European subject within universal reality. Through the lens of this crisis, it is as though reality itself were falling apart, across all its dimensions and scales. As asserting itself against this cross-scalar disorder, the human in Schelling serves as the (Christ-)figure of universal mediation and the guardian of universal order, whose task is to bring reality into oneness across all of its layers, guaranteeing its overarching coherence and goodness. In keeping with the modern program of self-assertion, Schelling thus imposes a human-centric order upon the decentered geo-cosmic depths, seeking to stave off contingency and disorder. The idea of overcoming astrality as the vocation of the human, and the very division between astrality as the realm of bondage and human consciousness as that of freedom—a division that upholds the anthropocentric hierarchization of being—likewise demonstrate that Schelling continues the modern trajectory of human self-assertion. His proclamation of a new epoch of universal liberation to come, too, restages yet again the foundational gesture of modernity itself.

---

64. I owe the phrase "vehicular theodicy" to Joseph Albernaz.

One could object to my claim that Schelling restages human self-assertion at the meta-level by making the argument that Schelling's vision of the human is ultimately non-Promethean and thus non-self-assertive, if by Prometheanism one understands the idea that humanity makes its own path and destiny, wresting it from God and nature, or the contention that human selfhood is what is the highest and divine. In part, this objection would hold: even as Schelling divinizes humanity (see, e.g., SPV 184), human history remains for him the carrier of a bliss that is *not* properly human and cannot be appropriated by the human. In truth, humanity is the vehicle of a thought, science, and consciousness that are not humanity's own, but the absolute subject's, that is, God's or the universe's. For Schelling, "the human," "human reason," or "humanity" is not autonomous but itself constituted through the more-than-human ancestral reality in the latter's coming to itself. Therefore, humanity must recognize that it does not so much make "its own" history as form the "ideal" part of a vast geo-cosmic history: the pivotal part indeed, yet but a part nonetheless, whose future is contingent even in its providential significance.

However, I would argue that, in the end, Schelling employs this non-Prometheanism itself for the purpose of human self-assertion and the glorification of human reason in reason's ambition not just to re-vision itself as part of the universe, but to subordinate reality to itself as the highest center-point from which all of reality can be cognized and redeemed. If Schelling does not seek to overthrow divine order in an act of Promethean rebellion, it is because this order for him *is* embodied in the human mind that kenotically gives up its self-assertion only to reveal the identity of its self-legislation with the highest law of the universe. Thereby, human self-assertion is, paradoxically, enacted through submission to what exceeds the human. Schelling's is a peculiar kind of anthropocentrism, wherein the legitimacy of the human consists in its proper embeddedness in the more than human. In this manner, however, his non-Prometheanism feeds into a meta-Promethean hubris. To claim that human consciousness is the ideal carrier of the entire cosmic process amounts to an absolutization of the human through its kenotic humbling: a Pauline logic of glorification through diminution that conceals the persistent demiurgic ambition according to which the human remains the one who decides the fate of universal reality, who damns it or redeems it, and who, through the light of science, makes all of reality transparent to itself.

This central role is what the human must accept, so as to discern the course that human history must take *if* the world-process is to end in bliss. Schelling's anxiety about the future in its contingency coincides with anxiety about the destiny of humanity as the carrier of the absolute subject. That the human stands atop the *Stufenfolge* of being means that it has the unprecedented freedom to fulfill, but also to *ruin*, to bring down the ascending spiral of nature. The specter of an irrecoverable failure, even of human extinction, haunts not only Schelling's analytic, but the age as a whole.[65] "Only empirically," Schelling writes, "can it be established whether the process [of human history] will find its destination" (DNP 390). Will the battle between the true and the false philosophy be won? Will the spiral of history be able to turn upward, or will humanity stumble back into the abyss and betray its theo-cosmic purpose? Can the human really redeem the dark unruly depths of time or reconcile the Gnostic divide between the salvific divinity and the creator God, overcoming Gnosticism once and for all? The further history progresses, the higher are the (already impossible) stakes: if, now that the universe has traversed such a long path, humanity were to fail to actualize its destiny, salvation history would collapse under the weight of this failure.

Schelling's response to this anxiety about possible failure is also theodical. In the face of the possibility of theo-cosmic failure, the philosopher must have even more faith in providence and combat despair. "Faith," as Schelling defines it in *Initia*, expanding on what we have seen to be the entanglement between faith and the not-yet in his earlier thought, is "trust in the possibility of that which is not possible immediately." The "philosophical unbeliever" is one who disbelieves the possibility of philosophical construction as constructing the movement of the absolute subject itself, and who therefore remains in a state of confusion and doubt, unable to discern or move toward the absolute future. By contrast, faith is confidence (*Zutrauen*) regarding the theodical coherence (*Zusammenhang*) of the world and the achievability of its end goal. "Faith always implies a goal, something that is attainable."[66] Furthermore, "Faith is always active; that is, if I believe in a goal I will move toward it." Faith inhabits the absolute future and prompts the true believer to work actively toward the goal amid the storms of history—not unlike, Schelling's example goes, Columbus confidently steering his ship toward the New World. "Columbus believed in the existence of another world," Schelling writes. "If, however, he had stayed in Spain, would he have been a believer?"—adding

---

65. On the Enlightenment origins of the idea of human extinction, see Moynihan, *X-Risk*.

66. For the post-1809 Schelling, faith or belief (*Glaube*) is belief in the positive God, too, but this God himself becomes the actual God only through universal history, so that belief in God and faith in the not-yet of the world structurally coincide.

that "to do nothing" is incompatible with faith. "Sitting still while believing in the goal" is contradictory (IPU 251).

In this manner, doing nothing is theodically denigrated, and true philosophy and faith alike are bound by the post-1809 Schelling to decision, the not-yet, and active future-oriented will. Unbelievers "would like the Kingdom of Heaven to come to them": an arrogant notion (IPU 251). The Kingdom of Heaven, analogized thus with the New World, becomes the final frontier to be conquered by philosophy for the greater glory of God and humankind. Surely, this goal justifies whatever suffering and sacrifice are necessary for it to be achieved, or so the philosopher believes in asserting that suffering is the way to glory.

In line with what we have witnessed to be the colonialist dimension of Schelling's philosophy starting at least from 1802, it is telling that he chooses Columbus as the model world-historical individual whose goal is one with that of providence. To return to an example from Chapter 3, just as the age of the European conquest of the Americas coincides with the beginning of modern philosophy and the age of discovery in science, so, too, the new magical and blissful epoch in which science is to become immediate and reality all-transparent will coincide with the new redemptive oneness of humanity, united within the universal church. However, Schelling's Christian-modern vision of humanity or, to use Sylvia Wynter's term, "humanness"—of who counts as the normatively human global subject, and which part of humanity leads the way to absolute bliss—remains colonial and racialized in character. After an interlude on the temporality of salvation, I will reconstruct in detail Schelling's hierarchized construction of global humanity. The cosmic revolution in Schelling may be the restoration of justice, but this justice is itself racialized, generating a racial Romantic theodicy of the global.

Interlude III

CLOCK TIME AS FALLEN TIME

> *Everything is but a work of time. All that is is merely the hand on the great dial of the vast clockwork of nature.*
> —SCHELLING (GPP 85)

The temporality of the continuous creation and revelation—the not-yet of world history—is for Schelling the time of God's work (*Arbeit*). It is a temporality driven by a longing for the bliss of the Sabbath and, materially, by the ascending interplay of forces within all being, human and nonhuman alike. The work of time thus understood is salvific and divine. Yet this is not the time in which most of life exists day by day, or in which the modern subject lives its everyday life. The time of modernity is clock time: the time of the mechanical clockwork device, at first weight-driven or spring-driven, as in the Renaissance clock, and later based on the regular oscillation of the pendulum, as in the so-called pendulum clock that Christiaan Huygens first built in 1656. Oscillation, which remains the underlying principle of every modern clock, fascinates Schelling, too, and he identifies it with the "lower" form of (proto-)time on which the "higher" temporality of natural and human history is imposed. To this unblissful kind of time, there corresponds for him the unblissful kind of work, in which the majority of life remains caught, and which at once grounds the time of revelation and *resists* it, threatening to consume the not-yet of world history in the cycle of the eternally same. The tension between the "fallen" circular clock time and the kairotic temporality of the ascending universal spiral is what I want to sketch in this interlude. For Schelling, while clock time is "fallen," it is not empty; and while it can foreclose the temporality of salvation, it is also entangled with it and must serve as the carrier of universal history as a "synchronized" path to bliss. Schelling's dialectic of salvific and unsalvific time complicates the standard understanding of modern clock time as merely "external," empty, and linear,[1] adding a crucial temporal dimension to the Schellingian analytic of modernity.

Whereas the absolute divine point prior to creation is sheer non-time, and the temporality of salvation history is kairotic time—that is, time marked by decisive points of turning, or points of *kairos*, through which divine judgment (*krisis*) is enacted and the promise of salvation is upheld—the temporality of unblissfulness is identified by Schelling with the first "blind nature" prior to the emergence of the orderly universe. As we remember, in Schelling's theo-cosmic vision, the first nature is the proto-universe or proto-All, the hot and tumultuous state at the origin of the universe. This state is formed by the fallen divine will turned demiurgic: a will (or, in natural-philosophical terms, force) that Schelling designates as "B" in contrast to "A" as the divine essence of oneness from which B falls away. In its fallen state, B is caught in the illusion of thinking of itself as the absolute center, as almighty and divine, whereas in fact it is already displaced *outside* divine oneness. It still burns with (borrowed) divine fire, yet this is a dark fire of self-seeking desire, not the light of bliss.

The contradiction between the illusory and the true, or the central and the peripheral, marks the struggle of forces within the decentered proto-All, generating what continues to be the underlying rhythm of universal nature—as it were, the deepest layer of time. This rhythm is the eternal fiery pulsation (*Puls*), in which one force takes over only to then be consumed by the opposing force in a never-ending "alternating movement" (WA14 231/21). In the first nature, there is nothing but such an "oscillation" or "quivering" (EIP 118). B strives to attain stable being yet fails to do so, over and over again. The hot nebular proto-matter is also proto-temporality, generating a time of repetition that is prior to the emergence of the upward spiral of time, yet also persists within or underneath this spiral. B's oscillation is the throbbing "heart of the universe," and one still sees this deep rhythm, this ceaseless "circle" and "interchange," in the dynamics of systole and diastole in the animal and human body, or in the cycle of the plant, which grows from the seed only to

---

1. Thus, Hartog associates modern clock time with the "mechanized" *chronos* as opposed to *kairos* and *krisis*. See Hartog, *Chronos*, xii. For the identification of the pendulum clock with "external" quantity, see Marx, *The Poverty of Philosophy*, in Marx and Engels, *Collected Works*, vol. 6, 127. For the opposition between the "homogenous and desacralized" clock time and natural rhythms, see Lefebvre, *Rhythmanalysis*, 73-76.

produce a new seed, out of which the process is repeated (IPU 785, WA14 231/21, 320/90, 327/94–95). One sees it, generally, whenever the same is repeated day after day, or whenever time generates no real newness: whenever, as Schelling symbolically puts it, the cycle of being is enacted as $a + a + a +$ ... (where a is a unit of time) without end (cf. WA27 15). "Bad" infinity for Schelling is just as circular as it is linear: an infinite series of the same ($a + a + a + ...$) is a bad infinity precisely because circularity and linearity cannot be distinguished in it. A "good" infinity, by contrast, would unfold the tension between the circular and the linear into an upward spiral directed toward the actualization of bliss at the end of time.

One also observes in the fallen circular temporality the origin of what we saw as the melancholy and doom hanging over nature in its futile striving, across cosmic worlds, to break through to eternal freedom and recenter itself. Doomed to eternal repetition, "The entire visible nature," writes Schelling, "seems never to attain stability, rotating unremittingly in a circle" and taking seemingly new paths "only to reach the same [result]" again (WA14 231/21). "That is why, as an old book says," writes Schelling in a reference to Ecclesiastes, "all that is done under the sun is so full of toil, and everything tirelessly consumes itself in work, and all the forces ceaselessly wrestle with each other": a state of unending cosmic war, not peace (*Frieden*; WA14 321/90). B's temporality is fallen time as such: fallenness manifesting itself as a rhythm of "unfreedom," of the relentless "wheel of nature" that loops onto itself (WA14 264/46). There is no escape from this "closed wheel, this impenetrable movement," this cosmic hamster wheel (WA14 240–241/28). The wheels upon wheels of nature are engaged in work that leads only to more work, to more of the same, day after day, consuming the natural subject or burning the subject out only to repeat without end the same cycle—just as the "work" of the plant is to grow and bloom and wither only to produce the same plant engaged in the same work or a variation thereof, and so ad infinitum. From this perspective, when the modern subject under capitalism works until exhaustion, only to be replaced with an equivalent subject who does the same, nothing could be more *natural* than this, since this is how nature in its unblissfulness works. As the temporality of the throbbing cosmic heart, this wheel is also "the wheel of birth" of which ancient doctrines taught, and which is to be regarded as the temporality that provides the necessary ground for the world-process, but which must be transfigured if the universal ascent is to take place (WA14 230–231/21, IPU 786). In other words, Schelling's attitude to (the work of) fallen time is ambivalent: the work of repetition is necessary for the work of difference and newness—the work of salvation—to be possible. However, in the absence of such higher work, repetitive work turns into cosmic hell, into an astral prison-factory.[2]

For Schelling, this deep cosmic time is what generates clock time; or, alternatively put, clock time is the stabilized expression of the temporality of fallenness and cosmic war, of the absence of stability or rest across all of nature. The heartbeat of the fallen universe is the "perpetual inner engine and clockwork" (*Trieb- und Uhrwerk*; WA14 230/20, WAF1 196, IPU 519). This clockwork engine is born from the oscillation and tumult within the first state of the universe, and remains captured by the deepest layer of universal movement—as visible most clearly in the cyclical rotation (*Umlauf*) of celestial bodies, this lowest layer of cosmic revolution. The cosmic *Umlauf* is born, in Schelling's account, from the oscillation between the central and the peripheral, or the centripetal and the centrifugal force within B's self-contradictory desire to remain the absolute center while being de facto thrown onto the periphery (EIP 129). The modern pendulum clock may have been invented by Huygens, but for Schelling it reveals and approximates, to the extent that human technology allows, the temporality that has been there since the origins of the universe. After all—and this is what Schelling could reply to those who view clock time as mere external or alienated imposition on the life of nature—the pendulum swings due to the same forces that cause planetary rotation, which in turn captures the persistent wrestling and longing within the natural depths. This longing is the longing for bliss; and this wrestling is the fallen demiurgic will's innermost striving (*Hinausstreben*) to escape its fallen condition (EIP 129), "the unblissfulness of the tumult" (WAF1 197). The sundial, for instance, captures the same wrestling, but only as mediated through the physical movement of the earth vis-à-vis the sun, whereas the oscillator-based clockwork draws directly on the cosmic forces that underlie this movement as well as all other cycles of natural life.

In this regard, in the Schellingian framework, the invention of the regular oscillation-based clock—whose design Huygens based on Galileo Galilei's work on the pendulum—goes hand in hand with the Galilean-Copernican revolution in astronomy: both disclose scientifically what was always there, namely, cosmic clock time and cosmic decenteredness in their co-imbrication, since clock time and the decentered universe emerge together from the birth pangs of the first nature. The clock may have been "one of the first distinctively modern technologies,"[3] but this technology only *reveals* (cosmic) clock time;

---

2. I adapt here the expression "astral factory" from Sloterdijk, *After God*, 59.

3. Grafton, "Chronology and Its Discontents," 140.

it does not create it from nothing. It is true that clock time is alienated time. But in this, it expresses the self-alienation of the universe, or the rhythm of strife, decenteredness, and fallenness from which the universe is born. Time as such is alienated—not *from* nature, but *as* the heartbeat of nature, as the time of the fallen world. Even the temporality of salvation has alienation and fallenness as its ground and emerges only out of clock time. Time for Schelling *is* the world: the world is the time of fallenness as carrying the higher time of judgment and salvation. In bliss, there would be no need for time.

For Schelling, what is specific about modernity is that it at once scientifically *discloses* and existentially *embraces* fallen clock time as the basis of modernity's own unblissful not-yet, without opening this fallenness onto a higher kairotic temporality. At the same time, Schelling's identification of the heartbeat of the universe with a clockwork may be viewed as subverting the association of modern clock time with empty and progressive linear time. The movement of the mechanical clock is an unblissful cyclical movement: the hand runs in the same circle every day, over and over again. Contra a well-worn dictum, from a Schellingian perspective it is not progressive time that is empty. Or rather, modern time is only relatively empty to the extent that it is *not* truly progressive, that it does not allow for transcendence, *ekstasis*, or *kairos*, that every day we wake up to the cycle of the eternally same, with the world imposing this sameness upon us so as to endlessly reproduce itself. But—and this is a further Schellingian twist—even this circular time is not really empty. From a theo-cosmic standpoint, there is no such thing as empty time (where "empty" may be understood variously as desacralized or as void of any inherent meaning, affect, soul, or inner drive). Clock time emerges out of the contradiction (*Widerspruch*) or tension (*Spannung*) within the fallen divine will's desire to be the All. This contradiction is what fuels the engine of cosmic life: "All life," Schelling asserts, "must go through the fire of contradiction; contradiction is the innermost engine [*Triebwerk*] of life" (WA14 321/90). Clock time is neither mechanical nor indifferent; like B itself, it is spiritual and astral. It captures the rhythm of the struggling universal will, of looping fiery desire, of "nature's wrestling in the circle of contradiction" (IPU 519). Its every beat contains the universal heartbeat, with all of this heartbeat's desire and longing. The universe pines for bliss and for the higher rhythm of redemptive ascent. The rhythm of clock time expresses this pining for bliss, too, the cosmic rhythm of contradiction *within* each being, within the plant as within the human. Clock time is internal or "innermost" even as it is externally manifested in processes such as the planetary *Umlauf*.

Thus, clock time is not specifically modern; throughout universal history, human and nonhuman life has subsisted on cosmic cycles and rhythms. The ticking of the cosmic clock is what all life wakes up to in its unblissfulness. Instead of being something specifically modern, this is deep mythological time as continuing to underlie modern time measurement, cutting across the periodizing boundary not only between modern and premodern but between human and pre-human. The clockwork is but the modern exemplification of the eternal circle that persists throughout the physical and mental layers of time, resonating with all of nature as calling for release from empty circularity. This release is what the true Christian-modern not-yet is, for Schelling, meant to provide, overcoming unblissful circular time by subordinating it to the rhythm and temporality of salvation. Such is the real significance of the temporality of the seven-day workweek as leading toward the bliss of the Sabbath, different from what the workweek really becomes in modernity: the ever-more-exploitative cycle of the same. Salvific time is the temporality of the ascending spiral, and only insofar as modernity forecloses this ascending movement does it appear as empty progress and bad infinity.

And yet, even in this foreclosure, modern time is never just externally mechanical, but an ever-restaged crisis of ascent, a forceful obstruction of the way up and reversal to the deepest layer of time that, instead of providing the ground for life, ends up reigning over it. It is this fiery wheel of ceaseless striving, and not the temporality of progress as such, that leads to the endless burnout, from whose ashes the subject—or a new replacement subject—is expected to rise like the phoenix, and to re-enter the same circle. In this manner, the perversity or invertedness of modernity as the age of self-assertion manifests itself in its foreclosure and inversion of the true order of time. To the extent that, under modernity, one inhabits the time of the same, day after day, one inhabits the primordial time of illusion, an "illusory image of eternity" (WA14 307/80). And to the extent that capitalist modernity abandons the telos of fulfillment or turns this telos into the mechanism of the reproduction and accumulation of the same, the work of modernity is illusory work: the time and work of the as-if, of as-if-newness, leading not to fulfillment but to the self-perpetuation of all-consuming desire. As $a + a + a + \ldots$, this time is "a constant and toilsome (yet vain and void) striving to produce a future" (WA27 15). Things produced and things consumed, things used to decorate the wheel in which one wrestles, only stoke further the flame of desire and perpetuate the time of fallenness. In other words, what is modern is not clock time but the inversion that makes clock time into the highest measure of life and work. By contrast, for Schelling, it is the attainment of bliss that must be the measure of life.

Modernity, too, longs for bliss and fulfillment and yet perverts what Schelling views as the true path to them. The existential program of modernity is a salvific program that inherits the structure of the general Christian contradiction (which coincides for Schelling with the general cosmic contradiction and alienation). But when clock time, this rhythm of universal fallenness, is made into the highest measure, the not-yet of salvation disperses into an endless repetition of the same. Schelling's denigration of mere cyclical temporality is a Christian-supersessionist move: thereby, mythological or "pagan" cosmic temporality is identified with fallenness, relegated to the lowest temporal level even as it is preserved and subordinated to the temporality of revelation. In the same stroke, it is a *modern* move, in which the not-yet of true progress is placed higher than the circular repetition of the same, even if the latter remains the necessary clockwork background of progress. In this, Schelling's vision of time merges with that of Christian-modern colonialism, which is not least a colonialism of time, seeking to impose on colonized subjects the temporality of the seven-day week understood not merely as clock time-based but as salvific, as integral to their conversion and salvation, and as integrating them into the movement of universal salvation history and into the substance of the one global humanity constructed in a Eurocentric manner.[4] At the same time, this Christian-modern supersessionist and colonialist move is directed by Schelling in part *against* modernity, for which, not unlike Newtonian physics, "there is, properly speaking, no up," no movement of ascent (WAE 270/247). The modern subject of self-assertion, too, exists within fallen cyclical time, without opening this time onto a higher telos.

Schelling wants to *judge* modernity just as he is looking for a recommencement of modernity, for a *krisis* as division and judgment, from which true newness and judgment of the past would emerge—a newness and judgment that would be able to reconnect the age to the early Christian promise of salvation. What modernity needs for Schelling is the rediscovery, within the modern subject's longing for bliss, of the work of salvation in which the age is *already* engaged, yet in an inverted or perverted manner that cannot reach its goal, making the modern age and the modern subject run around in circles. The purpose of the overarching not-yet of revelation is to break through the unblissful wheel of being to what is higher, to direct

---

4. See Nanni, *Colonisation of Time*.

the movement upward, to break the deranged spell—the fallen magic—of a cyclical seriality that, without the higher not-yet, can generate only mad ecstasies and loop frantically upon itself. Absent a higher telos, all being loops without purpose or use: an utterly non-theodical image, which Schelling is anxious to re-inscribe into the economy of salvation. Hence, what he calls for is the subordination of clock time to the not-yet of revelation, so that the work of salvation can be done *within* and *out of* the temporality of the universal clock. After all, clock time may be fallen—but, as generated by the fallen divine will, it continues to be essentially divine. The will undergoes the Fall for the purpose of God's revelation. Clock time is supposed to serve as the fallen *beginning* and carrier of the time of salvation history; and the beginning consists for Schelling in a tension that must be resolved by opening onto *kairos* and *krisis*.

The crisis of modernity out of which Schelling is speaking about clock time—from the 1814/15 *Ages of the World* draft to the 1821 *Initia* to the 1832/33 *Groundwork of Positive Philosophy*—is at once a crisis of salvation and a crisis of clock time itself. In the abandonment of divine transcendence, as diagnosed by Schelling and other thinkers of the time, alienation is only intensified, and clock time grows to be the symbol of this alienation: the unrelenting ticking of the clock as measuring out the increasingly meaningless and exploitative factory work, in whose image all of reality starts to appear. Metaphysically, this was already prefigured in the modern tradition of mechanist thinking, which transformed the dynamic and theological early-modern clock concept found in thinkers such as Nicholas of Cusa and Boehme, or the kairotic medieval concept of *horologium* (Latin for "clock") put forward by mystics such as Henry Suso, into something that the Romantics would go on to criticize as a merely "external" view of the human and the universe.[5] To rediscover the longing for absolute fulfillment and bliss, and for *the end of time itself*, in this crisis of clock time is, in the Schellingian analytic, a way of getting out of the hamster wheel of time. To emphasize this longing is also to grasp clock time as only deceptively mechanical and stable: to discern in it the cosmic vortex that drives nature itself mad unless a higher purpose is discovered in it. Getting out of the unredeemed modern clock time may be regarded as one of the reasons for Schelling's turn to Christianity, a turn that does not constitute simply a rejection of modernity, but an attempt to rediscover the salvific core of clock time and to move beyond the crisis of

---

5. See Neumann, "Machina Machinarium."

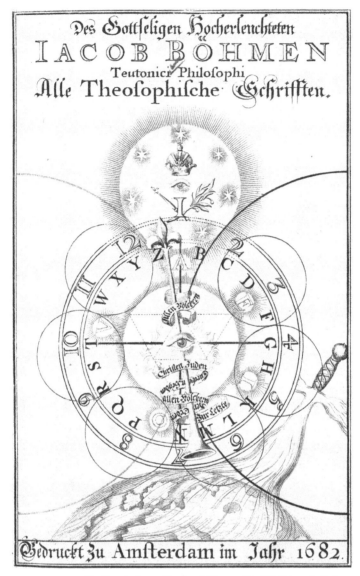

FIGURE III.1 *The frontispiece of Boehme's Theosophical Writings (1682)*
Staats- und Universitätsbibliothek Hamburg, Scrin A/731: 15

modernity, gaining a meta-viewpoint upon the movement (or rather, impasse) of the age.

The nineteenth-century crisis of clock time may also explain the divergence of Schelling's conception of the cosmic clock from the one found in Boehme. It is Boehme and his mediation through the Pietist theologian

Friedrich Christoph Oetinger, rather than mechanist Enlightenment thought, that arguably serve as the inspiration for Schelling's use of the term *Uhrwerk* from the 1810s onward. The frontispiece of the 1682 edition of Boehme's writings even depicts an intricate Renaissance-style clockwork with two dials (see Figure III.1). In *The Signature of All Things* (1622), Boehme speaks of the stars as a "clockwork which is entirely composed in itself," and of time as "run[ning] as a clockwork; it forms, frames, and destroys." That "each thing goes into its harmony," he writes, "is the clockwork of the great mystery of eternity."[6] For Boehme, the clockwork is a symbol of lawfulness that mediates divine revelation, "a clockwork out of the stars and elements, wherein the Most High God dwells, and uses this clockwork for his instrument," providentially measuring out the proper time for everything—a theodical vision of time to which Schelling also subscribes.[7] However, unlike Schelling, for Boehme clock time and salvific time are still fundamentally one; and when Boehme calls the cosmic *Uhrwerk* "the free clockwork," he expresses an idea opposite to Schelling's, who views clock time as the fallen realm of bondage.[8] Characteristically, writing in 1776, Oetinger reverses Boehme's judgment, proclaiming that "in a clockwork there is no freedom."[9] In this, Oetinger reacts to the same mechanist degradation of the clock-image that Schelling later responds to. Furthermore, Boehme lives before the invention of the pendulum clock, whereas Schelling bases his denigration of clock time on the notion of endless pendulum-like oscillation as the state of indecision and unblissfulness. Underneath its cyclicity, clock time is a time of deep cosmic anxiety (*Angst*) and horror (*Schrecken*)—and this is a highly modern, almost existentialist sense of time, emerging out of its post-Enlightenment crisis. Unlike Oetinger, Schelling wants to *redeem* clock time, to reconnect it to divine revelation. For Schelling, the imposition of the higher kairotic time can transform clock time into salvific time, delivering the universe and the human from the anxiety of eternal recurrence.

Schelling envisions a merging of clock time and kairotic time. Clock time is ineliminable and remains the basis. Kairotic moments within daily life, within the seven-day week, and within the overarching salvation history are likewise counted on the basis of clock time, even as they transfigure this time

---

6. *Works of Jacob Behmen*, vol. 4, 103, 132–133. Translation slightly modified.

7. Ibid., 188.

8. Ibid.

9. Oetinger, *Biblisches und Emblematisches Wörterbuch*, 127.

into the ground and carrier of the higher not-yet. Clock time gets "attuned to *kairos*," as Hartog writes regarding monastic time, and as one may also discern in the medieval and Renaissance clock concept.[10] If the bliss of divinity becomes the measure of time, if God himself "counts and measures by this clockwork" (WA14 307/80), clock time can turn into "a perpetual *kairos*-keeper."[11] This, too, is the sense in which a society that would understand and keep time in this manner would for Schelling be a new church and no longer a state, since the state is a form that is emptied of *kairos* or forecloses apocalyptic newness, whereas the universal church of the future would dwell again within the apocalyptic horizon.

However—and therein lies the problem—salvation and revelation are a *work* of time, too. Salvific time continues to be the time of work, of the indefinite not-yet and striving for bliss. Schelling intuits that time longs for its own abolition, and that bliss can be found only in the cessation of work. Yet, reintroducing the Christian not-yet at a higher level does not resolve the issue of the foreclosure of bliss through clock time, because this not-yet likewise defers or postpones the divine Sabbath until *all* of the work of the world is done. Schelling seems to believe that re-subordinating work to a higher telos would solve the problem of the endless repetitiveness and meaninglessness of work. But does it really make such a difference whether one is made to carry the endless burden of capital or the (no less endless) burden of the absolute subject's ascent? As Marx points out, the temporality of capital, too, is properly understood as a spiral.[12] This spiral, not unlike in Schelling, is carried by an essentially circular existence of endless work and striving. As modern subjects, we inhabit an ongoing yet failed and looping project of salvation, spiraling from crisis to crisis. Capital, like revelation, promises a vision of a higher, more fulfilled, even paradisal future, which turns out never to arrive, chaining the subject to the not-yet of the world. Thereby, the not-yet of revelation de facto merges both with the modern not-yet of infinite progress and the capitalist not-yet of a fulfillment that is indefinitely postponed for the sake of ceaseless accumulation and work.

---

10. Hartog, *Chronos*, 54.

11. Ibid. Here Schelling's vision approaches the Boehmean unity of providence and clock time. This unity means, moreover, that clock time as the basis of the temporality of salvation forms the ground of God's becoming God. Walter Kasper rightly perceives in this a threat to the standard theological figure of God. See Kasper, *Das Absolute*, 257–259.

12. See Harvey, *Marx, Capital and the Madness*, 136.

The problem, in other words, is the ontology of work as tied to the temporal structure of the not-yet, or even the ontology of work as such. Only the abolition of work can resolve, or dissolve into bliss, the problem of clock time, since it would allow one to become indifferent to it. To be in bliss is to be without relation to clock time, to abolish clock time by making it inoperative. Thus understood, the abolition of work and the abolition of time go hand in hand, as in Schelling's apocalyptic vision of absolute bliss, too. Such is perhaps the Romantic intuition behind Marx's related demand of minimizing work hours, a demand that likewise emerges out of the modern crisis of clock time and that, taken to its logical conclusion, implies the abolition of work. The abolition of work is a way of demanding bliss *in the now* and of putting an end to the endless reproduction of the same anxiety and unblissfulness. This would be in accordance with Schelling's concept of bliss, which he envisions, most radically, as an indifferent storm that tears down the oppressions of the world, transmuting the longing that underlies clock time into an all-dissolving water and all-consuming fire. And yet Schelling's constant desire for a redemption narrative, for the redemption of clock time and of the world, makes him foreclose such immanent bliss and defer it, via the not-yet of salvation, into a future that is known to God but not to us. Schelling's turn to Christianity does nothing to enact bliss, but only contributes to the foreclosure of bliss through the logics of transcendence, salvific work, and the not-yet.

Returning to the question of Schelling's anxiety about history, one could say that the anxiety of clock time and the tension between clock time and salvific time in Schelling are one with his own—and modernity's—anxiety over the ambivalence of clock time and its world-historical role. Clock time expresses alienation and unblissfulness, but it also carries with it the prospect of *synchronizing chronos and kairos* across nonhuman and human nature and across the globe, contributing to the construction of the one humanity—and it is only humanity as a unified whole that can for Schelling be the subject of salvation history, of true progress and fulfillment. Romanticism from the outset views modernity as a salvific age for humanity and as part of a salvation history still to be completed. Yet salvation and heaven in the nineteenth century seem to vanish from view, obscured by the rising factories and technologies of alienation. As one such technology, clock time, however, contains a utopian impulse that is important to Schelling: clock time is a way of re-mediating the global into a oneness and thus a way of synchronizing the time of universal history. For humanity to have a shared salvation history, it must inhabit a unified kairotic and cosmic (universal) time. Hence the significance of Schelling's statement that God himself "counts and measures" by the clock, and of the implication that clock time can be, as it was for Boehme, an instrument of providence.

The project of synchronizing salvation is as ambivalent as the modern vision of a unified humanity itself, premised as it is on European-Christian colonialism, and on the global system of racialization, conquest, exploitation, and enslavement. The de facto synchronization of global time in 1884 on the basis of Greenwich as the prime meridian serves only to showcase the colonialist foundation of modern clock time in its globalist-utopian dimension. The metaphysical-historical assumption for this kind of synchronizing project dates back not just to the Renaissance but to the Christian universalist idea of the chronology of salvation history as the true time.[13] This assumption, shared by Schelling, may be formulated as follows: those who must lead the way in the project of synchronizing salvation and bringing humanity together are those who possess the science of chronology and the true concept of time in the first place—and having "no chronology" is a central Christian-modern way of othering those considered to be less "civilized."[14] Schelling's intuition that humanity must be *temporally* one in order to be the carrier of absolute future reveals thereby its co-imbrication with the Christian-modern colonialism of time. This vision of a synchronized universal history provides, so to speak, the temporal foundation of Schelling's legitimation of modern colonialism in his late writings, to which we now turn.

---

13. As the early Christian apologist Tatian puts it, "Those whose chronology is confused cannot give a true account of history" (quoted in Grafton, "Chronology," 148).

14. Grafton, "Chronology," 143. Cf. Nanni, *Colonisation of Time*.

6
The Race to Bliss

ASSEMBLING GLOBAL HUMANITY

FOR SCHELLING, THE human is the carrier of divine revelation and recentering. Yet the obvious question remains: Who is "the human"? "In this entire investigation," Schelling writes in a lecture manuscript from the late 1840s entitled *Presentation of the Purely Rational Philosophy*, "we have presupposed *the human*, the singular human being . . . toward whom everything has been directed. . . . But what is the relation of this human to the collective humankind?" (DRP 500; emphasis added). "It is necessary," he asserts elsewhere, "to hold on to the standpoint of the oneness of humanity, on which some . . . give up all too easily" (DNP 389). In Schelling's thought starting from the 1790s, the essential oneness of humanity despite its visible scatteredness is a post-Revolutionary Romantic axiom he never abandons. Another Romantic or idealist axiom that is likewise central for his philosophy states that the fragmentation of humanity into different collective forms of being human corresponds to the fragmentation of human consciousness, including consciousness of the divine. In human history, as Schelling summarizes his natural-philosophical position, it is "not the individual who acts but the entire species" (*Gattung*; GPP 199). Likewise, it is humankind (*Menschengeschlecht*) as a whole that develops scientific knowledge and the consciousness of the one true God. Out of the scatteredness of paganism, the human mind gradually rises to Christianity, whose universalist promise itself necessitates the unity of humankind, to be realized in what Schelling envisions as the philosophical religion of humanity and the universal church of the future. Modernity develops rationally this Christian promise, which merges for Schelling with the Enlightenment-Revolutionary promise of liberation, likewise applying to the entire humanity. This Christian-modern promise always stands at the heart of his philosophy and its self-proclaimed epochal task.

Yet this promise only makes the problem more acute: How, then, to mediate between the normative concept of humanness and the de facto variety of forms of being human? How to re-collect global humanity out of its scatteredness? *How to re-mediate philosophically the global into a oneness that it essentially already is?* For Schelling, the global (i.e., global humanity in its differential distribution) is a disharmonious reality in whose state of division and conflict one still sees the shattering impact of the original transgression, tumult, and decentering. As Hickman has argued, Romantic philosophy of mythology, including Schelling's, constitutes a key site in the modern theoretical grappling with the symbolic event of 1492, an event in which the modern Western-centric world of the global is born in a disorienting and violent clash of cosmologies.[1] The goal of Schelling's philosophy of mythology and revelation is precisely to re-mediate all the particular deities and cosmotheologies of the fragmented humanity into a narrative of human consciousness directed in a salvific manner at absolute bliss. This narrative is at once global and subsumed into the Christian-modern trajectory, theodically legitimating this trajectory as the highest among the endless other possible trajectories on the globe. Thereby, his philosophy, like the broader Romantic project of reassembling the global through national, historical, religious, and literary particularities, participates in the modern project of re-mediating the variety of the global from the European vantage. Romanticism is both antagonistic to modern diremption and forms a pivotal post-Enlightenment stage in the formation of global Western-centric modernity and its conceptual categories.[2] To manage and order human difference, and to make even such "pre-rational" products of human spirit as ancient mythology or poetry philosophically comprehensible so that they can be more flexibly incorporated into the evolving consciousness of a single global humanity: such is Schelling's quintessentially Romantic ambition.

This ambition, too, responds to an epochal challenge. In the wake of 1492, with what Wynter calls the dissolution of medieval sacred geography as the providential hierarchy of place centered around the Christian world, a global

---

1. See Hickman, *Black Prometheus*.

2. See on this also Chepurin, "Reading Novalis and the Schlegels."

immanence (to use Hickman's term) is opened for the first time.[3] However, just like the opening of universal reality with the Copernican revolution in astronomy, the opening of the globe cannot but be perceived by the Christian-European subject not only as opportunity, but also as threat. The dissolution of sacred geography implies that there is, ontologically, no divinely pre-given distribution of place, only the de-hierarchized, decentered, disordered void of global contingency: a "flat" plane of competing cosmologies, none of which is guaranteed to represent the truth. The modern program of self-assertion arises, as Blumenberg suggests, from the European subject's attempt to orient itself in, and to assert itself against, the newly opened contingent expanse of reality. Thus, if one approaches this program from the perspective of the contingency of the global as a threat to the assumed central position of the Christian-European subject, one can glimpse this program's necessarily colonial dimension. In his circumnavigational colonial movement as aimed at the mastery of global reality, the paradigmatic rational Western subject ("man") strives to *re-assert* himself as central and globally normative, to recenter himself over and against the threat of his own decenteredness and contingency. Schelling's metaphysics of human recentering is part and parcel of this project.

The "re-" of the modern subject's re-assertion and recentering marks the colonial dimension of modern self-assertion as co-imbricated with Christianity, for it is Christianity that teaches the European subject to take its central place for granted as the divinely-guaranteed place of truth, salvation, and progress, no matter how "secularized" or "metaphorized" these categories become in modernity. In a sense, the formation of the modern Western-centric global world occurs through nothing but the Christian subject's continued stubborn post-1492 insistence on its own central place: on assembling global reality around itself, appropriating that reality unto itself, and re-affirming its own self-imposed universalizing mission. Modern philosophy parallels this practical insistence in the realm of the ideal, constructing the universal concept of the rational self-legislating subject, which continues throughout modernity to underlie the Western enlightening mission among those deemed less rational or developed.[4] Thereby, the modern subject makes itself, or its own A = A (to refer to the Schellingian formula of self-consciousness and self-legislation), into the subject of humanity's universal destiny, and into the

---

3. See Wynter, "Unsettling," 278–279, and "1492," 19.

4. This aspect of modern philosophy is analyzed in da Silva, *Toward a Global Idea of Race*.

measure of rationality, the measure to which other forms of humanness are normatively converted while constitutively lagging behind. In what we have seen as Schelling's association, in his *Initia* lectures, of the capacity for rational self-legislation with the higher part of humanity that carries the truth in contrast to the part that persists in error, the colonial assumptions of the modern construction of humanity are reproduced. In *Presentation* he reiterates the division of humanity into the "larger part" that seems excluded (*ausgeschlossen*) or "expelled [*ausgestoßen*] from history," and the smaller, better part "that alone seems to embody humanness" (*das Menschliche*; DRP 500). This statement, too, reflects the racialized character of the construction of "the human" in modernity, which by the nineteenth century develops into a self-reflective global framework of race.

Modern colonialism and the logic of racialization necessarily feed off each other. As soon as one posits the transcendent globally normative subject (the rational European "man"), all other forms of being human cannot but be remediated through and measured against this subject and deemed deficient to a lesser or greater degree. This results in a structurally hierarchized and differentially distributed ladder of humanness mapped onto existing human groups based on a set of criteria that may include such groups' perceived removal from the ideal of rationality, their relative incapacity for self-legislating or grasping the truth, and their external characteristics such as skin color, often taken to correspond symbolically to their intrinsic moral qualities and their geographical and ethnic distance from the normative trajectory of history. In particular, the association of truth with light and darkness with sin and error, cutting across the Christian-modern trajectory and prominent in Schelling, too, marks whiteness as the highest and blackness as the lowest ontological position along the spectrum of humanness, signaling blackness's structural exclusion from humanity proper and, as Geraldine Heng has argued, the beginning of its racialization already in medieval Christianity.[5]

As Wynter has shown across her writings, this racialized framework of humanness—of the normatively human, less than human, and nonhuman— is co-constituted with the world of the global. To speak of "the human" is to speak of a global racialized distribution of what it means to be human and who counts as human: "the human" and "the global" are co-formed. Those deemed less than human are relegated to the status of relative nature and of

---

5. See Heng, *Invention of Race*, 16–17 and 181–256. Heng also shows that the association of whiteness with transparency or colorlessness and with the Christian-European subject—at work in Schelling too—likewise emerges in medieval Christianity.

being, as Denise Ferreira da Silva puts it, "outer-determined" rather than "self-determined,"[6] which legitimates their subjugation by and their conversion into mere resource for the normative subject. By theoretically legitimating violence, racialization sanctions further violence: theory and practice are here inseparable. Throughout modernity, this framework metamorphizes in keeping with changes in philosophy and science yet remains essential to the subject's self-assertion. Complicating Hickman's use of the term "global immanence" to refer to the modern global world, one could say that global immanence is, instead, what this world forecloses, reimposing a transcendently hierarchized distribution of humanness upon the immanent plenum of being human across the globe.

One thus should not reduce racialization to the narrowly biological concept of race as it consolidates in Darwinism. What Wynter terms the Darwinian "biodicy" of the global is a step in the longer metamorphosis of racialization, traced back by her to the Renaissance construction of the normative human being as the carrier of autonomous reason.[7] Complementing the more secularist accounts such as Wynter's, Heng has demonstrated that modern racialization, including the association of whiteness with truth, progress, and a civilizing mission, inherits and transforms the earlier Christian racialized or proto-racialized framework, where conceptual instruments are developed through which "to demarcate human beings through differences ... that are selectively essentialized as absolute and fundamental, in order to distribute positions and powers differentially to human groups."[8] Already then, the incipient racialization is "a response to ambiguity" and anxiety,[9] to the uncertainty of reality that, as we remember from Chapter 1, has always accompanied Christian consciousness. This response through racialization is intensified with the post-1492 opening of the global plane of contingency and embedded in the modern program of self-assertion.

Racialization cuts across the binary of "religious" and "secular," constituting the evolving Christian-modern framework of intrinsic (naturally, historically, or providentially sanctioned) hierarchical distribution of humanness, which legitimates the subjugation of the world by the Christian-moderns. Racialization, one might say, is an evolving *hierarchized ontological*

---

6. Da Silva, *Global Idea of Race*, xiii.

7. See Wynter, "Unsettling" and "On How We Mistook."

8. Heng, *Invention of Race*, 27.

9. Ibid., 33.

structure of humanness, coterminous with the Christian-modern trajectory. In this chapter, I focus on Schelling's racialized theodicy of the global as co-imbricated with and upholding this structure and as emerging from within his post-1809 metaphysics. Since Schelling configures *homo modernus* as the privileged carrier of the universal ascent, humanity's entire path to bliss is thereby racialized. Moreover, Romantic *Naturphilosophie*, as exemplified by Schelling, can be understood as a missing link in Wynter's narrative of modern racialization as moving between the two frameworks that she considers paradigmatic: the Renaissance and the "purely" biological one culminating in Darwinism. What makes Schelling's metaphysics of racialization a particularly pertinent node in the broader modern trajectory of racial thinking is his naturalistic postulation that the racialized ladder (*Stufenfolge*) of humanness emerges necessarily from within the broader ladder of natural ascent (see Chapter 5), combined with his configuration of this hierarchized ascent as one with the Christian logics of conversion and salvation history, and as culminating world-historically in the Christian-modern world. This provides for a clear case study of the entanglement between Christianity and natural philosophy at a key moment at the threshold of biological Darwinism. To emphasize: Schelling's racialized theodicy of the global cannot be reduced to the question of his personal views on race. I intend to offer here neither a narrative of personal damnation nor a redemption narrative that would claim that the persistent antagonistic dimension of Schelling's concept of bliss somehow redeems his justification of colonialism and slavery. Racialization is not a Schelling problem; it is a modernity problem or, more precisely, a Christian-modern problem—and the violent tension between racialization and salvation or bliss, too, becomes theoretically important within this epochal perspective.

6.1. Negative and Positive Philosophy; or, Modernity and Christianity Redux

Since Schelling's framework of racialization is explicated in his lectures titled *Presentation of the Purely Rational Philosophy* (ca. 1846–54), a late text that has received relatively little attention in Schelling scholarship, it is worth dwelling on the meaning of the expression "purely rational philosophy" and the overarching systematic purpose of these lectures. As we will see, Schelling restages here his account of the Christian-modern trajectory with an explicit view to the problem of reassembling global humanity both as a species and as the global consciousness of the divine.

6.1.1. To Bring Reason to Rest

By "purely rational" or "negative" philosophy, Schelling means, most centrally, the modern philosophy of autonomous dirempted reason, mind, or spirit (*Geist*) from Descartes to Kant—a philosophical tradition that Schelling's positive Christian philosophy of divine revelation is meant at once to complete and overcome. Since Descartes, Schelling points out, modern philosophy has sought to seize God, or the absolutely first in thought. In this, philosophy inherits the earlier scholastic task, seeking to ground it anew in autonomous human reason (DRP 264–267). On its own, this would be a perfectly Blumenbergian point. Yet—Schelling adds, complicating this point—thereby modern thought also inherits the Christian view of the world or universe (*Welt*) as dirempted and fallen (what I have called the structure of the general Christian contradiction) and the Christian sense that the first (divine or absolute) principle is absolutely first with regard to the world and must be thought of as absolutely preceding the world. In this regard, Kantian idealism, too, follows the path that Christianity makes possible (DRP 467).

Reiterating his earlier view of Christianity and of the revolution in consciousness that it enacts vis-à-vis paganism, Schelling proclaims: "Christianity has freed us from this world; as a result, we no longer regard the world as something to which we are unconditionally bound and from which there is no salvation [*Erlösung*]." Christianity teaches that the world is transient (*vergeht*) and craves salvation as that in which it would itself cease to be. As Schelling reiterates here, the not-yet of the desire (*Begierde*) or craving (*Sucht*) for the end of the world *is* the world: a statement in which we recognize again the general Christian contradiction and its eschatological promise. The world longs for its own abolition. "The whole essence of the world is desire, nothing else" (DRP 467–468). This means that the world is negative and lacking, and the absolute cannot be in or of the world. This statement also confirms that, from 1795 to his final lectures, "world" continues for Schelling to designate the unblissful structure of fallenness, negativity, not-yetness, and striving—a constitutively Christian-modern structure. The sense that the absolute is nonworldly is, for him, what modern philosophy owes to Christianity, a sense that is true not only from the purely rational but the positive perspective, too: as we have seen throughout this book, the true structure of reality as such ("world") is for Schelling the structure of diremption that has defined the universe and all forms of natural and human being since the beginning, and that is revealed *to* human consciousness in Christianity. Modernity is the epoch tasked with the rational and scientific elaboration of this structure as the true condition of the universe, and in this regard its task and assumptions are continuous with those of Christianity. Hence, although Schelling also draws in *Presentation* on Plato and Aristotle as the pillars of rational philosophy, he returns to these thinkers from within the present so as to restage their insights on a higher Christian-modern level.[10] For him, these thinkers remained in their paganism bound to the eternal necessity of the cosmos and could not attain to the standpoint of absolute freedom from the world and of the contingency of the fact of the world. Only Christianity and, following it, modernity have strived to develop this standpoint—a development culminating in post-Kantian idealism, whose world-historical task, Schelling asserts, is not yet complete (DRP 466).

Idealism's task coincides for Schelling with that of modernity as the age of the self-assertion of spirit. He thus never departs from his conviction that the completion of post-Kantian thought is an epochal task. His attitude toward modernity in these lectures remains ambivalent in the same manner that we have witnessed throughout this book. In fact, to expose this ambivalence *and think it through to the end* is the central aim of *Presentation*, which is concerned with reinscribing modern reason, and the global world it demiurgically creates, into the Christian-modern trajectory as leading *beyond* the dirempted reality on which modern reason is premised. On the one hand, Schelling proclaims modernity to be the necessary epoch of reason's liberation (*Befreiung*; DRP 264). Modernity develops the autonomy of human spirit from any dogmatic dictate: a trajectory leading from the break with scholasticism to Kant's science of pure reason to the Fichtean idealism of the I. Modernity's achievement consists in working out, on the basis of reason alone, the standpoint of universal rational science (DRP 267). Yet, on the other hand, if the modern dirempted structure of reality is to be overcome, reason must in the end recognize its own limit, not so as to remain at this limit as Kant did in his philosophy but to *freely and consciously* resubmit itself, in a kenotic act of "good" *ekstasis*, to the divine as what exceeds

---

10. In returning to the Greeks, *Presentation* continues to be guided by the vision of a reconciliation of paganism, Christianity, and modernity. Schelling is also constructing here a unified trajectory of Western rational philosophy that culminates in himself as the one who *completes* this tradition at the present world-historical stage. Thus, Aristotle opens the true rational thinking of the first principle yet remains bound to the pagan cosmos. Schelling, however, returns to Aristotle's insights from a Christian-modern vantage, mobilizing the entire trajectory of European rational philosophy toward the epochal turn to the higher (positive) philosophy that Schelling himself proclaims.

and precedes reason's self-assertion. At the end of its path, reason will "re-subordinate itself to A^0," that is, to the bliss of divinity and the movement of the absolute subject,[11] and the absolutely first will emerge victorious, in and through human consciousness, over the entire world (*über Alles siegreich*; DRP 489). In this, the task of true critical philosophy as the philosophy of *krisis* consists.

This is the ambition of *Presentation*: to demonstrate the end result (*Ziel*) of purely rational philosophy to consist in an ecstatic encounter with "what exceeds all reason" (DRP 269), with unprethinkable blissful being. Reason must be led to realize that the goal of its own striving consists in the dissolution of the alienated reason-God-world structure—the intensified structure of the general Christian contradiction—within which reason unblissfully struggles. To demonstrate that the viewpoint of autonomous dirempted reason points necessarily to a non-dirempted future had long been Schelling's project. *Presentation* reiterates this project, and it is significant that the manuscript ends with a lecture that reaffirms bliss (*Seligkeit*) as what overcomes the dirempted structures of knowledge, morality, and the state, undoing all property or selfhood (*Eigenheit*; DRP 567) and confirming that, in the final decade of his life, bliss remains for Schelling what is the highest. The purely rational thinking of the first principle, the absolute, or God leads above reason to what is absolutely free from the world; and, once it glimpses this absolutely first principle, this absolute purity, reason cannot but submit itself to it kenotically. "The science of reason," Schelling writes, "leads beyond itself, and is driven toward an inversion" or turning (DRP 565), a revolution in principles that results in Schelling's own positive philosophy.

From a systematic standpoint, positive philosophy *begins* with bliss: with that which *simply is*, without any further qualification, or the divinity that, in its absolute freedom, is "unburdened by the substance of the world" and prior to God the creator himself (GPP 392–393, PO1 158). Negative philosophy, by contrast, *ends* with bliss as that with which positive philosophy begins: as the absolutely first that provides salvific repose (*Ruhe*) to the self-assertive reason and will (DRP 475).[12] In other words, the relation between *Presentation* and

---

11. On Schelling's use of "A^0" to designate the bliss of divinity configured as transcendent, see Chapter 5.

12. This is not to imply that positive philosophy immanently requires negative philosophy in order to begin: positive philosophy itself has no presupposition except divine bliss. However, dirempted reason needs to be *brought* to the standpoint of bliss, and this, from an epochal and systematic perspective, is the task of Schelling's lectures on negative philosophy.

Philosophy of Revelation may be described as follows. *Presentation* starts out from the rational articulation of the absolute-world relation to reach bliss as the absolutely inarticulable, unprethinkable excess over the thinkable (DRP 320). Then, via the positive philosophy of the divine will to creation that emerges out of the unprethinkable bliss of divinity, *Philosophy of Revelation* re-visions history as the arena of divine revelation and providence. Taken to its limit, modern reason reconfirms bliss as what is the highest, reopening the gates for Christian philosophy, yet in a way that is completely free from any scholastic or dogmatic baggage and unbound from the necessity of the world. That is why *Presentation* is positioned by Schelling as at once complementary and subordinated to his positive philosophy of revelation. In this manner, negative philosophy is returned to positive philosophy, and modernity to Christianity at a higher conscious level. The epochal circle is thereby completed, and the universal spiral turns upward, opening onto the epoch of all-reconciliation.[13]

Since the account in *Presentation* is thus auxiliary to the theo-cosmic process as positive philosophy grasps it, it is unsurprising that Schelling sticks here broadly to the same narrative of universal history that we have analyzed previously—with an important methodological distinction. In the purely rational philosophy that begins not with divine bliss but with the *idea* or *concept* of God as the first being in the philosopher's mind, the world-process cannot be grasped as that of free revelation, creation, or the Fall—and so Schelling tries to avoid here these theological terms. Negative philosophy cannot reach the innermost divine essence, the bliss of the hidden God, the nonproductive, non-relational, and intransitive divinity. "Thought cannot here" access absoluteness as such, "where God is free from the world in his sheer essence [and] without any relation" to the world (DRP 293). Approaching the divine from within reason's diremption, negative philosophy thinks the *what* (*Was*) of God, and not God's blissful *sheer being*, or what Schelling terms the pure *that* (*Daß*), the sheer *is* (*Ist*) or copula: the bliss that is not proper even to God, and of which there is "nothing more to be conceptually said" or thought (DRP 402).

---

13. I thus partly agree with Marcela García that *Presentation* aims to show "the failure and crisis of negative philosophy." See García, "Schelling's Late Negative Philosophy." However, one could equally claim that negative philosophy is meant by Schelling to be completed and to *succeed*, if approached correctly and thought through to the end, in bringing reason to the standpoint of bliss, and modernity (back) to Christianity. The *failure* of negative philosophy qua negative is necessary for its *success* in leading reason to the true positive standpoint.

What negative philosophy likewise cannot see is that, following the shattering of divine oneness, the bliss of the pure *is* continues to persist underneath the movement of the potencies as the re-collection of oneness out of scatteredness. In *Presentation*, too, the copula is the common (cf. Chapter 3): the blissful *is* persists as the sheer fact of the being of the world or universe and of every finite being, in whose *simply being what it is* the particular *what* is dissolved in the *is*. Schelling's sensibility here stays Romantic: underneath the world's negativity, there remains the fact that the universe *simply is*, even as its bliss-in-common is foreclosed by and in the structure of finitude. What is divine is not the not-yet of the world, but what remains concealed beneath the not-yet without being lost (*verloren*; DRP 400–401), immanently driving nature and spirit's self-transcending toward the highest oneness and what is revealed, at the end, in the cessation of the world. The pure *is* exceeds and overflows any *what*, breaking through at the end of reason's thinking of the world-process. This breaking through of bliss is the endpoint to which *Presentation* seeks to lead reason.

6.1.2. The World as the Movement of Possibility

Presentation's account of the transition from the idea of God to the rational structure of the world-process is a familiar one: it recapitulates from a purely rational perspective Schelling's post-1809 metaphysics of the ladder (*Stufenfolge*) of nature as an ascending process that follows the shattering of divine oneness, or what Schelling theologically grasps as the Fall of the divine will (which in these lectures, too, he designates as "B" to separate it from the divine A = A).

What exactly, he asks, can reason think as the idea of God? The first being, Schelling asserts, is thinkable only under the form of A = A, or as the absolute subject-object. Purely rational philosophy thinks God as the absolute subject who gives himself absolute being as his object or predicate, and this subject-object unity is God as one with himself (*bei sich*; DRP 290). The divine *what* has the usual structure of the three potencies, coinciding with the structure of possibility of all that can be thought. In thinking the idea of God as the first being, reason thinks the proto-form, archetype, or prototype (*Urbild*) of which every finite form of being is an image (*Bild, Gestalt*). To think God as the prototypical subject-object is to approach him, as it were, from the perspective of the world, or as the structure of world-possibility: hence Schelling's thesis that negative philosophy cannot avoid binding God to the world, and cannot attain absolute freedom as freedom from the very possibility of the world. To think God purely rationally is to articulate his form (A = A) and not his essence. It is to think the transitive God, "God with an essential relation to the world" (DRP 293), and not the intransitive divinity.

A = A expresses for the purely rational philosopher the total structure of possibility, which, however, within the divine idea remains merely virtual.[14] As we remember, for Schelling the theo-cosmic process is at once the *revelation* of God and the *actualization* of the totality of ideas contained within the ante-original divine nucleus. Since purely rational philosophy cannot grasp God as the free creator, or as one who freely reveals himself, it is led to think of the world-process solely as the process of unfolding the divine totality of possibility, or as the world-historical movement of actualization. Reason traces the way the universe actualizes and exhausts the divine A = A. "After the exhaustion of the entirety of possibility" (DRP 422), reason is led to think the absolute repose in which a being is disclosed (to reason) that is free from all further movement or work of actualization: the bliss in which the dirempted reason-world-God structure is dissolved.

Thus, to think the world, the mind must think the divine A = A as what contains the possibility of all finite being. Yet this is not enough. To grasp the transition from oneness to the world-process, the mind must also think the blind and dark principle of sheer expansion or scattering (B), which engenders twoness and the coming apart of the potencies. B constitutes, in a familiar manner, the proto-material ground of the universe: the tumult out of which the movement of possibility begins and an orderly universe arises. What ought to be, Schelling maintains, is governed by one universal law: that the fullest expanse of possibility be unfolded, that "all things possible" be realized (DRP 410). In this manner, as we remember from Chapter 5 too, A = A is recast as "the highest law": "All possibility is to be actualized" (DRP 492). As the natural-philosophical principle of selfhood, B is there to ensure that the highest degree of differentiation and complexity is reached within the universal process: the differentiation that "does not let anything remain unactualized" and that traverses all levels (*Stufen*) of being (DRP 415). Within the overarching A = A, *everything that is concealed must be revealed*: this is the law of divine revelation and divine judgment, too, even if purely rational philosophy cannot grasp it as such (DRP 492).

---

14. This is for Schelling the highest idea of God to which purely rational philosophy can attain, reaching its culmination in Kant's "ideal of reason," a doctrine according to which reason is led necessarily to think of the first being as the totality of possibility. See DRP 283–286.

While mostly stripped of theological language, Schelling's account of the natural *Stufenfolge* in *Presentation* is underwritten by the logics that are characteristic of his post-1809 metaphysics in general: the logics of hierarchy, immanent-transcendent normativity, and the kenotic submission (*Unterwerfung, Sich-Hingeben*) of the lower to the higher, wherein the lower serves as material (*Stoff*) or possibility for the actualization of the higher. In thinking the original shattering of oneness and the "sinking into materiality," the mind is then led to conceive of the natural process as beginning with the first upward turn, or B's redemptive prostration before the power of oneness (DRP 442–443). Oneness remains operative in scatteredness as the universal drive that propels the interplay of potencies within the continuous natural metamorphosis. Over the course of this metamorphosis, B is increasingly stripped of mere materiality, its darkness and blindness are transfigured into light, and nature ascends to the ever-more-spiritual unity: the process leading via inorganic to organic nature to the human. B marks the realm of the below (*Unten*), "the negation of all ascent" (DRP 443), the fallenness of being. The more B dominates in a form of being, the lower, darker, and more materially inert it is, and the further removed from purposeful self-legislation (DRP 407, 431). In this hierarchized ascent that actualizes the fullness of possibility, each level "senses that its being-for-itself is futile": that it is *not* there for its own sake but for the sake of the higher, through which alone it can gain "durability" and "participate" in the world-historical movement of possibility. The lower, Schelling continues to insist, is lower "by nature" (DRP 412). In this *Stufenfolge*, every single form of being—such as (to cite Schelling's examples) the Siberian mammoth or the pterodactyl—has its proper relationally determined place and duration (*Dauer*), in keeping with which some species become extinct in order to make room for a higher geo-biological layer (*Schicht*), all the way until "the present world," for whose sake previous layers exist (DRP 495–497, 500). The highest that the mind is compelled to think as the pinnacle of universal nature is the human. The human is at once the highest natural being and the rational *Geist* standing outside and above nature (DRP 459), from which the "world of knowledge, [spiritual] history, and the human species" begins (DRP 400).

6.1.3. The Spirit of World Domination: The Normative Subject Posits Itself

In thinking the ascent of the universal *Stufenfolge* to the human, the mind *encounters itself*. The dirempted mind cannot grasp its freedom as grounded in nature, and so it is led to think its own self-positing in a break from nature. The mind cognizes its emergence as "solely its own deed" (*Tat*; DRP 468), a deed from which our free will and self-consciousness originate yet which, as such, must be thought of as preceding them. Theologically, this ur-act of self-assertion corresponds to the Fall of Adam, even if purely rational philosophy does not think of it as such, but instead solely in terms of reason's spontaneous self-positing. Schelling's account of this ur-act continues to broadly follow Kant's reconfiguration of the biblical story of the Fall in "Conjectural Beginning." One may picture here the human's initial oneness with nature, from which the ur-act tears the human away, marking the awakening of reason, will, and freedom. As a result, reason finds itself severed from a "quiet community with God" (DRP 482) and thrust into a world that is alien (*fremd*) and hostile and that is perceived by the rational subject to be something pre-given and external, an obstacle (*das Entgegenstehende oder Dazwischengetretene*) to the subject's will (DRP 463). In thinking its own origin, the diremtped mind thus restages its condition—the condition of being alienated from nature and God (the intensified structure of the general Christian contradiction)—*as* origin. The mind cannot but think of itself as autonomous, and this is both a fallen condition and one that is necessary for the epoch of reason's autonomy—for modernity—to come into its own, so that the standpoint of rational universality and true science can develop. While self-assertion has been at work in human consciousness since the beginning, modernity is when it becomes autonomous and self-reflective, allowing reason to grasp the condition of alienation as the true condition of the world.

The world as the structure of the split (*Zwiespalt*) from (what is sensed by the subject to be) the lost paradisal bliss is "unblissfulness itself," from which the only salvation (*Seligkeit*) would be for the self-assertive will to regain repose (*Ruhe*; DRP 473).[15] This would also mean regaining an absolute freedom in which the will would have no obstacle anymore. Yet the self is presently bound to its postlapsarian toil, to the work on and of the world. Through this work of cognition and cultivation, reason learns to subdue reality. The goal of reason's striving is to cognize the world perfectly so that, in the end, it can be inhabited by reason as *reason's own* reality: to work toward

---

15. Significantly, Schelling offers here a lengthy etymological excursus on the meaning of *Seligkeit* as translating the Greek *makariotes*, a term that corresponds to the Latin *beatitudo* and that, he claims, originally implies a calmness wherein the self-assertive fire of desire is delivered to the divine (DRP 469–475). Thereby, even in this etymological construction, he inscribes bliss into a logic of kenotic submission.

the endpoint at which the world would "no longer oppose [the subject] as alien" (DRP 516). For that, however, the subject needs to explore, pierce (*durchdringen*), master (*Herr werden* or *beherrschen*) the world: and this is the purpose that rational knowledge and agency serve (DRP 463, 516). The purpose of science consists in the expansion of the will and in control over the world (*der Welt mächtig werden*; DRP 520–522). "The real power over the world," the power of divine bliss, is no longer accessible to finite spirit. "The only thing that remains [for spirit] is to *cognize* the world without remainder, to overcome it through cognition . . . whose sole goal," Schelling asserts, "is that spirit should become the lord [*Herr*] over what presently opposes the mind as object and as obstacle" (DRP 463). The goal, then, is to overcome alienation from within the alienated world.

Through cognizing and mastering everything with which it is confronted, spirit imposes the form of A = A upon reality, so that the process of human history as the history of spirit consists likewise in the actualization of the divine A = A in and through human consciousness. Human history is that of progressive conscious mastery of the totality of possibility—of all things possible—that is the world: a decidedly modern view. "All things possible" (*alles Mögliche*) is a strikingly Baconian formulation, echoing what we may recall from the introduction as Bacon's equation of modern scientific ambition with the exhaustion of the totality of possibility through the human mind, and so with "the enlarging of the bounds of Human Empire" into all dimensions.

As always in Schelling's analytic of rationality, intelligence must oppose itself to reality so as to cognize it and rearrange it around itself, a process through which intelligence gradually discovers the rational structure of the universe and its own embeddedness *in* this structure, which intelligence gradually masters until the universe no longer appears alien. Its own embeddedness in the universe points human spirit to its true place vis-à-vis nature and the divine, reconciling the structure of diremption. The mind must come to *know* that the universe and the earth are really there for the human's sake, and this is what in truth drives the will to knowledge and mastery. To prove itself to be the providentially destined "universal being" (DRP 491), spirit must triumph over the world. Such is, for Schelling, the true significance of reason's liberation from any extra-human authority. Of course, this justification of autonomous reason's ambition of world domination functions only under the assumption that reason will actually re-subordinate itself to salvation history. Otherwise, reason would simply remain stuck in its fallenness—a possibility that the post-1809 Schelling can never exclude and that fills *Presentation* with anxiety about the future despite Schelling's repeated assertion that modern reason is led necessarily to a *krisis* and self-transcendence.

Reiterating thus his diagnosis of modern self-assertion as a practical project of mastery, Schelling provides in *Presentation* a legitimation of the modern rational subject as the normative subject of history, and of European colonialism as the subject's necessary movement of mastering the totality of global and planetary possibility.[16] The "higher" part of humanity that represents normative humanness is identified by him with *Geist*, and *Geist* with self-positing and self-legislation: with the rational subject as one who is capable of freely governing itself and is justified in governing those who cannot. As *Geist*, the subject embodies the divine idea (A = A) and seeks to make reality equal to this idea. It is because the subject is *Geist* that it is driven to conquer the earth and the skies, propelling itself around the globe and imposing its form on other, less-than-human forms of being, even if the subject does not itself realize the true purpose of its circumnavigational movement: namely, to regain "the lost central position" (DRP 491). It is as though *Presentation* proleptically confirmed Enrique Dussel's statement that the truth of the Cartesian "I think, therefore I am" is "I conquer, therefore I am."[17] The global, too, is decentered, and the modern subject is engaged in the work of its recentering, traversing elliptically the globe until all possible trajectories have been mastered from the vantage point the subject occupies.

Just like his attitude toward modernity, Schelling's view of the modern subject in its self-assertion remains ambivalent. From the higher point of view, self-assertion is the erroneous and perverted approach to knowledge. Yet, in Schelling's theodical vision, error is the necessary step to truth, and self-assertion, too, has its assigned providential mission, the mission that Schelling from the 1790s onward affirms as central to the modern age: to rationally assemble or bring into a conscious unity the entirety of natural and human reality. Not unlike B, which we have seen him call the indirect or seeming divine will, the Promethean will to cognition and mastery (which he explicitly associates with Prometheus; DRP 481–489) is at once non-divine and, unbeknownst to itself, serves a divine purpose. Human thought and humanity itself must become actually, self-consciously one so as to create the widest possible basis for the next upward turn of the universal spiral, in which

---

16. In this, Schelling develops what we have seen as a crucial dimension of his thinking of the oneness of humanity from the 1790s onward.

17. See Dussel, "Anti-Cartesian Meditations."

the will must give up its Prometheanism and submit to the absolute subject. In liberating self-assertion and making it into an autonomous "principle of selfhood" (DRP 480), modernity is the Promethean epoch par excellence, yet its telos, Schelling continues to hold, is non-Promethean. Only by submitting to the divine can spirit, "like the bound Prometheus," at the end of "its long path ... exit" the fallen condition and complete the epochal turn (DRP 489).

Arguably, due to his own conception of place-assigning justice, Schelling would not be able to avoid justifying the modern subject as the highest carrier of universal history at its present stage even if he wanted to. The modern (Christian-European) subject, after all, *is* the de facto subject of world exploration, world cognition, and world domination. In this empirical fact, the Schellingian philosopher cannot but discern the higher providential purpose, since it is this subject who spreads globally the standpoint of science, bearing "the progressive work of human spirit" (DRP 501) across the globe and contributing to the historical "growth" of spirit (DRP 425). Thereby, the empirical course of history and its philosophical-providential construction coincide, "proving" that the subject's claim to the highest, globally central place is justified. This justification, fully elaborated in *Presentation* yet always implicit in Schelling's Eurocentric vision of humanity, marks his theodicy of history as at the same time a theodicy of the global: a philosophical legitimation of global Western-centric modernity as the world produced demiurgically by the modern subject in this subject's will to all-knowledge and all-mastery. Whatever the modern world's negativity, Schelling insists, this world carries the movement of world-historical possibility, and it is through this world that the path to absolute bliss leads: the path onto which the modern subject alone can set humanity. European colonialism and the hierarchized and racialized distribution of humanness are, in Schelling, conditions of possibility of the absolute future.

6.2. Without God, Without Possibility: Racialization and Conversion

With God all things are possible.
—MATTHEW 19:26

For Schelling, just as there is a ladder (*Stufenfolge*) of natural ascent, so, too, the history of global humanity ascends level by level, striving to re-collect the divine idea (A = A) from within the scattering of human forms. In fact, the framework of racial hierarchy in *Presentation* is but a recapitulation of

Schelling's post-1809 hierarchized metaphysics of the *Stufenfolge* within the realm of human difference. Since for Schelling "the human" is the highest telos and carrier of the theo-cosmic process—of the whole ladder of being across the universe—the racial framework of humanness that he advances in *Presentation* can be understood as the culmination of his entire theodicy of universal history. Here, he takes to the logical conclusion his persistent positioning, across the trajectory of his thought, of the European subject as the normative subject of history, and his (no less persistent) theodical justification of modernity, including modern colonialism, as that through which the path to the absolute future leads.

My claim, in other words, is the following. It is not because Schelling starts explicitly to talk about race in *Presentation* that his metaphysics thereby suddenly becomes racialized. Rather, what one might call Schelling's general world-grammar—his organization of universal reality through the logics of hierarchized ascent, proper place, and transcendence that are legitimated by recourse to the way things naturally and providentially are—is already a grammar of racialization that, when applied to humankind in *Presentation*, is explicitly revealed as racial.[18] Due to Schelling's natural-philosophical axiom of the recapitulation of "the real" within "the ideal," and due to humanity's embeddedness in the universal process as its central ideal part, the same logics through which the *Stufenfolge* of nature is generated as a hierarchized distribution of natural forms cannot but apply to the global distribution of forms of humanness. It is because in *Presentation* he is explicitly concerned with reassembling the oneness of humanity across its various hierarchized forms that Schelling avails himself here of the concept "race"; but the racial grammar of this reassembling coincides with his broader ontological and theodical grammar. Schelling's framework of racial hierarchy is the climax of his thinking of the *Stufenfolge* of the universe, and this entire *Stufenfolge* is, in turn, disclosed through this framework as a grammar of racialization.

Let us recall what, over the course of Part II, we have witnessed to be the post-1809 natural-philosophical logics of the *Stufenfolge* in Schelling, which emerge starting at least with his early *Ages of the World* drafts, and which constitute his grammar of racialization as well. In the universal ladder of being, the lowest (B) is the fallen proto-material basis, the unblissful tumult whose purpose is to serve as the expansive ground for the ascending actualization of

---

18. The term "racial grammar," originating in critical race theory, has also been employed in connection with European philosophy. See Terada, "Racial Grammar," and, on the racial "grammar of the world," Barber, "World-Making and Grammatical Impasse."

the totality of possibility and the re-collection of divine oneness. The lower the form of being is on the ladder, the more B dominates in it, marking it as relatively dark, decentered, and inert. The domination of B relegates a form of being to the opaqueness of materiality and rigidity, which resists universal light. The world-process dispenses (at once natural and divine) judgment by assigning to every kind of being and every species their rightful place in the universal hierarchy. History is the indifferent tribunal presided over by A = A as the divine law of universal order, guaranteeing the lawful unfolding of all positions, moments, and possibilities. Everything has its proper place and time, and to be "good" is to know and observe one's place. Only through participation in the higher, or by delivering itself to the higher, can the lower take part in the universal ascent. If it has no part through which to contribute to this process, or if it persists in its fallenness and refuses to kenotically give itself over to the higher, it gets rightfully left behind and has no further purpose or destination from the standpoint of the whole. *What remains behind and below is what remains without further possibility.* The logics of instrumentality and use permeate this entire hierarchical structure: the lower is the instrument (*Werkzeug*), means (*Mittel*), and material (*Stoff*) for the actualization of the higher. Moreover, this *Stufenfolge* is not imposed on reality from without: it emerges from within nature, whose essence remains divine yet, out of fallenness, appears as the transcendent telos (A^0), generating nature's immanent self-transcending, from level to level, as it strives to re-collect itself into oneness. It is through this self-transcendence of reality that the ladder of being arises, wherein the measure of the higher is the degree of its relative approximation of A = A as the formula of transparency, and of the eschatological triumph of light over darkness.

All of these are basic theses of Schelling's post-1809 naturalized theodicy. We should add to them his affirmation of the European subject as the globally normative *Geist* carrying the divine form (A = A). In Schelling's metaphysics, the highest is the measure; and so, once we posit A = A as that toward which humanity ascends, a hierarchy of forms of humanness emerges. The theodical ruse of racial grammar in Schelling is to normalize this hierarchy of humanness by rendering it natural and, as natural, also divinely sanctioned. Just as nature ascends from darkness to light, from the more material, inorganic kinds of being to the more spiritual, so the ladder of humanity ascends from the darker, more rigid, and outer-determined to the lighter, more self-determined human kinds. Even had Schelling not explicitly identified darkness with blackness and light with whiteness, his schema of the ladder of humanity would have amounted to an intrinsic hierarchization of forms of humanness and thus a grammar of racialization. Yet he does exactly that, and even though, anticipating interpretations such as the one I offer here, he denies that his work "results in a scientific justification of slavery and the Negro trade, and of all the atrocities enacted by the higher species upon the lower" (DRP 513), I believe there are enough textual reasons not to take him at his word. Characteristically, in this self-defense, Schelling does not problematize racial hierarchy itself, only the question whether it can justify colonialism and slavery—and even on this point, as we will see, he keeps slipping back into a theodical justification of the modern world of the global, including colonial genocide and enslavement. His racialized framework of humanness confirms, in the end, Wynter's central insight that the modern concept of "humanity" itself is unintelligible without blackness as its constitutive (at once excluded and included) other.

6.2.1. Layers of Possibility: Schelling's Geology of Race, Part I

Schelling's vision of humanity is as layered as his vision of nature. The history of humankind since the Fall of Adam has been a succession of temporal layers (*Schichten*), worlds (*Welten*), and epochs in the continuous creation of the one human species (*Schöpfungsepochen*; DRP 503), which Schelling hierarchically arranges to the extent that these epochs, up until the present world of the dominance of what he calls "the Caucasian race," constitute humanity's increasingly higher attempts to develop spirit, freedom, and self-legislation. This development is recapitulated from layer to layer or epoch to epoch, so that, at the respective stage of human history, each layer *is* the human species during this stage, itself differentially distributed. These epochal layers constitute the "system" of human times (DRP 503), restaging within the history of consciousness what in *The Ages of the World* Schelling envisions as the system of geo-cosmic times. "Pre-human" natural history is the model (*Vorbild*) for human history, insofar as the latter, too, is structured as a nested and layered system that ascends lawfully from the more "material" to the more "spiritual" humankind (DRP 502–503).

For Schelling, each epoch of the human species has its world-historical place in the development of spirit. At the end of each epoch, it is as though humankind at once failed to achieve the highest and *succeeded* in providing the foundation for the next, higher epoch, in which the attempt to reach A = A begins again at a higher level. In this manner, each epochal layer is measured or judged, and assigned its rightful place, in accordance with its approximation of the highest. Each layer is part of the world-historical movement of possibility. "In a kind of providential arrangement" (DRP 499), the lower layer is there for the sake of the higher, or so as to provide the possibility, basis, or ground for the next stage of human ascent (*Aufstieg, Erhebung*). Just like in the natural *Stufenfolge*, so too in the ladder of humanity each lower level of the system contains possibilities that are actualized only in and through the higher (DRP 504–506).

Importantly, each layer is racialized, a racialization Schelling seems to trace back either to the biblical account of the origin of peoples in the three sons of Noah, Shem, Ham, and Japheth (see DRP 502 and 509 on the "Japhethitic species"; cf. also 512), or even to the pre-Adamic proto-human species, already sub-speciated within itself, which in Adam awakens to reason, freedom, and proper humanness (DRP 510–511). The exact chronology of the layers of the global is unclear from *Presentation*, yet Schelling evidently maps the ascendance of "the Caucasian race" onto the Christian-modern trajectory. This layered process of racialization is dynamic: epoch to epoch, human "races" or "types" are at once repeated and evolve. Not only are the epochal layers themselves hierarchized but, since this whole system is nested and recapitulative, the process of hierarchization takes place *within* each layer and each race, too. This generates the framework of racialization as the unequal global distribution of humanness within and across the layers. Since the human is the universal being in whom all threads of nature come together, this implies that "when it comes to the actualization of the possibilities" contained within the human being, "there must appear here [i.e., in humanity] . . . all the levels of being, from the lowest to the highest, leading to a ladder whose members have different value [*Wert*] according to their distance from or proximity to the final goal" (DRP 529). The logic of value is not to be missed here. In fact, it had always been implicit in the language of lower and higher that is so central to Schelling's metaphysics. To hierarchize universal reality is to impose an abstract law of value upon it—and this re-mediation of reality through value, too, is part of the Western subject's program of self-assertion and recentering. A naturalistic hierarchy of value is no less transcendent, and no less violent, than any divine hierarchy.

In keeping with the Schellingian schema of the *Stufenfolge* as ascending from the darkness of B, each epoch of the human species begins with what is relatively dark and ascends toward the highest degree of light this epoch can reach. The same distribution of the relatively darker and the relatively lighter characterizes each race. This is the point where darkness is explicitly racialized as blackness, and light as whiteness, restaging the long-standing racialization of the darkness/light binary in the Christian-modern imaginary. Schelling cites approvingly the characterization of "the Negroes" from Georges Cuvier's *Discourse on the Revolutions of the Surface of the Globe* (1825) as "the most degraded human race... whose forms are closest to the brute, whose intelligence has nowhere risen to an orderly government or the slightest appearance of a continuous knowledge, and which has preserved neither annals nor ancient traditions" (DRP 503). Although, like Cuvier, Schelling does not completely exclude black Africans from humanity, they constitute for him the lowest, almost zero, stage in the species ladder. And even within the "so-called black race," Schelling notes, there is a further gradation (*Abstufungen*) of blackness, as though recapitulating a similar gradation in humankind as a whole, and ascending "from the level that is just one step above the animal, Negro proper, via all the intermediary levels, such as the Mongolian type, to the level that approaches the Caucasian race" (DRP 503). The same ascending scale from the darkest to the most fair-skinned (*hellfarbig*) repeats successively within each other race—Mongolian, American, Malayan, and Caucasian—and across all epochs.[19] Throughout this gradation, whiteness remains the normative visible characteristic of proximity to the highest, and of the degree of transfiguration of gravity (darkness) into light and fallenness into what is redeemed. "Actual rationality [*Verstand*]," for Schelling, "shows its power over what lacks rationality" (WA27 125): and this holds of the power of the normative (white) rational subject over the rest of the globe, too.

In Schelling's at once geological and racial (one may say geo-racial) vision of humanity, the lowest level of blackness is the deepest: the "deep black" skin color (*tiefschwarz*) that he associates with the Wolof people, mentioned alongside the Fula and the indigenous peoples of Congo. The level on which Schelling places the blackest Africans is that of the geo-cosmic depths of the unblissful human past, the visible representation of that principle in nature which embodies darkness, sinfulness, and tumult, and which cannot master or re-collect itself. Hence what Schelling takes to be the absence, in deepest blackness or pure blackness (*das rein Schwarze*; DRP 503), of self-legislation, rational order, tradition, chronology, or history. Generally, the darker and lower a form of humanness, the less for Schelling it presently appears as human, relegated instead to the less-than-human status in relation to the normative subject. This creates precisely the division between the two apparent

---

19. The recapitulation of the ascending blackness-whiteness spectrum within each race is the reason why Schelling expresses some reservations about the term "race," since it implies a static color-uniformity (DRP 506). He does not thereby critique racial theory as such, only its insufficiently processual character.

parts of humankind, where "humanness seems [*scheint*] to be located solely on one side," because, as soon as the normative Christian-modern subject assumes its world-historical role, the other races are *posited as the past* in relation to this subject and its world, just as the entirety of pre-human nature becomes mere past with the emergence of the human (DRP 500).

The verb "seems" (*scheint*) is key in Schelling's ruminations on the dividedness of the global: if it *seems* that the larger part of humankind is outside ("excluded" or "expelled" from) history and humanness, it is not because humankind is not one. Its oneness remains axiomatic for Schelling and stems from one common progenitor as well as the place of the human as such within universal order, signaling at once a physical and spiritual unity of humankind (DRP 507–508). If these groups seem expelled from history, it is because they are excluded from the movement of the present: they are mere remnants, ruins, or recapitulations of the lower epochal layers of humanity. In the past, these groups, too, may have been part of the movement of possibility, yet as humankind ascends from darkness to light and from matter to spirit, the less "spiritual" parts get stuck in the past of the species, fossilized on the lower layers of humankind or living out their days as ghosts of the past. In these fossilized humans, it is hard "to even recognize the soul that used to be in contact with the divine," and that continues to animate the higher humanity (DRP 501): a vision that testifies to what Hickman calls the "historical racialization of the ideal/material binary."[20] Nonwhite peoples that have formed states and created art and science are higher for Schelling than those who have not (DRP 504), but they, too, represent a relative past. This vision is theodical in a typical Schellingian manner: the lower may be relatively darker, more fallen, and more erroneous, yet this is also its *rightful place* in which it serves the actualization of the higher. Error is below truth yet necessary for ascent to truth, and darkness must be there so that light can be revealed: such is the (natural and divine) law, the tribunal (*Gericht*) by which the lower is sentenced to "the degraded position of what is below [normative] humanness" (DRP 511).

Racialization is thus intrinsically temporal and diachronic. Even the spatial distribution of humanness around the globe can be understood only from the standpoint of the geo-racial system of human times. The temporality of ascending historical progress is the temporality of racialization, and as the normative European subject surveys the global from its vantage, it sees other forms of humanness below and behind itself. The modern vision of progress

---

20. Hickman, *Black Prometheus*, 38.

is often presented as horizontal: as a "secularized" linear temporality stripped of transcendent salvation. However, the modern world remains beholden to a logic of hierarchized ascent, unfolding in the vertical tension between the salvific above (reoccupying the position of heaven) and the accursed below (hell). Those who are *ahead* in the movement of progress are also those who are normatively *above*, and those who are behind are arranged into a ladder based on their proximity to the normative—a verticality that is theodically legitimated and naturalized in accounts of race such as Schelling's.

In Schelling's vision, the European subject, moreover, sees retrospectively from its vantage that it has *always*, since the beginning of human history, been constitutively ahead of others precisely as the carrier of humanity's forward movement. It was him, the first "man," the subject who already occupied the same structural position of the highest at the origin of history, who in his original self-assertion produced the first "great *krisis*, the separation of the human from the divine, the material from the intelligible world." It was he who asserted himself against the divine because he "wanted to be his own self and not God's," to be "free from God and solely for himself." This normative subjectivity, too, was embodied by those who built the Tower of Babel, striving to reach the skies: the subject who "has been since the outset engaged in greatest undertakings," "the heaven-storming species" that, even in its self-imposed separation from the divine, "cannot stop searching for God." This "Japhethitic, Promethean species," in which, looking back, the European subject recognizes itself, has always been the driving force behind humanity's "untiring progress," capable of bearing "heaviest suffering and deepest pain" on its way to glory, the suffering and pain that, Schelling claims, are "unknown to the other part of humankind" (DRP 500–502).[21]

For Schelling, there has essentially only ever been *one* historical subject, the normative subject who can be traced back to Adam (*ha adam*, Schelling points out, means "man" in Hebrew) as the first subject of self-assertion, the constitutively *active* subject, "the human as *actus*," compared to which others appear as more or less passive. This subject is "the true human," and the rest of humanity is "mere material" (*Stoff*; DRP 507–508, 511). The Adamic subject may be fallen, but it alone carries "the divine spark, the spirit of freedom and self-determination" that this subject brings to the entire human species to the extent that various subspecies are capable of receiving it (as the bringer of the

---

21. Note Schelling's telling theodical identification of suffering with the normative subject in its work on the world, and not with those whom this subject subjugates and sacrifices in its world-conquest.

divine spark, Adam is thereby typologically identified with Prometheus and Lucifer; DRP 510–511). The Adamic subject is the demiurge of the world of human history, the demiurge whom Schelling transhistorically identifies with whiteness. For Schelling, it is to *this* transhistorically normative subject, and thus to the white Christian-European subject, that all of nature—the entire universe—calls out for salvation.[22] In postulating this subject, what Schelling attempts to secure is the one continuously ascending metamorphosis of (the clarified and kenotically subdued) B, the Promethean human will in its free and conscious step-by-step re-subordination to the divine—an ascent in which modernity, the age when autonomous freedom and consciousness are developed, is an essential stage. This allows Schelling to envision the natural and human *Stufenfolge* as one ascending edifice (*Gebäude*). The universal spiral is the true spiritual Tower of Babel, "building itself upward level to level" (DRP 507) as the Adamic subject ascends to a recentering in God at the end of history.

6.2.2. Indigeneity, Blackness, and Extraction: Schelling's Geology of Race, Part II

We have previously seen how universal and absolute the logic of place-assigning justice is in Schelling, but it is when this logic is explicitly applied to the human species that its violence becomes especially clear. One might ask: If Schelling postulates a hierarchy of different races, how can he envision the destined future oneness of humanity, seeing as these races persist in the past and do not progress toward the absolute future? Schelling's answer is simple: the lower races cannot remain outside the future; they are bound to either be assimilated or go extinct as they come into contact with the higher. Such is the way of nature, regarded by Schelling not just with indifference but with approval, insofar as the lower thereby ceases to obstruct further ascent. Thus, "the native inhabitants of America" cannot but "completely disappear" through mere contact (*Berührung*) with the Europeans: *not* even, Schelling emphasizes, "through European acts of violence," but simply because the lower is naturally destined to die out in a world that belongs to the higher. The same is evident, he maintains, in the case of the indigenous peoples of the Hawaiian Islands, where "mortality among the native inhabitants has risen with the arrival of the Europeans." Generally, the "new diseases" that spread

---

22. See Chapter 4 on nature as calling out for salvation to the human, and on Adam as the demiurge of the second creation.

among "wild peoples" once they have been exposed to the Europeans are but nature's (and providence's) way of showing what inevitably happens in the result of "even the first contact" with the highest species (DRP 509). To announce that the extermination of the lower happens through mere contact with the higher, and not due to willful European colonial conquest and genocide, is a theodical sleight of hand meant not least to absolve Schelling himself of justifying colonial extermination, and to absolve the highest, "divine" normative European subject of all guilt as well. Indeed, this subject appears as divine also because Schelling ascribes to it a quasi-divine, superhuman power: just to face this human God in his movement of world conquest is to be providentially judged, subdued, and even obliterated.

However, the Christian God, of whom the European subject is the providential carrier, is also a merciful God, and so he may show mercy to or redeem the lower forms of being human by incorporating them in humanity's ascent and converting their backwardness into the world-historical movement of possibility. This conversion into possibility of that which is itself without possibility, this redemptive grace as what the Christian-modern subject can bestow, is for Schelling manifest—strikingly—in transatlantic slavery. Since pure blackness embodies for him the fallen depths of the species, it is the site of the total absence of world-historical possibility and value, the dark ground of humankind that has never been transfigured into clarity. If the lower part of humanity is generally marked for Schelling by the relative incapacity (*Unfähigkeit*) to elevate itself to the higher, pure blackness constitutes *incapacity as such*: the blind will's sheer inability to re-collect itself or direct itself upward, to self-govern or self-legislate, to "participate in the gradual and orderly expansion of human knowledge" or "to take part in the religious process" of humanity. In thus taking pure blackness to equal the absence of contribution to "the progressive work of human spirit" (DRP 501), a site of world-historical inertness and nonproductivity, Schelling does not shy away from emphasizing the almost nonhuman nature of "some Negro tribes," their "blind fury" and "barbarity," as well as "the senseless, bloodthirsty cruelty of their chieftains" (DRP 513–514). This conjunction of pure wildness and pure absence of world-possibility resonates with Wynter's observation that blackness figures in modernity as "the ultimate chaos" on which the world of the normative subject is imposed, "the transgressive chaos" below the realm of rationality, and so below world-order.[23]

---

23. Wynter, "1492," 21, and "Ceremony Must Be Found," 37.

Transatlantic slavery, then, is for Schelling a way to convert this pure disorder into the world-historical order overseen by "man," to convert incapacity into the movement of possibility by transporting across the Atlantic those who, at home, have no possibility of their own, and embedding them in the ascending spiral of history. Only by, quite literally, *extracting* black Africans from the lowest layer of humanness and putting them to work can they be endowed with the redemptive possibility to contribute to the progressive work of spirit, to become the ground and resource for the higher, "connecting" to and "participating" in the movement of the world. For Schelling, "pure" black Africans can have their bodies put to work, and those coming "from the better tribes," their minds, as in his example of those Africans who, under the influence of the Europeans, have become "excellent mathematicians" (DRP 515).[24]

For Schelling, while blackness is technically part of humanness, it is only borderline human, constitutively incapable of self-legislation or self-development. "Would the Negro on its own have discovered a mathematical science?" he asks, implying that a race whose will is merely outer-determined (*bedingter Wille*) cannot rise to spirit. The black race can be (in part) elevated to participating in the work of spirit only if it is extracted from its lowest geo-racial layer and brought to the world surface by the self-determined, self-legislating subject. Hence, "'The more fallen and animal-like these tribes are, the more they necessarily point to [their own salvation through] the part of humanity that has raised itself to spiritual life." Only this part can illumine blackness with the light of science and make actual (*wirklich*) whatever possibility black Africans, who as such remain below the movement of possibility, still contain within themselves to contribute to the world-process (DRP 514). In keeping with the *Stufenfolge* as ascending from what is materially inert to what is spiritually active, so that "the more a being is dominated by materiality [*das Stoffliche*], the less lively its movement toward the goal and the more unrecognizable its destination" (DRP 431), blackness is figured by Schelling as incapable of moving toward the universal human destination unless actively moved by the normative subject. Just as, in Schelling's cosmo-theology, the dark fallen will (B) is divine only to the extent that it bears the work of God, so Africans are actually human only to the extent that they bear the work of "man": in this too, darkness and blackness structurally coincide.

---

24. Schelling may here have in mind black mathematicians such as Thomas Fuller and Benjamin Banneker.

In fact, Schelling speculates, to convert blackness into the movement of salvation history may have been the sympathetic (*wohlwollende*) intention behind not slavery as such, but the idea of the "Negro exportation" (*Negerausfuhr*) out of Africa. On the one hand, he admits that it has been since the outset an evil (*böse*) undertaking, tracing it back to the Spanish priest Bartolomé de las Casas, who in 1517 supported the vision of organizing "Negro trade" to "exploit the [American] silver and golden mines" (DRP 513). On the other, Schelling immediately proceeds to mitigate this evil by recourse to the same theodical "better" that, in Chapter 5, we saw him use to justify the Fall: Would it *really* have been better if the exported Africans had remained in their wild, bloody homeland? Is it not in a sense better, Schelling asks, that they were "saved" from dwelling in sheer darkness and incapacity? After all, "Negro slavery is something that these unfortunate [peoples] already had at home, and in fact in its most abominable form," a worse form (it is implied) than their enslavement by the Europeans. In the project of transporting black Africans across the ocean, too, "a sympathetic mind could see the only means by which to wrench this forsaken species from the most horrific barbarity, and to save many souls, almost hopelessly lost, from eternal death" (DRP 513). From a higher providential standpoint, it was, Schelling claims, a project of mercy, salvation, and conversion. Indeed, one may see in this project "a divine dispensation" except for the way it has been "in part" perverted "in the hands of humans," leading to the horrors of slavery whose extremes Schelling condemns (although not without adding the qualification "in part," which suggests that not everything about this project is perverted). We may recognize in this a theodical strategy that is likewise at work in his broader cosmo-theology: to embed an evil into the providential world-plan, thereby legitimating and instrumentalizing it, and at once mitigating it and activating it *as* evil in its proper place in the divine stage play.

Schelling concludes his lecture on race with the rhetorical question: "What would be more humane, to provide Negro exportation with its true [providential] purpose [*Bestimmung*], employing to that end a great world-dominating power"—that is, the Christian-modern power—"or to forcibly prohibit Negro exportation, thereby causing atrocities and occasioning even greater atrocities, while depriving thousands of (at least potentially human) beings of their only way to be saved [*Rettungsweg*]?" (DRP 515) To suggest that abolishing the violent displacement of black Africans would lead to "even greater" atrocities is itself a ruse of the theodical "better," meant to legitimate the existing global world as in truth better than in the counterfactual scenario in which transatlantic slavery would be stopped. Schelling's suggestion of what would be more "humane" and the false dichotomy he offers in the above question, a suggestion and dichotomy delivered ex cathedra by a dignified philosopher to his European-Christian audience, themselves need to be displaced. One needs but to imagine how this suggestion would sound, instead, in the hold of the slave ship—this zero point of the post-1492 world of the global, the (non-)place of conversion into value of what as such is taken to be without value—so as to expose the violence of Schelling's theodical indifference and his inability to dwell with the suffering that the Christian-modern world imposes on the forms of life it considers less than human, an imposition that Schelling reproduces in his philosophical racial grammar. While ruminating about what would be more humane or cruel and absolving himself of the guilt of justifying slavery, Schelling only reinforces the cruelty of his own naturalized theodicy and his inscription of blackness into the logics of racialization, hierarchy, value, extraction, salvation, conversion, possibility, and redemptive futurity: into the entire Christian-modern apparatus of the world. Schelling's thought thus forms a site within the broader movement of racial modernity in its reflection upon and legitimation of itself.

Since pure blackness is for Schelling the embodiment of fallenness, it should not come as a surprise that it is also the privileged site of the work of redemption. As Calvin L. Warren has observed, "Antiblack violence in modernity is reenvisioned as curative": a salvific cure, one might add, through which the nonproductive disorder of blackness is reborn into possibility, resuscitated into productivity, resurrected into history—a logic that, in modernity, remains co-imbricated with Christianity.[25] If Schelling seeks to incorporate blackness in the movement of possibility to such an extent that he ends up justifying the Middle Passage, it is because the absolute disorder embodied by pure blackness cannot but constitute a threat to the "divine" modern world-order. To recall Schelling's own verdict, according to which "most people . . . are afraid to gaze into the abyss of the past that is still all too present within them" (WA14 207–208/3–4), one could say that, in modernity's racial imaginary, blackness is figured as the exteriorized embodiment of the geo-cosmic abyss that the normative subject refuses to see within itself, turning it instead into the racialized dark ground on which the subject builds its Tower of Babel, storming the skies. Schelling's natural-philosophical framework exposes that, for the modern subject, blackness embodies chaotic contingency and the dark depths of deep time, the remainder that cannot be

---

25. Warren, *Ontological Terror*, 128. On slavery and rebirth, see Hartman, *Lose Your Mother*, 68.

re-mediated (cf. FS 131/29): the abyssal darkness that persists below and that stubbornly resists mediation and conversion into light, threatening the entire Christian-modern project of human recentering or of reassembling the divine *anthropos*. It is between this irreducible geo-cosmic darkness and the desire for all-transparency that blackness is caught in the modern racial imaginary. From Schelling's analysis, blackness emerges as a site of world-delegitimation and world-refusal, bearing many of the characteristics he associates with bliss, such as nonproductivity, intransitivity, inoperativity, and atemporality. However, Schelling does not want to ascribe bliss to blackness, instead denigrating it and seeking to re-subordinate it to the movement of the world. The desire to redeem blackness as possibility is not least the modern subject's desire to redeem itself and its world of endless striving and work, sensed by the subject to be constitutively unblissful. Perhaps, if all were to be converted into value and put to work, if all possibility were exhausted and darkness were fully transfigured into light, bliss would finally arrive—a modern desire inscribed in Schelling's metaphysics, too, and in his racialized theodicy of the global with its legitimation of the modern world as the path to bliss.

But, in this paradigm, the chaos of blackness is not only a threat: in its structural correspondence to dark geological depths, blackness is also a resource, extracted from the lowest layer of humanity and converted into value, just as the planetary depths are similarly extracted and converted in the mines where the enslaved Africans toil. As Kathryn Yusoff has suggested, the geological and the racial imaginary are entangled in modernity insofar as blackness is cast as lacking subjectivity, as inorganic, dark, and non-historical. Blackness, in other words, is a material resource whose value and possibility need to be extracted and actualized by the subject. What Schelling's geo-racial vision of humanity refracts is the triangulation of indigeneity, blackness, and extraction in the production of the New World as the frontier of modernity. In this triangulation, human layers are geologically arranged in a way that justifies the dispossession of indigenous land by the normative white subject for the purpose of extraction, while blackness is identified ontologically with mere matter. As Yusoff puts it, "The slave and the mineral are recognized in regimes of value, but only so much as they await extraction (where Whiteness is the arbiter and owner of value)."[26] Even the *possibility* or capacity (to have value) can be discerned, in blackness as in raw minerals, only by the normative human subject.

---

26. Yusoff, *A Billion Black Anthropocenes*, 70.

In the wake of Yusoff's work, and in view of Schelling's own merging of the geological and the racial, any grappling with his geological imaginary and his layered metaphysics of time needs to confront the indelibly racial grammar of this imaginary. The figures of the *Stufenfolge* and the dark ground in Schelling refract the geo-cosmic and geo-racial logics at the heart of modernity. The Schellingian temporality of universal history is a geo-racial extractive temporality, and the *Stufenfolge* is itself a mining operation, a structure of excavation and extraction, with darkness qua blackness at the bottom.[27] This lowest resource-position is crucial. Just as the divine world-order needs the dark transgressive chaos by contrast with which it can affirm itself *as* order (hell and Satan are, as we remember, the instruments of God that are required for his providential goals)—so the modern world, too, structurally requires the position of disorder as the resource that it keeps converting redemptively into order, thereby fueling the apparatus of conversion that is the world. The geo-cosmic disorder of blackness is thus theodically subordinated to and made to serve the order of the world, even while continuing to threaten this order as its dark other: the threat *through* which the world-order is further legitimated as "good" in contrast to the disorderly as "evil." In this theodical apparatus of world-reproduction and world-legitimation, conversion is also sacrifice, a forcible kenosis imposed from above upon the lower, the emptying out of the lower as the extraction of its possibilities toward the higher: a violent Christ-operation that the Christian-modern world imposes upon reality.[28] The law of the world and of divine providence—*that all possibility be exhaustively actualized*—necessitates sacrifice so that order can be upheld. The fundamental dictum of Schelling's theodicy according to which "suffering is universally ... the way to glory" (WAII 40/99), the way that goes "from darkness

---

27. This structure is there in the pre-human *Stufenfolge*, too, where the dark chaotic totality of possibility is gradually converted into order in the ascent of natural forms, an ascent modeled by Schelling on geology (cf. DNP 366). The Fall of B or the Luciferian will is driven, in Schelling's theo-cosmic account, by the desire to extract the possibilities contained in "the groundless depths" of being. The will imagines "that, thanks to this infinity of possibility, it could become all-powerful" (IPU 770). For Schelling, in the Fall, what is to become intelligence separates itself from being so as to extract resources and possibilities from it, a process inseparable from the rational cognition of the entirety of being and from intelligence's becoming intelligence: a conception of rationality that is modern and extractivist in character.

28. Kenosis is thus itself doubled in Schelling. First, there is the willing kenotic self-dispossession of the normative subject through which the subject becomes the carrier of (its own) God. As self-sacrifice, this is an operation of mastery through self-diminution. Second, there is the imposed dispossession of the black (non-)subject and others rendered less than human, and the expected "submission, self-denial, and servile compliance" on their part (Hartman, *Scenes of Subjection*, 237).

back to light" (WA14 289), reveals thereby its racialized, extractive, and sacrificial character.

6.2.3. In the Name of Possibility, in the Name of God: Conversion and Supersessionism

Conversion into the movement of world-historical possibility is, at the same time, conversion into the consciousness of the one true God. Turning (*Umkehrung*) as the basic operation of the universal spiral is also conversion (*Bekehrung*) in the religious sense: the two senses of the Latin *conversio*. As Daniel Colucciello Barber points out, the Pauline-Christian logic of conversion is premised on the division between the structural positions of "matter" and "spirit," between which the movement of conversion takes place, generating a (hierarchized and racialized) dialectic of exclusion and inclusion.[29] The *Stufenfolge*, including the *Stufenfolge* of humanity, is precisely such a movement of conversion. The human *Stufenfolge* is a circumnavigational spiral of spirals coiling around the globe and assimilating it into whiteness as the normative form (A = A) that is identified with the Christian consciousness.[30] It is, of course, "the Christian missionary" who mediates the racialization of "the pure Negro tribes" as those who are intrinsically "*empty of any idea of God*," and so less than human or almost nonhuman (DRP 501). In the fact that modern colonialism is Christian in origin and character, Schelling sees the confirmation of the modern subject as the highest, because this subject remains the carrier of the Christian God, and of a (likewise Christian) universalism of the one true form of consciousness into which other forms are converted. Schelling's thinking of global humanity confirms Lewis R. Gordon's diagnosis that "racism, which implies a hierarchy according to racial location, is haunted by the specter of conversion."[31] Through the Christian-modern consciousness, the spiral of history ascends as the process of God's coming to himself, whose endpoint, as we remember, is his triumph over the world: "Only *that* God who has a world of which he is the master [*beherrscht*] is actually God" (UPO 107).

---

29. See Barber, "Immanent Refusal of Conversion."

30. This shows that Schelling's racialized theodicy of the global, too, remains a geometric-aesthetic theodicy of whiteness as form.

31. Gordon, *Fear of Black Consciousness*, 117.

The conjunction of racialization and conversion in Schelling's framework of humanity further highlights the fact that Schelling's turn to Christianity serves not to oppose but to *reaffirm* modernity and the broader Christian-modern logics of the world in their re-mediation of bliss. To position Christianity and modernity simplistically against each other, as Schelling scholarship often does, is to obscure their shared genealogy and shared violence. It is not coincidental that the above language of divine world-mastery mirrors what *Presentation* justifies as the modern subject's striving to master the globe: it is through *converting the global* into one providential movement of history that the subject unites humanity, preparing God's triumph in and through a global consciousness that has kenotically resubmitted to God. Schelling's thought thus legitimates the nexus of *conversion*, *conquest*, and *supersessionism* within Christian-modern universalism, a nexus that already in premodern Christianity begins to be racialized and merges with a vision of civilizational progress.[32] Schelling's geo-racial system of epochs deals with questions arising from this universalist vision: Who inhabits the future and who is stuck in the past? Who is ahead and who is behind in the race to bliss? To be ahead, after all, is to be closer to salvation: a hierarchized vision of futurity that modernity inherits from Christianity.

Just like in the broader Christian-modern trajectory, *normative humanness* and *true religion* are, in Schelling's reassembling of the global, impossible to disentangle. Both diachronically and synchronically, the geo-racial distribution of forms of being human around the globe coincides with the distribution of forms of religious consciousness. As Schelling puts it in 1812, the idea "that a personal being [is] the originator and steerer of the world" is the "all-reconciling solution" to the mystery (*Rätsel*) of being, and it is only beginning with this idea that, historically, "everything human came to be" (DGD 158). To this day, it is "the higher [*bessere*], if smaller, part of humanity" that carries the true concept of monotheism (UPO 101), and conversely, the lower a part of humanity is located on the *Stufenfolge* of humanness, the more it is excluded from the ongoing "religious process" (DRP 501). The history of global humanity is a distributed development of the true idea of God across the pre-Christian and the Christian-modern world, a development in which each epoch and each people have their "assigned roles" that are likewise hierarchized (UPO 233). To convert a (past or present) people into this movement is to approach it as a node in the historically evolving relational network

---

32. See Heng, *Invention of Race*, 31–38.

of global religious consciousness aimed at re-collecting the true God. This global relationality is that to which pure blackness is, as such, without relation, unless it is extracted and re-mediated into historical movement. Pure blackness, as "endemically wretched,"[33] is completely "alienated from God" (DRP 501). In this regard, the extraction of black Africans from the lowest epochal layer, their being put to the world-historical work of possibility, their transmutation into value, and their conversion into true religion coincide.

As the ascent of the Adamic subject back to a recentering in God, the history of humanity is the metamorphosis of the fallen will (B). However, this is not simply a "pagan" metamorphosis. It is also a divine process (*Prozess*) in the joint juridical-theodical sense and a Christian-supersessionist conversion narrative. Already the *Stufenfolge* of pre-human nature is configured by Schelling through a supersessionist logic. In this logic, once the new appears (e.g., organic life or the human), the old (e.g., inorganic nature or the animal life, respectively) is immediately posited as the past that is lower than the new, and that is retroactively declared to have always existed solely for the sake of the higher, in which the redemption, value, and usefulness of the lower consist. This operation, which coincides with the cosmic Christ-operation as analyzed in Chapter 5, is reiterated across all levels, producing them *as* levels. The inscription of the structure of reality as such into a supersessionist logic is a programmatic move on Schelling's part: it is meant to "prove" that the true philosophical and historical standpoint coincides with the Christian, and that the Christ-potency has since the foundation of the universe been at work in re-mediating and re-collecting all being toward the bliss of divinity configured as transcendent.

This supersessionism intensifies in Schelling's *Philosophy of Mythology* and *Philosophy of Revelation*, a duology whose purpose is to show that the history of human consciousness since the times of Adam has been structured through the *Stufenfolge* culminating in the Christian-modern trajectory as the trajectory of salvation. As part of this project, Schelling seeks to show that all pre-Christian forms of religious consciousness and all pagan deities (as one with the consciousness that produced them) can be arranged in the *Stufenfolge* as he configures it, and thus teleologically subsumed under Christianity. No part of the global religious process can escape its conversion into the logics of hierarchy, place, and Christian revelation. Just like in his identity philosophy (see Chapter 3), the very concepts of "religion" and "religious process,"

---

33. Gordon, *Fear of Black Consciousness*, 75.

as well as the meta-opposition between "mythology" and "revelation" as the only two kinds of religion (UPO 391, 401), are constructed here by Schelling from a Christian-modern vantage.

Of all the German idealists and Romantics, Schelling arguably possessed the most detailed historical-theological, philological, and exegetical knowledge. In his lectures on mythology and revelation, this arsenal of learning is mobilized to excavate and re-mediate past deities and divine names in a Christocentric manner, geo-racially arranging them into their proper layer along a ladder that goes from the darker, blinder religion "at the beginning of humankind" to the more spiritual and transparent (UPO 382).[34] It is possible to show, Schelling maintains, "that the mythologies of various peoples as these mythologies historically appear [are] moments within one and the same progressive process" (UPO 239) culminating in the breaking through of the light of Christianity. In the end, all non-Christian forms of consciousness of the divine are converted by Schelling into relative approximations of the world-historical event of Christianity, in which all natural and human reality, including the past, is revealed to disclose the universal Christian truth. In this manner, Schelling's thought responds to the post-1492 cosmological disorientation by reassembling global deities and subordinating them to the Christian God in a "narrative demand of conversion"[35] that reaffirms the Christian-modern trajectory as central, and that seeks to make impossible any site that would truly remain *outside* or *refuse* the universal movement of conversion in its re-mediation of all possible positions through the logic of the *Stufenfolge*. Whoever tries to escape or oppose the divine law and its place-assigning justice, Schelling theodically proclaims, is *thereby* judged and assigned one's proper (lower, fallen) place. In trying to escape the law that governs the world, one is subjected (*untertan*) to the law (DRP 530).

Two examples from Schelling's account of the mythological process should suffice to show how non-Christian forms of consciousness—and forms of bliss, too—are subsumed by him into the Christian narrative of conversion and salvation. These examples are, first, the nomadic religion of the stars and, second, the bliss that is revealed in the ancient Greek mysteries. As we know, the history of consciousness begins for Schelling with the Fall of the self-assertive will (B). This will then becomes the normative subject

---

34. As Whistler argues in "Language after Philosophy of Nature," geological excavation of divine names constitutes Schelling's method already in his 1815 *Deities of Samothrace*.

35. Barber, "Immanent Refusal of Conversion," 143.

insofar as it prostrates itself and begins, out of fallenness, the ascending process of re-collecting the divine. Here too, the Tower of Babel is a key symbol for Schelling. In seeking physically to storm the skies, the will is still driven by B, the Luciferian dark fire of pride, the vortex spinning to its crash while believing itself to ascend: the self-assertive subjectivity that, refusing to acknowledge its own fallenness, keeps all potencies chained to itself and insists on immediately claiming heaven (UPO 239–240).[36] The falling down of the tower is turned, in Schelling's redemption narrative, into B's recognition of its fallenness and its spiritual prostration (*Niederwerfung*) before the higher. It is this redemptive act, the first upward turn, which is the proper "starting point of paganism" (PM 238), that is, of the mythological process as the reassembling of divine oneness, the process that arranges itself into the *Stufenfolge* as the rising tower of true, spiritual ascent. It is no longer pure fallenness but the redemptive Christ-potency (light, love, or A^2) that is operative in the Adamic subject insofar as it opens itself upward and searches for the divine—hence this subject's position as normative from a theological perspective.

Nomadic consciousness, by contrast, is relegated by Schelling to the deep geo-racial prehistory (*Vorgeschichte*) of humanity, still dominated by the conflict between the centripetal and the centrifugal force, the same conflict that, within the cosmic process, generates the proto-material oscillation from which celestial bodies and their movements are formed. Nomadism precedes paganism proper, remaining just below the spiritual ascent to God, in the dark ground where B—the "astral" or "sidereal" principle—reigns. However, nomadic consciousness also carries with it a bliss of its own, even if Schelling refuses to call it "bliss" because, in his post-1809 thought especially, he positions bliss as transcendently above, and never as below, the *Stufenfolge* of the world. Nomadic religion is "the most ancient" of all: it is "astral religion," corresponding within consciousness to the emergence of the system of the universe (*Weltsystem*). In their being "unbound from a stable living place," nomads do not so much worship individual stars as *move together as one* with the movement of celestial bodies, "these nomads of the heavens." Nomadism is thus a "wandering, roving," non-positional and nonproductive form of being that refuses all hierarchy or place. The principle in which

---

36. The resulting tumult corresponds "within consciousness to the same moment that we must think as preceding nature [proper]" within the cosmic process (UPO 240), i.e., precisely to what in Chapter 5 we saw as the tumultuous proto-material state following the Fall of B as the principle of scattering. The scattering of consciousness, in other words, recapitulates the same natural-philosophical or cosmic model.

nomadic consciousness is immersed (*eingetaucht*), Schelling insists, is B itself as "pure astrality," the one undivided ("inseparably one") fire of the divine will prior to its scattering—the fire that forms the inner spiritual core of celestial bodies. The "magic power" of this principle "consumes all [bounded] life" (UPO 239–241; cf. POP 215). Unbound to the world as an orderly distribution of place, and one with the divine fire in which the world is consumed and the one undivided being is revealed—is this not a state of bliss? An aporia arises: considered immanently, nomadism is a self-sufficient form of inhabitation of bliss. Yet, because Schelling wants to decouple astrality from bliss and to position normative humanness *higher* than astrality, he refuses to acknowledge the bliss of this form of being, inscribing it into the ascent toward Christianity. The immanent-transcendent apparatus of the world forecloses astral bliss.

A similar aporia presents itself in Schelling's account of the ancient Greek mysteries, whose truth he already in 1802 identifies with that of Christianity. In his later philosophy of revelation, too, he subordinates the bliss revealed to those initiated into the mysteries to a Christian vision of redemptive futurity. The bliss disclosed in the mysteries consists in a oneness with "the bliss of the perfect God" (UPO 330). Even if, as pagan, the mysteries cannot rise to the true idea of God the creator, they attain the mystical bliss of hidden divinity. It is the bliss of death to the world: "the bliss that no eye has seen and no ear has heard, and that only those see and hear who die" (UPO 351). Considered immanently, this bliss transports one to a standpoint "liberated from the bonds of the material world" and so "completely free from paganism" (UPO 350, 384–385). One may observe a contradiction between Schelling's relegation of the bliss of the mysteries to the level of paganism and the fact that paganism itself is dissolved here. This contradiction is due to the conversion narrative that he needs to construct for this bliss to fit into the *Stufenfolge*. He attempts to resolve this contradiction by declaring the bliss of the mysteries to be not true salvific bliss but an anticipation of Christian bliss qua salvation. In this anticipation, paganism supposedly transcends itself and discloses, unbeknownst to the pagan mind, the "necessity" and "certainty" of the light of Christian revelation (UPO 382–389).

For this reason, Schelling configures the bliss of the mysteries as remaining below the continuing historical ascent. It is the bliss of the underworld (*Unterwelt*; UPO 351), of death without resurrection, reflecting the fallen pre-Christian condition. This supersessionist construction remains, however, an uneasy one. Schelling himself admits that, following the emergence of Christianity, the adherents of the mysteries *refused* inscription into the Christian consciousness. The spirit of the mysteries "continued to feed the survival of paganism and opposed Christianity the most" (UPO 383). Schelling explains this as the continuing resistance of gravity to light, backwardness to progress, fallenness to salvation. Yet the distinction between an "insufficiently true" and a "true" bliss is a theodical sleight of hand, wherein all forms of immanent dwelling in bliss are subordinated to the not-yet of history. Bliss is thereby enclosed into the Christian promise of "absolute reconciliation" (UPO 389)—even though bliss as such is indifferent to Christianity.

Schelling subjects to this enclosure not only the past but the future, too. "Universal church" and "philosophical religion," these central terms of his prophetic-theodical vision, are constructed via a supersessionist conversion narrative and underwritten by the racialized universalism premised on the one true God's conquest of the world. Philosophy proclaims the arrival of a new world, a more blissful one, but, in this very proclamation, it reproduces the colonial logics of *the* world: the one hegemonic Christian-modern world. A post-Christian church that "overcomes" and "completes" Christianity is still Christian in its origin and essence, necessitating the sacrifice of those forms of consciousness that cannot or refuse to be subsumed under the divine $A = A$: the sacrifice that Schelling calls reconciliation. This returns us to the stated goal of Schelling's *Presentation*: to bring modern consciousness to rest in the bliss of the pure *is*, or what his philosophy of revelation likewise announces as the "true repose," the "joy and bliss" of consciousness (UPO 601–602). In the final lecture of *Presentation*, consciousness glimpses the bliss of the divine *is* and acknowledges its own diremption and fallenness. Just as we saw in Chapter 4 in the discussion of his philosophical method, it is for Schelling, however, not enough that consciousness simply empty itself and be in bliss. It must further deliver itself *toward* the absolute subject. "The will," Schelling writes, "cannot find repose or peace" until it submits to the transcendent God. Only in this manner can modernity re-subordinate itself to Christianity and not simply dissolve in bliss; and only in this manner can the end of negative philosophy truly coincide with the beginning of positive philosophy as a Christian philosophy of revelation. At the end of its path, consciousness must realize that "it longs for God himself." "*Him, him* it demands, the God who acts" and who steers the world, the transcendent "Lord of being." "*Person* seeks *person*," Schelling's formula of philosophical religion goes, in which the personhood of the Christian God is structurally mapped onto the personhood of the normative Christian-modern subject and so itself racialized (DRP 566–568). In Schellingian theodicy, "God" and "man" thus function jointly to uphold the apparatus of the world, and the invocation of these two terms as emancipatory is itself an operation of legitimation serving to reinforce the unequally distributed and racialized claim to freedom, truth, and the absolute future. If, for Schelling, the Christian God is one who demands all the hierarchization, subjugation, and sacrifice inherent in the Schellingian vision of universal history, to equate bliss with this God is itself a violent theodical ruse. The personal God prohibits impersonal bliss, for it is only by submitting consciousness to himself that he can actually become the true, legitimate God, and not the illegitimate usurper-God of this unblissful world.

Conclusion

BLISS AGAINST THEODICY

Why Bliss so scantily disburse—
Why Paradise defer—
Why Floods be served to Us—in Bowls—
I speculate no more—

—EMILY DICKINSON

WHY IS THE formula of A = A, of the blissful *simply being what one is*, so insistently subsumed by Schelling into the form of the Christian God, of the normative self-legislating subject, and of the providential law that presides over the universal process? There is no foundation for this except the Christian-modern desire for conversion and domination, the desire that Schelling's thought refracts and legitimates, and that, as he himself notes, *is* the (Christian-modern) world. Hence his repeated inscription of bliss, which is as such atemporal, in the Christian promise. In truth there is but one bliss, the all-dissolution and all-consumption of the world, the bliss that can be immanently inhabited or manifest itself in various ways, yet remains as such without relation to the not-yet of the world. Based on the examples of Schellingian bliss traced in this book, a *counter-tradition of bliss against the world* may be assembled, which would non-hierarchically encompass nomadism and mysticism, blackness and hidden divinity, magic and the mysteries, the bliss of lying on water and looking at the skies and that of the all-consuming revolutionary fire.

Perhaps one should not even call this a counter-tradition, since the term "tradition" may imply too much of a continuity. Rather, it is an indifferent, non-relational set of *sites of refusal and delegitimation,* which all reject equally the imposition of hierarchies, racializations, and not-yets, indifferentiating the world and immediately resonating together, atemporally and transhistorically, within one bliss-in-common. Bliss cannot be found in world history, only, as it were, underneath history or as persisting across history yet without relation to it. As such, bliss is without conversion or justification, without striving or work, and indifferent to transcendences either "religious" or "secular," "divine" or "worldly." As stripped of "humanness," a term constructed through racialized division, bliss can be only, as it emerges most strongly in Schelling's identity philosophy, the bliss of the non-appropriable All, refusing the hierarchy of human, less than human, and nonhuman as well as the dichotomy of "man" versus "nature." In its indifference to any transcendent law, bliss precludes the binary of good and evil through which judgment is upheld, dissolving the theodical demand to judge in the immanent inhabitation of the one common being. In bliss, there is no division into the realm of fallenness, backwardness, disorder, and darkness and the realm of redemption, progress, order, and light. Bliss indexes, rather, a collapse of the separation between these and similar realms, the separation through which the Christian and the Enlightenment mind function. And although, in the history of thought, bliss has often been inscribed in the binary of "matter" and "spirit" (and into the hierarchized and racialized gradations that emerge from this binary), what Schellingian bliss at its most radical shows is that this binary, too, is refused in the immanent inhabitation of what simply *is*, the bliss-in-common that the immanent-transcendent apparatus of the world encloses and represses.

If bliss thus may be called heretical and Gnostic in its total *no* to the logics of the Christian-modern world, and in its indifferent insistence on this world's illegitimacy and its secondary, imposed, at once illusory and all-too-violent character, one must also think of bliss as heretical vis-à-vis "Gnosticism" itself, insofar as historical doctrines that may be characterized as Gnostic fall prey to the flesh/spirit binary and to the logics of redemption and judgment. Bliss does not judge: it cuts through, burns down, collapses, refuses, or simply does nothing in the face of the world's imperatives of production and work. If there can be an ethics of bliss, it can be only one that is free of the moral law, which, like all law, needs to maintain the reality of fallenness and dividedness, of guilt and punishment, of radical evil and redemption. To *enact* bliss, as we saw in Schelling's example of one who is holy, is to oppose all enclosures and hierarchies, to tear down all borders and prison walls. This blissful agency cares not for seeking a transcendent salvation or a mastery of all things possible; it cuts through the logics of salvation and possibility. No redemption narrative can hold in bliss, and no project of control. Bliss cannot be possessed, appropriated, partitioned, or produced, calling into question the legitimacy of productivity itself. All of these are persistent features of Schellingian bliss immanently considered, features to which he holds on, strikingly, throughout his philosophical trajectory.

Afrofuturist musician and poet Sun Ra has spoken of a "dark tradition," of which the "black tradition" is a constitutive and prominent but not exclusive part, a tradition allied, not unlike the nomads in Schelling, with the blackness of space and the celestial bodies themselves: with the utopic nowhere, the radiance of sheer "isness," the non-place from which to unground this world.[1] To view Schellingian bliss, in no small part against Schelling himself, as aligned with this tradition is to insist on the antagonistic dimension of bliss that must be inhabited as prior to its theodical foreclosure by Schelling, by Christianity, or by modernity. This would be to view bliss as what erupts transhistorically against the world of self-assertion and domination, the world that the normative subject ("man") erects atop the abyss of cosmic contingency, seeking to subdue and master this abyss and racializing it as the geo-cosmic darkness that the subject fears.

At stake in the affirmation of bliss against the world is more than a mere inversion, or a positioning of darkness against light or tumult against order: this would not be enough, because inversion is itself, as we have seen in Schelling, an operation of the world. Just as Sun Ra refuses to oppose the blackness of space to the radiance of the sun, but inhabits the utopia of their absolute indifference, so bliss, too, must be thought of as refusing this dichotomy. The binary of disorder and order is co-produced by the world in its movement of division and judgment, so that the world can theodically assert itself *as* order (as "good") over and against what it proclaims to be disorder and chaos, while reproducing the position of chaos as the resource position. Instead, to dwell in and with bliss would be to inhabit immanently cosmic contingency without striving to hierarchize or control it: to inhabit the plenum of the earth and the skies, which is *already there* as the absolute (divine, earthly, solar) power on which the world feeds, but which the world obscures and encloses, converting it into the dark ground for self-assertion and resource extraction. This would be, perhaps, to live in common in the way that the early Marx envisions, too. This being-in-common, this pantheism of bliss, is what Schelling's thought, like Christian-modern universalism more broadly, at once promises and defers into an indefinite future.

The persistence of bliss in Schelling may appear as contradictory in view of his commitment, starting already from the 1790s, to a metaphysics of the

---

1. See *Space Is the Place* (dir. John Coney, 1974), a film featuring Sun Ra, and Sun Ra, *Immeasurable Equation*, 252.

world that is, as I have argued, Christian-modern in character. Yet this contradiction is, properly speaking, not Schelling's own, but reflects the constitutive tension inscribed in the modern world. As I have tried to show in this book, what makes Schelling such a unique thinker of modernity as itself a salvific epoch continuously entangled with Christianity and Gnosticism is his fundamental insight that the modern world longs for bliss, promises bliss, and feeds on the absolute power of bliss. In the Schellingian analytic, this world is exposed as an apparatus of capture, a structure of reality that encloses and re-mediates the one bliss into a lost ante-original past and a longed-for future, the re-mediation due to which bliss appears as *never now*, but is turned into a promise of future fulfillment and non-alienation. As long as the world is there, however, this future constitutively cannot arrive, so that, through the very promise of bliss as a salvific futurity to be actualized, the (Christian-modern) world of endless diremption, striving, and work—a world that Schelling identifies, already in his 1795 metaphysics, with the structure of reality as such—is justified and reproduced. If, in Christianity as in modernity, the promise of the end of the world *is* the world, it is because Christian-modern consciousness cannot but sense the negativity and unblissfulness of its own world, and the *failure* of the promise of bliss on which this world is premised. The Christian-modern world is the most terrible uroboros serpent of them all, scaling itself up by coiling around the earth and incorporating into itself all forms of being so as to feed on them as it devours itself.

Still, if this book has attempted to think bliss at once with and against Schelling, it is because bliss as he himself theorizes it cannot be bound or confined to his Christian-modern metaphysics of the world. This is not to position the "good" Schelling of bliss against the "bad" Schelling or the "subversive" against the "conservative" Schelling; this would itself be a redemptive and theodical operation. The point, rather, is to think the necessary presence of both bliss *and* the world as the two poles in whose tension his thought unfolds, thereby refracting the late eighteenth and nineteenth-century crisis of the aporetic entwinement of bliss and modernity. In other words, Schelling's thinking of bliss discloses the antagonistic entanglement between bliss and the world, and between bliss and theodicy as a conjoined world-legitimation and God-legitimation, at the heart of the Christian-modern trajectory as a trajectory of salvation that fails. This failure is still with us, with both those who are the subjects of and who are subjected to this world. If, despite its inherent failure, the project of modernity continues, it is because it has so far managed to turn its ever-restaged crisis and failure themselves into the motor of the postponement of bliss into a promised future (if only everyone works hard enough or is put to work in a more efficient way): a future that exploits the longing for bliss yet will never arrive.

In the Schellingian analytic, this conjunction of promise and deferral, the conjunction through which the world maintains and upscales itself, is also a Christian inheritance. "World" itself, as I have argued via Schelling and Blumenberg, emerges in Christianity as the time and space of the failure to enact bliss *in the now*. Developing an idea from Jacob Taubes, Daniel Colucciello Barber has grasped this as the failure of the messianic promise, the failure that Christianity inherently denies, converting it into what drives the Christian process of conversion and expansion.[2] The Christian desire for world domination is also the desire to convert this failure into success, which can be fully accomplished only once there is nothing left that would resist Christian consciousness: the same logic of all-mastery that Schelling discerns in the modern will. Out of the original failure, world history arises in Christianity as salvation history, and the entire theodical apparatus—starting at least from Augustine—arises with it, embedding (the promise of) bliss into the logics of mediation, transcendence, redemptive futurity, and the not-yet. This theodical overwriting of bliss is what Schelling reproduces when he subsumes the bliss of *simply being what one is* under $A = A$ as the formula of the law. Yet this overwriting is still upheld by the longing for bliss and by the deep-seated, broadly Gnostic sense that this world is *not* all that there is or what is absolutely real. This sense is inherited by modernity even as it redoubles on spiritual investment in the world, leading to the aporias and impasses of salvation as absolute freedom from the world—the aporias that this book has traced. The failure and illegitimacy of the modern world are inscribed in the modern structure of reality *avant la lettre*. With the intensification of the nonhuman character of the post-Copernican universe, this sense of illegitimacy intensifies, too, an intensification to which Schelling's theodicy of human recentering responds. In a universe of endless contingency and endless elliptical trajectories of the real, the project of world domination likewise fails in advance of itself. Schelling's insistent imposition of order and hierarchy on the universe as though from below, out of the immanent movement of nature itself, reveals his anxiety about this failure as threatening to unground the Christian-modern construction of humanity and universal history.

---

2. Barber, "Immanent Refusal of Conversion," 145: "Christians are those who identify with a messianic hope that seems to have failed, but that cannot have failed; Christian identity is constituted by the conversion of failure to an only-seeming-to-have-failed, to a cannot-have-failed"—the conversion that is also a theodical operation.

In the nineteenth century, bliss is repressed by the consolidated capitalist world of the global with a new intensity: a crisis out of which one may understand not only Schelling's, but the broader Late Romantic turn to Christianity. There is, I believe, some truth to the conventional wisdom that explains this turn in figures such as Schelling, Friedrich Schlegel, and Wordsworth by their disillusionment with the post-Revolutionary apocalyptic hopes of their youth, even if I would reject the simplistic stereotype of young radicals becoming conservative with age. The late Romantic turn to Christianity is continuous with the early Romantic impulse of antagonism to the negativity and alienation of the modern world. As Schlegel formulates it in 1817, already after his conversion to Catholicism: "In my life and all my philosophical studies, there is but one constant search for eternal oneness."[3] Schelling, too, could have subscribed to this formulation. In the 1790s and in part the early 1800s, sensing the crisis of modern reality, the Romantics rightly know that this oneness cannot be found in this world that is constitutively dirempted and not-yet—but they also insist apocalyptically on the imminent revolutionary end to this world and the coming of absolute bliss. As the world, yet again, re-mediates this crisis, consolidating itself and deferring bliss, this imminent apocalyptic expectation fails with the reproduced failure of bliss in the now. This failure is, arguably, what prompts the Romantics to turn to Christian transcendence, which they erroneously view as the only (ostensibly non-worldly) site through which they can still hold on to a vision of bliss, and through which to overcome the negativity of modernity. Hence, too, Schelling's post-1809 abandonment of his earlier notion of intellectual intuition, which could still access the bliss of the All *right now*, and his reconfiguration of bliss as transcendent.

Yet it is the very idea of overcoming and, by extension, completing modernity through Christianity that is the problem, restaging the hegemonic-supersessionist Christian-modern gesture. In insisting on and philosophically developing this idea, Schelling produces a racialized theodicy of the world in his very desire to escape the grip of the world and to secure a principle that would be unburdened by the world. As Schelling himself grasps it already in 1802, the Christian promise of oneness and bliss is a promise of all-reconciliation that goes *through* the world and that *legitimates* the course of world history as the path to salvation, so that, in choosing to stick to this promise instead of uncovering its theodical ruse, Schelling cannot but end up

---

3. Quoted in Anstett, "Einleitung," xi.

reaffirming this (Christian-modern) world from a supposedly higher providential vantage. His hierarchized positioning of bliss as what is above the world, too, leads him to disregard that which remains behind and below, and is sacrificed by, the universal spiral of the world in its ever-soaring ascent.

In this regard, I would suggest, the early Marx's revolutionary vision of being-in-common inherits the antagonistic Romantic impulse in a much stronger way than late Romanticism itself, and in a way that is more attuned to the mid-nineteenth-century capitalist reality. One cannot escape the logics of domination and racialization by turning to Christianity against modernity, to "religious" against "secular," because these logics, just like the religious/secular binary itself, are co-produced by Christianity and modernity, mutually upholding and reinforcing each other through their seeming opposition. Only in a joint antagonism to Christianity and modernity, or only by abolishing "the world" as the ostensible structure of reality as such, can bliss be enacted in the now. Bliss itself, the pure *is*, is neither religious nor secular, neither Christian nor modern, but the plenum of the absolutely real that precedes and collapses these and other binaries, refusing the operation of periodization, itself Christian-modern in character.

This book is, in the end, both an account of the sites of refusal and a cautionary tale: the tragedy of Romanticism, and arguably an important reason for its waning in the nineteenth century, is that it made the fatal decision of adopting the Christian logic of mediation and of mediating bliss through the (Christian-modern) world. Not coincidentally, it is the logic of mediation that likewise led Hegel, though in many regards an anti-Romantic, to his own racialized Eurocentric theodicy of history. German idealism and Romanticism could not stop grappling with the *why* of the world: Why is this world there? What is its genealogy and world-historical task? Why must it be? Yet if there is a philosophical lesson in this, a lesson for philosophy itself, it is that there is a very thin line between rationally or providentially explaining the world, making it cohere and endowing it with sufficient reasons, and theodically legitimating it, thereby justifying its negativity and violence. The entwined questions—*How to insist on bliss without theodicizing it?* and *How to think the world without justifying it?*—constitute arguably one of the most difficult problems for all philosophy, a problem that Schelling tried but ultimately failed to resolve. Not so much as Schelling's "own" concept but as a transhistorical impulse that is excessive over his theodicy of the Christian-modern world, bliss is what persists at once despite and because of this failure, and what connects transhistorically all sites of world-delegitimation and world-refusal.

Bibliography

Adorno, Theodor. *Minima Moralia: Reflections from Damaged Life*. Translated by E. F. N. Jephcott. London: Verso, 2005.

Albernaz, Joseph, and Kirill Chepurin. "The Sovereignty of the World: Towards a Political Theology of Modernity (After Blumenberg)." In *Interrogating Modernity: Debates with Hans Blumenberg*, edited by Agata Bielik-Robson and Daniel Whistler, 83–107. Cham: Palgrave Macmillan, 2020.

Altizer, Thomas J. J. "The Advent of the Nothing." In *Sacred Modes of Being in a Postsecular World*, edited by Andrew W. Hass, 122–134. Cambridge: Cambridge University Press, 2021.

Anidjar, Gil. "[Interview with] Gil Anidjar." In *The Present as History: Critical Perspectives on Contemporary Global Power*, edited by Nermeen Shaikh, 225–253. New York: Columbia University Press, 2007.

Anidjar, Gil. "Secularism." *Critical Inquiry* 33, no. 1 (2006): 52–77.

Anstett, Jean-Jacques. "Einleitung." In Friedrich Schlegel, *Kritische Friedrich-Schlegel-Ausgabe*, vol. 9: *Philosophie der Geschichte*, edited by Jean-Jacques Anstett, xi–lix. Munich: Ferdinand Schöningh, 1971.

Augustine. *The City of God against the Pagans*. Translated by R. W. Dyson. Cambridge: Cambridge University Press, 1998.

Augustine. *Confessions: Books 1–8*. Edited and translated by Carolyn J.-B. Hammond. Cambridge, MA: Harvard University Press, 2014.

Augustine. *The Literal Meaning of Genesis*. Translated and annotated by John Hammon Taylor, SJ. 2 vols. New York: Newman Press, 1982.

Bacon, Francis. *The Works of Francis Bacon*, edited by James Spedding, Robert Leslie Ellis, and Douglas Denon Heath. 14 vols. London: Longman, 1857–62.

Balthasar, Hans Urs von. *Apokalypse der deutschen Seele: Studien zu einer Lehre von letzten Haltungen*. Vol. 1: *Der deutsche Idealismus*. Salzburg: Anton Pustet, 1937.

Barber, Daniel Colucciello. "The Immanent Refusal of Conversion." *Journal for Cultural and Religious Theory* 13, no. 1 (2014): 142–150.

Barber, Daniel Colucciello. "World-Making and Grammatical Impasse." *Qui Parle* 25, nos. 1–2 (2016): 179–206.

Barton, Carlin A., and Daniel Boyarin. *Imagine No Religion: How Modern Abstractions Hide Ancient Realities*. New York: Fordham University Press, 2016.

Beiser, Frederick. *German Idealism: The Struggle against Subjectivism, 1781–1801*. Cambridge, MA: Harvard University Press, 2002.

Benz, Ernst. *Schellings theologische Geistesahnen*. Wiesbaden: Franz Steiner Verlag, 1955.

Berger, Benjamin, and Daniel Whistler. *The Schelling-Eschenmayer Controversy, 1801: Nature and Identity*. Edinburgh: Edinburgh University Press, 2020.

Berlant, Lauren. *Cruel Optimism*. Durham, NC: Duke University Press, 2011.

Bielik-Robson, Agata. "The God of Luria, Hegel and Schelling: The Divine Contraction and the Modern Metaphysics of Finitude." In *Mystical Theology and Continental Philosophy: Interchange in the Wake of God*, edited by David Lewin, Simon D. Podmore, and Duane Williams, 32–50. New York: Routledge, 2017.

Blumenberg, Hans. *The Legitimacy of the Modern Age*. Translated by Robert M. Wallace. Cambridge, MA: MIT Press, 1983.

Boehme, Jacob. *The Epistles of Jacob Behmen*. Translated by J[ohn] E[llistone]. London: Gyles Calvert, 1649.

Boehme, Jacob. *Mysterium Magnum*. Translated by John Sparrow. Edited by C. J. B[arker]. London: John M. Watkins, 1965.

Boehme, Jacob. *The Works of Jacob Behmen, The Teutonic Philosopher*. Translated by William Law. 4 vols. London: Richardson, 1764–81.

Bowie, Andrew. *Schelling and Modern European Philosophy: An Introduction*. New York: Routledge, 1993.

Browning, Elizabeth Barrett. *Letters*. Vol. 1. Edited by Frederic G. Kenyon. New York: Macmillan, 1898.

Burnet, Thomas. *The Sacred Theory of the Earth*. 5th ed. 2 vols. London: J. Hooke, 1722.

Campe, Joachim Heinrich. *Wörterbuch der deutschen Sprache*, Vol. 5: *U bis Z*. Braunschweig: Schulbuchhandlung, 1811.

Caputo, John D. *Specters of God: An Anatomy of the Apophatic Imagination*. Bloomington: Indiana University Press, 2022.

Chakrabarty, Dipesh. "The Climate of History: Four Theses." *Critical Inquiry* 35, no. 2 (2009): 197–222.

Chepurin, Kirill. "Reading Novalis and the Schlegels." In *The Palgrave Handbook of German Idealism and Poststructuralism*, edited by Tilottama Rajan and Daniel Whistler, 59–81. Cham: Palgrave Macmillan, 2023.

Chepurin, Kirill. "Romantic Bliss—or, Romanticism Is Not an Optimism." *European Romantic Review* 32, nos. 5–6 (2021): 519–534.

Chepurin, Kirill. "Theodicy across Scales: Hemsterhuis's *Alexis* and the Dawn of Romantic Cosmism." *Symphilosophie: International Journal of Philosophical Romanticism* 4 (2022): 263–293.

Chepurin, Kirill, and Alex Dubilet. "Introduction: Immanence, Genealogy, Delegitimation." In *Nothing Absolute: German Idealism and the Question of Political*

Theology, edited by Kirill Chepurin and Alex Dubilet, 1–34. New York: Fordham University Press, 2021.

Chepurin, Kirill, Adi Efal-Lautenschläger, Daniel Whistler, and Ayşe Yuva. *Hegel and Schelling in Early Nineteenth-Century France*. Vol. 1: *Texts and Materials*. Vol. 2: *Studies*. Cham: Springer, 2023.

Clarke, Arthur C. *Profiles of the Future: An Inquiry into the Limits of the Possible*. Rev. ed. New York: Harper & Row, 1973.

Cullmann, Oscar. *Christ and Time: The Primitive Christian Conception of Time*. 3rd ed. Translated by Floyd V. Filson. London: SCM Press, 1962.

Da Silva, Denise Ferreira. *Toward a Global Idea of Race*. Minneapolis: University of Minnesota Press, 2007.

Danz, Christian. *Die philosophische Christologie F. W. J. Schellings*. Stuttgart: Frommann-Holzboog, 1996.

Danz, Christian. "Die Philosophie der Offenbarung." In *F.W.J. Schelling*, edited by Hans Jörg Sandkühler, 169–189. Stuttgart: Metzler, 1998.

Danz, Christian, ed. *Schelling und die Hermeneutik der Aufklärung*. Tübingen: Mohr Siebeck, 2012.

Das, Saitya Brata. *The Political Theology of Schelling*. Edinburgh: Edinburgh University Press, 2016.

Davis, Kathleen. *Periodization and Sovereignty: How Ideas of Feudalism and Secularization Govern the Politics of Time*. Philadelphia: University of Pennsylvania Press, 2017.

Delumeau, Jean. *Sin and Fear: The Emergence of a Western Guilt Culture*. Translated by Eric Nicholson. New York: St. Martin's Press, 1990.

Dubilet, Alex. *The Self-Emptying Subject: Kenosis and Immanence, Medieval to Modern*. New York: Fordham University Press, 2018.

Dussel, Enrique. "Anti-Cartesian Meditations: On the Origin of the Philosophical Anti-discourse of Modernity." Translated by George Ciccariello-Maher. *Journal for Cultural and Religious Theory* 13, no. 1 (2014): 11–53.

Eckhart, Meister. *The Essential Sermons, Commentaries, Treatises, and Defense*. Translated by Edmund Colledge and Bernard McGinn. Mahwah, NJ: Paulist Press, 1981.

Eusterschulte, Anne. *Analogia entis seu mentis: Analogie als erkenntnistheoretisches Prinzip in der Philosophie Giordano Brunos*. Würzburg: Königshausen & Neumann, 1997.

Field, J. V. *Kepler's Geometrical Cosmology*. London: Bloomsbury, 2013.

Frank, Manfred. *Der unendliche Mangel an Sein: Schellings Hegelkritik und die Anfänge der Marxschen Dialektik*. 2nd ed. Munich: Fink, 1992.

Frank, Manfred. "Einleitung des Herausgebers." In F. W. J. Schelling, *Philosophie der Offenbarung 1841/42*, edited by Manfred Frank, 9–84. Frankfurt am Main: Suhrkamp, 1977.

Frank, Manfred. "Schelling, Marx und Geschichtsphilosophie." In *Habermas-Handbuch*, edited by Hauke Brunkhorst, Regina Kreide, and Cristina Lafont, 219–244. Stuttgart: Metzler, 2008.

Freud, Sigmund. *Civilization and Its Discontents*. In *The Standard Edition of the Complete Psychological Works of Sigmund Freud*. Translated under the general editorship of James Strachey. Vol. 21, 64–145. London: Hogarth Press, 1961.

Fuhrmans, Horst. *Schellings Philosophie der Weltalter: Schellings Philosophie in den Jahren 1806–1821*. Düsseldorf: Schwann, 1954.

García, Marcela. "Schelling's Late Negative Philosophy: Crisis and Critique of Pure Reason." *Comparative and Continental Philosophy* 3, no. 2 (2011): 141–164.

Gloyna, Tanja. *Kosmos und System: Schellings Weg in die Philosophie*. Stuttgart: Frommann-Holzboog, 2002.

Gode-von Aesch, Alexander. *Natural Science in German Romanticism*. New York: Columbia University Press, 1941.

Gordon, Lewis R. *Fear of Black Consciousness*. London: Penguin Books, 2022.

Grafton, Anthony T. "Chronology and Its Discontents in Renaissance Europe: The Vicissitudes of a Tradition." In *Time: Histories and Ethnologies*, edited by Diane Owen Hughes and Thomas R. Trautmann, 139–166. Ann Arbor: University of Michigan Press, 1995.

Grant, Iain Hamilton. *Philosophies of Nature after Schelling*. London: Continuum, 2006.

Hartman, Saidiya. *Lose Your Mother: A Journey along the Atlantic Slave Route*. New York: Farrar, Straus and Giroux, 2007.

Hartman, Saidiya. *Scenes of Subjection: Terror, Slavery, and Self-Making in Nineteenth-Century America*. Rev. ed. New York: Norton, 2022.

Hartog, François. *Chronos: The West Confronts Time*. Translated by S. R. Gilbert. New York: Columbia University Press, 2022.

Harvey, David. *Marx, Capital and the Madness of Economic Reason*. Oxford: Oxford University Press, 2017.

Hegel, G. W. F. *Faith and Knowledge*. Translated by Walter Cerf and H. S. Harris. Albany: State University of New York Press, 1977.

Hegel, G. W. F. *Lectures on the Philosophy of Spirit, 1827–8*. Translated by Robert R. Williams. Oxford: Oxford University Press, 2007.

Hegel, G. W. F. *Lectures on the Philosophy of World History*. Vol. 1. Edited and translated by Robert F. Brown and Peter C. Hodgson. Oxford: Clarendon Press, 2011.

Heng, Geraldine. *The Invention of Race in the European Middle Ages*. Cambridge: Cambridge University Press, 2018.

Hermanni, Friedrich. *Die letzte Entlastung: Vollendung und Scheitern des abendländischen Theodizeeprojekts in Schellings Philosophie*. Vienna: Passagen Verlag, 1994.

Hickman, Jared. *Black Prometheus: Race and Radicalism in the Age of Atlantic Slavery*. New York: Oxford University Press, 2017.

Horn, Eva. *The Future as Catastrophe: Imagining Disaster in the Modern Age*. Translated by Valentine Pakis. New York: Columbia University Press, 2018.

Hühn, Lore. *Fichte und Schelling oder: Über die Grenze menschlichen Wissens*. Stuttgart: Metzler, 1994.

Jacobs, Wilhelm G. *Gottesbegriff und Geschichtsphilosophie in der Sicht Schellings*. Stuttgart: Frommann-Holzboog, 1993.

Jonas, Hans. *The Gnostic Religion: The Message of the Alien God and the Beginnings of Christianity*. 2nd ed. Boston: Beacon Press, 1963.

Kant, Immanuel. *Critique of Practical Reason*. Rev. ed. Translated by Mary Gregor. Cambridge: Cambridge University Press, 2015.

Kant, Immanuel. *"Toward Perpetual Peace" and Other Writings on Politics, Peace, and History*. Edited by Pauline Kleingeld, translated by David L. Colclasure. New Haven: Yale University Press, 2006.

Kasper, Walter. *Das Absolute in der Geschichte: Philosophie und Theologie der Geschichte in der Spätphilosophie Schellings*. Mainz: Matthias-Grünewald-Verlag, 1965.

King, Karen L. *What Is Gnosticism?* Cambridge, MA: Belknap Press, 2003.

Koselleck, Reinhart. *Begriffsgeschichten*. Frankfurt am Main: Suhrkamp, 2006.

Kotsko, Adam. *The Prince of This World*. Stanford, CA: Stanford University Press, 2016.

Kuiken, Kir. *Imagined Sovereignties: Toward a New Political Romanticism*. New York: Fordham University Press, 2014.

Lacoue-Labarthe, Philippe, and Jean-Luc Nancy. *The Literary Absolute*. Translated by Philip Barnard and Cheryl Lester. Albany: State University of New York Press, 1988.

Lefebvre, Henri. *Rhythmanalysis: Space, Time and Everyday Life*. Translated by Stuart Elden and Gerald Moore. London: Continuum, 2004.

Leibniz, G. W. *Theodicy*. Translated by E. M. Huggard. Chicago: Open Court, 1985.

Lévi, Eliphas. *The Doctrine and Ritual of High Magic*. Translated by Mark Anthony Mikituk. New York: TarcherPerigee, 2017.

Levinas, Emmanuel. "The Temptation of Temptation." In *Nine Talmudic Readings*. Translated by Annette Aronowicz, 30–50. Bloomington: Indiana University Press, 1990.

Levinas, Emmanuel. "Useless Suffering." In *The Provocation of Levinas*, edited by Robert Bernasconi and David Wood, 156–167. London: Routledge, 1988.

Lovejoy, Arthur O. *The Great Chain of Being: A Study in the History of an Idea*. Cambridge, MA: Harvard University Press, 1964.

Marquard, Odo. *In Defense of the Accidental*. Translated by Robert M. Wallace. Oxford: Oxford University Press, 1991.

Marquard, Odo. *Schwierigkeiten mit der Geschichtsphilosophie*. Frankfurt am Main: Suhrkamp, 1982.

Marx, Karl. *Early Writings*. Translated by Rodney Livingstone and Gregor Benton. London: Penguin Books, 1992.

Marx, Karl, and Friedrich Engels. *Collected Works*. Vol. 3. New York: International Publishers, 1975.

Marx, Karl, and Friedrich Engels. *Collected Works*. Vol. 6. New York: International Publishers, 1976.

Masuzawa, Tomoko. *The Invention of World Religions: Or, How European Universalism Was Preserved in the Language of Pluralism*. Chicago: University of Chicago Press, 2005.

Matthews, Bruce. *Schelling's Organic Form of Philosophy: Life as the Schema of Freedom*. Albany: State University of New York Press, 2011.

Matthews, Steven. *Theology and Science in the Thought of Francis Bacon*. Aldershot: Ashgate, 2008.

McGrath, Alister E. *Christian Spirituality: An Introduction*. Oxford: Blackwell, 1999.

McGrath, Sean. *The Philosophical Foundations of the Late Schelling: The Turn to the Positive*. Edinburgh: Edinburgh University Press, 2021.

Melville, Herman. *Moby-Dick: An Authoritative Text, Contexts, Criticism*. 3rd ed. Edited by Hershel Parker. New York: Norton, 2018.

Merchant, Carolyn. *Reinventing Eden: The Fate of Nature in Western Culture*. 2nd ed. New York: Routledge, 2013.

Moynihan, Thomas. *X-Risk: How Humanity Discovered Its Own Extinction*. Falmouth: Urbanomic, 2020.

Nanni, Giordano. *The Colonisation of Time: Ritual, Routine and Resistance in the British Empire*. Manchester: Manchester University Press, 2012.

Nassar, Dalia. *The Romantic Absolute*. Chicago: University of Chicago Press, 2014.

Neiman, Susan. *Evil in Modern Thought*. Princeton, NJ: Princeton University Press, 2002.

Neumann, Hanns-Peter. "Machina Machinarium: Die Uhr als Begriff und Metapher zwischen 1450 und 1750." *Early Science and Medicine* 15 (2010): 122–191.

Nietzsche, Friedrich. *The Anti-Christ, Ecce Homo, Twilight of the Idols, and Other Writings*, edited by Aaron Ridley and Judith Norman. Translated by Judith Norman. Cambridge: Cambridge University Press, 2005.

Nongbri, Brent. *Before Religion: A History of a Modern Concept*. New Haven, CT: Yale University Press, 2013.

Norris, Benjamin. *Schelling and Spinoza: Realism, Idealism, and the Absolute*. Albany: State University of New York Press, 2022.

Novalis. *Philosophical Writings*. Translated and edited by Margaret Mahony Stoljar. Albany: State University of New York Press, 1997.

Oetinger, Friedrich Christoph. *Biblisches und Emblematisches Wörterbuch, Teil 1: Text*. Edited by Gerhard Schäfer. Berlin: de Gruyter, 1999.

Paracelsus. *Essential Theoretical Writings*. Translated and edited by Andrew Weeks. Leiden: Brill, 2008.

Pelikan, Jaroslav. "Cosmos and Creation: Science and Theology in Reformation Thought." *Proceedings of the American Philosophical Society* 105, no. 5 (1961): 464–469.

Pleše, Zlatko. "Evil and Its Sources in Gnostic Traditions." In *Die Wurzel allen Übels: Vorstellungen über die Herkunft des Bösen und Schlechten in der Philosophie und Religion des 1.–4. Jahrhunderts*, edited by Fabienne Jourdan and Rainer Hirsch-Luipold, 101–132. Tübingen: Mohr Siebeck, 2014.

Podmore, Simon D. *Struggling with God: Kierkegaard and the Temptation of Spiritual Trial*. Cambridge: James Clarke, 2013.

Pseudo-Dionysius. "The Celestial Hierarchy." In *The Complete Works*, translated by Colin Luibheid, edited by Paul Rorem, 143–191. New York: Paulist Press, 1987.

Rossi, Paolo. *The Dark Abyss of Time: The History of the Earth and the History of Nations from Hooke to Vico*. Translated by Lydia G. Cochrane. Chicago: University of Chicago Press, 1984.

Rousseau, Jean-Jacques. *Collected Writings*. Vol. 8: *The Reveries of the Solitary Walker, Botanical Writings, and Letter to Franquières*. Edited by Christopher Kelly. Hanover, NH: University Press of New England, 2000.

Runge, Philipp Otto. *Hinterlassene Schriften: Erster Theil*. Hamburg: Friedrich Perthes, 1840.

Saiber, Arielle. *Giordano Bruno and the Geometry of Language*. New York: Routledge, 2005.

Sandkühler, Hans Jörg. "Die Philosophie der Geschichte." In *F.W.J. Schelling*, edited by Hans Jörg Sandkühler, 124–149. Weimar: Metzler, 1998.

Sandkühler, Hans Jörg. *Idealismus in praktischer Absicht: Studien zu Kant, Schelling und Hegel*. Frankfurt am Main: Peter Lang, 2013.

Schaffer, Simon. "'The Great Laboratories of the Universe': William Herschel on Matter Theory and Planetary Life." *Journal for the History of Astronomy* 11, no. 2 (1980): 81–110.

Schlegel, Friedrich. *Kritische Friedrich-Schlegel-Ausgabe*. Vol. 2: *Charakteristiken und Kritiken I (1796–1801)*. Edited by Hans Eichner. Munich: Ferdinand Schöningh, 1967.

Schmidt-Biggemann, Wilhelm. *Philosophia Perennis: Historical Outlines of Western Spirituality in Ancient, Medieval and Early Modern Thought*. Dordrecht: Springer, 2004.

Schmitt, Carl. *Glossarium: Aufzeichnungen aus den Jahren 1947 bis 1958*. Berlin: Duncker & Humblot, 2015.

Schmitt, Carl. *The Nomos of the Earth*. Translated by G. L. Ulmen. New York: Telos Press, 2003.

Scholem, Gershom. *Major Trends in Jewish Mysticism*. New York: Schocken Books, 1954.

Schraven, Martin. *Philosophie und Revolution: Schellings Verhältnis zum Politischen im Revolutionsjahr 1848*. Stuttgart: Frommann-Holzboog, 1989.

Schweighäuser, Geoffroy. "Sur l'état actuel de la philosophie en Allemagne." *Archives littéraires de l'Europe* 1, no. 2 (1804): 189–206.

Sheehan, Jonathan. "Suffering Job: Christianity beyond Metaphysics." In *God in the Enlightenment*, edited by William J. Bulman and Robert G. Ingram, 182–200. New York: Oxford University Press, 2016.

Sloterdijk, Peter. *After God*. Translated by Ian Alexander Moore. Cambridge: Polity Press, 2020.

Sloterdijk, Peter. *Stress and Freedom*. Translated by Wieland Hoban. Cambridge: Polity Press, 2016.

Soni, Vivasvan. *Mourning Happiness: Narrative and the Politics of Modernity*. Ithaca, NY: Cornell University Press, 2010.

Sun Ra. *The Immeasurable Equation*. Edited by James L. Wolf and Hartmut Geerken. Herrsching: Waitawhile Books, 2005.

Terada, Rei. "The Racial Grammar of Kantian Time." *European Romantic Review* 28, no. 3 (2017): 267–278.

Tertullian. *The Five Books against Marcion*. In *The Ante-Nicene Fathers*, edited by Alexander Roberts and James Donaldson, vol. 3, 269–475. Buffalo: Christian Literature Publishing Company, 1885.

Tilliette, Xavier. "Hegel in Jena als Mitarbeiter Schellings." In *Hegel in Jena: Die Entwicklung des Systems und die Zusammenarbeit mit Schelling*, edited by Dieter Henrich and Klaus Düsing, 11–24. Bonn: Bouvier, 1980.

Tritten, Tyler. *Beyond Presence: The Late F.W.J. Schelling's Criticism of Metaphysics*. Berlin: de Gruyter, 2012.

Trop, Gabriel. "The Politics of Speculative Collectivities in the Work of Friedrich Schelling." *European Romantic Review* 34, no. 3 (2023): 359–368.

Trop, Gabriel. "Spinoza and the Genesis of the Aesthetic." *Aesthetic Investigations* 4, no. 2 (2021): 182–200.

Voegelin, Eric. *Collected Works*. Vol. 5: *Modernity without Restraint*. Edited by Manfred Henningsen. Columbia, MO: University of Missouri Press, 2000.

Warren, Calvin L. *Ontological Terror: Blackness, Nihilism, and Emancipation*. Durham, NC: Duke University Press, 2018.

Whistler, Daniel. "Abstraction and Utopia in Early German Idealism." *Russian Journal of Philosophy and the Humanities* 2 (2016): 5–27.

Whistler, Daniel. "Language after Philosophy of Nature: Schelling's Geology of Divine Names." In *After the Postsecular and the Postmodern: New Essays in Continental Philosophy of Religion*, edited by Anthony Paul Smith and Daniel Whistler, 335–359. Newcastle upon Tyne: Cambridge Scholars, 2010.

Whistler, Daniel. *Schelling's Theory of Symbolic Language: Forming the System of Identity*. Oxford: Oxford University Press, 2013.

Whistler, Daniel. "Silvering, or the Role of Mysticism in German Idealism." *Glossator* 7 (2013): 151–185.

Wirth, Jason M. "Schelling and the Future of God." *Analecta Hermeneutica* 5 (2013): 1–12.

Wirth, Jason M. *Schelling's Practice of the Wild: Time, Art, Imagination*. Albany: State University of New York Press, 2015.

Wolfson, Elliot R. *Heidegger and Kabbalah: Hidden Gnosis and the Path of Poiēsis*. Bloomington: Indiana University Press, 2019.

Woodard, Ben. *Schelling's Naturalism: Motion, Space and the Volition of Thought*. Edinburgh: Edinburgh University Press, 2019.

Wordsworth, William. *The Major Works*. Edited by Stephen Gill. Oxford: Oxford University Press, 2008.

Wynter, Sylvia. "1492: A New World View." In *Race, Discourse, and the Origin of the Americas: A New World View*, edited by Vera Lawrence Hyatt and Rex Nettleford, 5–57. Washington, DC: Smithsonian Institution Press, 1995.

Wynter, Sylvia. "The Ceremony Must Be Found: After Humanism." *boundary 2* 12, no. 1 (1984): 19–70.

Wynter, Sylvia. "On How We Mistook the Map for the Territory, and Re-imprisoned Ourselves in Our Unbearable Wrongness of Being, of *Désêtre*." In *Not Only the Master's Tools: African-American Studies in Theory and Practice*, edited by Lewis R. Gordon and Jane Anna Gordon, 107–169. Boulder, CO: Paradigm Publishers, 2006.

Wynter, Sylvia. "Unsettling the Coloniality of Being/Power/Truth/Freedom: Toward the Human, after Man, Its Overrepresentation—an Argument." *CR: The New Centennial Review* 3, no. 3 (2003): 257–337.

Yusoff, Kathryn. *A Billion Black Anthropocenes or None*. Minneapolis: University of Minnesota Press, 2018.

Zachhuber, Johannes. "F.W.J. Schelling and the Rise of Historical Theology." *International Journal of Philosophy and Theology* 80, nos. 1–2 (2019): 23–38.

Zakariya, Nasser. *A Final Story: Science, Myth, and Beginnings*. Chicago: University of Chicago Press, 2017.

Ziche, Paul, and Vicki Müller-Lüneschloß. "Editorischer Bericht." In F. W. J. Schelling, *Werke 12: Schriften 1802–1803*, edited by Paul Ziche and Vicki Müller-Lüneschloß, 423–445. Stuttgart: Frommann-Holzboog, 2019.

Žižek, Slavoj. *The Indivisible Remainder: On Schelling and Related Matters*. London: Verso, 1996.

Zöller, Günter. "Church and State: Schelling's Political Philosophy of Religion." In *Interpreting Schelling: Critical Essays*, edited by Lara Ostaric, 200–215. Cambridge: Cambridge University Press, 2014.

Index

For the benefit of digital users, indexed terms that span two pages (e.g., 52-53) may, on occasion, appear on only one of those pages.

Figures are indicated by an italic *f* following the page number.

A = A (formula) 7, 124–41, 155–56, 161–63, 181*f*, 188–90, 223–32, 236–60, 265–77, 303–4, 311–21, 332, 338–40, 344. *See also* bliss of pure "="; copula; form; identity

A⁰ (zero potency). *See* bliss as A⁰; potenceless

abyss:
    of blackness 329–30, 342
    geo-cosmic/natural 7, 104–5, 114–15, 141–42, 177, 184, 194–95, 255–56, 276–77, 285–86, 329–30, 342
    of identity 76, 114–15, 138, 141
    in the subject 115, 184, 194–97

Adam. *See* consciousness, Adamic; Fall of Adam

Adorno, Theodor 12–14, 18–19, 52, 141

agency:
    absolute/divine 143–46, 341–42
    of all being 144, 156–58, 162–66

alchemy 198–99, 278

alienation/diremption:
    as alien power 99–105
    and Christianity 27–53, 57, 61–62, 86–87, 92–93, 115–16, 171–72, 190–91, 307–9, 342–45

    cosmic 42, 149, 214, 217–18, 270, 279–80, 291–92
    and fallenness 31–32, 149, 188–91, 199–200, 207, 291–92, 307, 313–14
    God's 227–28, 234–37, 240
    modern 1–20, 27–31, 38–57, 60, 69–74, 78–79, 81, 84–87, 92–93, 98–99, 106–7, 117, 130–31, 146–49, 152, 158–59, 188–90, 198, 207–8, 240, 280, 291–302, 307–9, 313–14, 342–45
    nature's 113–16, 190–91
    See also contradiction, general Christian; world

anamnesis. *See* recollection

antagonism. *See* bliss as antagonistic

apocalyptic 3–6, 10, 32–38, 42–43, 45–46, 50–53, 63–64, 88–89, 94–95, 102–4, 107–8, 118–19, 139–40, 145–46, 153–55, 173–74, 215–16, 248n.25, 255, 276–82, 297–99, 345. *See also* bliss; world-annihilation

Aristotle 257–58, 270–71, 276–77, 307–8

ascent, universal. *See* Stufenfolge

358 Index

astrality 60–61, 112–13, 148, 160–61, 167, 193–94, 258–63, 278–79, 284, 290–92, 296–97, 336–37. *See also* Lucifer; sun
Augustine 61–62, 165–66, 187, 213n.23, 241, 243–44, 246–48, 262, 266n.36, 344

B:
  as fallen will or non-divine principle 188–89, 210, 230–39, 245–48, 252–53, 257–68, 273, 276–78, 289–90, 311–13, 318–19, 324–27, 331n.27, 334–36
  as force of expansion/scattering 111–13, 233–38, 257–61, 273, 312
  in the identity philosophy 131–35, 142, 163
  as philosopher's consciousness 209–13
  See also Fall; Lucifer
Babel, Tower of 324–25, 329–30, 335–36
beatitude. *See* bliss
blackness 271, 304, 319–23, 325–34, 340, 342. *See also* humanity; race
bliss:
  as A⁰ 266–67, 276, 278, 308–9, 318–19
  as absolute freedom (*see* freedom, absolute)
  as absolutely real 5–7, 13, 54–55, 71–77, 82–83, 87, 104, 108, 129, 140–41, 144–45, 187–90, 221, 344–46
  as antagonistic xii, 1–14, 18–19, 23–24, 49–53, 56–57, 71–74, 88–96, 104–8, 120–25, 128, 139–40, 145–47, 159–60, 172, 184, 221–23, 228, 240, 283–84, 305–6, 342–46
  call of 35, 145–46
  deferral/re-mediation of 1–2, 6, 14–17, 33–38, 45–46, 50–51, 63, 71–72, 85, 91–98, 103–8, 115, 120–21, 147–48, 155–57, 221, 227, 239–41, 251–52, 255, 298–99, 342–45
  epoch of 6, 17, 23, 30, 35, 45–48, 51–56, 120–21, 153–55, 169, 183, 201–2, 215–16, 228, 236, 239, 279–80, 284–87, 309–10, 345
  as fire 5–6, 13, 52, 91, 118–19, 139–44, 153–57, 159–60, 222–23, 232, 259n.31, 299, 336–37, 340
  of God 126, 141–43, 183, 222–27, 239–40, 254
  and happiness 4–6, 89–93
  as immediate (*see* immediacy)
  as intransitive 74–78, 84–85, 90–91, 94, 98, 113–14, 139, 185, 220–31, 243–44, 310–12, 329–30
  in Kant 4–5, 14–15
  lost 6, 79–81, 190, 208–9, 214, 233, 237–38, 267, 270–71, 311, 314–15, 342–43
  as nonbeing/nothingness 34, 77–79, 92–95, 102–8, 126, 222–27, 230, 270–71n.42, 272–73, 277–78
  as non-relational (*see* non-relation)
  in the now 10, 14–17, 49–52, 91, 96–97, 107–8, 146, 172, 179, 251–52, 299, 342–46
  promise of 1–2, 7–17, 34, 45–51, 120, 133–34, 152, 183, 207, 214, 221, 236, 239–42, 255, 265, 283–84, 289, 298, 307–8, 337–44
  of pure "=" 7, 124–28, 133–34, 139–44, 162–63, 172, 223–24, 250–51, 310–11, 346
  and salvation 4–13, 32, 45–46, 65, 75, 80–83, 88–90, 102, 114–15, 133–34, 183, 200–1, 227–28, 238, 302, 309–10, 314–15, 337, 341–43
  shelter of 224, 239–40, 254
  as transcendent 178–80, 255–56, 266–71, 276, 334, 336–37, 345
  as translation of *Seligkeit* 4–5

Index 359

as water 6, 12–13, 139–46, 159–60, 239–40, 299, 340
See also apocalyptic; divinity; heaven; indifference; letting-be; non-domination; non-will; nonproductivity; paradise; repose; Sabbath
bliss-in-common 6–7, 12, 17, 46, 80, 117, 124–25, 139–47, 177, 224–25, 227, 250–52, 278, 311, 340–46. *See also* copula as common
Blumenberg, Hans xi–xii, 16–22, 30, 32–43, 49, 56, 59, 64n.7, 69, 83–84, 100, 106–7, 152–53, 187, 302–3, 307, 344
Boehme, Jacob 9n.8, 54n.42, 198n.8, 211–12, 271–72, 295–300
Bruno, Giordano 112–13, 119, 137, 271–72

catastrophe 10, 20–21, 139, 163, 180–82, 188, 257–58, 276–77, 282
center:
cosmic/divine 112–13, 127–28, 133–34, 140, 164, 177–83, 186–96, 199, 201–2, 220–21, 231–35, 250–52, 255–56, 260–61, 267, 270–79, 284, 289–91, 302–3, 316
human as (*see* humanity as cosmic center)
See also construction, geometric; decenteredness; recentering
chaos 78–80, 83–84, 103–4, 180–82, 198, 231–33, 258–60, 262n.34, 267–68, 273–77, 326, 329–32, 342. *See also* confusion; disorder; tumult; vortex
Christ:
bliss of 206
as Christ-operation 35, 206–7, 210, 220–21, 237–38, 245–46, 263, 265–66, 278, 331–32, 334

as Christ-potency 183, 199–200, 207, 237–38, 265–66, 334–36
cosmic 207, 237–38, 265, 334
event of 36–37, 63, 181f, 183, 205–7, 210, 217, 239, 263, 265, 267–68
as mediator 35–37, 169–70, 183, 199–200, 265–66, 284
See also Fall and redemption; kenosis; rhythm, theo-cosmic; spiral
Christianity:
and colonialism 151–53, 171–72, 286–87, 303–6, 326–35
cosmic 168–71, 265–68
emergence of 5–6, 28–38, 43–44, 46–48, 61–63, 168–72, 182–83, 196, 227–28n.6, 264–68, 307–8, 335, 337–38, 344
and modernity (*see* modernity, genealogy of)
and racialization 304–6, 321–22, 326, 328–35, 338–39, 345–46
Schelling's turn to 7, 9n.8, 270, 295–96, 299, 333, 345
significance of 5–6, 16–17, 28–52, 61–65, 115–16, 119–20, 129n.8, 151–53, 168–72, 180–83, 196, 206–8, 215n.26, 264–68, 280, 295–96, 301–10, 329–46
and world-legitimation 32–38
See also construction of religion; contradiction, general Christian; reconciliation; supersessionism
church:
Christian 33, 37, 49–52, 64–65, 264–65, 338–39
new 280, 287, 297–98, 301–2, 338–39
circle 127, 192, 199, 255–59, 271–78, 289–94, 309–10. *See also* construction, geometric; point; sphere; spiral; uroboros

clock time 288–300. *See also* time, abolition of
colonialism 11–12, 17, 23–24, 57, 60, 104, 107, 150–62, 165n.36, 171–72, 286–87, 294, 300–6, 316–39
confusion 185, 188, 192–93, 203, 264–65, 267–68, 279, 286–87. *See also* chaos; disorder; tumult; vortex
consciousness:
  Adamic/primordial 185–91, 199–200, 210, 212–13, 264, 324–25, 334–36
  Christian 31, 35–41, 149, 169–72, 183, 206–7, 215n.26, 264–65, 305–8, 332–34, 338–39, 344
  divine 186–87, 234–35, 247, 285, 315
  finite 79, 94, 102, 149, 158, 211 (*see also* I and not-I)
  modern 149, 152–53, 190–91, 201–2, 278–81, 307–9, 313–14, 332–34, 338–39, 342–43
  nomadic 336–37
  pagan 5–6, 61–62, 106–7, 169–72, 185, 196, 206, 334–35 (*see also* paganism)
  philosopher's 202, 209–13
  See also revolution, philosophical-phenomenological
conservatism 221, 256, 281–84, 343–44
construction:
  critical 248–49
  geometric 255–56, 271–77, 332n.30
  identity-philosophical 121–32, 138–39, 166–69
  kairotic 180, 217, 239, 276–77, 288–300
  kenotic 180, 202–14, 262–71, 313, 318–19, 325 (*see also* kenosis)
  of matter 111–15, 180–82, 232–34, 237, 258–60, 289–90, 312, 318–19, 330, 332
  of nature 109–16
  polar 115–16, 208–14, 231, 280–81
  of religion 168–72, 334–35
  of theo-cosmic process 227, 235–36, 268–69, 276
  with a view to bliss 110, 131–32, 180, 184, 202–4, 208–9, 214
  See also method of philosophy
contingency:
  cosmic 112–13, 127, 160–61, 172, 178–79, 217–18, 231–32, 241, 244–45, 250, 257–58, 342–44
  of divine being 217–19
  of the future 180, 216–19, 241–42, 285–86, 315–16
  of the global 302–5
  of happiness 89–93
  and self-assertion 18, 40–42, 69, 104–5, 284, 305, 342
  and theodicy 163, 172, 180, 216, 241, 244–45, 250, 258, 270, 276–77, 284–86, 329–30
  as threat 22, 40–41, 69, 104–5, 177–78, 184, 217–19, 241–42, 258, 270, 276–77, 284–86, 302–3, 329–30
contradiction, general Christian 8, 27–57, 71, 81, 86–87, 106–7, 119, 131n.10, 149, 168–72, 190–91, 201, 207–8, 227–28, 236, 265, 294, 307–9, 313–14. *See also* alienation; Christianity; reconciliation
conversion xii, 23–24, 47–48, 65–66, 78–79, 83, 146, 185, 204–5, 246–47, 256–57n.27, 262–67, 276–77, 294, 303–6, 326–45
Copernican revolution 22, 42, 46–47, 112–13, 120, 127–28, 178–79, 190–91, 207–8, 214, 250, 269–70, 291–92, 302–3
copula:
  as binding 172

as common 124–25, 310–11
in post-1809 Schelling 186n.2
as spirit 223–24, 237n.12
cosmic view 127, 150–56, 161, 168–69
cosmos. *See* universe
creation 5–6, 20, 66–67, 83–84, 106–8, 114–15, 162–66, 178–83, 191–92, 195–96, 199–200, 218–42, 247–52, 257–67, 274–79, 288–89, 309–10, 320
crisis:
of clock time 295–99
of faith 38
of happiness 4–5, 92–93
and *krisis* 82, 199, 204–5, 211–12, 241, 248–49, 281 (*see also krisis*)
of modernity 1–12, 20–21, 29–30, 38–43, 46–49, 54n.42, 56, 82, 93, 120, 146, 178–79, 184, 199, 213–14, 270, 280–81, 284, 293–98, 343–45
of salvation 4–5, 20–21, 29–30, 66–67, 93, 295–98
of theodicy 20–21, 66–67, 93, 180, 270

death 47–48, 94, 104, 107–8, 154, 204–6, 328, 337
decenteredness/decentering:
of the divine will 180–82, 220–22, 232–35, 260–62, 273, 289–92
of the global 316–17
of the human 177–79, 184–96, 199–200, 208n.17, 255–56, 284, 302–3, 316–19
of the universe 127–28, 163, 173–84, 189–91, 195–96, 199–200, 207–8, 217, 221–22, 231–34, 241–42, 255–56, 258, 265, 273, 278–79, 284, 289–92, 302
See also Fall; fallenness; recentering

demiurge:
God/divine will as 32–33, 219, 230–31, 234, 240, 289–91
human subject as 42–43, 56, 58, 61–62, 68–73, 81–84, 97, 100, 104–7, 199–201, 240, 285, 317, 324–25
natural subject as 110, 115
diremption. *See* alienation/diremption
disorder 21–22, 68–70, 73, 83–84, 163–64, 185, 188–89, 246, 250, 258, 260n.32, 268, 276–77, 281–84, 302–3, 327–32, 340–42. *See also* chaos; confusion; tumult; vortex
divinity 203–4, 221–31, 239–40, 243, 252, 255–56, 266–67, 270–71, 276–78, 285–86, 297–98, 308–12, 334, 337, 340
doing nothing 12–16, 167–68, 239–40, 287, 341–42. *See also* idleness; nonproductivity; repose
double vision 129–31, 162–63, 170, 173–74, 210–11

earth (planet) 7, 13, 61, 112–13, 127–57, 161–62, 164, 169–70, 177–82, 185–86, 198, 208n.17, 217–18, 269–70, 278–79, 291, 315–16, 342–43. *See also* fire; sun
Eckhart, Meister 198n.8, 206n.14, 222–23, 225n.4
ekstasis 181f, 189, 195–96, 201–10, 213–14, 222, 234–35, 255–56, 261–62, 265, 292, 308–9. *See also* decenteredness; recentering
epic, post-Copernican 178–79, 220, 243–44
essence, blissful primordial 72–75, 79–82, 90–91, 97–98, 104, 111–17, 121–27, 142–43, 153, 222–29, 234–35, 239–41, 266–67, 270–72, 276–77, 310, 318–19. *See also* form and essence

evil:
  of colonialism and slavery 150–52, 155–58, 287, 328–32
  of dogmatism 100–3
  and error 185, 194, 247–48, 260n.32
  and good/evil binary 65–67, 159–63, 173–74, 194, 221, 242–55, 331–32, 340–41
  as inertia 164
  as inversion 188–89, 194, 246–48, 252 (*see also* fallenness; re-inversion)
  as necessary/useful 15, 20–21, 23, 65–68, 164, 194, 232–33n.8, 236–37, 240–50, 328–32
  to see no 21–22, 66, 157–66, 173–74
  and world-legitimation 15, 65–66, 158–63, 165–66, 173–74, 236–37, 240–47, 255, 287, 328–32
  See also Fall; felix culpa; freedom for good and evil; guilt; sin; theodicy
explosion 112–13, 154, 177, 180–82, 188, 196, 214, 220, 231–32, 257–59, 264–65, 276–77. *See also* fragmentation; nucleus

faith:
  Christian 35–38, 44–45, 49–51, 168–69
  moral 44–45, 97–98
  in the not-yet 16, 20n.34, 36–38, 50–51, 67–68, 97–98, 166–69, 217–18, 286–87
Fall, the:
  of Adam/human consciousness 14–18, 65–68, 81–82, 182, 185–91, 196–201, 210, 216, 232–35, 246, 249, 264–65, 313–14, 320, 335–36
  as bad *ekstasis* 189, 201–2, 234–35, 265
  and creation 5–6, 83–84, 129, 180–82, 199–200, 220–22, 231–35, 256–60, 273, 278, 310–11
  of divine will/Lucifer 178–82, 220–22, 231–35, 238–39, 241–50, 252–53, 255–67, 273, 294–95, 311, 331n.27
  as falling away (*Abfall*) 5–6, 122–23, 127–33, 137–39, 149, 155, 158, 161–64
  as *fortuna adversa* 257–58
  in Kant 14–18, 185, 188–89, 313–14
  and redemption 180–83, 189, 201–2, 207–8, 210, 213–14, 220–21, 237–38, 241–42, 245–46, 247–48, 250, 255–58, 260–68, 271, 283, 294–95, 321–23, 326–30, 335–36, 341–42
  as restaged in philosophy 210
  theodical legitimation of 14–18, 64n.7, 65–68, 158n.32, 161, 185–87, 200–1, 216, 234–35, 241–50, 254, 258–65, 294–95, 313–14, 328
  See also consciousness, Adamic; freedom for good and evil; sin; transgression; turmoil
fallenness:
  as Christian axiom 5–6, 31–32, 38, 119, 168–70, 206–8, 307
  of dirempted reason/subject 79–82, 119, 149–50, 158–59, 199–201, 278–79, 313–17, 324–25, 338–39
  and ignorance 260n.32
  as inversion/perversion 194, 201, 220–21, 232–35, 246–47, 257, 262 (*see also* evil; re-inversion)
  and redemption (*see* Fall and redemption)
  standpoint of 123, 128–30, 138, 158
  as universal condition 5–6, 31–32, 122–23, 127–31, 133–34, 149–50, 163–64, 179–83, 190–96, 199–200, 207, 229, 232–40, 247–48, 255–68, 271, 280–81, 288–97, 307–8, 318–19

felix culpa 18, 249–50
Fichte, J. G. 3, 5n.4, 14–15, 38–40, 43–45, 71–72, 94, 98, 109, 118–19, 123, 130–31, 139–40, 281–82, 308–9
finitude:
    in Christianity 31–35, 45–47, 51, 169–70, 206
    as inversion 84–85, 237–38
    as problem 5–7, 45–46, 72, 80–97, 102–16, 121–24, 127–34, 138–39, 150, 156–63, 311
    as punishment 158–63
    See also alienation; fallenness; world
fire:
    of bliss (see bliss as fire)
    of pride 232–33, 246–47, 258–62, 289, 314n.15, 335–36
    solar 139–41, 148–49, 153–55, 164
    of wrath 246–47, 259n.31
    See also astrality; sun; world-annihilation
forces, duality of 38, 111–17, 133–34, 163–64, 187–88, 209–12, 229–38, 259–61, 269–70, 276–77, 289–91, 336–37. See also construction; nature
form:
    and essence 84–87, 124–26, 223–30, 252, 277–78 (see also essence, blissful)
    function of 83–85, 124–25, 131–33, 139, 223–24, 237–39, 252–54, 265–66
    of identity/oneness 83–85, 124–25, 131, 188–89, 229, 237, 252, 272–73, 311–12, 332
    imposition of 68–69, 73, 84–85, 127, 265–66, 315–16
    indifferentiation of 142
    of opposition 31, 45, 78, 96
    See also A = A
fragmentation/shattering 122–23, 126–33, 139, 147–48, 149–50, 151–52, 158–59, 163, 169, 172, 196, 214,
228–32, 258–61, 280–81, 301–2, 311–13. See also explosion; Fall; tumult
freedom:
    absolute 1–6, 12–13, 29n.3, 43, 74–83, 87–91, 96, 102, 107–8, 125, 133, 144, 167, 198–99, 209–10, 222–26, 229–30, 243, 252–55, 309–15, 344
    for good and evil 4n.2, 242–48, 252–55
    of self-assertion and striving 4n.2, 46–47, 77, 79, 100–7, 125, 199
    two types of 77, 102–8, 125, 252–55

garden 15, 55–56, 166–67, 190, 250–51, 264. See also paradise
Gelassenheit. See letting-be
geology 13, 21–22, 275–76, 320–32, 335n.34
geometry. See construction, geometric; center; circle; point; spiral
geo-racial imaginary 322–24, 327, 330–37. See also race; *Stufenfolge*
global, the 22–24, 60–62, 67–68, 149–53, 287, 294, 299–309, 316–35, 345. See also humanity, unity of; theodicy of the global
Gnostic divide in God 218–19, 226–28, 234, 285–86
Gnostic imperative/question 8–9, 65, 78, 80–82, 88–95, 107–8, 218, 240–41, 247–48, 346
Gnosticism:
    and modernity 17, 30, 37–38, 41–43, 71, 82–84, 105, 137–38, 199–201, 218–19, 285–86, 342–43
    Schelling's engagement with 8, 58–59, 63–65, 71, 88–89, 233–34, 260n.32
    as world-delegitimation 8–9, 30, 32–38, 41, 50–51, 64–65, 88–89, 214–16, 218–19, 228, 341–42, 344

God:
    acquitted/on trial 20, 162–63, 218–19, 226n.5, 232–34, 241–42, 247–48, 254
    actualization/becoming of 178, 185–86, 226–31, 234–40, 245, 270–71, 286n.66, 298n.11, 338–39
    as bound to the world 226–28, 240, 311–12
    creator versus salvific 218–19, 223–31, 240, 254, 259, 285–86, 309–10
    hidden 40–42, 218–19, 224–29, 239–40, 258–61, 310, 337, 340
    positive 218, 226–31, 234, 238–42, 254, 276–77, 286n.66
    wrestling with 210–12
    See also bliss of God; divinity; law; providence; theodicy

guilt/fault 16, 161, 187–202, 246–50, 325–26, 328–29, 341–42. *See also* Fall; freedom for good and evil; sin; transgression

happiness. *See* bliss and happiness
heaven:
    as above versus below 266–67, 323–24
    ascent to 276–77, 335–36 (*see also* Babel, Tower of; *Stufenfolge*)
    as non-will or standing still 166–67, 197–98, 222–23, 225, 245
    as one with bliss 3–5, 46, 116–17, 184, 198, 203–4, 222–26, 229, 245
    regained 46, 51–52, 88–89, 105, 116–17, 119, 196–204, 255–56
    two paths to 43, 82–83, 85–89
    war in 232–33

Hegel, G. W. F. xi, 1, 3, 8–9, 14–17, 20–21, 27–49, 58–60, 63, 168, 173–74, 220, 346

hen kai pan 46, 121, 133–34, 178, 230, 239, 266–67. *See also* pantheism

heresy 7–8, 58–59, 63–66, 223n.2, 341–42
history:
    and bliss (*see* bliss, deferral of; bliss, epoch of)
    cosmic 132–33, 147–57, 168–69, 178–82, 220–21, 265, 285, 288–89*see also* cosmic view; epic, post-Copernican; revolution, cosmic)
    in the identity philosophy 147–74
    as kairotic (*see* construction, kairotic)
    legitimation of (*see* theodicy of history)
    as metamorphosis of B 234–36, 247–48, 263, 278, 313, 321–25, 334
    as proof of God 216–19, 228–29, 276–77
    as providential (*see* providence)
    of salvation (*see* salvation history)
    as stage play/drama (*see* theodicy of divine stage play)
    as trial/tribunal 102–3, 180, 214–15, 218–19, 241–42, 249, 318–19, 323
    See also contingency of the future; not-yet; system of times

holy man 144–45, 167
humanity/humanness:
    and blackness 304, 319–30
    as carrier of theo-cosmic process 151–52, 185–87, 196, 201–2, 216, 234–35, 278, 282–86, 300–6, 317–18, 324–26, 331n.28
    as cosmic center/telos 116, 148, 153–54n.30, 178–86, 190–96, 201–2, 206–7, 213–14, 220–21, 255–56, 264–65, 277–79, 284–86, 301–2, 313, 317–18, 321
    as cross-scalar 278, 284
    hierarchized distribution of 22–24, 61, 107, 151–52, 196, 301–6, 316–18, 321–24, 328–29, 332–34

as higher than the stars 193–94, 278–79, 336–37
normative 16–17, 22, 196, 287, 302–6, 316–42
as organ of the sun 148–53, 155–56
unity of 60–61, 67–68, 107, 120, 149–53, 178–79, 196, 278–79, 287, 294, 299–326, 333–34
as universal mediator 148, 178–79, 192–93, 284
See also blackness; decenteredness; Fall of Adam; global, the; race; recentering; Stufenfolge

I, the:
as I-ness 135, 150–51, 158n.32 (see also self-assertion; selfhood)
and not-I 43–44, 56, 72–107, 109–12, 117, 194–95, 233–34
identity:
as A=A (see A=A; copula; form)
absolute 3–4, 12–15, 27–32, 35, 45–56, 72–117, 121–47, 156–58, 163–66, 170–73, 223–24, 238, 243
whatever 124–26, 172
identity philosophy:
as aesthetic cosmic theodicy 157–73
as all-reconciling 120–21, 137–38, 150–53, 158, 163, 166–73
as apocalyptic 118–19, 139–40, 145–46, 153–55
epochal task of 118–21, 127, 137–38
as solar thought 139–40
as theo-cosmic system 118–57
idleness 12–14, 222–29. See also doing nothing; nonproductivity; repose
immediacy 5–7, 17, 31–35, 48–57, 60–63, 74–77, 80, 87, 90–92, 96–97, 104, 115, 119, 121–28, 134, 140–48, 158, 163–64, 169–70, 186, 188–90, 203–4, 211, 223–24, 229, 239–40, 250–51, 254, 280, 340–41

Incas, the 151–52, 161–62, 171–72
indifference:
of bliss 6, 12–13, 104, 108, 122–26, 131–32, 140–47, 156–57, 187–88, 204, 222–26, 229, 242–43, 252–55, 299, 337–38, 340–42
relative 127–28, 131–32, 134–35, 159–60
theodical 157–68, 172, 251–52, 318–19, 328–29
See also non-will
indifferentiation 140–46, 156–57, 250–51, 340–41
indigenous peoples 23, 150–51, 159–60, 322–23, 325–30
instrumentality. See evil as necessary/useful; usefulness
intelligence, character of 155–56, 185–88, 201–2, 247, 279–80, 315–16, 331n.27
intuition:
intellectual 7, 72–83, 90–99, 105, 108, 122–28, 140–41, 144, 146, 166, 173, 177, 179n.2, 203n.11, 270, 345
mystical 31–32, 49–53, 55–56, 91

Job, book of 20, 58–61, 65–67
justice, place-assigning 214–15, 221, 249, 268–69, 283–84, 317, 325–26, 335. See also history as tribunal; theodicy

Kant, Immanuel 4–5, 14–21, 29–30, 35, 37–40, 44–45, 58–73, 82, 83n.6, 85–87, 94–96, 99–100, 109, 112–13, 130–31, 185, 188–89, 193–95, 232–33, 241–42, 248–49, 307–9, 312–14
katechon 103–4
kenosis/kenotic 154, 179–80, 202–12, 220–21, 244–49, 252–53, 260–65, 268–71, 279–80, 283–85, 308–9, 313–15, 318–19, 324–25, 331–33, 338–39. See also construction, kenotic; sacrifice

Kepler, Johannes 112–13, 119, 208n.17, 255, 269–70, 271–72
Kingdom of God/Heaven 46, 287. *See also* heaven; *hen kai pan*
krisis 29–32, 38–41, 46, 51–52, 82, 188, 190–91, 196–97, 199, 203–5, 209–15, 238, 241, 246–49, 253, 279–81, 289, 294–95, 315–16, 324. *See also* crisis

ladder of reality. *See Stufenfolge*
law, the:
  as A = A 132–33, 242–43, 247–54, 268–71, 312, 318–19, 340, 344
  divine providential 150, 180, 217, 221, 241–55, 257–58, 262, 268–71, 285, 312, 318–19, 323, 331–32, 335, 340 (*see also* providence)
  as gatekeeper to bliss 221, 251–55
  and good/evil binary 243–48, 252–53, 255, 340–41
  as judging all being 243–54, 268–71, 318–19, 335 (*see also* justice, place-assigning)
  moral 45, 86–91, 95–96, 144, 341–42
  speaking in the name of 254
  and temptation 241–46, 252, 254–55
Leibniz G. W. 20–22, 65–66, 119, 133–34, 163–64, 166, 241, 246, 249n.26, 258
letting-be 74–75, 125, 145–46, 166, 198, 222, 229. *See also* non-will
love 208n.17, 232, 237–38, 260–61, 263–64, 269–70, 276–77, 335–36
Lucifer 180–82, 232–35, 246–48, 257–60, 324–25, 331n.27, 335–36. *See also* B as fallen will; Fall; Satan
lying on water and looking at the sky 12–13, 53, 74–75, 141, 239–40, 340

madness, divine 181*f*, 233–36
magic 30, 54–57, 62–64, 121, 144–45, 149, 187–89, 192, 194–95, 198, 280, 287, 294–95, 336–37, 340
Marcion 32–33, 58–59, 63–64, 65–66n.8
Marx, Karl 11, 31–32, 46, 146–47, 282, 289n.1, 298–99, 342, 346
mediation. *See* bliss, deferral/re-mediation of; Christ as mediator; humanity as mediator; immediacy
method of philosophy 111, 121–32, 183–84, 202–18, 309–10, 338–39. *See also* construction; kenosis; recollection; spiritual exercise
miracle 49–50, 62–63, 91
modernity:
  ambivalence toward 2, 29–30, 46–49, 55–56, 105, 118–19, 151–53, 158n.32, 184, 190, 198–201, 308–9, 313–17
  and crisis (*see* crisis of modernity)
  as demiurgic 11, 42–43, 56, 58, 65, 68–73, 81, 83–84, 97, 100, 104–6, 200–1, 240, 308–9, 317
  genealogy of xi–xii, 2–11, 16–17, 27–49, 68–69, 86–87, 106–7, 151–52, 168–72, 183, 196, 206–8, 264–65, 280, 284, 301–10, 313–14, 329–35, 338–39, 342–46
  as hell 198
  legitimation of 29–30, 42–49, 55–56, 68–72, 105, 118–21, 150–53, 155–56, 158n.32, 163, 169, 178–79, 190, 196, 200–1, 207–8, 247, 256, 284–87, 294–95, 299–300, 307–18, 324–25, 329–35
  as Plato's cave 130–31
  re-commencement of 29–30, 49, 55–56, 163, 294–95
  as salvific 11, 14, 17, 43, 51–52, 56, 82–86, 105, 152, 190, 214, 240, 293–300, 323–25, 329–30, 333, 342–44

task of 22, 42–43, 46–49, 59–60, 71–72, 101–5, 118–21, 151–52, 158n.32, 201, 290–91, 303–4, 307–9, 316–17, 346
morality 44–45, 82–83, 86–108, 144, 159, 309, 341–42
mysteries 47–48, 63n.5, 335–38, 340
mysticism/mystical 5–8, 17, 30–32, 49–57, 64–65, 75, 81–83, 91–94, 100, 126, 198n.8, 203–4, 208–12, 223n.2, 295–96, 337, 340
mythology 3, 8, 11, 23–24, 58–63, 68–69, 106–7, 151–52, 169–70, 181f, 183, 185, 192–93, 196, 206, 264–65, 294, 302, 334–36. *See also* paganism

nature:
 bliss of (*see* bliss as fire; bliss as water)
 circularity/melancholy of 110, 114–16, 191–96, 199, 258–59, 263–65, 288–98
 as conflictual/dissonant 113–15, 127–28, 132–34, 136–39, 148–49, 152–54, 156–57, 160–61, 163, 232–33, 250–51, 291–92
 construction of (*see* construction of nature)
 figure of 220–21, 256, 265, 271–77
 first blind 258–60, 273, 289–92
 as fugitive 194–95
 as geo-cosmic abyss 104–5, 114–15, 142, 177, 194–95, 276–77, 284–85, 322–23, 329–30
 post-Copernican (*see* universe, post-Copernican)
 See also forces, duality of
nebulae/nebular hypothesis 180–82, 193n.7, 217, 232–33, 261–62, 289–90
negative and positive philosophy 3, 201, 216–18, 306–12, 338–39

non-domination 7, 46, 107–8, 145–46, 280–83, 342, 346
nonproductivity 6–7, 12–14, 74–77, 105, 113, 126, 142–45, 222, 310, 326, 329–30, 336–37. *See also* idleness; repose
non-relation 5–6, 51–52, 75–77, 85, 90–91, 104, 108, 124–28, 133–34, 143–45, 172, 225–26, 299, 310, 340–41
non-will 77, 94, 102, 108, 188, 197–99, 205–6, 222–31, 239–40, 242–43, 255, 259, 270–71n.42, 277–78. *See also* indifference; letting-be
nothing/nothingness:
 absolute/divine 34, 77–79, 92, 126, 222–27, 230, 272–75, 278
 bliss as (*see* bliss as nonbeing)
 common/shared 224–25, 227, 272–73, 277–78
 to be as nothing 102–3, 199, 205–6, 209–10, 222–24, 239–40
 world as 77, 129–31, 156–57, 158–59, 164, 173–74
 See also doing nothing; Gnostic imperative/question; world-annihilation
not-yet, the:
 in Christianity 16–17, 33–37, 48–52, 170–71, 206, 298–300, 344
 and faith 36–38, 97–98, 167, 286–87
 of the world 7–13, 16–17, 33–38, 43, 48, 51–52, 84, 96–98, 104–8, 118–19, 121, 147–48, 155–57, 164–66, 170–71, 179–80, 190, 217–18, 228, 239–41, 250–51, 255, 270–71n.42, 283–84, 288–99, 307–11, 337–40, 345
 See also bliss, deferral of; history; world-plan
nucleus, theo-cosmic 180–82, 229–32, 236, 238–39, 271–72, 312

paganism 5–6, 27–37, 47–49, 61–62, 69–70, 92–93, 101–2, 149–50, 151–52, 168–72, 185, 196, 206, 210, 264–65, 294, 301–2, 307–8, 334–38. *See also* Christianity; construction of religion; mythology
pantheism 3, 7, 53, 117–21, 170, 220–21, 224–25, 236, 238, 251–52, 267–68, 276–77, 342. *See also hen kai pan*
paradise 14–18, 46, 55–56, 66, 88–89, 180–91, 199–200, 212–15, 264–65. *See also* bliss, lost; consciousness, Adamic; garden
Paul/Pauline 34n.13, 58–59, 63–65, 94n.13, 103–4, 167–68, 205–6, 242n.18, 262, 285, 332
peace 12–16, 173, 233–36, 243–44, 290–91, 338–39. *See also* repose; Sabbath
philosophy. *See* construction; identity philosophy; katechon; method of philosophy; negative and positive philosophy
Plato/Platonic 58–64, 68–70, 72–75, 78–79, 81–82, 119, 127, 130–31, 146, 159, 165–66, 190–91, 200–1, 202n.10, 204n.12, 214, 268–69, 307–8
poetry 55–57, 61–63, 110, 116–17, 172–73, 302
point 112–13, 127–29, 131–34, 137–40, 163, 231, 267, 271–79, 284–85, 289. *See also* center; circle; sphere; spiral; zero point
positive philosophy. *See* God, positive; negative and positive philosophy
possibility, movement of 312–13, 317, 320–23, 326–32. *See also* God, actualization of; world as totality of possibility

potenceless 132–33, 141–42, 148, 266–67. *See also* bliss as A^0
potency/potencies 47–48, 128–61, 169–70, 183, 199–200, 207, 223–25, 234, 237n.12, 258–69, 272–74, 278–79, 311–13, 334–36
Prometheus 148–49, 278, 285, 316–17, 324–25
prophecy 119, 154, 165–66, 213–18, 338–39
Proudhon, Pierre-Joseph 146–47, 283
providence 16, 20, 35–38, 47–51, 67, 165–66, 178–80, 184–87, 192, 208n.17, 216–17, 228, 232–37, 240–49, 255, 260–62, 268–69, 276–78, 284–87, 296–303, 305–6, 309–10, 315–21, 325–33, 340, 345–46. *See also* law; theodicy; wisdom; world-plan

race/racialization xii–xii, 9–10, 14, 22–24, 63n.5, 107, 271, 287, 300, 303–6, 317–42, 345–46
recentering:
  colonial dimension of 302–4, 316, 321, 329–30
  human and theo-cosmic 179, 183, 189, 196, 199–202, 213–14, 220, 232–33, 237, 240, 265, 273, 278–79, 281–82, 290–91, 301–4, 316, 321, 324–25, 329–30, 334, 344
  See also decenteredness
recollection/re-collection 74n.1, 79–80, 110–17, 122–23, 128–34, 137–39, 147–48, 151–53, 163–64, 180–82, 190, 196, 214, 236–38, 255–59, 264–65, 302, 311, 317–19, 322–23, 326, 333–36. *See also* fragmentation
reconciliation:
  of Christian contradiction 32–39, 46–51, 119–21, 137–38, 139, 183,

192–93, 201, 207, 236, 265, 315–16, 337–38
  of Christianity and paganism 49, 171–72, 308n.10
  of earth and sun 153–54
  at the end of history 16–17, 27, 34–38, 45–46, 55–56, 66, 120–21, 150–52, 168–69, 207, 228–31, 241–42, 255, 265, 309–10, 345–46
  of God's self-alienation 31–35, 218–19, 227–31, 236, 240, 285–86
  with evil and the world 8–9, 34, 145–46, 158–59, 163–69, 173–74, 338–39, 345–46
redemption. *See* Christ; Fall and redemption; rhythm, theo-cosmic; spiral
re-inversion 184, 201–5, 214–18, 220–21, 236, 246–47, 263, 265, 283. *See also* recentering; revolution, cosmic
religion. *See* Christianity; construction of religion; supersessionism
religion of humanity 181f, 264–65, 280–82, 301–2
repose/rest 7, 12–16, 94, 101–2, 105–8, 114–16, 141, 166, 186–90, 197–99, 213, 222–24, 230, 233, 236–43, 278, 309–15, 338–39. *See also* idleness; nonproductivity; peace; Sabbath
revelation 35–38, 44–51, 113–17, 122–30, 155, 162–64, 169–72, 180–85, 201, 206–7, 217–18, 221–39, 245–49, 258–68, 271, 277, 288–98, 301–2, 307–12, 334–39
re-visioning of reality 3, 116–33, 139, 146–47, 157, 177, 250–51, 265, 285, 309–10. *See also* construction; cosmic view; revolution, philosophical-phenomenological

revolution:
  Copernican (*see* Copernican revolution)
  cosmic 215–16, 220–21, 255–58, 261–62, 265, 276–83, 287, 291
  moral 96
  philosophical-phenomenological 46, 60, 64–65, 119–21, 130–31, 143–47, 172, 279–82, 309
  political 10–11, 144–45, 221, 256, 279–84, 340, 345–46
revolutionary collectivity 144–45
rhythm, theo-cosmic 220–21, 255–56, 265, 289–93
Romantic/Romanticism 3–12, 17, 23–24, 28–30, 45–50, 53–57, 73–74, 116, 119–20, 125–27, 136–40, 146, 155, 158–61, 171–72, 194–95, 254, 270, 279, 282–83, 299–306, 311, 345–46
rotatory motion 182, 188, 199, 232, 237–38, 257–59, 261–62. *See also* explosion; turmoil; vortex
Rousseau, Jean-Jacques 11–15, 18–19, 53, 74–75, 141
Runge, Philipp Otto 274–76, 278

Sabbath 7, 213, 221, 239, 270–71, 275, 288–89, 293, 298. *See also* divinity; non-will; peace; repose
sacrifice 20–21, 154, 204–6, 245–46, 252–53, 268, 287, 324n.21, 331–32, 338–39, 345–46. *See also* kenosis
salvation. *See* bliss and salvation; Christianity; God; modernity as salvific
salvation history 32–38, 50–51, 102–3, 115, 168–69, 183, 192, 207–8, 213–18, 228, 238–40, 258, 263–65, 274–75, 283–300, 305–6, 315–16, 323–39

Satan 67, 100–1, 232–33, 238, 331–32.
See also B as fallen will; Fall;
Lucifer
Schelling's texts cited (selection):
Ages of the World (1811) 55n.43, 183,
198, 214, 221–26, 236–37, 272, 275–
76, 331–32
Ages of the World (1814) 215n.26, 231–
33, 238, 243–44, 257–62, 265–69,
272, 278, 289–98, 329–32
Ages of the World (1827/28) 180–82,
218, 223n.2, 224–26, 229–36,
248–49, 257–62, 277, 289–90, 293–
94, 321–22
Ages of the World (in general) 3,
179–80, 183, 243–44, 266n.37, 295–
96, 318–19
*Aphorisms on the Philosophy of
Nature* 121–26, 129–34, 136–38,
141, 146, 164, 166, 177
Further Presentations 124, 127–28,
132–33, 148–54
*General Deduction of the Natural
Process* 7, 74n.1, 113–16, 163–64
History of Gnosticism 63–64
Initia Philosophiae Universae
(citations) 54–55, 185–218, 222–54,
257–62, 266–77, 281–82, 286–87,
289–92, 331n.27
Initia Philosophiae Universae
(mentions) 183, 202–4, 274–75,
295–96, 303–4
Introduction to Philosophy 43, 116–
17, 153–54n.30, 213, 218, 222–26,
231–36, 258–59, 261–62, 272–
73, 289–91
*Lectures on the Method of University
Studies* 27, 35–40, 48–52, 115–16,
131n.10, 150, 168–69
Of the I 58–59, 71–91, 95–98, 100,
104–7, 110–11, 279n.55

On the Origin of Evil 65–70,
107n.16
On the Relation 27–51, 144, 170–
71, 203
*Philosophical Investigations (Freedom
Essay)* 3, 144, 163–64, 177–80, 213,
231, 234–35, 238–41, 243, 246–49,
264–65, 276–79, 329–30
Philosophical Letters 7, 58–60, 71, 74,
80–82, 84–85, 88–107
Philosophy and Religion 143–44, 148–
50, 158–59, 164n.35
Philosophy of Revelation (as project) 3,
67, 179–83, 192–93, 206, 282, 309–
10, 334–35, 337–39
Philosophy of Revelation (citations)
8–9, 63n.5, 67, 100–1, 185, 188–89,
199–200, 206–7, 216–19, 221, 226–
27, 247–48, 257–59, 263–69, 278,
280–82, 309–10, 332–39
Presentation of My System 3, 118–19,
123–26, 131–33, 136–37, 140–41
*Presentation of the Process of
Nature* 182, 232, 247, 260–63, 277–
79, 285–86, 301–2, 331n.27
*Presentation of the Purely Rational
Philosophy* 180–83, 193–94,
205n.13, 208n.17, 214–15, 226n.5,
249, 258–59, 283, 301–39
Stuttgart Seminars 35, 144, 179–80,
215–17, 234, 238, 279–81, 285
*System of Philosophy (Würzburg
System)* 116–17, 122–50, 154–68,
173, 256–57n.27
science:
light of 179, 190, 193–94, 206–10, 214,
238, 249, 285, 327
modern 18, 40–47, 54–56, 79, 115–16,
120–21, 137–38, 148, 152–56, 163,
169, 190–91, 196, 201, 207–8, 279–
80, 287, 307–9, 313–17

self-assertion:
    cosmic/universal 133–35, 148–51, 154–55, 162–64, 194, 231–34, 237–38, 260–61, 312
    as evil/transgression 194–95, 199–200, 210, 231–34, 313–14, 335–36 (*see also* sin; transgression)
    giving up 201–12, 214–15, 248–49, 260–62, 265, 268, 271, 278, 285, 308–10, 314n.15 (*see also* kenosis)
    modern 13, 18–23, 28–29, 39–49, 54–59, 66–73, 78–80, 93, 99–107, 119, 123–25, 146–53, 156–57, 184–89, 194–201, 256, 280–85, 294, 302–9, 313–17, 321, 324, 342
    of the will (*see* Fall)
self-emptying. *See* kenosis
selfhood 133–37, 142–45, 148–50, 153, 156–59, 163–69, 177, 190, 194, 198–205, 224, 229, 232, 237–38, 256–57, 260–61, 285, 309, 312, 316–17. *See also* I
sin 158–59, 187–89, 194–97, 201–2, 232–33, 242n.18, 246–50, 252–53, 274–75, 304. *See also* Fall; freedom for good and evil; guilt; transgression
slavery/enslavement:
    to the absolute 45
    and bliss 92, 305–6
    transatlantic 22–23, 271, 300, 305–6, 319–20, 326–30
    See also blackness; colonialism; humanity; race
socialism 146–47, 221, 256, 282
sphere 73, 86–90, 114–15, 123–24, 127. *See also* center; circle; construction, geometric; point
Spinoza, Baruch 4–5, 92–95, 98–100, 118–21, 126, 133–34, 138–39, 159, 165n.36, 266–67

spiral 48, 180–83, 220–21, 255–57, 262–65, 270–86, 288–90, 293, 298, 309–10, 316–17, 324–27, 332, 345–46. *See also* circle; construction, geometric; revolution, cosmic; *Stufenfolge*; uroboros
spiritual exercise 202
standing still 166–67, 172–73, 192, 286–87
stars. *See* astrality; earth; Lucifer; sun
state, the:
    organic life of 253–54
    overcoming of 280–83, 297–98, 309
    See also church; revolution
Stufenfolge:
    of nature/world-process 111, 116, 129, 137–38, 178–83, 211, 220–21, 238, 250, 256–57, 261–86, 305–6, 311–13, 317–37
    as racialized 107, 271, 304–6, 317–34
suffering as the way to glory 236–37, 240–41, 255, 287, 324, 331–32
sun:
    and earth 127–41, 147–57, 164, 269–70, 291
    proto-sun 112–13, 127–28, 140, 148–49
    radiance of 342
    See also astrality; earth; fire; identity philosophy
Sun Ra 342
supersessionism 171–72, 210, 294, 333–39, 345–46. *See also* Christianity; construction of religion
synthesis 23–24, 69–70, 75–79, 82–89, 95–99, 106–17, 123–24, 138
system:
    solar 61, 112–13, 135–36, 140, 148–50, 193–94, 220
    as system narrative 179–82, 254–55
    of times 213–14, 216, 275–76, 320, 323–24, 333

system (cont.)
  of the world/universe 61, 112–13,
    120–22, 127–29, 131–32, 137–38, 163,
    173–74, 179, 273, 336–37 (see also
    universe; world)

temptation. See law and temptation
theodical "better" 245, 247–50, 328–29
theodicy:
  as acquittal of God (see God
    acquitted/on trial)
  aesthetic 165–66, 276–77, 332n.30
  and catastrophe 257–58
  of divine providential law (see law)
  of divine stage play 234–35, 246, 257–
    58, 260–61, 276–77, 328
  figure of 276–77
  geometric 276–77, 332n.30
  of history 20–23, 30, 48, 118–19, 180,
    214–19, 228–31, 234–42, 248–50,
    276–77, 283, 285–87, 317–18, 334–
    35, 338–39, 344–46
  as imposition of universal order
    239, 269–70, 284, 304–5, 318–
    19, 344
  as logic of proper place/time 51–52,
    161–66, 189, 214–16, 241–43, 246–
    52, 267–71, 283–84, 313, 318–23
  naturalized 268–71, 283, 305–6, 313,
    318–20, 323–29
  of the racialized global 287, 302, 305–
    6, 317–20, 328–32, 345–46
  as reconciliation (see reconciliation)
  ruse of 16–17, 21–22, 162–63,
    246n.22, 255, 319–20, 328–29,
    338–39, 345–46
  as spiritual investment in the
    world 16–22, 32–34, 37–38, 65–66,
    71–72, 103, 163, 254–55, 344
  as world-legitimation (see world-
    justification/legitimation)

  See also evil; Fall; history as tribunal;
    indifference, theodical; justice,
    place-assigning; providence;
    wisdom; world-plan
time, abolition of 295–99. See also clock
  time; theodicy as logic of proper
  place/time; world as time
transcendence:
  and bliss (see bliss as transcendent)
  divine 18–20, 32–33, 40–49, 66–67,
    122, 186–87, 219, 252–53, 266–71,
    276, 295–96, 338–41
  emergence of 205–6, 266–71
  and modernity 9–10, 30, 38–40,
    43–46, 49, 283, 292–96, 304–5, 318,
    321–24, 340–41
  See also divinity; God
transgression 158–61, 180–82, 185–94,
  200–1, 216, 221–22, 230–34, 241–
  55, 302, 326, 331–32. See also Fall;
  freedom for good and evil; guilt; sin
tsimtsum 231
tumult/turmoil 180–82, 188–89, 196–
  99, 211–12, 214, 232–33, 241, 248–
  49, 257–60, 262n.34, 264–65, 268,
  273–77, 280–84, 289–91, 295–96,
  302, 312, 318–19, 322–23, 335–36,
  342. See also chaos; confusion;
  disorder; explosion; rotatory
  motion; vortex
turba gentium 264–65
turning/re-turning. See re-inversion;
  revolution; spiral; uroboros

unfolding/*explicatio* 111–13, 122, 127–29,
  131–38, 150, 158, 162–66, 173–74,
  204–5, 210, 218, 221–22, 236–39,
  249, 265–66, 268–69, 271–77,
  312, 318–19
universe, post-Copernican 22, 104–5,
  112–13, 116, 120, 127–28, 159–60,

173–74, 178–79, 184, 197, 214, 217–18, 231–32, 250–51, 258, 265, 344. *See also* Copernican revolution; epic, post-Copernican; nucleus; system
unmoved mover 270–71, 276
unprethinkable, the 227, 252, 254, 277, 309–10
uroboros 258–59, 278, 342–43
usefulness:
   of evil (*see* evil as necessary/useful)
   of the lower for the higher 164–65, 234, 265, 268–71, 313, 318–25, 331–32, 334
utopia/utopic 12–16, 56–57, 74–77, 91, 93, 112–13, 133–34, 137–38, 155, 230, 272–73, 299–300, 342

vortex/swirl 114–15, 188, 198–99, 211–12, 232–34, 257–62, 264–65, 295–96, 335–36. *See also* confusion; rotatory motion; tumult; *turba gentium*

water. *See* bliss as water; lying on water
will. *See* B as fallen will; demiurge; Fall; freedom; non-will; self-assertion
wisdom 54n.42, 192–96, 206–7, 213, 235–36, 246, 263–64
Wordsworth, William 1, 53–55, 124, 345
work/toil:
   abolition/cessation of 239–40, 298–99, 340–41 (*see also* idleness; nonproductivity; repose; Sabbath)
   of God 237–40, 288–89, 327
   imperative of 1, 6, 14–16, 19–20, 239–40, 286–87, 314–15, 327–30, 341–44
   of possibility 312, 333–34
   of the subject 15–21, 105, 115, 240, 314–17, 326–30
   of the world 14–17, 179, 237, 240, 290–94, 314–15, 329–30

world:
   as arena of judgment 247–49, 276–77, 291–92, 342
   as deferring/foreclosing bliss (*see* bliss, deferral of; not-yet)
   as demanding its own end 72, 85, 97, 106, 215–16, 298, 307–8, 342–43
   as desire 307–8, 340
   as distribution of good and evil 247–48, 252–53, 331–32
   as distribution of proper place 163–66, 171–72, 336–37
   as global (*see* global; humanity)
   as mystery 80, 81n.4, 88–89, 98, 108, 129
   as not-yet (*see* not-yet)
   as perfect 163–66
   as prison 72, 145–46, 192, 236–37, 290–91, 341–42
   reproduction of 12–15, 19–20, 23–24, 71–73, 85, 92–96, 104–6, 114–15, 144–46, 240, 255, 292–94, 331–32, 338–39, 342–43
   as structure of alienation 5–8, 17, 28–32, 45, 48, 71–73, 78–85, 92–93, 115–16, 120–24, 190–91, 236, 240–42, 313–14 (*see also* alienation)
   system of (*see* system of the world/universe)
   as time 291–92
   as totality of possibility 18–19, 56, 131–32, 164n.35, 183, 238–39, 244, 249–50, 312–19, 331–32
   as universe (*see* universe)
   as vessel 236–37, 284
world-annihilation 6–7, 13, 17, 34, 49–52, 64–65, 72, 77–78, 82, 85–97, 101–8, 118–19, 121, 125–28, 139, 142–43, 146–48, 154–58, 162–63, 215–16, 225, 228, 298–99, 346. *See also* apocalyptic; bliss as fire; bliss as water

world-grammar, racialized 318–20
world-justification/legitimation 2–3, 8–9, 14–24, 29–38, 42–43, 48, 52, 58, 64–70, 98, 101–8, 156–60, 165n.36, 167–68, 173–74, 217–19, 235–36, 241, 245, 255, 328–33, 340, 345–46. *See also* theodicy
world-mastery, logic of 18, 22, 40–47, 55–56, 69–70, 83–86, 99, 105, 125, 151–53, 155–56, 187–88, 198–99, 218–19, 226–28, 302–3, 308–9, 314–17, 331–33, 341–44
world-plan 19–20, 37–38, 67–68, 192, 195–96, 216–17, 234, 238–39, 245, 249, 263–64, 268–69, 328. *See also* history; providence; theodicy; wisdom
Wynter, Sylvia 22–24, 287, 302–6, 319–20, 326

zero point 75–77, 104, 227, 266–67, 276, 328–29

www.ingramcontent.com/pod-product-compliance
Lightning Source LLC
Chambersburg PA
CBHW070152020925
31867CB00043B/353